$15.00

REVOLUTIONARY JUSTICE
THE SOCIAL AND POLITICAL THEORY OF P.-J. PROUDHON
Robert L. Hoffman

Pierre-Joseph Proudhon (1809-65) was the most important French theorist of socialism and the true "father" of anarchism. Yet his ideas have not received the comprehensive treatment ordinarily accorded a philosophy of such magnitude. Hoffman here puts Proudhon's ideas in a context which conveys their real spirit and reveals their continuing force and appeal.

Proudhon's published works include well over 20,000 pages, and the whole appears as a "perplexing welter of disorder." Hoffman integrates and clarifies the work, showing how Proudhon developed a grand vision of man, society, and justice which goes far beyond the attacks on political and economic oppression for which he is best known. Hoffman's comparative consideration of Marx and later theorists suggests the continuing significance of Proudhon's thought in intellectual history and in contemporary political theory.

"The best overall study of Proudhon in English." — Aaron Noland, The City College, New York.

ROBERT L. HOFFMAN is assistant professor of history at the State University of New York at Albany. He has also edited the book *Anarchism* (1970).

UNIVERSITY OF ILLINOIS PRESS   Urbana Chicago London

ISBN 0-252-00240-7

Jacket illustration of Proudhon by Honoré Daumier; courtesy of Harvard College Library.

Revolutionary Justice

THE SOCIAL AND POLITICAL THEORY
OF P. - J. PROUDHON

Revolutionary Justice

THE SOCIAL AND POLITICAL THEORY OF P.-J. PROUDHON

Robert L. Hoffman

UNIVERSITY OF ILLINOIS PRESS

Urbana : Chicago : London

Contents

Preface

THE PUBLISHED WRITING of Pierre-Joseph Proudhon comprises well over twenty thousand pages; the unpublished manuscripts available to me include nearly two thousand more. Topics covered by him seem beyond number. No subject is immune to his attention, however restricted his knowledge, and in his books every useful argument occurring to him is explored at length, however limited its actual bearing on the major theses he develops. His various works repeat one another endlessly, though a development of his thought is perceptible. While his basic beliefs remain constant and consistent, his statements of ideas often seem contradictory. Taken in small portions his writing is lucidly rational and orderly, but the vast whole appears as a perplexing welter of disorder.

How, then, is one to write about Proudhon's thought? It is too immense and unwieldy to be compressed and straightened into the neat patterns of summary and interpretation that would comprise the usual academic monograph. And its intricacies are too important to be washed out in the process of simplification, selection, and regrouping of ideas into readily manageable forms. All of it cannot be reproduced, surely, but the subject demands a method that will re-create the whole in form like that of the original, though with briefer span.

Both Proudhon and his writing were undisciplined, erratic, over-flowing with passionate response to the times. He found himself in a new, rapidly changing world and reacted in quite distinctive ways. Those of his contemporaries who contributed most to ideas that prevailed then and since welcomed the new age; he did not, rejecting the form rather than the fact of change, but was ambivalent about both attachments to the past and prospects for the future. Whether or not they welcomed social change, most of his contemporaries thought about it in terms of ideas shaped in an earlier age; though much affected by the same ideas also, Proudhon on the other hand responded to change with nearly three decades of vigorously creative intellectual activity.

It is this remarkable creative response, in so many ways distinctively different from what others produced, which makes Proudhon fascinating. Because he continually modifies his thought, and because these changes are so responsive to his experience, I believe that he is best understood in the context of this developing experience.

This alone could determine my approach, but another reason is no less vital. I think that much of the man's thought remains alive and important today, but if we examine it apart from the way it was created it may not appear so. Nothing becomes dated as readily as the ideas of a man thinking in radical reaction to contemporary events. However, Proudhon saw problems in terms of questions which remain compelling and without satisfactory solutions. He tried to resolve them in novel ways, with results different from alternatives which have been repeatedly proposed and variously applied ever since. Even when his answers were inadequate, as they often were, they simultaneously revealed the inadequacies of alternatives and opened the way to more satisfactory solutions. Such qualities of his thought apply to its relevance today as well as a century ago. If he is to be understood thus, then I think Proudhon must be seen as a man trying to discover answers to the problems of man and society *as* he encounters them.

These conclusions lead me to a method which has a chronological and biographical orientation, but not a conventional one. A chronological ordering of material is employed, but it is dropped when other forms are better. I give much biographical information, but many important things in his life are omitted here, for I devote attention only to those aspects of it which clarify his philosophy. Biography is introduced irregularly, with some chapters devoting much space to it and others omitting it altogether. This chronological and biographical method may appear haphazard but is deliberate; the consequent fault is not disorder but extension of this book's length, a result I would rather have avoided but believe necessary under the circumstances.

Biographical interludes are also used as a device to include theoretical and programmatic issues not vitally important in themselves, but very helpful in understanding the growth of Proudhon's thought. His various positions on whether workers should vote in elections are an example. Many subjects to which he devoted much labor are omitted here, and I place much less emphasis than he did himself on some aspects of his thought—his mutual credit schemes, for instance.

Coping with the complexity of Proudhon's writing might have been made much easier—and this book shorter—had I employed quite another approach. I could have classified and interpreted his ideas in categories selected in order to make analysis simpler and more straightforward, and possibly of more obviously direct relevance to issues frequently debated today.

The model here would be procedures typically employed by political scientists, whose work on the thought of past theorists most often is primarily concerned with how these ideas can contribute to efforts of theorists today. To accomplish this purpose they employ categories of analysis and interpretation derived from the ways social science now attacks the relevant problems.

At its best such an approach can be marvelously illuminating, but I have discarded recurring inclinations to make more use of it, despite the fact that my interests in theory and history are determined by my concerns with the present. The chief problem with this analytic method here is that it is essentially anti-historical and, even though often used with some historical perspective, runs into grave danger thereby. The theorists of yesterday did not have the same orientations or employ the same analytic categories as those of today; then the more we rely on present categories, or on ones invented for the sake of straightforward explanation, the more likely we are to distort the original meaning and intent of the works studied. These difficulties are familiar to historians, but too often forgotten in matters where most are as partisan and involved as in questions of socialist thought. The consequent distortion may be insignificant for some purposes, though it is bad history, but I believe that we cannot make use of Proudhon's thought until we understand quite well what he himself meant. He is too close to the world around him, and too different from other philosophers, for us to do otherwise—and the complexity and disorder of his work make the dangers of distortion exceptionally great.

Another factor leads me to employ my genetic, descriptive method. When writing for an audience of scholars about a Locke or a Rousseau, one can assume readers have sufficient familiarity with the original texts and a plethora of secondary works for a new book to concentrate on interpretive analysis. We can play around with new arrangements of the familiar, with uncovering of the previously neglected in both the familiar and in "minor" works, with comparisons between writers. But Proudhon is familiar to very few, especially outside of France, and those acquainted with him at all usually know too little of the variety of his ideas. Thus I take my chief task here to be integration and simplification of a diverse and disordered subject, and this task has peculiar demands if the product is not to be a misshapen one.

Doing this obviously is a process of abstraction, as any historical effort must be, and this too has dangers. My interpretive categories may be close to the original ones, but I select and restructure the material in order to speak of it, and thus can end by distorting it. When I write in two pages what Proudhon thought about a matter, it is often a distillation of what he himself wrote in several hundred pages, in many different forms and places. Such "distortion" need not be objectionable, if the real spirit of the original is still conveyed: the purpose of historical study should be to *illuminate* the past—and thereby the present as well—not to *reproduce* it.

Historians of ideas ordinarily give much of their attention to comparisons between thinkers and to tracing the filiation of developing ideas from one writer to another. I have avoided much of what one might expect in this regard, for several reasons. First, such studies could easily treble the length of an already long book. More-over, they would have less than the usual value because, as ex-plained later, Proudhon had most idiosyncratic ways of engaging the thought of others. Finally, such pursuits often display erudi-tion without adding much to understanding; then they have the quality of idle academic games. I have played the game sometimes, where it seems clearly to reveal something of Proudhon; I probably have done so too much—one's academicism is difficult to keep in check.

There are also other hazards whose consequences I may not have avoided altogether. In selecting, simplifying, and resolving difficul-ties in interpretation, I can render the man's philosophy more com-prehensible and consistent than it appears on casual study—but I may do so to a greater extent than is warranted by the original. Or, another danger, it is all too easy to explain imperfectly conceived ideas of Proudhon in terms of the similar but more developed con-ceptions of others, especially Marx. Finally, there are the problems of partisanship, for no one can be neutral in speaking of Proudhon's philosophy. I admire the man and his ideas, and I do not try to hide this. I think some sympathy and fondness for them are essential to understanding. This once said, I have still to avoid the opposite faults of partisan blindness and pleading on the one hand and, on the other, sterile attempts to remain objectively detached. I have tried to solve the problem as best I can; others will do it differently, but with a subject like this it could not be otherwise.

The best though incomplete edition of Proudhon's works is the *Oeuvres complètes de P.-J. Proudhon,* nouvelle édition (Paris: Marcel Rivière, 1923–61). This is the labor of love of a group of very fine French scholars who were more or less Proudhonist at heart; they gave the edition excellent lengthy introductions and notes, although it does have some textual faults. Most of Proudhon's important work is here, but there are significant omissions; publica-tion was suspended before the editors' plans had been fully realized, and there appears to be little chance that the edition will be com-pleted.

Wherever possible this edition is the one used and cited. The volumes were not numbered by the publisher; the volume numbers used here are by order of publication in this edition, a practice used in library cataloging and binding.

There is an earlier, more complete edition, the *Oeuvres complètes de P.-J. Proudhon* (Paris: A. Lacroix, Verboeckoven, et Cie., 1867–70), twenty-six volumes, including nearly all of the work first published in the author's lifetime. It is augmented by eight volumes of the *Oeuvres posthumes de P.-J. Proudhon* (Paris & Brussels: A. Lacroix; and Paris: Garnier Frères, 1866–75). This consists of unfinished, unpublished work left in manuscript by Proudhon at his death; it was assembled and edited by his friends. They also published the *Correspondance de P.-J. Proudhon* (Paris: A. Lacroix, 1875) in fourteen volumes.[1] There are few notes or comments in these editions. Mgr. Pierre Haubtmann has had the opportunity to compare the collected *Correspondance* with many of the original manuscript letters. He found frequent errors in transcription, and the collection obviously has been carelessly edited in other ways. I have had to rely on it despite the possibility of errors, although in some cases circumstances permit their correction.

Since the Lacroix collections appeared, a substantial quantity of additional Proudhon material has been published. Some of it is in the Rivière edition, but most is in separate books and a great number of periodical publications. The material includes extensive notes and rough drafts for books never completed, and many additional letters.

There is a treasure of Proudhon manuscripts which has remained in the possession of his family. The most important seem to be eleven *carnets*, notebooks which he kept from 1843 to 1862. These were available to just a few scholars until the death of Proudhon's daughter Catherine in 1947 (at the age of 97), after which they were given to the Bibliothèque Nationale (Nouvelles Acquisitions Français, nos. 14265–75). These are in the process of being published as the *Carnets de P.-J. Proudhon*, with Mgr. Haubtmann the editor (Paris: Marcel Rivière, 1960–). The three volumes printed

1. My footnote citations use abbreviations: "*Oeuv.*" for the Rivière edition of *Oeuvres complètes*, "*Oeuv. (Lacroix)*" for the Lacroix edition, and "*Corresp.*" for the collected correspondence. With the Rivière edition, single works in multiple volumes are cited with a major and a minor volume number, e.g., "*Oeuv.*, VIII, vol. iv."

thus far include roughly half of the material in these notebooks, terminating at *carnet* no. 8, p. 138 (August 13, 1850).[2]

These *carnets* are simultaneously daily diaries, copybooks for reading notes, workbooks with drafts of material for publications or speeches, notes of diverse thoughts, address books, and notebooks for matters of business, both his own and those of his employers. They are an extremely rich source for the study of Proudhon, making possible better comprehension of ideas which sometimes are rather obscured by the elaboration added in preparation.

As far as I can determine, very little of the rest of the family archives has ever been accessible to anyone writing about Proudhon except Mgr. Haubtmann. He describes them and includes extensive extracts in two unpublished Sorbonne theses which I have not seen. I am indebted to Aaron Noland, professor of history at the City University of New York, for permitting me to examine his notes on Haubtmann's work, whose contents I was not aware of until after having nearly completed my own research.[3]

The most important of these Proudhon manuscripts seems to be the "Cours d'économie," a rough draft in three large volumes written between 1850 and 1855. Haubtmann says that this could better be called "Le Cours de sociologie." Also in the collection are forty-one notebooks, written 1826–42 and 1844, with reading notes and comments, and extracts from the books read. (Though I have not seen the books, Proudhon's personal library is now in the Bibliothèque Municipale de Besançon, *dons* 34.904–35.913. Not only did he annotate these volumes, but one can guess how much of a book he actually read by seeing what pages have been cut.) The family archives include many other unpublished manuscripts: rough drafts

2. The *carnets* contain over 3,400 pages, with more than 1,800 yet to be published. They are written in an almost miniscule and frequently illegible hand. Many individual words and some entire sections (especially those written with a dull pencil) are impossible to read or can only be guessed at. All my references to the *carnets* cite the volume and page numbers of the MSS., which are included in the published editions. They are cited simply as "*Carnets.*"

3. Pierre Haubtmann, "P.-J. Proudhon, sa vie et sa pensée," 8 vols., and "La Philosophie sociale de P.-J. Proudhon" (*thèse* and *thèse complémentaire* respectively, Paris, Faculté des lettres et des sciences humaines, 1961), Bibliothèque de l'Université de Paris—Sorbonne, W-1961 and W-1961(5). His *Proudhon: Genèse d'un anti-théiste* (Paris and Tours: Mame, 1969) makes some use of the unpublished material, which he mentions on pp. 8–9. Mgr. Haubtmann is rector of the Institut Catholique de Paris.

which got no further except in other works, diverse collections of notes, and letters. Finally, the original manuscripts for most of Proudhon's published works are here, with annotations and corrections.

From what I have been able to learn of this family archive, I think the parts of it relevant to my work could not add much except additional support for what is already amply demonstrated by available material. It should be most useful for biographical study, however. Mgr. Haubtmann apparently has used it for this, his eight-volume principal thesis covering Proudhon's life and thought through 1849.

In my bibliography I gave appropriate details for everything I could discover which has been written by or about Proudhon. It is hard to see how anyone could use all of this compilation, but for lack of any such bibliography I have had to go through much wasteful effort. This one is offered to save others the trouble, thus making me feel better about the time spent putting it together.

There are half a dozen men to whom I feel especially indebted in connection with the preparation of this book: Lewis Coser, Michael Cherniavsky, Frank Manuel, Herbert Marcuse, George Fischer, and Edward Mills Purcell. While only the first two were directly involved, the others made vital contributions to the process which brought the work to fruition. I prefer to specify to each man privately the nature of the obligations I feel, but I must take this opportunity to express my deepest thanks to all six.

A Note on the Chapter Openings

All the caricatures in this book originally were published in *Le Charivari*, a daily satirical newspaper, between 1848 and 1850. They are reproduced here through the courtesy of the Harvard College Library. Following are the captions, English translations, and publication dates for the caricatures printed here on the initial page of each chapter. These and most of the other caricatures were drawn by "Cham" (Amédée de Noé), who did close to 200 cartoons of Proudhon for *Le Charivari* during this period.

Chapter 1—March 4, 1849

LA RECRÉATION DU MONDE PAR P.-J. PROUDHON. P.-J. Proudhon crée un homme et une femme à son image. (*C'est fort laid.*)

"THE RE-CREATION OF THE WORLD BY P.-J. PROUDHON. P.-J. Proudhon creates a man and a woman in his own image. (*It's very ugly.*)"

Chapter 2—March 18, 1849

PROUDHON GROS-PIERRE. *Le vrai paysan.*—Prolétaires . . . réacchionaires . . . c'est pa du patois d'cheu nous . . . J'vous comprenons point!

"PROUDHON GROS-PIERRE. *The true peasant.*—'Proletarians . . . reactionaries . . . We ain't got no lingo like that . . . I don't understand you nohow!' "

Chapter 3—August 27, 1848

L'ABOLITION DU TALENT. (*M. Proudhon*).—Quel est le misérable qui a commis ce chef-d'oeuvre?—Raphaël, monsieur. (*M. Proudhon*).—Je vais faire arrèter le citoyen Raphaël comme un infame réactionnaire; vite son adresse, puis qu'on le pende!

"THE ABOLITION OF TALENT. (*M. Proudhon*).—'Who is the wretch who perpetrated this masterpiece?'—'Raphael, monsieur.' (*M. Proudhon*)—'I am going to have Citizen Raphael arrested as an infamous reactionary; quickly his address, seeing that they are hanging him!' "

Chapter 4—March 18, 1849

UNE MYSTIFICATION DU BAL DE LA MI-CARÊME. P.-J. Proudhon Considérant Victor.

"A HOAX OF THE MID-LENTEN BALL. P.-J. Proudhon Considering (*Considérant*) Victor."

Chapter 5—August 6, 1848

Aspect de l'assemblée nationale pendant que le citoyen Proudhon est en train de développer ses petites idées.

"View of the National Assembly while Citizen Proudhon develops his little ideas."

Chapter 6—December 24, 1848

CASTIBELZA-PROUDHON.—Le vent qui souffle à travers la montaaaagne m'a rendu fou . . . oui, m'a ren-en-endu fou! . . .

"CASTIBELZA-PROUDHON.—"The wind which blows across the mountain-n-n-n has made me crazy . . . yes, has ma-a-ade me crazy!' "

Chapter 7—December 2, 1849

POLÉMIQUE ENTRE P.-J. PROUDHON ET LOUIS BLANC. P.-J. Proudhon propose à son adversaire d'engager une lutte corps à corps.

"POLEMIC BETWEEN P.-J. PROUDHON AND LOUIS BLANC. P.-J. Proudhon proposes to his adversary that they engage in a hand-to-hand struggle."

Chapter 8—January 13, 1850

Le mariage et ses suites ramènent, après quelques années, P.-J. Proudhon aux idées de famille.

"Marriage and its sequels bring P.-J. Proudhon back, after a few years, to ideas about the family."

Chapter 9—August 20, 1848

LE CHRISTIANISME FAISANT PLACE AU PROUDHONISME.

"CHRISTIANITY GIVING WAY TO PROUDHONISM." (Inscription over altar: "We adore Proudhon.")

Chapter 10—February 18, 1849

DÉCLARATION.—Je fais serment devant Dieu et devant les hommes, sur la Constitution et sur l'Evangile, etc. (*Le diable n'y comprend plus rien.*)

"DECLARATION.—'I take my oath before God and before men, on the Constitution and on the Gospel, etc.' (*The devil understands nothing of this.*)" (Proudhon holds a paper which reads: "God is infamous.—Proudhon.")

Chapter 11—February 18, 1849

Il est institué auprès de la *Banque de peuple* un comité de *jusrisconsultes* choisis uniquement parmi les *travailleurs*.

"Close to the *People's Bank* a committee of *jurisconsults* is instituted, chosen solely from among the *workers*."

Chapter 12—February 18, 1849

La *Banque du peuple* encourage et soutient de ses avances toute entreprise industrielle, scientifique et *autres*.

"The *People's Bank* encourages and sustains with its advances every industrial, scientific, and *other* enterprise."

Chapter 13—August 20, 1848

SANS RIEN ÉCOUTER, M. PROUDHON VA TOUJOURS DROIT SON CHEMIN.

"WITHOUT PAYING ATTENTION TO ANYTHING, M. PROUDHON ALWAYS GOES RIGHT DOWN HIS ROAD." (He is headed toward Charenton, the famous insane asylum.)

Revolutionary Justice

THE SOCIAL AND POLITICAL THEORY

OF P.-J. PROUDHON

one: Introduction

> Of *system*, I have none, I do not want any, I formally reject the supposition.[1]

PROUDHON PLAYED a curious, anomalous role in the several histories in which he was an actor. In the history of developing social and political ideas leading from the eighteenth-century Enlightenment to the present he was an integral part of an evolving tradition, following very closely the convictions and assumptions of his predecessors and contributing in varying degrees to those of his successors. Yet at the same time he stood self-consciously aside from that tradition, reacting against it, discovering its faults, and articulating, often with brilliance and eloquence, the dissatisfaction with it half-felt but ill-recognized by many of his contemporaries and successors.

In that violently revolving whirlwind of social and political events that might variously be called the history of revolutions, of the social movement, or of the emancipation of mankind, he helped to mark and make the transition from "liberal democratic revolution" to "social revolution." He fathered that side of the latter which is called anarchism, acting as a major source of inspiration for the labor movement in France and, on occasion, elsewhere. Yet

1. *Oeuv.* (*Lacroix*), XVIII, 54.

3

in a certain significant sense he was not a revolutionary, while in another way he was the truest revolutionary of all. He was not a socialist any more than he was a bourgeois liberal, yet he was a more honest socialist than anyone else. One might almost say that he was not even an anarchist, yet that word has little positive meaning that he did not create for it.

He is none of these things and all of them because he gave to each term his own unique meaning—so unique that few can be said really to have followed him or even fully understood him, so idiosyncratic that to assign him with others to a category marked "socialist," "revolutionary," or even "anarchist" is to mislead through generalization which necessarily is too inclusive. Proudhon was not only the individualist *par excellence;* he was the individual who defies abstraction from his individuality.

If Proudhon is taken as a piece of an essentially nonhistorical, academic discipline called political theory or philosophy, then he generally merits a place, usually secondary (as befits the creator of so fruitless a movement as anarchism), in any complete account or collection of readings for university students. Not only did he negate government itself, but he proposed such intriguing if impractical ideas as "Property is theft" and that of free credit as a panacea. Some have even put him forward as a foil to Marx, as the one who really first conceived of all the important ideas with which the latter so upset the world. Yet the creative constructs of Proudhon may be less significant for political philosophy than the light he shed through his negative criticism of widely accepted theories.

Proudhon was very much a creature of his time. Most of what he wrote, especially in the last and most creative third of his life, was produced in response to the events and ideas that swirled about him. Much of this is so particular to the moment that it has by now lost most of its life and interest. He was directly involved in the politics of the Second Republic, and to a much lesser but still significant extent in the politics of the Second Empire; his ghost loomed over the brief, tumultuous life of the First Socialist International. Yet he was as remote from all of this as any "political man" of the time could be. Moreover, he perceived much of what the future held in store only dimly, or even not at all. In a country which was industrializing rapidly, his mentality was that of a pre-industrial artisan and peasant; the mass society of the twentieth century was largely alien to his imagination, while the foretastes of this future in his own time were almost equally strange to him.

Despite these observations, Proudhon can seem remarkably independent of his times. Studying him while trying to associate him with these several histories of which he was a part and from which he was apart—and while contemplating the condition of man today—can lead to the suspicion, even the conviction, that he speaks to that condition as few others have done.

Just because he was so independent of the world about him, yet so intimately conscious of it and moved by it, Proudhon's thought has a universality and relevance that transcends time without separating from it. He is history in the best sense, because he is an important part of the past we must know if we are to comprehend the present.

Proudhon is a contradiction, just as his work is a tissue of contradictions. Contradiction is his essence, his glory, and his limitation. He is a great figure and a constricted one. He built no system, yet he surpassed system-building. Possibly the most important aspect of his legacy is not what he thought, but what he leads us into thinking for ourselves.

To introduce Proudhon and his work as a fabric of contradictions not only defines the essential character of the subject; it also poses a series of questions or problems to be resolved. If the preceding paragraphs are to be more than a rhetorical device, then they should not be left without additional comment, and such comment follows.

However, the problems are not to be resolved easily. The body of his writing is too large and too complex to do more at this point than sketch additional details in the picture. The rest will unfold gradually, in chapters structured to facilitate this process.

One could do much with a simple analytic approach: this is the biography; here are the main sources of intellectual influence upon him; these are the principal elements of his philosophy, one by one; and there are the significant connections which tie diverse points together. In part, this is what must be done, if the result is not to be as disordered as his books sometimes are—but it is not enough.

Proudhon was not a systematic thinker, yet he did have a unitary and comprehensive view of man and society which animated all his work and integrated it.

In a similar vein one of his admirers wrote of "the master idea . . . which constantly dominates and orders this effervescence of seemingly contradictory ideas."[2] The master idea, if just one is to be named, is Justice, but this is more a complex of ideas or, indeed, an entire philosophy, whose definition evolves continually throughout his career. It needs to be understood in terms of the process of its evolution.

It also can seem as if Proudhon had not one, but several philosophies—parallel, perhaps, but sufficiently distinct for his successors to pick out one philosophy to make over for their own while repudiating or ignoring the rest. Such has been done, and he has been the darling of the radical right as well as of the radical left where he is more naturally placed. Yet these supposedly parallel philosophies are, rather, intersecting facets of a unitary, all-embracing world view, aspects of a concept of Justice at once complex and simple.

His philosophy is not fundamentally abstruse; it is difficult primarily because of the way it is set forth, at such length and unsystematically, and secondarily because of the encumbering intellectual baggage that many have brought to its study. By defining some of the problems at the outset, this introduction should make the remaining chapters more illuminating.

Placing this man in a developing tradition stemming from the Enlightenment *philosophes* serves better to explain Proudhon than it does to define the tradition, and serves better to explain what he thinks, but does not say, than what he does say. He is a maverick, adapting a heritage of received ideas to his own idiosyncratic patterns, or straying from it far enough to criticize many of its principal elements, while still colored by its effects. He assumes uncritically the validity of some notions of Enlightenment philosophy while subjecting others to close scrutiny, and it is the uncritical assumptions which connect him to the tradition most closely. His

2. Georges Guy-Grand, introduction to *De la Justice dans la révolution et dans l'église, Oeuv.*, VIII, vol. i, 47.

greatest departures from it involve his attacks on his contemporaries for conceptions stemming from the same Enlightenment ideas that he has incorporated and adapted in his own thought.

He adopts the profound faith of the *philosophes* in the power of enlightenment, and their excitement over its possibilities. They believed that all human problems can be conquered through the increase of ordered knowledge, and the extension of that knowledge to all men through education. Typical of the tradition and of Proudhon is this emphasis on knowledge, as opposed to mere technique or to the operations of Fate, the Divine, or some particular human authority. Intellect replaces faith and the guidance of divine or external human agency.

The relation of knowledge to experience here is different from that which was customary in earlier philosophy. Just as human life and action are to be based on knowledge, rather than on instinct or unreflective obedience to the law of God or man, so too the subject of philosophy is the actuality of human experience, and the goal of knowledge the mastery of problems confronting mankind. Ideas, however abstract, are not valued in abstraction.

Moreover, this ordered knowledge is derived *from* experience in the spirit of the New Science of Galileo and Newton. Law, whether of nature or of God, is not *prior to* phenomena, but discovered *in* them. Discovery of regular relation and consequent law in nature is the process by which knowledge increases—a revealing to human understanding of the essential rationality of the universe. This rationality or reason is the structure of regular relationship between the elements and phenomena of existence, and laws the statements of such relationships.

Proudhon regards knowledge and reason in essentially this way; it is necessary to recall this deliberately from time to time, for the emphasis he places on ideas in themselves sometimes makes them appear as if rather distant from experience, in conception if not in application. This is more true of his earlier writing, where some of his concepts are not yet fully developed and his philosophy is technically weak, than it is of his later work, where he scorns those who he believes divorce their theories from actual, daily human experience.

Quite vital is his characteristically Enlightenment view of reason as determination of structure, not the sum of divinely given ideas prior to all experience: such structure is not fixed. Rational determination is always modifiable and modifying. One structure dissolves into another; law is a statement of existing but changeable relationship, not of absolutes fixed for all time. The world is not "all in." Thus, this notion of reason and of rationality of existence incorporates an assumption that *process* is essential to reality, and fixity alien to it. If process is the nature of things, then it is possible and even easy to go on to rejection of any status quo and still further to claim the inevitability of revolution.

The idea of progress, if not necessarily of revolution, is the obvious consequence of this conception of process in reality combined with enthusiasm for the potential of enlightenment. Proudhon's approach is progressivist, of course, but, although basically optimistic about man and his future, he usually avoids the naïve optimism common to both his own contemporaries and their Enlightenment forebears. For him, though knowledge can make progress possible, it hardly guarantees it, and great obstacles block the way.

Crucial here is the degree of optimism about human nature: a large measure of such optimism is required by any socio-political theory which is not conservative. In simplest form, common in the eighteenth century and ever since, this optimistic approach regards man as fundamentally unflawed, though perhaps soiled by bad institutions and by material, cultural, and spiritual deprivation. All such evil influences are remediable, and existing flaws in human nature are thus capable of reduction to the vanishing point.

This is Proudhon's initial view, but experience in time makes him more skeptical about human nature and less hopeful about progress. His mature skepticism represents not a departure from the progressivist faith but a modification of the more naïve form in which it often appears. In the naïve form it is supposed that the expansion of knowledge and its successful application, together probably with the modification of institutions, will ensure progress indefinitely. Imperfections in human nature are superficial and will gradually disappear as their external causes do. Proudhon concludes, on the other hand, that men must change themselves before progress is possible: institutional changes and both individual and collective moral regeneration are necessary for each other and for progress.

He differs from conservatives in believing that substantial improvement in individual morality is possible and that potential human nature is sound; he just is not continually enthusiastic about the immediate prospects of fulfilling that potential. Thus he is skeptical about present manifestations of human nature and about improving it solely through external instrumentalities, but he retains the humanist faith in his positive view of human potential, which in its implications is an affirmation of belief in a fundamentally good human nature. Not only does Proudhon retain the humanist orientation of many eighteenth-century *philosophes;* he also develops some humanistically oriented lines of thought much further. His philosophy may be one logical extreme of the humanist tendency. Naturally enough, the religious skepticism of the Encyclopedists continues undiminished in Proudhon's work, where it is greatly reinforced by republican anticlericalism and his own sharply negative reaction to any authority.

While retaining hope for progress in his own peculiar way, he departed more radically from the tradition born of the Enlightenment in his ambivalent attitude toward revolution. The principal current of the Enlightenment heritage in France leads from the Encyclopedists through the Revolution of 1789 (both directly and by way of Rousseau) to the countless variations of "enlightened" thought ranging from that of some Orleanists and Bonapartists on the one side to insurrectionary Blanquists on the other. Each of these variations viewed the Revolution of 1789 as a positive development, a major progressive step. More generally, those whose thought lay within this range of opinion regarded some form of revolution as a suitable, even an excellent or necessary, means to attain a desired political system not yet realized, though most of the same men deeply feared an "excess" of revolution. Furthermore, for many Frenchmen the Revolution of 1789 was a basis of great national pride and the origin of their personal fortunes. The hopes and fears of revolution were of primary emotional importance for quite a number of men.

Proudhon's attitude toward revolution and the Revolution is more complicated, though not truly inconsistent. In some respects he accepts the Revolution of 1789 and subsequent revolutionary developments as progressive, but his acceptance is much qualified. He feels that at best they only brought *genuine* revolutionary change—which is yet to be seen—a little nearer, while at worst they merely substituted forms of tyranny for each other, at some points retrogressively.

Except in 1848 and 1849 he remains for the most part detached from revolutionary action; he declines to assume the mantle of leadership for the French workers' revolutionary movement, which is virtually his for the asking from then on. Both his prior convictions and the experience of the 1848 Revolution make him distrust the revolutionary process profoundly and distrust its putative leaders even more. After 1848 he believes that revolution has not fulfilled its promise and cannot do so unless a very different approach is followed, one involving the moral regeneration of mankind.

Nevertheless, he does seek change which is revolutionary beyond all question, probably more so than that sought by most other revolutionaries. He envisages a revolutionary process of accomplishing these changes, though he thinks forcible insurrections unlikely to achieve them. He consistently argues for concepts which are in effect the most radical logical extremes of the revolutionary principles of others. Undeniably he is a revolutionary as uncompromising as any other, and more so than most. That he also condemns revolutions is a paradox easily understood. Less apparent, but explicable on similar grounds, is the consistency of his revolutionary approach with his maintenance of a number of positions, such as partial approval of the *coup d'état* of Louis-Napoleon Bonaparte, ordinarily associated with more moderate or even conservative philosophers.

Proudhon stands in lines of development that pass from the eighteenth-century Enlightenment through Turgot and Condorcet to Saint-Simon and Fourier, to Comte and to the Saint-Simonian school, and through Rousseau to the Jacobins, Montagnards, and on to bourgeois republicanism and to the socialism of Louis Blanc. In considering the line through Rousseau and the Revolutionary republic, Proudhon is dissatisfied with what he regards as an essentially political approach to problems originating in social and economic iniquities. He has little use for solutions imposed or organized by the State and no expectation that a new governmental constitution will itself provide a fruitful basis for change. The nationalism associated with the Revolution of 1789 repels him.

With the utopian socialists he has fewer differences, but these disagreements are profound nevertheless. He believes that the various socialist schemes for a better society would necessarily result in unacceptable repression of individual liberty. His radical individualism is devoid of egoism, and thus distinguished from bourgeois liberalism, but the resemblance is too strong for him to have escaped having the petit bourgeois label applied to him.

To say that Proudhon is not a socialist may be an exaggeration, though the term is sufficiently vague to exclude or include almost anyone. His departure from the main currents of socialist thought is sufficiently great to exclude him; yet this would be a mistake, if humanism and a libertarian ideal are accepted—as I think they must be—as the core of any variety of socialism. Proudhon adheres so closely and consistently to the humanitarian-libertarian theme, and follows it so determinedly, that he could be called the truest or most honest of socialists.

His relation to anarchism is also a peculiar one. He is the "father" of anarchism: although there were earlier anarchists or near anarchists, most notably William Godwin, they had little or no influence on the movement when it developed. Godwin's main effect was that on English Romantic poets, and on Thomas Malthus, who wrote his *Essay on the Principle of Population* in response to Godwin and Condorcet. Proudhon's role has been very different: not only have anarchists learned much directly from his work, or from précis of it, but the scope of his thought is so broad that they have been able to say little that he has not already discussed thoroughly, except in their venting of negative and destructive impulses.

While Proudhon is unflaggingly anarchist in the term's negative sense of opposition to all forms of government, anarchism is also a positive theory of how an ideal society is to be achieved in the virtual or total absence of government. He develops such a theory, but his faith in it is circumscribed by his skepticism about human behavior and revolution. Only fitfully does he show the kind of ardor characteristic of the revolutionary enthusiast, and he would have lacked sympathy for much of what evolved after his death in revolutionary anarchist movements. However, he would have been at home, if not burning with zeal, with some of the forms that anarchism has taken.

It should be becoming apparent that Proudhon, even more than most men, can hardly be fully understood or soundly appreciated apart from the integral context of the whole man and his work. Too much of what has been written of him lacks this integral comprehension; this is particularly true of British and American writing, and of the work of Marxists, who often have known Proudhon chiefly through Marx's negative comments about him. Surveys of political theory and intellectual history have tended to focus on especially novel or startling ideas of the French anarchist, often without achieving even a superficial *aperçu*.

One reason for the difficulty in appraising him adequately is that he does not conform to any of the patterns which one customarily perceives for a French man of ideas. Not only his ideas, but also his prejudices differ from those of other ideologues. Georges Guy-Grand has described him as "a Franc-Comtois peasant, an opinion-ated artisan, a Frenchman of the old stamp, the incarnation of the genius of the French people." [3] While these terms hardly constitute a complete characterization, they do indicate some of the distinctive coloring of the man, and they help to explain his moralism, individualism, and difficulty in adjusting his thought and imagination to the peculiar problems created by a new industrial age.

His personality was unusual in many ways. His intellectual detachment (almost an estrangement) from the actual daily world is common among men of ideas, but in him this remoteness was combined with an intimate consciousness of daily events and a deep, responsive interest in them resulting in thousands of pages of topical writing and substantial effects on his "timeless" theory.

He had little personal ambition, foregoing more than one opportunity to gain positions normally much sought-after, and showing little taste for fame and public acclaim. He was reluctant to be a man of action, on grounds both of temperament and theory, and he soon regretted his one experience as a politician, when he served as a deputy in the National Assembly of the Second Republic. As an ideologue he was not combative; though a frequent polemicist, he

3. Ibid.

avoided acrimony, vituperation, and vindictiveness in controversy, usually keeping debates at an elevated level.

Probably most important is the recognition that Proudhon was a highly moral man as well as a moralistic one. He would do harm to no man willingly, and he seems to have been immune to sensual temptations and avarice alike. He was a passionate man, but his passions were those of social and intellectual concerns, while in personal matters he remained essentially puritanical. Marrying a girl he chose for her simple virtue, he was a model husband and father, a paragon of domestic rectitude. A selfless man who was good to the core, his abundant virtue would make him seem dull were it not relieved by a few sins: a naïve sort of pride, stubbornness, blindness to others' points of view, a certain intolerance for human failings, and an occasionally immoderate temper.

That he was fundamentally a virtuous man helps to explain much about him, especially a moralism so uncompromising as to lead more cynical and "practical" men to regard his ideas as too innocent and unsophisticated. The following, written by him in his mature years, typifies his approach:

> Purity or clarity of reason, purity or innocence of heart, purity or health of body, purity or justice in actions and sincerity in words, purity even in justice, that is to say, modesty in virtue; that is the morality of Progress, that is my religion. It supposes a continual effort upon itself, and it admits all transitions, it agrees in all places and at all times. Morality, monsieur, mark it well, is the only thing I regard as absolute, not with regard to the form of the precept, always variable, but with regard to the obligation it imposes. Now, this Absolute is still only a transcendental conception, having for its goal the ideal perfection of the human being, through fidelity to law and to progress.[4]

Another facet of the man's makeup that should be kept in mind is the idiosyncratic way he used and responded to the things he read in his extremely wide and eclectic studies. Guided by an extensive but not universal curiosity and an appetite for material to be used in his writing, he was, however, limited in his learning by a lack of intellectual receptivity and flexibility, and of the discipline supposed to be acquired from the formal education of which he had

4. *Philosophie du progrès, Oeuv.*, XII, 83.

too little. Additionally, he was unable to read any modern language except French, although he knew Latin, Greek, and Hebrew. This meant that modern writing not available in French or Latin was inaccessible to him, or known only in derivative form in French secondary works.

We can tell fairly well what he read, though for the most part we can do little more than guess in identifying which works most influenced him and how they did so. He read most widely in classical philosophy, the Scriptures and modern theological commentary, jurisprudence both ancient and modern, and just about anything modern in the categories of speculative philosophy, politics, economics, and social theory. He was not notably discriminating in his selection of reading matter, taking the obscure and dull along with the distinguished.

Religious writings certainly contributed to his moralism, though their effects on his work must have been largely indirect. Speculative philosophy helped form the general outlook discussed earlier. Rousseau seems to have influenced him deeply, although Proudhon is very critical of the other's concepts. He also learned much from liberal economists, notably Smith, Ricardo, Say, Joseph Garnier, and Adolphe Blanqui, and from Sismondi. To other French socialists, especially Fourier and some of the Saint-Simonians, he no doubt owed most of all,[5] but as they were nearest to him it is most difficult to appraise the nature of the debt.

While the quantity of Proudhon's reading was huge, it would seem that his assimilation of the material was quite limited and that he often read hastily, probably reading few books in their entirety or with any desire to understand the author's views in all their details. When one compares the reflections of the other men's ideas in his writings with the original sources, it is apparent that the "reflections" are just that: he interpreted a source in terms of his own preconceptions and preoccupations, and did not try to understand it on its own ground. He read only to discover more about those things which interested him, and he was more likely to find there reinforcements for his prior conceptions than he was to be struck

5. Hegel and Marx are often alleged to have had major influence on him. This will be considered at length in Ch. 4.

by fresh inspiration or a need to change his mind. As a result his insights into the work of others were frequently acute, but he often also ignored or misunderstood important ideas which were relevant to his own theses.

Such limitations in reading are common enough; they are especially likely to be faults of someone like Proudhon, an autodidact of circumscribed perceptivity and strongly held convictions of his own. While rarely insistent on his own views to the point of dogmatism, the firmness of his beliefs made it difficult for him to recognize the virtues of alternative ideas.

In discussing the work of other authors in his own writing, which he does often and at length, usually his purpose is only to provide useful hooks on which to hang his arguments or to afford targets for his darts. He takes no care to represent the views of others accurately and is careless about quoting them correctly.

Whether with deliberate purpose, or simply out of bias and restricted perceptivity, he distorts the shapes of others' views into whatever it is that he wishes to argue against, rendering the refutation easier. This he does frequently, and not just in polemics.

Prolonged discussions of others' work are usually parts of his sometimes almost obsessively comprehensive attempts to cover every aspect of a subject and marshal every conceivable argument in support of his cause. These, together with his detailed attention to topical matters of transitory significance, make his writing tiresomely prolix in many parts. With his often excessive verbiage, as well as his occasional neologisms and peculiarities of style and diction, Proudhon could have benefited greatly from the services of a good editor. Friendly criticism of the substance of his work before publication could also have sharpened its cutting edge and increased its impact.

Nevertheless, despite all its faults, Proudhon's writing is extraordinarily powerful. He often speaks with remarkable eloquence, both his individualistic style and the passion of his convictions giving his words exceptional impact. At his best the logic and unfaltering moral force of his arguments put them beyond refutation, and the clarity of his reasoning easily transcends his tendency to wordiness. Even his private correspondence often displays such excellence, and in both private and public writing the emotional appeal of the many eloquent reflections of personal conviction can be quite moving.

Potent as his writing is, it is hardly surprising that he has had many disciples and admirers. Yet no coherent and lasting movement was actually based primarily on his philosophy, as some have been based on the thought of Marx, Saint-Simon, Fourier, and others. At first glance, the explanation is simple: Proudhon did not create a complete, integral philosophical system, and the practical ideologies of movements should be systematic, in order to provide both programs for action and foundations for the conversion and enduring faith of adherents. Proudhon, however, wrote:

> Of *system*, I have none, I do not want any, I formally reject the supposition. We shall know the system of humanity only at humanity's end. . . . What interests me is to know its route and, if I can, to mark the path.[6]

His rejection of system-building requires explanation and qualification, however. "A system in the nineteenth century was by definition an attempt to encompass all knowledge and to dictate rules for a new order"[7]—by this definition Proudhon did come very close to being a system-builder, though he did not succeed in being thoroughly systematic. In an intermediate period of his intellectual development, during the mid-1840's, he did indeed try to create precisely the sort of system just defined. Failing to achieve his goal and recognizing at least in part the futility of his attempts, he discarded the deliberately systematic approach.

Nevertheless, his philosophy does have the integral coherence intended for systems and much of the all-encompassing scope pretended for them. If it lacks the "science" sought by him at one time and claimed by a Marx or a Comte, it does have principles with the universality though not quite the same sort of certainty sought by a science. His certainty is, rather, that of a man who has no doubt of the essential rightness of his convictions, without really relying on the force of inductive demonstrations or claiming unimpeachable authority.

6. Lettre aux citoyens rédacteurs du Populaire," *Le Peuple*, March 21, 1849, 1; in *Oeuv. (Lacroix)*, XVIII, 54.
7. Frank E. Manuel, *The Prophets of Paris* (Cambridge, Mass., 1962), 1.

Proudhon's philosophy does prescribe the forms to be taken by a new and just order, and the means for getting there; but he lacks the confidence of other system-builders in expectations that man will indeed arrive at the new order. The very nature of his beliefs prohibits such confidence, though enthusiasm sometimes gives it to him for a while. A century of added experience and increasing self-knowledge have made his new order seem no nearer and almost surely less realizable than in his day.

The overall difficulty of thoroughly comprehending his work and the plethora of contradictions there make it hard to see how complete and integral his world-view actually is. While summarizing the tens of thousands of pages might bring order out of the apparent chaos of his verbosity, the contradictions would remain to perplex and confuse.

These contradictions are of many sorts. Some are apparent inconsistencies which vanish when closely examined; examples of these have been discussed above. Some result from rhetorical devices he loves to use in order to startle and to provoke fresh thought. "Property is theft" involves the best-known use of such a device. Perhaps some contradictions and inconsistencies are irreconcilably problematical, though in the end it is hard to see how any of these seriously detract from the effectiveness of his ideas.

The most important contradictions, however, he regards as inherent in the nature of things and of human relationships. Thus contradiction must ultimately be perceived as the core of his philosophy, though in a way far different from that of Hegelian or Marxian dialectics.

So Proudhon's philosophy partakes of most of the marks of systematization distinguishing the great nineteenth-century speculative theories on social systems. However, to his mind there is one crucial difference: his philosophy is not absolute, but insistently non-dogmatic. It knows no certainties except moral obligation, and it assumes that no knowledge or concept is final. There is at once a rejection of the dogmatism and fatalism of then traditional thought and of the positivism born of modern science.

His is a readiness to admit fallibility, while distrusting a positivism that prescribes and demands in accordance with the logic of a science which will not recognize the waywardness, irrationality, emotionalism, and variability natural to man. It is thus in an important way more humane than the unitary systems he rejects.

Today much of the political left reflects a weariness, even disgust, with a century of dogmatic ideology and its political consequences; it expresses a revulsion against statism and the technocracy born of the positivist temperament, whether the state is a "people's democracy" or a bulwark and instrument of capitalist enterprise. The result has been an intense storm of theoretical innovation and reappraisal of old ideas, both marked by a new humanism.

In this context, and perhaps even in a wider one, Proudhon's humanism has a fresh relevance:

> One cannot do what he wants with a system, though he may invent it a thousand times: nothing is more rebellious, more inflexible, and, if I dare say so, more obstinately total. Man, by virtue of his free will, has the faculty of avowing and disavowing, of coming to terms with everything; he can infinitely modify his thought, his will, his action, his speech; his life is only a succession of transactions with his fellow men and with nature. An idea, on the contrary, a theory, a system, a constitution, a pact, all that which receives from language and logic expression and form, is a thing defined and consequently definitive; an inviolable thing, which does not bend, which does not yield; which cannot be given up for another, but which cannot assume new properties, that is, which does not become another while remaining itself.[8]

8. *Contradictions politiques, Oeuv.,* XIII, 159ff.

two: Early Life and Work

We are little bousbots.—
Who used to go about in sabots . . .[1]

All that I am I owe to despair. Fortune depriving me of the means
of gain, I wanted, from the scraps picked up during my brief studies, one day to create for myself a science all my own.[2]

PIERRE-JOSEPH PROUDHON was born on January 15, 1809, at Besançon, the principal town of the Franche-Comté. He was the oldest
son in a poor family, his father a cooper and his mother a cook,
both employed at a large brewery.

The Franche-Comté, one of the last regions incorporated into
France, is a mountainous area whose people had a spirit of independence and little love for royal authority. Jacobin republicanism
was strong there, as was a rebellious temper. Other celebrated men
with distinctive, radical social concerns also came from Besançon or
nearby at about the same time: utopian prophet Charles Fourier,
literary giant Victor Hugo, and realist painter Gustave Courbet.

1. Edouard Droz, "Hommage des petits bousbots à Proudhon et à Fourier,"
lyrics of song performed by public-school children at a soirée sponsored by the
local Université Populaire, Besançon, June 29, 1904; Bibliothèque Municipale de
Besançon, Manuscript Collection no. D 16968. "Bousbots" is a local slang word
denoting poor vineyard workers or, by extension, the very poor generally.
2. Written by Proudhon in his youth. Quoted in Daniel Halévy, *Essais sur le
mouvement ouvrier en France* (Paris, 1901), 157.

Proudhon was to be the printer of the first, friend of the second, and both friend and literary collaborator of the last.

The Proudhon family on both sides was of plain artisan and peasant stock, with that tradition of honest rectitude and individualism often associated with such a background. For a time Pierre's father operated his own small brewery and tavern. Later the son was to say that this venture failed because his father would sell only to honest customers and at a just price—his costs plus a modest amount for his labor.

The family was republican; the boy's mother, Catherine, loved to tell the children of the exploits of her father, a bold revolutionary to whom Pierre gave heroic stature in his later writing. A cousin was a Jacobin Club leader and a Freemason. For the Proudhons, as for many Comtois, Jacobinism meant an egalitarian promise of universal justice and a new age, not the bloody conflicts that made many others fearful of a revived republicanism in later years.

For a time after the Proudhon brewery's failure the family lived on the farm of Catherine's father, near Besançon. Until his twelfth year Pierre lived mainly a peasant's life, herding cows and helping his father in farm work.

Catherine Proudhon appears to have been a remarkable person, "a superior woman, endowed with a heroic character." [3] She was the leading figure in the household, a powerful positive influence on her children, even more than most mothers are. Pierre always retained a deep veneration for her. Probably she was the most important formative factor in his early life. It was she who made him enter the *collège* at Besançon in 1820, although such an education must have been unusual in the family, and they could hardly afford the fees. The parish curé obtained for young Pierre a *bourse d'externat*, which made this course of study possible, although still a financial strain.

The boy had no money to buy books, so he had to do without. Later Proudhon recalled doing his Latin exercises at home without a dictionary, then looking up the unknown words at school before classes. His lessons he copied from books borrowed from classmates.

3. C.-A. Sainte-Beuve, *P.-J. Proudhon, sa vie et sa correspondance, 1838–1848* (Paris, 1872), 16.

Many times he was punished for having "forgotten" to bring his books to class. He had to leave his wooden sabots at the classroom door in order not to disturb the class with their noise.

Although set apart from the other boys in the *collège* by his social station and poverty, Pierre was a successful scholar and an especially good Latinist. His formal education was cut short when he was seventeen, however, after an unsuccessful lawsuit completed his father's financial ruin. The youth returned home after receiving the school's principal prize for excellence, only to hear the news of the adverse judgment.

As the oldest child it was now necessary for him to go to work. Despite having to give up his education and its fruits, he seems to have cherished the independence he gained by being self-supporting, although years later he was to have heavy burdens of debt and the support of his parents. Having adequate learning and a love of books, he began work as an apprentice at one of the several printing firms in Besançon. He soon learned the work of a compositor, and he followed the trade of a printer for some years. His employers published a number of theological works, for which young Proudhon's Latin expertise was most useful. It was during this period that he acquired a thorough knowledge of the Bible and of Greek and Hebrew.

The work of setting type and correcting proofs for the theological books increased his interest in religious writings. It seems that Proudhon continued to study intensively and that the bulk of his reading for several years was theological. It is difficult to assess his religious beliefs in the early part of his life, or the actual effect on him of his reading, for our source of information is his later recollections, written at a time when he had become a most severe critic of religion and of the Church.[4]

Proudhon indicated that the appeal to him of the Church lay not in its mystery or ceremony but in the supposition that all are equal in the Church and can find solace there. However, in his actual experience he found in the Church not equality but social-

4. Some of the information on his early life is derived from the brief "Mémoires sur ma vie," written in 1841 (*Carnets*, I, 1–9). Most of the rest comes from various recollections written after 1848.

class preference. He ceased practicing religion at the age of sixteen, resuming it a few years later with his intensive theological reading. Whatever the truth of these recollections may be, it seems that he concerned himself with spiritual ideas rather early and found in theology his first important contacts with philosophy. He recalled that, since reading Fénelon's *Démonstration de l'existence de Dieu* at fourteen, "I have remained a metaphysician." This is characteristic hyperbole, but the background of religious and spiritual modes of philosophy remained a significant element of Proudhon's thought throughout his life, although he did claim that orthodox theology stimulated him into heretical lines of thought.

In any case, the retrospective picture of the author's youth passed on to us is not the typical one of a tormented young intellectual, but rather one of a spirited—and spiritual—fellow in love with life, having an inquisitive nature, living a somewhat hard life but without discontent or bitterness over lost opportunity. Daniel Halévy comments, "Bourgeois we are, and the renunciation of the bourgeois life seems to us the hardest of tests. A worker, Proudhon sees things from another viewpoint, and does not suffer. He takes a trade: it is quite natural." [5]

Major political controversy has revolved around the supposed social class identity of Proudhon and of Proudhonist thought. He has been called one of those rarities, a proletarian ideologue, since he was the son of a skilled worker and a peasant domestic servant, and he practiced a worker's trade himself for many years.

On the other hand, Karl Marx scornfully denounced him as a petit bourgeois. Proudhon did work for several years in a managerial job and for a while owned his own business. During the latter and creative half of his life he lived as a *publiciste;* although still very poor, he did little work in the printer's trade. Whatever the effects of early experience on him, he was no longer really a worker when he set forth his philosophy.

Nevertheless, according to the criteria—more or less Marxist in derivation—used in criticism of Proudhonism, it is class origin and ideological content that must matter here. If it would seem by the first that Proudhon's mind would have to be "proletarian," his

5. Daniel Halévy, *La Jeunesse de Proudhon* (Paris, 1913), 35.

ideas certainly are not to be deemed that in Marxian terms, and it is for these that he was called petit bourgeois. Proudhon's individualist, libertarian perspective and the philosophy resulting from it are not readily distinguishable in Marxian terms from the egoistic, liberal individualism of the petite bourgeoisie. While polemical purposes have caused Marxists to stress the allegation of petit bourgeois identity more than is warranted, the judgment is consistent with more detached Marxist theoretical premises.

Although a Marxist definition of "proletarian" was not ordinarily made so narrowly, in the most frequent usage (in reference to industrial or industrializing countries) the true proletarian was thought of as the worker employed in an *industrial* enterprise. The adjective is important because of the Marxist view that this proletariat has distinctive interests as a class, a distinctive perspective, and potentially a self-conscious, unique identity. From these assumptions come specifications about ideology appropriate to this proletariat, and denial that social and political ideas supposed to serve bourgeois class interests can be suitable for the needs of proletarians.

But this outlook relies on the assumption that the workers involved are completely integrated into and adapted to an industrial economy and the resulting social structure, and that this industrial system retains essentially the same kind of exploitive patterns defined in *Das Kapital*. If such is the case, there is a compelling basis for Marxist concentration on the claimed need for workers to develop and emphasize consciousness of their common needs and their potential opportunities as a class.

There is, however, a sharp discrepancy between historical reality and the theoretical premises involved here. Workers were not quickly integrated into industrial economies; they did not adapt rapidly to their positions in industrial societies. Rather, for decades and even generations they retained ideas, attitudes, and customs originating in the artisan workshops and peasant communities from which most of them had come. Those with artisan origins attempted, often successfully, to maintain previous work habits and patterns of social relationships, despite pressures from management and those resulting from their often miserable material circumstances, even though these customs were frequently ill-adapted to industrial conditions. Likewise, many workers with peasant roots maintained not only former habits and attitudes but also direct contacts with the villages from which they had come.

Neither artisan nor peasant attitudes were readily consonant with the perspectives of a class-conscious industrial proletariat in the Marxist model. Here we would do better to speak of a "pre-industrial" workers' mentality, insofar as it is possible to speak of a class-defined mentality at all. This pre-industrial quality of the proletariat persisted well into the period of industrialization, the times involved varying widely with the place.

Pre-industrial workers might and often did have a strong sense of common interests and group identity, even a "class consciousness" such as Marxists spoke of. However, they were likely to identify most closely with others in the same craft, with those who worked or lived in the same place, or with those who came originally from the same rural village or region. With these social sentiments went other attitudes which together made of these proletarians a "class" which was enough like the Marxist model to make the latter plausible, but not enough to make it a valid representation.

Thus the social categories employed in Marxist thought have had grave shortcomings, relying as they have upon suppositions that industrial workers had adapted to their circumstances more rapidly than in fact they did. The misconceptions involved here extend beyond Marxist analyses, for similar assumptions about the "industrialization" of working-class populations have been widely employed elsewhere. In passing, it may also be suggested that the Marxist view of the industrial proletariat discussed here does not correspond to reality in countries long since industrialized—what might be called "post-industrial" societies.

Proudhon's outlook here is a perfect example of a "pre-industrial mentality," although his philosophy eventually did include a more sophisticated understanding of industrial society than was usual among others whose ideas were pre-industrial in basis. Even his social origins—craftsman, son of a craftsman and a peasant mother, a youth in provincial town and on a farm—fit the pattern of the typical pre-industrial worker exactly.

Petit bourgeois he certainly was not. The bourgeoisie was alien to him; he never felt or understood the "bourgeois mentality" and did not even attempt to do so. He always thought of himself as one of the working class, but this class did not yet know modern industry—or else it reacted against what it did know of it. Besançon was a town of clock- and watchmakers, and even the Paris where he later made his home was still in the early stages of industrialization. Proudhon was always the artisan, once a country boy and a cattle-herder, who could not see or plan for a world of industry on a grand scale, for advanced technology, and for all their consequences. While he partly overcame this limitation in his final writings, the direction he took clearly reflects it.

This emphasis on the perspectives of pre-industrial working men is required because it explains much more than the character of Proudhon and his theory. Later we shall examine the extensive popularity of Proudhonism among certain groups of workers, who typically were also pre-industrial in their essential identities, even though many were employed in large factories. Still more significant is the fact that ideas like Proudhon's had a wide currency among workers where there is little or no reason to claim influence by him or his immediate disciples. His philosophy is important for the history of workers' movements, not so much because of his actual influence as because he gave voice and intelligent theoretical development to ideas and attitudes which were natural to large numbers of less-articulate working men for many years after initiation of large-scale industrialization.

Marxist confrontation and rivalry with Proudhonism and its anarchist descendants caused basic theoretical differences to be submerged in bitter polemics. Marxists could better have denounced Proudhonism and anarchism as uselessly obsolete because based on premises relevant only to pre-industrial society. Instead, they condemned by association with the bourgeois enemy. In so doing they failed to appraise adequately the true temper of many of the workers they sought to organize into a revolutionary movement. Without the conflict between Marxists and anarchists, the former might well have avoided the pitfall, for there is adequate basis in Marx's theory to make the needed distinctions between pre-industrial and industrial working-class mentalities.

Proudhon's retrospective portrait of his youth shows us an industrious, rather solitary artisan who spent his leisure hours in study and long walks in the country. He read Chateaubriand and was irritated by his apparent dishonesty and that of a Church which approved an unjust world. He was impressed by Bonald but saw discrepancies between the lessons of experience and that conservative's ideal. He remained religious, although his reading and reflections were leading him away from faith. The reading of the Abbé Pluquet's *Mémoires pour servir à l'histoire des égarements de l'esprit humain* (the so-called "Dictionnaire des hérésies") probably did not strengthen his orthodoxy. He does not seem to have been a good Catholic even then, but the idea of the sacred and of immutable law revealed by God was attractive to him for a while. He was attracted by a system of moral prescriptions, strengthened and elevated by ritual and the sense of the sacred: the humanist ideals of the Revolution sanctified and made eternal. When Proudhon discarded religious belief, it was in order to discover and embrace fresh foundations for his ideals.

A close friendship grew up between Proudhon and Gustave Fallot, a young philologist whom he met in 1828. The friendship itself and the direction which Fallot gave to the other's hitherto aimless study made the philologist a most important factor in his young friend's growth.

This association is particularly interesting because it seems to be the only one in Proudhon's life where there is clear indication of a really close relationship. Unquestionably he had many friends: we can see this from his extensive correspondence with some of them, from many other indications in his letters, notebooks, and published works, and from what the friends themselves said about him. Yet it is impossible to say what the nature of his personal relationships was, or how intimately he knew his various acquaintances. Proudhon wrote much about his experiences, both in private writing and for public consumption, but he revealed singularly little about his inner life or about those experiences and thoughts which were primarily personal and emotional rather than intellectual in import. It would be difficult, if not impossible, to write a biography of him that revealed his personality to the same degree as has often been done with other men of letters.

Friendship with Fallot led Proudhon to interest in philology himself. Typically, however, he turned philological studies into an instrument for the study of society and ethics. When Fallot went to Paris, he followed, but did not remain there long. He had a provincial's dislike and distrust of the capital, and he lacked funds besides.

Proudhon then spent a couple of years wandering around France and Switzerland as a journeyman printer. "For two years I have traveled around the country, studying, asking questions of the little people, to whom I find myself brought close by my social condition. . . ." [6] Returning to Besançon, he became a master printer for the firm of Gauthier et Compagnie.

It seems that his philosophical education was not limited to theology and philology; even his earliest publications reflect an extent and depth of learning remarkable for an autodidact like Proudhon, despite the limitations in his self-education discussed earlier. Moreover, even his remoteness from Paris cannot have insulated him altogether from the intellectual and political ferment of the 1830's. This period was one which saw the birth and growth of a new age in French radicalism.

> It is a very general opinion that 1830 is the date of a bourgeois revolution, and 1848 the date of a socialist one. This opinion is false. 1848 is the date of a painful, fruitless crisis, of a bloody liquidation of hopes: 1848 invented nothing. 1830, on the contrary, and the three years which followed, marked the true crisis, the intervention of ideas, the initiative for movements. Then Saint-Simonism, Fourierism, and Blanquism took shape in Paris as coteries and clubs. . . . [7]

Charles Fourier had devised a new system of "utopian socialism" based on small, carefully integrated communities called phalansteries and on his use of a novel "scientific" interpretation of individual and social psychology. His theories had wide influence extending beyond his declared disciples. Proudhon supervised the printing of the first edition of his *Nouveau Monde industriel et sociétaire* (1829) and set the type for an edition of his *Théorie des quatre mouvements*. He spoke with Fourier several times during the printing of the former. He was quite impressed with Fourier's ideas and considered himself a disciple for a time. The attachment soon di-

6. Letter to Muiron, undated (1832?), *Corresp.*, I, 2.
7. Daniel Halévy, *La Jeunesse de Proudhon*, 56ff.

minished, and Proudhon's written work is frequently and lengthily critical of Fourierism. He states in his recollections that his disaffection arose from the conflict between some Fourierist doctrines and the dictates of reason, and from the other man's exclusive emphasis on satisfaction of material wants.

Proudhon probably had Fourierist friends in Besançon, and not long after returning there he was asked to edit a Fourierist periodical, *L'Impartial*. Although pressed to accept, he declined, claiming lack of competence and indicating that he had differences with Fourierism which he did not think would permit him to satisfy both his sponsors and his conscience.[8] He also objected to official censorship imposed by the authorities.

Although Proudhon became increasingly distant from Fourierism, he always remained much affected by the conceptions of his fellow Comtois. The ideas of serial order and pseudo-mathematical method in Fourier's analysis of human society were to become, in a much-transmuted form, the center of Proudhon's theoretical efforts for a time, and they reappear in his work much later, as do other elements of Fourier's thought. Proudhon shared and exceeded the other man's libertarian passion; he may have owed some of it to the older radical's ideas, although perhaps they both owed much to the Montagnard spirit common in the Franche-Comté.

In 1836 Proudhon and a friend, Lambert, established their own small press, with a third man, Maurice, as silent partner. Later that year Proudhon went to Paris, where he began to write a *mémoire* on language. Fallot had just died, and his friend wanted to continue his work in order to "immortalize" him. Proudhon came back to Besançon before long, but the press did not thrive and he returned to Paris once more in January, 1838, to seek business for his press or a job for himself. In April his partner disappeared and Proudhon went back to Besançon to take over his place. Lambert was found, a suicide, and Proudhon had to offer the press for sale, although he was not able to dispose of it until five years later. The moribund business put him heavily in debt; even after the sale he was left with a deficit of eight thousand francs.

Proudhon printed his own first publication, an *Essai de gram-*

8. Letters to Muiron, undated (1832?), *Corresp.*, I, 1–7.

maire générale. It appeared as an appendix to his reissue of Bergier's *Eléments primitifs des langues.*[9] Proudhon did not put his name to this essay and later disavowed its basic premises,[10] but it did help to establish him as a scholar when, in May, 1838, he presented himself as a candidate for the Pension Suard.[11]

This *pension* of fifteen hundred francs a year was awarded triennially by the Académie de Besançon to a young man of the region to assist him in his studies. Fallot had been the first *pensionnaire.* Proudhon regarded the winning of this aid as crucial; with it he could devote himself to study and writing, while without it he expected that he would have to give up all thought of any life but a printer's. There was opposition to his candidacy, apparently because of his origins and reputation for radicalism, but in August he was awarded the *pension.* While he did not then give up the printer's trade altogether, it was not long before the distinction of the *pension* was followed by the notoriety of his startling *mémoires* on property. He could no longer be a simple provincial artisan.

Proudhon went with his award to Paris, where he occupied himself with intensive reading, as well as with attending lectures at the Sorbonne, the Collège de France, and the Conservatoire des Arts et Métiers, and with occasional proofreading. His tutor was the Academician Joseph Droz, who found him a difficult pupil, too self-willed and unconventional. In a letter Proudhon admitted, with typical self-dramatization, that "I have a difficult nature, a melancholy disposition, defiant, suspicious, and misanthropic." Droz did, however, express a high esteem for both the character and the ability of his proud charge.[12] Proudhon conceived several literary projects, not all fulfilled, including a "Revue de Franche-Comté." This was to be edited by him and printed on his press. In 1839 he revised and expanded his essay on grammar and submitted it in

9. (Besançon: Lambert et Cie., 1837). The *Essai* was later reprinted separately (Besançon, 1850). Brief extracts in *Oeuv.,* XV, 82–84.

10. Letter to Tissot, July 31, 1842, *Corresp.,* II, 57; letter to Bergmann, January 18, 1845, ibid., 174.

11. Letter to the Académie de Besançon, *Corresp.,* I, 24–30; also *Oeuv.,* IV, 9–16. The date in *Corresp.* is in error and should be May 31, 1838.

12. Letter to Pérennès, March 13, 1839, *Corresp.,* I, 103. Letter of Droz to Pérennès, December 24, 1838, quoted in Edouard Dolléans, *Proudhon* (Paris, 1948), 59ff.

February in the competition for the Prix Volney. No prize was awarded, but his entry was given honorable mention and praise by the judges.[13] He wrote twenty-nine or thirty articles on grammar, logic, religion, and biography for a Catholic encyclopedia,[14] and an article on the alphabet which was published in *L'Instruction publique*.

But Proudhon's efforts began to turn away from grammatical subjects, toward economics and politics. The Académie de Besançon had announced a contest on the subject, "On the utility of the celebration of the Sabbath, with regard to hygiene, morality, and familial and civic relations." As *pensionnaire* of the Académie, Proudhon felt obliged to submit an entry and did so in June, 1839. The entry was not what the academicians had expected, for Proudhon took the opportunity to express freely his ideas on justice and equality. His essay received only the bronze medal, being too radical for some of the judges. He printed two hundred copies himself.[15]

Proudhon, then thirty years old, saw his philosophical task as an undertaking of dedication:

> . . . to work without respite, through science and philosophy with all the energy of my will and all the powers of my spirit, for the moral and intellectual betterment of those whom I like to call my brothers and companions; to be able to propagate among them the seeds of a doctrine which I regard as the law of the moral world. . . .[16]

If this declared purpose seems grandiose, he was at least not ambitious in a simple, personal way. He declined to take advantage of

13. This thesis was titled "Recherches sur les catégories grammaticales et sur quelques origines de la langue française." About half was published in the *Journal de la langue française* (1839–40), but the journal ceased publication before the rest could appear. The editors of the Rivière edition thought that the manuscript of the essay had been lost (*Oeuv.*, XV, 85), but a draft in Proudhon's hand can be found in the Bibliothèque Municipale de Besançon, no. 1375; it has 52 sheets. Haubtmann reports another MS copy in the Proudhon family archives.

14. *Encyclopédie catholique* (Paris, 1839), II. Seventeen of the articles appear in *Oeuv.*, XV, 89–132.

15. *De l'Utilité de la célébration du Dimanche* (Besançon, 1839); 2nd ed., rev. (Besançon & Paris, 1841), *Oeuv.*, IV. After the publication of *Oeuv.*, IV, the original version of the first edition was rediscovered and the variorum, which are not important, printed in *Oeuv.*, X.

16. "Lettre de candidature à la Pension Suard," *Oeuv.*, IV, 16. See also the letter to Ackermann, September 16, 1838, *Corresp.*, I, 59–61.

the opportunity offered by his having won the Pension Suard to achieve status and material gain in a profession or as a man of letters,[17] nor did he in later life seek distinctions or wealth.

The early grammatical labors were an attempt to approach these moral goals. He hoped to discover through philology the story of mankind's origins and development. Together with what he thought to be scientific analysis of history and of the Christian and Hebraic traditions, this could lead him to discovery of primitive truths and of the true moral law, in the knowledge of which man could fulfill the dreams of the Revolution.

> Perhaps the fact, still so obscure, of the origin of language, once analyzed and better clarified, will lead him to the discovery of that famous *criterium*, object of so many investigations and of such ardent wishes. And who knows if near this always incomprehensible fact, the word, there does not lie some prodigious although unperceived psychological phenomenon, of which the precise knowledge and thorough observation in depth would suddenly change the face of opinions and beliefs.[18]

These efforts of his were comparable to Renan's in the latter's *L'Avenir de la science*. Proudhon believed that there had been an original language, an original religion and moral philosophy, and that the ages had obscured them in corruption and distortion. The elements of the religion of Moses and Jesus were sufficient for the needs of men's hearts and reason, but the Church and theologians had hidden the truth behind veils of falsehood.[19]

Proudhon sought to rediscover the original plan—to "rebuild the temple"—and from this to demonstrate the truths at the heart of the Christian and Hebraic traditions in their uncorrupted forms. More than this, he wanted to transform moral and social philosophy

17. Proudhon admonished a friend to address him in correspondence not as "man of letters," but as "printer" or "student," or by no title at all (letters to Maurice, April and August 18, 1839, *Corresp.*, I, 110–12, 147–49; see also the letter to Ackermann, September 16, 1838, ibid., 6off.).

18. "Recherches philologiques sur les catégories grammaticales," autograph MS, Bibliothèque Municipale de Besançon, no. 1375, sheet 52.

19. Proudhon planned a book on this, to be called *Recherches sur la révélation, ou philosophie pour servir d'introduction à une histoire universelle*. He closely studied and annotated the Bible, and was composing a life of Jesus when Renan's appeared. Much of this has been included in *Oeuv.*, XV. P.-J. Proudhon, *Portrait de Jésus*, ed. Robert Aron (Paris, 1951), is an attempt to reconstruct this life of Jesus which he planned, with the editor assembling fragments from surviving texts.

into an exact science. For some time afterward he labored on development of such a science; although in later years he no longer thought a precise and systematic science possible or desirable, he always tried to make his philosophy an ordered and coherent structure, comprehending the whole of the human condition. At first he simply searched for eternal truths, as if they lay written in some celestial book waiting to be discovered. Afterward he came to believe that the verities were not fixed but subject to evolution, and that they were to be discovered through the application of reason to experience; nevertheless, his approach remained close to that of an idealist, and he often strayed from the empirical approach he espoused. His anarchist rebellion against the established order was not in his view a rejection of the rule of law, but adherence to the higher law of reason. For him the laws of Church and State never had risen nor could rise to such a level.

With his philosophy putting him in opposition to both Church doctrine and the constitutional monarchy, Proudhon was from his early years republican, anticlerical, and hostile to religion in any conventional form, though not to the spiritual and moral components a purified religion might have. "I believe in universal confraternity. Every sovereign who does not fulfill this mission is for me a traitor, a liar, an enemy of the human race." [20] The blame for the country's moral deficiency and social unjustices lay with the Church and with the nation's leaders, not only because of false direction and teaching, but also because the people were hostile to them and not ready to heed wiser voices. Proudhon wanted not only to discover truth but to make the time opportune for its teaching.

This, then, was the "pre-philosophy" of the anarchist.[21] It sounds diffuse and naïve, even when compared to the work of an older Proudhon. But similar ideas had long been commonplace; "radical" thought still operated largely in the terms of the eighteenth-century ideologues, as did he at this point in the evolution of his thought. New modes were to come into being in the years soon after; Prou-

20. Letter to Muiron, undated (1832?), *Corresp.*, I, 14. On the preceding see this letter and also the letter to Pérennès, February 21, 1838, *Corresp.*, I, 38–45.
21. On this subject see C. Bouglé, "La Première Philosophie de Proudhon," *Revue de mois*, X (October, 1910), 424–34.

dhon contributed to them. His *mémoires* on property shocked just because they did seem so different.

De la Célébration du Dimanche is in a way a transition piece between Proudhon's "pre-philosophy" and the novelties of *Qu'est-ce que la propriété?* Yet the shift is not actually very great. After all, the last of the pre-philosophy, this "transition essay," and the beginning of the first *mémoire* on property were all composed in 1839. His pre-philosophy is pertinent because it was continued afterward with only limited change. He did drop the philological pursuits and look for the hidden truth less in the murk of the past than in the critical reexamination of concepts widely accepted in the present. But he continued to believe in the existence and knowability of moral law, in the ideals of his youth, and in the power of scientific inquiry to discover vital truth and, through this, to make it possible to end man's troubles.

In *De la Célébration du Dimanche* Proudhon makes Mosaic law his source of moral instruction, finding there the working of egalitarian principles. One can suspect that this essay is argued on this basis principally in order to impress the judges of the Académie de Besançon, but there is no reason to suppose that this approach is only a tactical device, particularly when we compare it with his earlier work. The character of Proudhon's writing is often shaped as much by considerations of rhetoric as those of logic, but he always remains sincere. In understanding him it is necessary to distinguish his matter from his rhetoric (and his method), while at the same time perceiving how the matter is involved in and helps determine the rhetoric and method.

Here Proudhon attributes to Moses a purpose which, with regard for what was to follow from Proudhon's pen, can be taken as a fair first approximation of the author's own goals.

> What Moses wanted for his young nation was not public assemblies and fairs; it was not only unity in government or community of customs: all that is the consequence rather than the principle; it is the sign, not the thing. What he wanted to create in his people was a communion of love and of faith, a fusion of minds and hearts, if I may put it thus. It was the invisible bond, stronger than all material interests, that is formed between souls by love of the same

God, the same conditions of domestic welfare, solidarity in their destinies, the same memories, the same hopes. He wanted, in short, not an agglomeration of individuals, but a truly fraternal society.[22]

This is an evolved form of the Revolutionary goal of *fraternité*. Proudhon was conscious of a lack of substance in the use of the slogan, "Liberté! Egalité! Fraternité!" He tried to give the words richer meaning, to discover a moral world that they truly denoted. Since in the next dozen years he emphasized the first two terms of the triad more strongly and in the most uncompromisingly extreme forms, it was easy to overlook the equal importance to him of *fraternité*. The oversight occurs all the more readily because we are conditioned by our knowledge of other theorists and of political movements to look more steadily for the attack on the existing order and for the libertarian individualism of Proudhonian anarchism. Yet, strong as was his demand for freedom, he sought with equal urgency a way in which men could form "not an agglomeration of individuals, but a truly fraternal society." The goal of a harmoniously functioning society is not readily compatible with an individualism as radical as Proudhon's; the effort to reconcile these conflicting ideals was always to preoccupy him. The apparent contradiction between individualism and fraternity forms a fundamental dilemma of his work. The problem of reconciling liberty and political or social obligation is the eternal stumbling-block of politics. For Proudhon the paradox is more difficult still, since he is so extreme in his demands for both sides.

It is one thing to perceive in *moral* terms a path for reconciliation, but quite another to find a *political* path. The moral formula is to a large degree a personal and voluntary prescription, but the political solution must go a long step beyond the moral *should* to a social *could*. An effectively operative plan for social organization requires more than principles of true justice and moral order. Proudhon was slow in realizing the implications of this. He was first of all a moralist. Through "science" he tried to give his moral law the same force as the laws of natural science. Failing in this, he would go on to gather the depth and power for his thought and the

22. *De la Célébration du Dimanche, Oeuv.,* IV, 41.

practical experience that his sort of science could not gain him. Proudhon's most important work came a decade and more after this 1839 discourse on the celebration of the Sabbath, but the tone and rhythm were already established here.

In this essay his focus on Hebraic law, especially the Decalogue, results in finding social unity—fraternity—and equality to be the basic ideals that the law is supposed to express. He recalls that when the Hebrew children asked the why of the Sabbath rites, they were told that these were the recognition of their joint deliverance and prospective prosperity.[23] The common observation of a day of rest was, says Proudhon, the symbol of common bonds and helped to unite the community. Further, the universal application of the Commandments made them a law for equality. He extends the injunction, "Thou shalt not steal," to a claim that unequal conditions are wrong because they cannot exist without what in effect is theft, taking from a man what is rightfully as much his as anybody's. The Sabbath law made men equal by making them brothers. Other aspects of Hebraic law are also said to establish equality. Equality— the "égalité des conditions"—conforms to reason and to the Christian as well as the Hebraic spirit; "the legislation of Moses proves that this goal can be attained." [24]

Proudhon is writing here primarily of economic equality: equal conditions and opportunities. He asks for limitation of the right of property and makes an impassioned plea on behalf of the exploited against inequality in general, and property and autocracy in particular. "Man certainly does not come into the world as a usurper and intruder; a member of the great human family, he seats himself at the common table: society is in no way a mistress who can accept or reject him." [25] Proudhon appears to be reacting against a famous statement of Thomas Malthus, whose *Essay on the Principle of Population* (1798) represents one school of thought to which he is most hostile:

A man who is born into a world already possessed, if he cannot get subsistence from his parents on whom he has a just demand,

23. Ibid., 41ff. Proudhon quotes, incorrectly, Deuteronomy 7:20–24.
24. Ibid., 59.
25. Ibid., 55ff.

and if the society do not want his labour, has no claim of *right* to the smallest portion of food, and, in fact, has no business to be where he is. At nature's mighty feast there is no vacant cover for him. She tells him to be gone, and will quickly execute her own orders, if he does not work upon the compassion of some of her guests. If these guests get up and make room for him, other intruders immediately appear demanding the same favor. The report of a provision for all that come, fills the hall with many claimants. The order and harmony of the feast is disturbed, and the plenty that before reigned is changed into scarcity; and the happiness of the guests is destroyed by the spectacle of misery and dependence in every part of the hall, and by the clamorous importunity of those, who are justly enraged at not finding the provision that they had been taught to expect. The guests learn too late their error, in counteracting those strict orders to all intruders, issued by the great mistress of the feast, who, wishing that all her guests should have plenty, and knowing that she should not provide for unlimited numbers, humanely refused to admit fresh comers when her table was already full.[26]

Malthus wrote this essay to argue against the egalitarian principles of William Godwin (*Enquiry Concerning Political Justice,* 1793), which are quite similar to those of Proudhon, and against the progressivist optimism of Condorcet. While admitting Godwin's principles to be attractive as abstract ideals, Malthus argues forcefully that natural limitations on the means of human subsistence not only make it impossible to establish a permanent egalitarian society but would make any attempt to do so productive of far more human misery than that existing in unequal societies. While his case is not unassailable, it is argued wholly on what are thought to be the practical, if unhappy, facts of nature. This approach is so alien to Proudhon's that he cannot in counterattack meet Malthus directly on this field of pragmatism; however practical Proudhon may sometimes be, his insistence on ideals prevents

26. Thomas Malthus, *Essay on the Principle of Population,* 2nd ed. (London, 1803), 53ff. This passage is not in the first edition and is omitted from later editions, possibly because of the criticism it aroused. Proudhon quotes the first three sentences of this statement in *La Philosophie de la misère* (1846), where he attacks Malthus at length (*Oeuv.,* I, vol. i, 83; vol. ii, 311–87). He returns again to this statement of Malthus in an article, "Les Malthusiens," *Le Représentant du peuple,* no. 98 (August 11, 1848); *Oeuv.,* VII, 386–91. Also in *De la Justice dans la révolution et dans l'église, Oeuv.,* VIII, vol. ii, 111–36.

his engaging an opponent on grounds of practical considerations alone. Thus is his response here, an argument which reduces to insistence on a fundamental principle of an equal right to live for all men.

All differences between men disappear before the right to subsistence. The conditions of life should be equal because the right to life is equal. It is a crime to deny a man means to earn his subsistence, or to make it more difficult for some men, easier for others. To suggest that some men may have no right to live is an outrage. That there could be insufficient food supplies to give life to all men is a thought Proudhon can hardly entertain, either. For him it is only a short step now to declaring that property is theft. Here he only says that it is the last of the false gods.[27]

To the authority of Moses he adds that of Jesus and the Gospels. Both Hebraic and Christian morality are said to be founded on a system of moral law which takes precedence over all else. This law establishes the right which Proudhon proclaims. He distinguishes himself here from Rousseau who, he suggests, places first emphasis on the relationhips of social contract and the will of the community, rather than on the basic rights of man. At this point Proudhon reverses the common order of argument by saying that unequal birth, strength, ability, and age are negated by the leveling out of any effect of these differences in the work of the whole society. The varied activity of society makes real human differences meaningless, and the paramount social purpose should be to protect equal human rights. Proudhon criticizes Fourierist and Saint-Simonian theories for subordinating equality in attempting to design an effective social structure.

His ideas are carried on to a form close to that of his later anarchism. Insisting that men should be ruled by eternal reason, not temporal and variable human will, he repudiates monarchy, oligarchy, and democracy. Whether few rule many or many rule few (as in a democracy), it is the rule of will. It is with this in mind that Proudhon concludes that the problem is:

> *To find a state of social equality which is neither* communauté, *nor despotism, nor fragmentation, nor anarchy, but liberty in order*

27. *De la Célébration du Dimanche, Oeuv.,* IV, 61.

and independence in unity. And this first point resolved, there will remain a second: to indicate the best mode of transition. There is the entire problem of humanity.[28]

Had Proudhon written nothing else, these early works would merit attention in their own right; as it is, they serve only to point the way to his later writing. Yet they are significant, for through their simplicity they illuminate what followed, since in them we can clearly see the basic concerns and ideals that later are wrapped up in a complex of extended argument and elaboration which more often than not has helped lead readers to misinterpret the author grossly.

Here we see his rationalistic approach, guided by a radical vision and purpose to seek not the more solid foundation of accepted ideas and customs, but their subversion by intellectual means. This is particularly intriguing when we consider the statement by him, quoted above, of the purpose of Mosaic law. Except perhaps for some nuances of wording (as in speaking of a *fraternal* society), this might well be a conservative's statement of organic social theory. In later chapters there will be many occasions to point out real or apparent links between Proudhon and conservatives—and to repeat the admonition, which should be obvious but has not been to many of those confronting the ideas in question, that there always remains in Proudhon's convictions the urge to change completely the existing society, not to conserve it. For him organic social unity is the goal to be achieved, and no society has ever realized it; the very elements of social structure that conservatives have sought to preserve or restore are the ones that Proudhon believes have prevented creation of social solidarity and effective unifying bonds between men.

Society will always be divided as long as men are unequal and ruled by others. Thus his emphasis on economic and social equal-

28. Ibid., 61. Proudhon often uses "communauté" to denote a community whose members are repressed by the whole. He regularly uses the word in this sense to refer to the social units envisaged by utopian communists like Fourier. Where the word appears with this meaning, it will be reproduced here without translation. "Anarchy" here has the traditional meaning of "chaos through lack of control," rather than "an orderly substitute for government through imperative authority," which is what he usually means by the word. See his explanation of the distinction, in "Explications presentées au Ministère Public sur le droit de propriété" (1842), *Oeuv.*, X, 263.

ity as well as the political and legal equality urged by the intellectual progenitors and heirs of the 1789 Revolution; and thus his
requirement that men be ruled by their own reason, not the will of
others. In stressing socioeconomic equality he insists on the radical
precepts that the right of all to the means of life stands above everything else, and that differences in individual ability are balanced
out in the overall functioning of a society. The implications of these
principles are fundamentally revolutionary, even if couched in
terms of an appeal to the primary elements of ancient Judeo-Chris-
tian tradition. They always remain the basic themes of his thought.

three: The *Mémoires* on Property

When the lion is hungry, he roars.

"WHAT IS PROPERTY?" asks Proudhon in the title of his first major work. On the first page is his answer: "It is theft." The epigram, together with the book it initiates, served to win him immediate and extensive notoriety. "Property is theft" has frequently been all that is remembered of him.[1]

Proudhon loved to use paradoxes and the shock force of strikingly exaggerated phrases; he became quite partial to the form of this one and employed it repeatedly with different nouns substituted. It served not only as an effective rhetorical device, but also as a hook on which to hang arguments so disturbingly radical that they might well be introduced by such extreme declarations.

By "theft" he is referring to income not earned by the productive labor of the man who receives it but derived from rents, interest, dividends, or the labors of employees. Such income is unjust; the present political, legal, and economic systems are based on prop-

---

1. *Qu'est-ce la propriété? ou recherches sur le principe du droit et du gouvernement,* premier mémoire (Paris, 1840); *Oeuv.,* IV. For disputes over the credit for originating this epigram, see the editor's note, *Oeuv.,* IV, 131ff. He points out that no one previously had used the epigram in the sense Proudhon intended.

erty and are unjust as well. What begins as a book attacking traditional academic arguments of legists and economists ends as a work of extreme egalitarian, libertarian political theory.

Two matters need to be noted at the outset. First, Proudhon was challenging an institution so deeply and firmly rooted and unquestioningly accepted that it was in a broad sense far more sacred than the Catholic Church. The Revolution had shaken the latter, but it had not questioned private property. In France in 1840 it was implicitly agreed that private property is universally rightful and necessary. The communism of primitives like the American Indians was considered an example of their backward ignorance. Ancient peasant communal holdings in Europe were condemned; where they remained they were being broken up, except in Russia, where the peasant commune was cherished as a conservative factor.[2] That Romanticism admired the primitive state of innocence and a few theorists had attacked individual and unequal property, even advocating renewed communism, did little to diminish the solidity of the bastion which Proudhon assailed. It was a bastion triply secured by bourgeois supremacy, peasant individualism, and aristocratic remnants.

Second, he was thinking primarily in terms of an agrarian economy. Such was the economy of France in 1840; there the industrial revolution was still in its early stages, and Proudhon had yet little occasion to be impressed by its manifestations. Although he was well read in contemporary political economy, the study of it had not yet made him think much about a factory society. His theory is intended to be universal, but his reasoning is not always directly applicable to nonagrarian situations. However, the most important points of the *mémoires* are not significantly affected by this limitation.

Qu'est-ce que la propriété? attempts a thorough analytic examination of a constellation of problems centered on the institution of property. It is primarily a work of destructive criticism. As an advocate of equality, he sees too little of it in an economic and politi-

2. In parts of the Balkans there were extended family groupings, called *zadrugas*, with communal holdings, and there were scattered instances of communal farming persisting elsewhere in Europe, usually on land too poor for successful individual cultivation. Only in Russia, however, did the multiple-family commune including the whole village thrive and even draw admiration from theorists.

cal system based on private property. This system is the enemy, and he attacks it with *élan*. His method is to show each of the enemy's defenses and pretensions worthless, to expose injustice under the facade of property. The enemy's champions are many, and Proudhon tries to meet each of them head-on. The result is argumentation in formidable abundance. Although the total effect may be obscured by excessive length, clarity usually remains in each part. He is less verbose than full of things to say, and often he speaks with great eloquence. The first *mémoire*'s editor remarks: ". . . if the reader has to take more trouble here than is usually required of him, he is well repaid by the grandeur, the variety of episodes and the liveliness of the battle which he witnesses. Combat in the Homeric style, where exhortations and even injuries to adversaries are not lacking." [3]

Actually, the title *Qu'est-ce que la propriété?* refers to not one but several *mémoires*. The first, and most notorious, appeared in June, 1840, with a second edition printed in August, 1841. The book aroused much outrage, and Proudhon escaped prosecution only through the agency of distinguished economist Adolphe Blanqui. Brother of the revolutionary Auguste Blanqui but himself no radical, he gave a laudatory report on the first *mémoire* before the Académie des Sciences Morales et Politiques [4] and interceded with an irate government on Proudhon's behalf.

"Property is theft" was an even more impressive phrase than Proudhon had expected. Few troubled to understand his meaning, but most of those who did were not quieted by what they read. He had chosen in his book to be vehement and aggressive in order to draw attention, and in this purpose he certainly succeeded. "Its style is harsh and bitter; the irony and anger make themselves felt too much; it is an irremediable evil. When the lion is hungry, he roars." [5] Moreover, the real substance of his ideas was indeed revolutionary; even the judicious praise of Blanqui did not keep him from becoming generally viewed as a *bête noire*.[6] The Académie de

3. Michel Augé-Laribé, Introduction, *Oeuv.*, IV, 103.

4. A long résumé of this report appeared in *Le Moniteur universel*, September 27, 1840 (not September 7, the date given in *Corresp.*, I, 259), 2020-21.

5. Letter to Ackermann, February 12, 1840, *Corresp.*, I, 183.

6. Letters to Ackermann, July 11, 1840, and to Bergmann, August 19, 1840, *Corresp.*, I, 224, 238ff. Published attacks on the book were many.

Besançon, addressed in the first *mémoire*'s "dedication," repudiated the book and debated withdrawing its author's *pension*, which completed its three-year term shortly afterward anyway.

After publishing the *premier mémoire* Proudhon immediately began composition of a second to continue and strengthen his arguments. In letters to friends he admitted that the violent tone of his first *mémoire* had been a mistake and promised to be more polite in the second, although he displayed less regret in his letter to the academicians of Besançon.[7] There he only granted that his language might frighten away some and be misunderstood by others, but he insisted that everything he had written was correct. In another letter he declared that when a man as impoverished as he discovers "suddenly, through his meditations, that the cause of so many crimes and so much misery lies entirely in a miscalculation," it is difficult to be gentle.[8]

In April, 1841, Proudhon published *Qu'est-ce que la propriété? Deuxième Mémoire*, subtitled *Lettre à M. Blanqui sur la propriété.*[9] It is more gentle, and is also briefer and less interesting, being principally a history and debate about property doctrines and laws. Relatively little furor greeted its issue, or that of a revised edition in February of *De la Célébration du Dimanche*. The latter has a new preface in which the "What is . . . ?" formula is extended to declare royalty a myth, religion a "dream of the spirit," God an eternal "X," and communism—death! [10]

The lion had not yet finished roaring. Throughout the remainder of the year he worked on yet another book on property, which was published in Besançon and Paris on January 10, 1842, and seized by the authorities in Besançon on January 18. In the first two *mémoires* Proudhon had been very critical of the Fourierists, then

7. Letter to the members of the Académie de Besançon, January 6, 1841, *Corresp.*, I, 270–86; *Oeuv.*, IV, 353–63.

8. Letter to Ackermann, November 15, 1840, *Corresp.*, I, 251. A closely similar expression of passion is in his second *mémoire* on property, *Oeuv.*, X, 20.

9. (Besançon, 1841). *Oeuv.*, X, 1–153.

10. *Oeuv.*, IV, 31. In a notebook of 1843 Proudhon extends the formula still further, adding that philosophy is a hallucination, democracy is chaos, criminal justice is a trap, God is an abstraction, immortality of the soul is despair and the connected resignation is the virtue of dupes, necessity is law, chastity is the highest expression of love, and marriage is the fullness of human personality. Association, justice, man, and evil are less succinctly characterized with the same formula (*Carnets*, I, 37–38).

led by Victor Considérant. (Fourier had died in 1837.) There had been replies in Fourierist periodicals, and in 1841 there appeared a complete counterattack, *Défense du Fourièrisme. Réponse à MM. Proudhon, Lamennais, Reybaud, Louis Blanc, etc.*[11] (Despite the title, the book is directed wholly against Proudhon.) Although the anonymous author had declared himself unknown to Considérant, Proudhon made his third *mémoire* a polemical response to this counterattack, addressing himself to the Fourierist leader. The new book is entitled *Avertissement aux propriétaires, ou lettre à M. Considérant . . . sur une défense de la propriété.*[12] It serves as an extension and defense of Proudhon's property theories, with much invoking of the authority of Adam Smith and his French disciples to support them. But more striking are the parts devoted to countering the Fourierist accusations against Proudhon; these sections are hearty polemics in the best French tradition.

The authorities in Besançon apparently found the polemics to be too hearty, and Proudhon was speedily brought to trial on charges of attacking property, disturbing the peace, exciting scorn and hate against certain classes and persons and against the government of the King, and of an outrage against the Catholic Church.[13] If convicted, Proudhon could have been sentenced to five years in prison and a fine of six thousand francs. Feeling against him was strong. (In a letter he mentions that at the courthouse a pretty girl fled at the sight of him!) At the trial he addressed the court for one and a half hours, presenting a carefully reasoned, relatively concise and restrained exposition of his ideas. Apparently the speech was effective, though perhaps not in the way intended: in announcing the jury's decision the foreman said, "This man is in a sphere of ideas inaccessible to the common herd." [14] It was decided that Proudhon was trying to convert proprietors and the government, not to start a revolution, and he was acquitted.

He published part of his trial address and described some of the

11. Anonymous, attributed to C.-M.-H. Dameth (n.p., 1841). Quoted at length by the editor in *Oeuv.*, X, 159–64.

12. *Oeuv.*, X, 155–248.

13. Henri Kuntz, *Un Procès de presse à Besançon en 1842* (Besançon, 1897); Louis Malnoury, *Les Procès de l'histoire comtois* (Besançon, 1930). Proudhon's letters describing the trial (*Corresp.*, II, 8–20, 40–56; XI, 371–73) are reprinted in part in *Oeuv.*, X, 159–64.

14. Letter to Ackermann, May 23, 1842, *Corresp.*, II, 44.

remainder in correspondence.[15] It constitutes a useful summary of his ideas and adds some new points, but the one really important work in this series is the *premier mémoire.*

The negative reactions to Proudhon's writing on property were to be expected, but there was positive response to them as well. Adolphe Blanqui was very favorably impressed, as was Joseph Garnier, also a prominent liberal economist. Besides a stir created among French socialists, the *mémoires* also were well received by socialists abroad. Karl Marx attacked Edgar Bauer at length in *Die Heilige Familie* for Bauer's criticism of Proudhon on property. Lorenz von Stein and Karl Grün devoted considerable space to Proudhon in their contemporary books on French socialism.[16] Although the *mémoires* no longer seem quite so remarkable today, they still can produce some of their original impact.

One might well wonder why there should be so much interest in *Qu'est-ce que la propriété?* As we noted above, attacking property was not a popular pastime in 1840, but it was no novelty. The communist utopians certainly wanted to transform property, and the Saint-Simonians sought such drastic changes as to abolish it, in effect.[17] There is criticism of property in works of classical philosophy and of the Church fathers. Godwin attacked it, root and branch. Of more direct pertinence to the French tradition than the classical sources or Godwin were several eighteenth-century French writers. The Curé Jean Meslier wrote vigorously against property, but this work was almost unknown until 1864. The Abbé de Mably and Morelly called for property's abolition and for more or less communist systems, as did Gracchus Babeuf and his Conspiracy of Equals of 1796. More influential was Jean-Jacques Rousseau, who in an early composition bitterly attacked property, insisting that it had destroyed natural liberty and is the first cause of inequality and

---

15. *Explications présentés au ministre public sur la droit de propriété* (Besançon, n.d. [1842]); *Oeuv.,* X, 249–75. The correspondence is cited above.

16. Karl Marx and Friedrich Engels, *Die Heilige Familie oder Kritik der Kritischer Kritik* (Frankfurt-am-Main, 1845); see below, p. 48. Edgar Bauer, "Proudhon," *Allgemeine Literatur-Zeitung* (Charlottenberg), Heft V (April, 1844), 37–52. Lorenz von Stein, *Der Sozialismus und Communismus des heutigen Frankreichs* (Leipzig, 1842; rev., 1848), 397–421 in the 1848 edition. Karl Grün, *Die Sociale Bewegung in Frankreich und Belgien* (Darmstadt, 1845), 401–71.

17. St.-Amand Bazard et al., *La Doctrine de Saint-Simon, exposition. Première Année* (1829), ed. C. Bouglé and Daniel Halévy (Paris, 1924), *séances* 6 to 8.

all its consequent evils.[18] However, he later adopted a more moderate view, allowing a limited right to property.

Another book has been the cause of much controversy over the originality of Proudhon. This is the *Recherches philosophiques sur le droit de propriété et sur le vol* . . . (1780) [19] of J. P. Brissot de Warville, the Girondin political leader of the Revolutionary period, guillotined by the Montagnards in 1793. Alfred Sudre in his *Histoire du communisme* (1849) claims that Proudhon took his ideas and his famous formula from Brissot.[20] This accusation has been repeated many times, although Proudhon denied any previous knowledge of the Girondin leader's book. By accusation or implication of plagiarism, prominent critics tried to show that Proudhon was not a man to be taken seriously.

Sudre, whose work is highly polemical, quotes at length from Brissot's book, but he takes considerable liberties with the original text throughout. The crucial passage is quoted by Sudre as ". . . car la propriété exclusive est un vol dans la nature." The original is, "Car cette propriété exclusive est un délit véritable dans la nature." [21] Of more importance than this inconclusive comparison of texts is the fact that Brissot's book is less an attack on property than a plea for more understanding and less drastic punishment for poor men who steal in order to live. He says that man has a natural right to the satisfaction of needs; when these needs are satisfied, there is no question of further right to equal rewards for labor—in

18. *Le Testament de Jean Meslier,* ed. Rudolf Charles (Amsterdam, 1864), 3 vols. Although written ca. 1733, this is the first publication in full. Extracts were published in the eighteenth century and after, but apparently these do not include the parts pertinent to property. There were several copies of the manuscript in Paris libraries, but Proudhon does not mention Meslier. For the Abbé de Mably, see especially his *Doutes . . . sur l'ordre naturel et essentiel des sociétés politiques* (Paris, 1768). Morelly, *Code de la nature* (n.p., 1755); *Prince ou systèm d'un sage gouvernement* (n.p., 1751). Filippo Buonarroti, *Conspiration pour l'égalité dite de Babeuf* (Brussels, 1828; Paris, 1830), 2 vols. J.-J. Rousseau, *Discours sur l'origine et les fondements de l'inégalité parmi les hommes* (Amsterdam, 1755), in *The Political Writings of Rousseau,* ed. C. E. Vaughan (Oxford, 1962), 169ff.

19. (Chartres, 1780). Few copies of this version were published, and all commentators seem to have read a revised edition published in Brissot's *Bibliothèque philosophique du législateur, du politique et du jurisconsulte* (Berlin & Paris, 1782–86), VI, 261–339; I have used this edition, as did Sudre.

20. (Paris, 1849), 273. Pp. 265–86 are about Brissot's book and 403–65 about Proudhon. For the latter's denial of the connection, see *Oeuv.*, VIII, vol. ii, 90–92.

21. Sudre, *Histoire du communisme,* 272; Brissot, *Bibliothèque philosophique,* VI, 293.

contrast to Proudhon's own demands. Although Brissot says that private property is not justified in natural law, he clearly states that he regards property as necessary to order, commerce, and the growth of wealth in civil society. He does not consider unearned income at all. An attack on him by the Abbé Morellet of the Académie Française, saying that he sought to abolish all property,[22] provoked an angry response from Brissot, insisting that he wished to maintain property in society:

> This little treatise had no other object than to prove that we punish too cruelly men whom need forces to steal. Examination of this question led me to that of property in civil and natural law, and I soon became convinced that civil property does not have the same base as natural property, that the latter is based solely on need, and limited by need, while the other has for its base the necessity of conserving order.[23]

Despite some similarity, the views of Brissot and Proudhon are basically very different. Furthermore, the latter was so compulsively comprehensive that he would surely have discussed the question of justifying property as based on need, an issue raised by Brissot, had Proudhon read the Girondin leader's work. The charge against Proudhon of plagiarism has no foundation.

(In a long digression from a salacious account of an erotic adventure, the Marquis de Sade comments sardonically on how only the weak are charged with theft, while in a vast variety of ways the strong rob the weak with impunity. He says that the property right originated in usurpation and that "theft is punished only because it attacks the right of property; but this right itself originally is only a theft." While his concern is much more limited in scope, de Sade's thoughts here are quite close to Proudhon's. However, it would be surprising if the latter had read this book, and I know of no mention of the connection between the two authors' views before a brief comment printed in 1951. Presumably the nature and restricted circulation of de Sade's unexpurgated work have kept

22. André Morellet, article in a supplement to the *Journal de Paris*, March 6, 1792. This article and the author's reply to Brissot's counterattack are in Morellet's *Mélanges de littérature et de philosophie du dix-huitième siècle* (Paris, 1818), III, 294–322.

23. J.-P. Brissot de Warville, article in *Le Patriote françoise*, no. 941 (March 8, 1792), 272–73.

his relevance from being noticed, so the connection between the libertine and the puritan is intriguing but insignificant.) [24]

Mably, Morelly, Meslier, Babeuf, and Godwin were egalitarians who condemned property on ethical grounds; Brissot did likewise, but redeemed it through economic and political considerations. Proudhon attacked it for both ethical and economic reasons, as did the Saint-Simonians.

In any case it is not of great importance who had or had not attacked property previously, or in what fashion they did so. *Qu'est-ce que la propriété?* won approval not because it was the first work to attack property, but because it did so forcefully and thoroughly, introducing fresh ideas in the process, ideas which went beyond the mere condemnation of property itself. Marx praised the *mémoires* in the following terms, written in 1844, before he and Proudhon became estranged:

> Proudhon now subjects the basis of political economy, private property, to a critical test, surely the first decisive, ruthless and at the same time scientific test. It is a great scientific advance which he has made, an advance which revolutionizes political economy and makes a real science of political economy possible for the first time. Proudhon's work *Qu'est-ce que la propriété?* has the same meaning for modern political economy which Sieyès' work *Qu'est-ce que le tiers état?* has for modern politics.[25]

Marx's remarks here need not be taken as entirely objective, but Proudhon's *mémoires* do have merits which make them unusually impressive. They are at the same time passionate and rational. Reasoned argument combines with the fiery cry for justice; "science" and humane righteousness march together. Proudhon's combination of argumentation so elaborately and closely reasoned with an emotively conveyed sense of outrage at social injustice was unusual, if not unprecedented. For many of those affected by shades of the French Revolution and schooled in the rationality of the Enlightenment, Proudhon must have seemed an exciting newcomer. Marx's

24. *L'Histoire de Juliette, ou les prosperités du vice*, in *Oeuvres complètes du Marquis de Sade*, ed. Gilbert Lely (Paris, 1967), VIII, 121. See Paul Schlesinger, "Proudhon et Sade," *Mercure de France*, June 1, 1951, 373–74. *Juliette* dates from 1792.

25. Karl Marx and Friedrich Engels, *Die Heilige Familie*, in Marx and Engels, *Werke* (Berlin, 1958–67), II, 33. Other remarks on pp. 23–36, 39–56, 165, 166.

professed enthusiasm is readily understandable; he was to employ the same combination, with far greater historical effect. Other characteristics of *Qu'est-ce que la propriété?* to be discussed later further assisted in making it influential.[26]

The theories and arguments developed in the *mémoires* on property can be divided for descriptive purposes into several categories: systematic criticism of all defenses of property; elaboration of the principles of justice in economic, political, and social life; the nature of the injustices involved in property; and revision of established economic theories of value and exchange. To these can be added the preliminary development of a methodology, and a category for polemical declamations of limited theoretical relevance. However, the real subject of these *mémoires* is not property, but justice.[27]

> . . . I make no system: I demand the end of privilege, the abolition of slavery, equality of rights, the reign of law. Justice, nothing but justice; such is the sum of my discourse; I leave to others the trouble of disciplining the world. . . .
>
> Justice is the central star which governs societies, the pole on which the political world turns, the principle and rule of all transactions. Nothing is done among men except by virtue of *right;* nothing is done without the invocation of justice.[28]

Such statements might be found in other writers, and would be unexceptional expressions of pious (but not very meaningful) sentiments with most of them. For Proudhon, however, "justice" must be the final and universally decisive criterion, and it must be defined in fully meaningful and universal terms. Like Socrates in Plato's *Republic,* though not so cleverly, he tries to expose the ways in which conventional conceptions of justice are empty, inconsistent, and contradictory, or in which they fail to specify adequately the conditions necessary for a society and its people to be just. Remedying these supposed failures was Proudhon's life work, and the explications of justice the real subject of all that he wrote.

The 1789 and 1830 French revolutions both sought to establish

26. C. Bouglé, "La Méthode de Proudhon dans ses premiers mémoires sur la propriété," *Revue d'économie politique,* XXIV (1910), 711–31.

27. For an examination of the significance of the *mémoires* for economic theory, see Aimé Berthod, *P.-J. Proudhon et la propriété* (Paris, 1910), the best of several studies available.

28. *Oeuv.,* IV, 134, 144.

just government by basing it on the rule of law, instead of on the monarch's will. The assumption made was that justice is constituted by the rule of law. Proudhon objects to this, claiming that justice is prior: law should always be a declaration and application of the just. If our ideas of justice are inadequately or falsely determined, then the laws will be unjust—and so, too, will the government. Under such government no one can truthfully speak of there being a rule of law and order; the law is false and the order illusory.

Natural-law theorists had taken a similar position: natural laws are universal rules determined by reason, while the laws actually employed in government should invariably be applications of natural law. Proudhon departs from this in attempting to discover a conception of justice more general than the usual compass of law, including specification of all conditions proper to relations between men. His position also is distinctive because of its total insistence on adherence to universal principles of justice without admitting any other bases for law, such as expediency or customary usage.

Proudhon's approach amounts to a kind of moral absolutism—something which has not usually been found acceptable in politics, however much it may be admired, because of conflicts between the apparent requirements of political practice and those of "abstract" principle. What Proudhon is getting to, however (although it is not fully developed here), is the determined conviction that such conflicts are illusory. To him, most of man's political problems are direct consequences of injustice itself, and not of something which prevents the full realization of just principles. When he says (in the excerpt quoted earlier) that "the cause of so many crimes and so much misery lies entirely in a miscalculation," he means that at present key ideas of justice are false—a "miscalculation"—and thereby our troubles arise.

Then the exposure of errors in ideas of justice and the discovery of its true principles is man's most important task. Proudhon believes that through this progress toward truth, and only through it, man can progress toward happiness and the ideal society. Belief in progress through the increase of knowledge is Proudhon's heritage from the *philosophes* of the Enlightenment, but he makes knowing justice the key to all else, rather than pressing with equal force for all kinds of knowledge. Unlike other prophets of progress, he has little interest in the potential of natural science and applied technology for the curing of man's ills.

In his view unequal conditions of human life are at the center of injustice. He makes property the focus of his attention because he regards it as the institutionalization of inequality.

Property, according to common usage in economics, is material wealth of lasting form not consumed or expended, and from which its owner derives revenue—or it is the right to such wealth. Its two chief forms are land and capital, which are in addition necessary instruments of production. Proudhon's own proposal of the best definition of property is one taken from Roman law. Property is the absolute, exclusive, and autocratic domain of a man over a thing.[29] He can use or misuse the property in whatever way he wills. Whoever else uses it does so as the proprietor's servant, in the sense that the user remains subject to the owner's will and works for his benefit. Even when not actually an employee, a user works for the proprietor because he owes the other compensation for the use of the property. The proprietor who works his property by himself is not criticized by Proudhon, except insofar as the former has a disproportionately large share of the available property, or when he misuses it.

There are in this interpretation three characteristics of property which are the objects of Proudhon's attacks. The first is the dominance of will, which permits the proprietor to misuse or not to use at all what can be put to other uses benefiting society or individuals. An example would be the great landowner who lets land go to waste or uses it as a private hunting preserve, while neighboring farmers have insufficient acreage for the community to sustain itself. Second is the exclusive character of ownership, unlimited in duration. The proprietor can exclude the landless poor from the land and the means of earning sustenance for as long as he and his heirs choose; this is another function of the dominance of the will. His timeless right is passed on to his heirs and cannot be curtailed, however powerful the reason for wanting to do so. Finally, the title to property makes possible income not earned by labor. Thus the theft involved in property is both the unearned income and the

29. *Oeuv.*, X, 80.

denial of property to the needy by those owning more than they themselves can use productively.

"Private property," understood as the fruits of man's labor and the right to dispose of them freely, is not in itself the object of stricture. To be able to dispose of these fruits freely is essential to man's control over himself and thus to liberty. But property instituted as it is permits not only the enjoyment of the fruits of one's own labors, but of others' labors as well. It allows and causes the enrichment of some at the cost of the impoverishment of others. Proudhon tries to show that, even if there is no impoverishment, there is only injustice in the unequal rewards for labor resulting from a property system.

He takes up in turn each of the arguments advanced by others to justify property rights. Through elaborate reasoning he seeks to demonstrate that none of these arguments is valid, and that all the supposed benefits of property are delusory. Property does not and cannot achieve the purposes intended by its advocates. Lacking a foundation of justice, property is said by Proudhon to be positively unjust. Economic inequality's many abuses of fundamental human rights are summed up in the institution of property. Finally, he reasons that property cannot be a viable institution and must destroy itself.

It should be realized that the contemporary defenses of property were not generally based on arguments of property's economic utility. Powerful defenses can be so founded, asserting the necessity of property for a flourishing commerce and agriculture. It can be said that only in a private-property system can the requisite initiative, energy, and responsibility for economic progress and prosperity be developed. Although Proudhon does rebut these conclusions, they are not the principal ones he had to counter. The extensive literature on the subject was rationalistic in nature, utilizing juridical arguments or identifying property as a natural right. Property was seen in terms of absolute principle rather than utility and expediency, and Proudhon disputes the question in like fashion. Although he can and does argue the utilitarian aspects of a case, principle remains the center of his orientation. Reason, right, and unwavering principle determine his concepts; his emotions—outrage

and compassion over misery in the world, anger at opponents—
never really distort this rationalism.

Proudhon first disputes with those who claim property to be a
natural right. He does not really question the notion that there
are natural rights—it is one of his own assumptions. Eighteenth-
century philosophy and the Revolution firmly established the concept that there are rights that are every man's simply because reason
has ascertained that they are part of the essence of universal human
nature. In pure form the idea of natural right precludes the possibility of any valid justification for abridging these rights.

Proudhon is too much a child of the Revolution not to continue
thinking in terms of natural right. He does, however, inquire afresh
into what rights man is thus entitled to enjoy. Ideas about rights
had become stale and banal; few thought deeply about what the
rights which they recognized as ideals actually entailed for the
individual or for society. Proudhon gives new life to these old ideals
and concludes that human rights have implications far more extensive than had previously been supposed. However, he believes that
there is no natural right to property, and that man's true rights
preclude rather than justify property.

The 1789 Revolution's "Declaration of the Rights of Man and
the Citizen" constituted for French republicans the fundamental
statement of rights, and property is included among them:

> Article 17: Property being an inviolable and sacred right, no
> one can be deprived of it, except when public necessity, legally
> determined, evidently requires it, and under the condition of a
> just and prior indemnity.[30]

Basic rights in the Declaration are *liberté, égalité, sureté,* and property. Proudhon contends that the last is not like the others at all.
Liberty, equality, and security are universal, absolute rights, inviolable and inalienable. As rights they are the primary conditions
of the state of man. But property right is for most people dormant
and unexercised, a right in potential only. Property lacks univer-

---

30. Final version of 1791. *La Grande Encyclopédie,* XIII, 1075. The Declaration
of Rights itself does not actually call property a "natural" right, or bracket it with
other rights; but it was common to do both, and Proudhon is not explicitly arguing against the Declaration.

sality, yet a natural right must by definition be universal. Still more important, property right is not absolute, inviolable, or inalienable. A right which can readily be curtailed, changed, or otherwise modified is hardly a right—or at least not one to be characterized as natural. Whatever else property may be, it is neither hallowed nor respected.

The state is continually abridging property right, chiefly through the imposition of taxes. It takes from the proprietor to give relief to the poor and even requires remissions of rent to do so. Is this not robbery? Should not charity be voluntary? Why should such forcible redistribution of wealth be necessary in a just system? The state is constituted to benefit everyone, but the rich must pay more to enjoy these benefits. Is this equality? The state usurps the alleged rights of citizens to enjoy and dispose as they will of their property.

Much of the first part of the *deuxième mémoire* is occupied by an account of the repeated failures of property institutions and of the violation of property right by government measures. Proudhon employs historical arguments to demonstrate that property is evolving toward extinction. His remarks are not distinctive, however; these discussions are included principally to give his theory respectability, for this second *mémoire* is in large part an apologia for the first.

Since Proudhon's time modern law has far extended the legal curtailment of property right, of which rent control and the public right of eminent domain are two examples. This is quite in accord with Proudhon's expectations. The Declaration of the Rights of Man says property right is limited by "public necessity." Proudhon's point is that any individual's property rights *must* conflict with the rights of others—with "public necessity"—and that the general interests of society are not served by the observation of property right, because the proprietor is benefited only at the cost of the propertyless who constitute the bulk of society. Property is antisocial; society cannot consistently respect it and does not do so.

Proudhon fails to perceive clearly that the conventional political thought he attacks rests on the assumption that all individual rights necessarily conflict with and even wholly contradict the interests and "rights" of society. Much of the task of politics then consists of reconciling this conflict, and it is usually thought that the solutions employed necessarily must abridge individual rights in some respects. Otherwise there can be no organized and ordered society, without which individual rights cannot be realized at all. By this reasoning, curtailment of property right does not negate the right but ensures its ultimate protection.

In its departure from this rationale, an important basis of liberal thought, Proudhon's theory made a more radical break than he seems to have realized. Liberalism had continued the belief in necessary contradiction between individual and social interests, while reversing tradition by preferring the demands of individualism to those of the social body. Proudhon accepted the individualist temper, but refused to admit either the necessity of irreconcilable contradiction or the derogation of the social.

He had not yet completed definition of the idea, but he was on his way to what in effect would deny the supposed contradiction between individual and social interests while refusing to limit the former. He would later insist that where interests conflict a balance between them could be achieved that would deny neither individual nor society. Property right is condemned by him because no such balance is possible with it: a few enjoy property rights only at the expense of the many and of society as a whole.

The implications of such a position are revolutionary simply because, if followed through without reservation as Proudhon does, they give us the conclusion that all true rights must be enjoyed in the same degree by all men, and cannot in fact be so enjoyed in existing society. If the position is accepted, then it is difficult to avoid going on with him to the further conclusions that both government and the property system must be abolished, and that society must be wholly reconstituted. Proudhon maintains that property perpetuates and aggravates society's division into rich and poor classes. War between the classes is the inevitable result, as the rich can only preserve their wealth by denying the poor the property they require. When the state aids the poor, using revenues gained in large part from the rich, it is forcing proprietors to aid their enemies. Property destroys itself by introducing class war.[31]

Since Marxism has focused attention on concepts of class war,

31. Proudhon gives many additional reasons for concluding that property is impossible and cannot survive. See esp. *Oeuv.*, IV, 242–97.

the notion expressed here assumes an appearance of substantial importance. However, Proudhon carries the idea little further at this point, and even though he later develops it much more, he does not ever take a position close to Marx's. In his own view, such social struggle makes revolutionary change both necessary and possible, but he does not see class war as the primary process involved in revolution.[32] Indeed, it is only late in life that he actually develops a clearly conceived theory of revolutionary process; even then he lacks the confident expectations engendered by Marxist determinism.

Before leaving the topic of natural right, Proudhon comments on the preoccupation of many writers with the origins of property. He protests that natural rights are always with us and do not have origins. Property's defenders say it is a natural right, yet cannot agree on its origin. Proudhon thinks this absurd.

The "absurdity" may be a quality not of property, but of the notion of "natural right" itself. Despite the continuing wide acceptance of notions about natural law and rights, such ideas have been subject to devastating philosophical criticism. While there has been a revival of natural-law theory in more sophisticated form, Proudhon's simplistic assumptions about rights would be difficult to sustain if arguments of modern analytic philosophy were brought to bear against them.

However, the important historical fact is that not only Proudhon but also a great many others have been convinced that there are natural rights which must be realized if justice is to prevail. Take them as articles of faith rather than philosophically demonstrable truths: they are in either case a major basis of political thought and action. For him such rights are *the* foundation; they are the fundamental postulates on which social philosophy must be based.

Having denied that there is a *natural* right to property, Proudhon goes on to say that the latter's claims to be a "right" are reduced to two: the right of occupation and the right to labor. The right of occupation is the right claimed for the first occupant of the land. He takes the land, improves it, makes it his home and means of livelihood; many say that it should be his property. But what of the latecomers who arrive on the scene when there is no more land

32. This subject will be further examined in later chapters.

available? There can be no right of occupation for them. Proudhon's arguments reduce once more to matters of principle. The right of occupation should be equal for all. The extent of individual occupation should be determined not by individual will but by the needs of all and the resources available to them. Since population varies, the limits of individual land possession cannot be fixed.

Land, like air and water, is necessary to existence; there can be no right to appropriate it for private use when this denies others an equal access to the means of existence. Individuals should not be able to take for their exclusive use the natural wealth of the land, which is offered free and which they did not create. Men should receive the use of the land from society, which alone has the right of disposal. Society should be free to redistribute the land whenever and however social needs suggest.

In connection with this, there also arise the arguments of many legists who support property as a necessary pillar of civil law and hence of any society solidly based upon the rule of the law. Although we shall not follow Proudhon's rebuttal through all its intricacies here, it should be noted that the topic held considerable interest for contemporary readers. The great critic Sainte-Beuve commented that he had felt that civil-law arguments of this sort constituted an excellent justification of property, perhaps the only good one, and that he found Proudhon's destruction of these arguments to be one of the most impressive facets of the book.[33] It is likely that Sainte-Beuve's reaction reflects that of many moderate liberal readers of the *mémoires*. For us the principal interest lies in the propositions, first advanced by Proudhon in this context, that neither "fact" nor universal consent makes a right.

Jurisprudence is said by him to recognize that fact does not make a right, yet it defends property law on the basis of its doing just that. This law recognizes two supposed facts: that the property system "works," and that custom approves or at least accepts it. Proudhon contends that the system does *not* work, as he subsequently tries at length to show. Property law actualizes what in reality is an abstract fiction and sanctions egoism—with evil results disastrous for the causes of justice and social order.

33. C.-A. Sainte-Beuve, *P.-J. Proudhon, sa vie et sa correspondance, 1838-1848* (Paris, 1872), 93.

The general dictum he advances here is that neither custom—however ancient it may be—nor the mere fact of an institution's existence can justify it. There is no reason to attribute perfection to man's first efforts at social and economic organization; that would be to eternalize chaos. Universal consent cannot justify property; a man cannot consent to surrender the means of life. Here is yet another instance of Proudhon's insistent reliance on principle: a man cannot even give up his rights voluntarily. This denial of universal consent assumes great importance in Proudhon's later anarchist theory, and particularly in his criticism of democracy.

Some defenders of property assert that a man's labors earn him a right to the fruits thereof—a point with which Proudhon agrees—and to the property with which he has toiled to make it fruitful. Proudhon protests that the farmer who rents his land from another gains no share in its ownership, although he has also added to its value (or kept its value from declining through disuse). If labor truly justified property right, this could not be so. Instead of gaining any right to the land, the tenant must pay for the use of it. Payments should only serve to compensate a previous occupier for whatever value he may have given the land.

By labor man creates *products;* by this he has a right to the products, but not to the *land* or to any other instrument of production: he did not create that. "The right to a product is exclusive, *jus in re;* the right to the instrument is common, *jus ad rem.*" [34] This distinction between the right *to* a thing and right *in* a thing is identified as the critical issue in questions of property right. Proprietary right is *jus in re,* the absolute right to claim a thing, no matter who is in possession of it. But possession is the element of property necessary for its use and enjoyment. Everyone has a right to possession of the means of production, a *jus ad rem* belonging to all equally. *Jus ad rem* is a limited right arising from some other law, in this case the rule that no one should be denied the means of securing his own survival and his family's.

Some of those objecting to the inequality of proprietary right would simply redistribute property on a basis of equality; Proudhon would abolish property right altogether. Possession without *jus in re* would remain: in his view this would amount to the destruc-

34. *Oeuv.,* IV, 210.

tion of property, because the possession—which would be granted and withdrawn by society—would entail none of the absolute and exclusive rights which by definition are property's. The right of occupation is equal for all, and possession should vary with the population.

Possession without proprietary rights: it is clear that Proudhon is not opposed to individual farm or workshop holdings as such. He is attacking revenue without labor, labor without revenue, and exclusive, absolute rights to instruments of production. However, he is convinced that property and these evils are inseparable, that they can be eliminated only by the abolition of property—or, to put it in Proudhon's own terms, correcting property's wrongs will destroy it altogether. This is why he aims his assault at the entire institution of property rather than specifically at the evils in the institution, as others did.

One such critic was Pierre Leroux, another typographer turned ideologue who had been associated with the Saint-Simonians, then split away from them. Proudhon expresses great admiration for Leroux's *De l'Humanité* (1840) and his ideals of equality and social solidarity. But Leroux thinks property can be reformed, and for this Proudhon strongly criticizes him; as regards property this is their only difference, but it is all-important.[35] Even the Saint-Simonians, who attack property fiercely, envisage their solution to be a transformation, not demolition, of property. The same issue is one of those dividing Proudhon from the Fourierists. The anonymous one of their number whose criticism provoked his *Lettre à Considérant* calls for reform, not destruction, of property; Proudhon responds with "proofs" that to reform it will be to destroy it, recalling his earlier reply to Adolphe Blanqui, that property is like a polygon. If you remove its corners you no longer have a polygon —you have a circle.[36]

Despite these differences with other reformist and revolutionary theorists over property, both in his conclusions and his insistence on making it the essence of injustice, the *mémoires* on property stand on common ground with the work of the Fourierists, Saint-

35. Pierre Leroux, *De l'Humanité, de son principe et de son avenir* (Paris, 1840), 2 vols. Proudhon, *Oeuv.*, IV, 106–11.
36. *Oeuv.*, X, 186–88; IV, 128.

Simonians, and other early socialists: all of them in one way or another protest and seek to end injustice in the ways in which men are rewarded for their labor. Privileges of the *noblesse* and the Church had been for the most part eliminated by the Revolution; in their place economic privilege and concomitant popular misery grew even as the economy flourished. The number and volume of voices of protest grew apace, and one does not need to seek out revolutionaries and utopians to find these voices. There were liberal economists like Adolphe Blanqui, Joseph Garnier, and Joseph Droz (Proudhon's tutor) who saw in economic inequality not only injustice but a bar to economic progress. Sismondi's *Nouveaux Principes d'économie politique* (1819) established a critical school of non-socialist economists who in succeeding years subjected the faults of liberal laissez-faire economic practices to thorough-going criticism. Such reports as Villermé's *Tableau de l'état physique et moral des ouvriers* (1840) [37] powerfully described the misery of the urban working classes, well before Marx and Engels made their own contributions.

The critical school of economists had great influence on socialist theory. While there is no direct evidence of influence by Sismondi or Villermé in *Qu'est-ce que la propriété?*, there is little doubt that they had their effect on Proudhon: he certainly knew their work and would have found it impressive, and he had close personal contacts with Blanqui, Garnier, and Droz. He takes up the spirit and substance of their criticism and carries it several steps further. In this area he is more in the line of the Saint-Simonians than of other socialists, and their criticisms of property are in many ways very similar. However, Proudhon rests his case more on ethical grounds than do either the Saint-Simonians or the critical economists. They share his view of land as an essential instrument of production and his objection to its misuse by some while able potential users are excluded. Nevertheless, Saint-Simonian objections are primarily directed against the undesirable economic effects of such abuses, while Proudhon's are directed against their injustice.

One of his major points of contention is his argument that lib-

---

37. J. C. F. Sismonde de Sismondi, *Nouveaux Principes d'économie politique* (Paris, 1819), 2 vols. Louis René Villermé, *Tableau de l'état physique et moral des ouvriers* (Paris, 1840).

erty is impossible without economic equality. This was to become a central article of socialist belief, especially through the theory of Marx; but when Proudhon wrote, his approach was a novel one. The Frenchman concentrates on the transactions of "commerce" —any exchange of goods or services. The premise of such transactions is that equal values are exchanged; no one would freely and knowingly enter into an exchange in which he suffered a loss. Thus unequal exchange results from either coercion or fraud.

Proudhon's claim is simply that men regularly enter disadvantageous transactions knowing their loss; because of unequal conditions they have no alternative. Then they are not free; rather, they are compelled by those with economic advantage over them.

> To be free: the man who is in possession of his reason and of his faculties, who is neither blinded by passion, nor constrained or impeded by fear, nor deceived by false opinion.
>
> Thus, in every exchange there is a moral obligation that neither of those involved gains at the expense of the other; that is, in order to be legitimate and true, commerce must be free of all inequality. This is the first condition of commerce. The second is that it be voluntary, the parties transacting with liberty and full knowledge.
>
> Then I define commerce or exchange as an act of society.
>
> The negro who sells his wife for a knife, his children for glass beads, and himself for a bottle of brandy—he is not free. The merchant of human flesh with whom he deals is not an associate but his enemy.
>
> The civilized worker who gives his labor for a piece of bread, who builds a palace in order to sleep in a stable, who makes the richest materials in order to wear rags, who produces everything in order to do without everything—he is not free. The master for whom he works does not become his associate by the exchange of salary and service between them, and is his enemy.
>
> The soldier who serves his native land through fear instead of through love is not free. His comrades and his chiefs, ministers or organs of military justice, all are his enemies.
>
> The peasant who rents land, the manufacturer who borrows capital, the tax-payer who pays tolls, gabelles, title and license fees, personal taxes, personal property taxes, etc., and the deputy who votes them have neither intelligence nor freedom in their acts. Their enemies are the proprietors, the capitalists, the government.
>
> Give men back their liberty, enlighten their intelligence, so that

they know the meaning of their contracts, and you will see the most perfect equality preside in their exchanges, without any consideration for superior talents and gifts. You will recognize that in the order of commercial ideas—that is, in the sphere of society—the word "superiority" is devoid of meaning.[38]

Thinking of social intercourse in terms of exchange and "contracts"—any agreements to undertake exchanges—is central to Proudhon's philosophy and vital to the suggested solutions of social problems he later develops. The social ideal of many theories—especially those of socialism—is a vision of individual differences submerged in collective action for the joint benefit of all. In speaking of exchange and contract Proudhon maintains the independence of individual identity, assuming that differences between men cannot be subordinate, and at the same time insists on the collective character of all productive work.

To liberals' claims that in market economies exchanges are indeed freely made, he would reply that the only free participant there is the one who can afford not to sell his goods or services at all until a clearly advantageous exchange is offered, and that few are in this position. To claims that some of those in commerce deserve richer rewards for what they give to it, Proudhon responds that only work contributes anything of value and thus only it deserves reward; because every labor depends on that of others, all work should be equally compensated.

Most men labor, produce, and are rewarded with barely enough to sustain themselves and their families—if that; other men labor no harder, often less or not at all, and gain enough to live in luxury. This disparity of incomes and the common misery of a large part of the population are the result of what the Saint-Simonians called the "exploitation of man by man." [39] Proudhon elaborates on the extent of this exploitation by pointing out that wage laborers and tenants can provide only for their present needs, while they are providing security and independence in the future for capitalists and proprietors, who not only can save from their greater incomes, but also have their present capital and property to provide security indefinitely. But workers are wholly dependent on their employers; their

38. *Oeuv.*, IV, 228ff.
39. *La Doctrine de Saint-Simon*, 223, 235.

incomes are too small for them to be provident. If a man's employer or landlord discharges or evicts him, he is helpless. Even benevolent employers cannot promise the security of permanent employment; business has its crises, and the promise often could not be kept.

Like most socialists Proudhon believes that only labor is productive, that land and capital are worthless without labor. There is no real basis for claims to a share of the product merely as compensation for the use of capital or any property. Proudhon has a kind of labor theory of value: that labor alone determines the value of products. "Labor is the only universal measure, the only exact measure of values. . . . Every product ordered must be paid for by what it cost in time and expenses, neither more nor less. . . ." [40] Of course, this theory is not original, nor does he claim that it is. Furthermore, it is not quite correct to characterize Proudhon's as a pure labor theory of value; he is inconsistent in his statements and visibly vacillates in his position. He does believe that the value of a product *should* be determined solely by the quantity of work expended in producing it, but he recognizes that there still are other determinants as well. He does not carefully think through all the implications of his conception. As a result, in matters of economic exchange his theory always remains technically weak.

However, he makes a novel contribution to ideas on value with his notion of "collective force," which he later stated to be the central idea of the first *mémoire*. When men work together, dividing the task amongst themselves, all share in the resulting income, but ordinary employees receive less relative to the amount of their labor than do the managers and owners of the enterprise. All may receive as much or more than any could working alone, but the distribution of what is gained by their joining of efforts is entirely unequal. There is a vast miscalculation involved: since men working together can achieve much more than they can separately, all are jointly, and hence equally, responsible for the additional production. None deserves a greater part of the resultant extra income.

> The capitalist, it is said, has paid for *the days of labor* (*journées*) by the workmen; to be exact it is necessary to say that the capitalist has paid for as many times *one day's labor* as he has employed workmen each day, which is not the same thing. For he has not

40. *Oeuv.*, X, 189; IV, 232.

paid at all for the immense force that results from the union and harmony of the workers, from the convergence and simultaneity of their efforts.[41]

The conventional economist will point out that harnessing this collective force is the function of an entrepreneur or manager; his greater income is said to be merited because it is he who makes it possible for labor to achieve its additional productive capacity. To this criticism one can object that many capitalists and proprietors do little or nothing to organize production, leaving that to employees, tenants, and the entrepreneurs who borrow their capital or use their property. The claim that invested capital is itself productive is ignored here, or rejected as a figment created to fit the needs of false economic analysis. The Saint-Simonians would change this situation by giving remuneration only for work performed, with the greatest compensation for the organizers and directors.

Proudhon not only attacks unearned income, but also rejects any kind of differential rates of compensation for work, however special the abilities required by a job may be. Here he finds himself set apart from the Saint-Simonians and Fourierists (as well as from more conventional theorists), and he devotes much of his work on property to combatting them on this subject. They suggest rewards for labor scaled on the basis of talent, with Fourierists also making provision for additional compensation to those who furnish the capital for their phalansteries. The Saint-Simonians say: from each according to his capacity, to each capacity according to his accomplishment; the Fourierists, to each according to his capital, labor, and talent.

Proudhon maintains that every man should be paid at the same rate, whatever his talent, because each worker performs a useful and necessary role in society, which depends on division of labor through differentiation of functions. With everyone who works performing an essential function, it is a misconception to suppose that some are more valuable than others: none is useful without the joint efforts of all. Instead of speaking of *inequality* of faculties, we should talk only of *diversity* of faculties.

The primary importance of the division of labor is one of the

41. *Oeuv.*, IV, 215.

first principles of classical political economy. "Division of labor" refers to the way in which every man performs specialized work, rather than attempting to accomplish all tasks. It is agreed that the division of labor is essential for any but the most primitive economy. Proudhon's point is that it is precisely the diversity of human faculties which makes the division of labor sensible and effective. Some best use intellectual faculties, some manual skills, and others sheer physical strength: all are necessary in modern society. Economic activity is always and above all a collective function ultimately involving the whole society. Individuals can lay no valid claim to special advantage or extra material benefit from their work, for they must depend on others to accomplish anything. Commercial exchange is as social in essential nature as is productive labor, and increase of income through clever trading is no more justifiable than extra pay for special talent.

Any fair exchange should bring equivalent and mutual benefit to all parties, and this is all the more true because every party needs the others. The employment of labor is as much an act of exchange as the sale of material products; the employer is buying service and depends upon it no less than his employees require what he pays them. With all work a social and cooperative process, there should be no relationships of masters and subordinates.

Since functions are varied, it is important to fit them to one another well:

> . . . in examining the law of exchange formulated by Adam Smith, and the objections it has occasioned, have we not seen that variations in values actually result from absence of organization and not at all from the intrinsic fact of exchange? Then there is reason to occupy ourselves with the formula of organization, and no longer with the formula of distribution.[42]

This is a shot aimed at Fourier. Proudhon's position resembles Fourier's because they both emphasize the complementary roles of diverse individuals working together, but Proudhon's insistence on equal remuneration is a vital distinction. In referring above to distribution formulas, he is scorning Fourierist concerns about how best to divide the products of collective industry.

42. *Oeuv.*, X, 198.

The French are narcissists, remarks Proudhon, meaning that they always want to feel superior to their fellows and to be recognized as such. Before 1789 blood raised some men above others. Since 1830 money has done so. If all fortunes were equal, then the French would invent new categories of distinction. There should be no need for either the distinctions of socialist ideologues or those of bourgeois society. Life is not a combat of man against man, but a fight fought by the entire society against nature, and men should aid one another without seeking special rewards. Working relations should be of specialist to specialist, rather than of superior to inferior, of coordination rather than hierarchy.

The professional man whose superior intellect and education are supposed to merit extra compensation is no different. Like collective force, his abilities result from a collective social process, for professional knowledge is the accumulation of learning by many men, an accumulation of social capital. The professional is co-possessor with society of his special faculties, not proprietor of them. When he practices his profession, he is using social capital invested in him. He should be adequately compensated by being free to devote himself to his science or art; society is compensated by the service he gives it. Moreover, the spiritual rewards of altruism and of self-fulfilling work should be far more precious than material wealth.

It should be added that recent study of vocational motivation suggests that Proudhon's position here has more of a claim to justification than moral principle alone. Self-fulfillment or altruism proves to be the major career incentive of many people, and not just those in ill-paid professions, fine arts, and public-service work. Corporate executives often seek advancement largely to find more challenging, responsible opportunities to exercise their administrative and leadership talents. Increased income is prized by them most of all because it is the most significant conventional indicator of success. Max Weber's well-known analysis of the motivations of capitalists also leads to the conclusion that, for entrepreneurs and many others in business, material wealth is only a secondary goal, except as a convenient measure of accomplishment.

When Proudhon says that labor destroys property, he refers to the consequences of mutual dependency in work. Since in all production every man is in debt to others for their labors, no one can claim an exclusive right to anything, including the products of his own labor. Because both talents and material wealth result from social processes, the whole society has a proprietary interest in them, and their enjoyment by individuals is limited by this interest and the obligations it may entail. Thus Proudhon's concept of possession without absolute and exclusive rights of use and abuse is extended from land to any property, including the immaterial.

Proudhon does not advocate the communism of men like Fourier or Cabet; he rejects this alternative emphatically. Communism would, he insists, repress individual liberty and engender mediocrity. In later years he submits communist ideas to extensive criticism, and he attacks them here at some length also. Society's proprietary interest does not have to be realized through communal possession.

This more complete vision of society, labor, and property which we have just outlined has far greater depth and significance than the simple statement, "Property is theft." It is here that we see the most important facet of the *mémoires* on property. The lengthy, often unwieldy arguments against property are transformed into a basis for a radically different conception of social justice and social relations, of equality and liberty. The distinctive character of his indictment of property results from the radical egalitarian concept of justice developed; despite the broadly common ground between Proudhon and other theorists, his ideal of justice makes his approach uniquely different and his vision of the good society a peculiar creation of his own.

Classical political economy, as formulated by Adam Smith, David Ricardo, and J.-B. Say, is a science of mechanics, the dynamics of exchange, production, distribution, force, growth. Humans are ciphers in a calculation, social organization one factor among many. Such economists may privately be humane and compassionate individuals, and personal elements do enter in their reckoning, but their science is essentially impersonal, not antisocial but nonsocial.

Socialists, on the other hand, focus on the uniquely human qualities of man and society, seen as something more than impersonal factors in calculations of force and structure in economics and politics. Individual and collective human needs are prior to considerations internal to political and economic science. Meeting these needs requires society's involvement and changes in its structure that neither purely political action nor economic growth of the society as a whole can bring about alone.

In 1840 socialism was not the potent force it was later to become —the word itself was just beginning to be used—but there were two important socialist "schools" well established in France, the Saint-Simonians and the Fourierists. Although their schemes for a new order were very different, they shared with each other and with Proudhon the common objective of a closely knit, wholly integrated social structure. He owed much to both schools.[43] But the equality sought by Saint-Simonians was essentially that of opportunity, and the Fourierists founded their theories mainly on considerations others than those of rights. Neither school placed primary emphasis on those issues of justice and right that so preoccupied Proudhon.

He offers no solutions here; he is still in a critical stage, trying to formulate principles and discover the faults of old ideas. His principles are basically old ones; what he does with them is novel. He has made justice his mistress and is devoted to her exclusively. To know her is no easy task, and Proudhon spends much of his life in the attempt to do so. In these *mémoires* we see the shape of the vision of justice which he is to fill out in succeeding years. Much of this shape is to be seen in the fifth and final chapter of the *premier mémoire*, "Psychological exposition of the idea of justice and injustice, and determination of the principle of government and right."

Following Aristotle, he defines man as an animal living in society. What, then, are the conditions and laws of human society? What is right (*droit*), and what is justice?

> *Right* is the totality of principles which rule society; in man justice is respect for and observation of its principles. To practice justice is to obey the social instinct; to perform an act of justice is to perform an act of society.[44]

43. Probably he knew only some of the quite varied conceptions developed by different members of the two schools. Over the years he discussed their ideas often but made significant omissions.
44. *Oeuv.*, IV, 300.

Other animals are often social, but unlike them humans reflect and reason about their society. Our reason and our instinct tell us that it is self-injurious and contrary to human nature to act anti-socially, but, knowing what is wrong, we still do it. More to the point for Proudhon's mission of bringing light to the world, our reasoning is often at fault; consequently we have systematized anti-social behavior.

Justice, he says, is the recognition in another of a personality equal to our own.[45] Society, justice, and equality are equivalent terms. We reason falsely when we suppose that a man's fortune is his own affair. Division of labor and specialized aptitudes form the essential basis of society. We are all of necessity associated and dependent on each other and cannot lay claim to greater rate of gain than our fellows. Such gain is antisocial because it thwarts the proper working of society. Worst of all is the wealthy idler who accomplishes no socially useful function. He is a parasite on society—a robber.

> Sociability is like the attraction of sensitive beings; justice is the same attraction, accompanied by reflection and knowledge. But by what general idea, under what category of understanding do we perceive justice? Under the category of equal quantities. . . .
>
> What is it to practice justice then? It is to make an equal share of the goods for each one, on the condition of labor; it is to act in association. . . .
>
> What is the right of occupation? It is a natural way of dividing the land while placing workers side by side according to how they present themselves: this right disappears before the general interest which, being the social interest, is also that of the occupant.
>
> What is the right of labor? It is the right to have oneself admitted to share in the benefits when fulfilling the required conditions; it is the right of society, it is the right of equality.[46]

The divergence of abilities and of functions among men tends to divide them, inequality making the separation and isolation far more acute. It is necessary to gather energies into the integrating of society, breaking down the walls between men and building a foun-

---

45. Ibid., 303. Cf. definitions given in his *magnum opus, De la Justice dans la révolution et dans l'Eglise* (1858).

46. Ibid., 306.

dation of equity where "superiority" is rewarded by esteem and where privilege of every kind disappears.

Proudhon realizes that, quite apart from the differences which are remediable, "society" is not a single organism which can be homogeneous in composition. Men have an assortment of concentric loyalties to a number of social entities: associates in work, neighbors, town, nation, and above all their families. Though he explicitly recognizes that society is actually quite complex, Proudhon's sociology is often simplistic; nevertheless, a more sophisticated sociology would not change his fundamental position. He does not think social complexity can change the basic nature of justice, for the latter rests on primary principles themselves in no way complex.

Proudhon bases everything on some simple ideals, attributing much of what is wrong in society to man's lack of understanding of these principles. Still, he does not suppose that injustice results only from mistaken ideas, or that justice can be realized solely through the correction of error.

Even if knowledge of truth were available, human wills would diverge and clash. Proudhon thinks that the conflict of wills is natural, and not necessarily contrary to the requirements of justice. The difficulty lies in the ways men's wills very often are exercised.

The individual will is capricious, vague, and subject to frequent unjustifiable shifts. Often governed by the passions, even when rationally determined the will often leads men astray because reasoning has been faulty or premises false.

Men tend to insist on their ideas when all experience and further reflection should show them to be wrong. Stubborn persistence in caprice and error has regularly made human life wretched. Thus the philosopher can build the foundations of the good society by replacing error and caprice with truth and rationally determined will.

But society itself causes the arbitrary and irrational to determine action, despite well-developed rationality among individuals. In asserting this, Proudhon assumes a distinctive position, differing from the Enlightenment tradition in which most of his notions about reason, passions, and will are commonplace. His idea is that the conditions of social intercourse are often such that men are required to do other than their reason dictates. Demands of commerce are often erratic, irrational, and arbitrary. Requirements of law, though intended to be reasonable, are frequently merely arbitrary.

A man cannot determine his most important actions through his own reasoning. However rational the original thought of others, when they impose their will on him, or when he is bound by largely impersonal processes like many of those in commerce, to him it is arbitrary and his reason is neglected. The only determinant of action should be one's own reason, the only rules those of rational principle. When the decision or the rule originates elsewhere, as with government and law, it amounts to a denial of man's very essence, his rationality.

The government of man by man instead of by reason can never be just, for it is always domination by the arbitrary and willful. Thus Proudhon arrives at anarchism.

What form of government are we going to prefer? —Eh! you can ask that, one of my younger readers doubtless asks; you are republican. —Republican, yes; but this word specifies nothing. *Res publica* means "the public business"; now whoever wants public business, under whatever form of government, can call himself republican. Kings are republicans too. —Fine! you are a democrat? —No. —What! Would you be a monarchist? —No. —Constitutionalist? —God protect me. —You are an aristocrat then? —Not at all. —You want a mixed government? —Even less. —What are you then? —I am an anarchist.

—I understand you: you speak satirically, addressing yourself to government. —In no way: you have just heard my profession of faith, seriously and fully thought through; although very much the friend of order, I am, in the whole force of the world, anarchist. . . .

Through teaching himself and acquiring ideas, man finally acquires the idea of *science*, that is, the idea of a system of knowledge conforming to the reality of things and deduced from observation. He seeks then the science or system of inanimate matter, the system of organic substance, the system of the human mind, the world system: how would he not also seek the system of society? But, getting to this, he understands that the truth or political science is something entirely independent of the sovereign will, of the opinions of majorities and of popular beliefs: the kings, ministers, magistrates and peoples, just as much as wills, are nothing for science and merit no consideration. He understands at the same time that if man is born sociable, his father's authority over him ceases on the day when, his reason being formed and his education done, he becomes the associate of his father. He understands that politics is a science, not petty trickery, and that in the last analysis the function of the legislator is reduced to methodical research into truth.

Thus, in a given society, the authority of man over man is rationally the inverse of the intellectual development this society has achieved, and the probable duration of this authority can be calculated by the more or less general desire for a true government, that is, a government according to science. And just as the right of force and the right of cunning are restrained before the ever greater determination of justice, likewise the sovereignty of will gives way before the sovereignty of reason, and ends by annihilating itself in a scientific socialism. Property and royalty have been in the process of demolition since the beginning of the world; as man searches for justice in equality, society searches for order in anarchy.

Anarchy, the absence of a master, of a sovereign, such is the form of government that we approach every day, and the inveterate habit of taking man for our rule and his will for our law, we have to regard this as the height of disorder and the expression of chaos.

Later, referring to these passages in his trial defense, Proudhon says that by anarchy he means the negation of human sovereignty, that is, the substitution of pure reason for arbitrary will in government.[47]

Thus far, the anarchist idea is not as clear as Proudhon tries to make it appear. It is apparent that he is opposed to any government which does not rule in every detail according to true rational principle, that these principles are as yet inadequately known, and that no government has ever fulfilled his requirements. But given a society in which the whole truth is known, when we recall how imperfect a creature is man, how is it supposed that he can govern without error and caprice?

"Anarchy" means no rule or no government. But if, as Proudhon says, some kind of order is to be maintained and there are to be

47. Ibid., 335, 338–39; X, 262n.

relations between men, then there must be decisions made by men about their society and about social relations. Whether or not some men rule others, decisions about social relations, together with the actions implementing these decisions, do constitute a "governing" of society. What, then, can anarchy be?

The answers to these questions are not clarified in these *mémoires*. We know that Proudhon opposes the government of man by man, saying that in any form it is oppression. He attacks monarchy and the contemporary government of France, a constitutional monarchy, but he does not acclaim democracy. Democracy, he says, wants to make everyone king when no one should be king, for none should rule or be ruled. Then he goes on to say that the people are the guardians of the law and the executive power.

He means that the people should guard and execute the law of eternal reason, but it is hard to see how this differs from ideal democracy. Somehow the answer is contained in the concept of association, visualizing society as a gathering of mutually dependent individuals. This vision is one of interchanged benefits and complementary functions, without any notion of persons ruling the operation. Repeatedly in these *mémoires* he speaks against the exercise of sovereign authority by anyone, saying that the sovereignty of the people is an empty abstraction. Proudhon looks for a society where *reason* rules, not men. How this can be effected, or why government cannot achieve it, he does not really tell us here. To find the details of his anarchism and a plan for an anarchist society we must look to later books.

Here he speaks indefinitely of the final and natural form of society, the form he calls liberty. Liberty is equality; it is anarchy, denying the rule of the will and admitting only the authority of the law of necessary reason. Liberty is universal tolerance and infinite variety, respecting the wishes of everyone, within the limits of this law. "*Sociability* in man, becoming *justice* through reflection, equity through engaging capacities, having *liberty* as its formula, this is the true foundation of morals, the principle and the rule of all our actions." [48]

The indefinite characteristics of Proudhon's anarchism are only clarified in the progressive development of his theories through the

48. *Oeuv.*, IV, 343.

years, a thorough scheme for the just society not being presented until *Du Principe fédératif*, which he published in 1863. This is quite in accord with his approach to social and political philosophy. Since all depends on right knowledge, it is his task to expose false ideas and then to discover the true ones. In consequence, it takes time to develop a complete theory. Thus his initial function is primarily a critical one, the enunciation of principle serving to provide critical criteria.

His lack of a system to defend is an advantage; with such radically different attitudes he can shake the solidity of a multitude of bastions and bring new light to bear on many questions. In these *mémoires* he has made a start by attacking property, and through this has established the ground for future battles.

Proudhon's critical position is that of a revolutionary, but his attitudes toward revolution always display an ambivalence which makes his thought both provocative in its subtlety and difficult to understand and appraise. While on the one hand he is a child of the French Revolution of 1789, on the other he is the most outspoken and original critic of its tradition among those with some sympathy for the Revolution's purposes. He believes that the Revolution and developments since have done too little to bring men closer to justice, and that most of its supposed benefits have been illusory. He wants the Revolution to accomplish its declared purposes and more, but he does not think it is ready even to make a beginning.

A philosopher first of all and only reluctantly a man of action, Proudhon took no part in the several revolutionary conspiracies of the 1830's.[49] Later he was to become engaged more directly, in the Second Republic and Empire, but he never was at ease in the activist's role. In part this was a matter of temperament and a consequence of the peculiar difficulties he faced in public activity. Probably more important were his conviction that the revolutionary movement first needed a new philosophy if it were to go anywhere, and his determination to develop this philosophy. It can be said that this life-long task was completed, but only on his deathbed, where

49. ". . . I am a man of meditation, not of revolution. . . . I declare myself outside the ranks of conspirators . . ." (letter to Bergmann discussing his trial, February 8, 1842, *Corresp.*, II, 13). These conclusions are the court's, and he does not object.

he dictated to a friend the notes for the final chapter of his last major work, *De la Capacité politique des classes ouvrières.*

In his later writing Proudhon becomes very much concerned with the actual revolutionary process of transition to a new society. Here he suffers from an ambivalence more profound than that with which he views the past tradition. He fears that revolution itself will not have the intended results, even if social philosophers have a true conception of what is required to establish justice. Experience makes him more skeptical than most of his socialist contemporaries about the readiness of mankind to accept the truths reason reveals and to act upon them. Thus he is increasingly concerned with how to translate these truths from the philosopher's texts to the minds and the spirit of the people.

However, before 1848 his attention is directed primarily to the discovery of truth and the establishment of a philosophy to guide the cause of revolution. He is still confident that the pure principles exist and are waiting to be discovered; as yet he has little doubt that their discovery and clear enunciation is sufficient for their acceptance. The following passages, written in 1841 and 1842, illustrate his conception then of the nature and function of social philosophy, pointing the way to his search during the next few years for a precise and systematic science of society.

> Since you have read my book, you must understand that there is no question of *inventing,* of combining in our brain a system which we shall present afterward; it is not thus that the world is reformed. Society can only correct itself by itself, that is, it is necessary to study human nature in all its manifestations, its laws, religions, customs, political economy; to extract from this enormous mass, *by the operations of metaphysics,* what is true; to eliminate what is vicious, false, or incomplete, and all the preserved elements; to form the general principles which serve as rules. This work will take centuries to be conducted to its completion. . . .

> Society advances, almost without perceiving it, to a political organization which is absolutely and divinely true, legitimate, perfect, eternal. It is not a question here of ontological aphorisms on equality, fraternity, the rights of man and the citizen, the sovereignty of the people, etc. The metaphysic of *The Social Contract* and *The Spirit of the Laws* is worn out; in the place of these hollow theories arises a new science, exact, mathematical, before

which the darkness of journalism and the storms of the tribune cease forever.[50]

Proudhon was to develop his theory much beyond what he achieved in the *mémoires* on property; although most of the major elements of his later thought are visible here, they are not yet fully realized. His views on property itself did not change substantially, however, though he returned to the subject many times.[51] Always property was but a focus of much more far-reaching concerns, as they are here. While the *mémoires* are themselves powerful expressions of his radical perspective, for understanding his philosophy they serve chiefly as an introduction, the foundation upon which Proudhon's mature philosophy was built.

The story of the literary career of *Qu'est-ce que la propriété?* is a different matter, however. In the next decade the first *mémoire* in particular was one of the books most often read by men interested in socialist ideas, and for many of them it probably was an important stimulus contributing to the radicalization of their thought. Though less influential in later years, it has always been one of the most frequently read of Proudhon's books. Since few of his other works have been translated into English, most Britons and Americans who have read any of his writing seem to know only *What Is Property?* [52]

Most intriguing is the intensity of the sensation created by these *mémoires* at the time of their publication. They were read—or at least talked about—by many others besides radicals. Published attempts to refute them were numerous, and Proudhon was prosecuted, even though his writing was not openly seditious. Since his expressed views would seem to have differed sharply from those then prevailing in literate society, the reaction to his tracts may not

50. Letter to Antoine Gauthier, May 2, 1841, *Corresp.*, I, 324ff.; *Oeuv.*, X, 266.
51. At his death he left an incomplete manuscript, published by his friends as the *Théorie de la propriété* (*Oeuvres posthumes*, II [Paris, 1865]). This book serves as a useful summary of his entire theory of property, while adding very little to what he had written before. The long introductory chapter gives a good résumé of the previous work; it was written by intimate friends of Proudhon, as a faithful reconstruction of notes for this book and of previous writings. Some have suggested that he had at the end of his life modified his condemnation of property to approve possession without absolute rights or unearned income. However, this was always his position.
52. Translated and published by Benjamin R. Tucker, a major American anarchist (Princeton, Mass., 1876).

appear surprising. No radical book is likely to have so sensational an effect and so diverse an audience in the United States today— but then we are more used to revolutionary pronouncements and more jaded by a surfeit of protests.

Yet France's actual experience with revolution was more intimate than our own; the 1789 Revolution had established a tradition dominant in French intellectual and political life. Proudhon's work was very much in the line of this heritage; though he departed from conventional interpretations and applications of the tradition, his ideas and values were no more than a further rational development of those already firmly incorporated there. Nevertheless, people either were unwilling to recognize them as a legitimate critical reformulation of familiar notions, or they seized upon them eagerly, as if they believed the tracts were something much needed but previously lacking. The reaction to Proudhon may be more revealing than it at first appears.

The commonplace explanation would be that this was a bourgeois society, with bourgeois views predominant, and his ideas did violence to the most sacred bourgeois beliefs, those involving property and the differential rewards of a "free enterprise" economy. This observation has some validity, but it is too much simplified. Such characterizations of social structure and ideology have long been used but no longer are adequate. France was not simply a "bourgeois society." Bourgeois Frenchmen did not all conceive of affairs exclusively in terms of self-interest and class values, and the revolutionary tradition was pervasive, potent, and not exclusively bourgeois in the definitions of it then current.

The revolutionary process which began in 1789 was not made exclusively by and for the bourgeoisie; its identification as a bourgeois revolution, so long the common currency of historiography, has not withstood the critical examination of recent historians. Their work has demonstrated that the interests of Frenchmen were too multifariously differentiated, as were significant strata of social and economic status, for class labels like "bourgeois" and "peasant" to have more than a preliminary analytic value.

Even where use of these broad class identifications is valid, the 1789 Revolution and the tradition it engendered were not simply bourgeois. Elements of the bourgeoisie did achieve political power, but they were not strong enough to do so unaided. Disaffected aristocrats helped, but the main force needed to dismantle the *ancien régime* came from urban plebeians, especially those of the capital city, and from the less direct but still very disruptive effects of rural discontent and turmoil. Among lower classes in both town and country there existed radical impulses and needs that far exceeded those of the higher social strata. This contributed in large measure to the Revolution's being pushed leftward beyond what can be explained as the securing of class interests by an economically powerful bourgeoisie. The interests and urges of rural folk and *sans culottes*, never close, eventually diverged altogether, with the latter isolated and submerged in the Thermidorean reaction. Their misery and potential for rebellion, however, remained an important element in French politics.

We may still say that the Revolution of 1789 and its sequels were bourgeois, and that France in 1840 was dominated by the bourgeoisie—if such statements are recognized as shorthand characterizations of prevailing trends, with more complex distinctions often necessary. The Revolution's outcome was indeed a state where the interests of property-owners superseded those of the propertyless poor, where seigneurial privilege had given way to more modern forms of economic privilege and relationships, and where royal and aristocratic prerogatives no longer formed the real basis of political authority, notwithstanding attempts to reverse this during the Restoration period. Political and economic power were not simply combined in the hands of the bourgeoisie, and the policies of the State were not determined merely by the needs of commerce. But various elements of the bourgeoisie were becoming steadily more powerful in government, the economy, or both.

Property-owners were not homogeneous, however, either in interests or in ideas and attitudes. The bourgeoisie was itself quite varied in needs and outlook. Farmers with small properties composed the most numerous economic grouping, and men with inherited or adopted aristocratic attitudes remained influential. In these widely differing groups there would always be many who thought their interests threatened or their conceptions of rights violated by one or another of the political and economic measures sought in a bourgeois revolution. Thus there was among the propertied classes a reservoir of discontent; most often the consequence was reaction in a conservative vein, but this was often not very different from the radicalism of the left—as with hostility to commercial banking or to some of the developments of industrialization. Classical liberalism in its several evolutionary variations has generally been conceived of as *the* bourgeois ideology, dominant in nineteenth-century France. In fact, however, such ideas and attitudes found only limited and *selective* acceptance among the propertied classes, whose members were too divided (and often too ambivalent and ignorant about political and economic realities) for there to be uniformity and confident beliefs shared by most of them.

Such conditions might not make them readily receptive to socialist ideas—especially any denying property rights—but they did make the political situation relatively fluid and unstable. Not only would French political history be tumultuous, but also the conditions in which socialist ideas and movements could grow are not suitably characterized by reference to "the dominance of bourgeois ideology." Proudhon's *mémoires* were sensationally provocative simply because there was no solid foundation of uniform beliefs among the literate. If there had been one, he could have been rejected or ignored as readily as other left-wing ideologues often have been in the United States.

Moreover, the tradition of the 1789 Revolution had powerful "subversive" components, even though its main themes had been those of bourgeois liberalism. The rights called for in the Revolution could not easily be denied afterward. As usually conceived these rights were quite circumscribed, but their definition was so vague that claims for rights more extensive than usual could be made readily and within the spirit of the tradition. Thus insistence on these rights could mean nothing more than confirmation of the overthrow of the *ancien régime*—or, if they were interpreted differently, the demand could become a call for overthrow of the new regime.

More radical interpretations of the rights of man were part of the Revolution's legacy. The extremism of the left in the Jacobin period was a kind of radical populism which was remembered positively by many after Thermidor. It was picked up and developed further by Gracchus Babeuf's Conspiracy of Equals in 1796, and enshrined in the fond images of Jacobinism retained by people like Proudhon's parents. Though Babeuf's conspiracy was easily suppressed and he was executed, his legend was perpetuated through the account published by his surviving associate, Filippo Buonarotti, in 1828.[53] Heirs of Babeuf engaged in a seemingly endless series of insurrectionary plots and secret clubs, from the 1820's on through the Paris Commune of 1871.

The ideological content of this conspiratorial activity was ambiguous. Babeuf did not develop his ideas very far, and neither did the principal figure in the later conspiracies, Auguste Blanqui. The latter actively plotted insurrection for half a century, but said relatively little about anything but the business of revolt itself.[54]

A lasting republic was not to be secured in France until late in the nineteenth century; indeed, republicanism has never been finally established there. Many wanted a republic, though what people saw as its promise was quite varied and often vague. In their desires for a republic many sought no radical change, but they could not readily forget the intoxicating and idealistic universalism of the years when French armies marched across Europe to liberate man from tyranny. In this idealism lay the truly radical and subversive elements of the Revolution's tradition.

The idealism might be caught up in Jacobinism of an essentially bourgeois temper, in a more radical populism, in the revolutionary though ill-defined communism of Babeuf and his heirs in the conspiratorial clubs, or in the more cerebral, less activist schemes and dreams of the early socialist prophets. Or it might simply find expression in the potentially rebellious dissatisfaction of the unlettered and usually passive poor. Whatever the case, the situation was an inchoate one; there were few sharp distinctions in varieties of belief among those who regarded the 1789 Revolution as a largely positive development. There was a wide basis for revolt against the status quo, but no common vision of what Frenchmen might be revolting for.

Under these conditions there should have been a substantial and potentially very receptive audience for fresh and contemporarily

53. Buonarotti, *Conspiration pour l'égalité dite de Babeuf.*

54. His fullest and most important statements were published only after his death in 1881. A complete bibliography is in Maurice Dommanget, *Les Idées politiques et sociales d'Auguste Blanqui* (Paris, 1957), 408–18.

relevant interpretation of the Revolutionary tradition. Proudhon provided this and thus elicited the excitement that he did. No doubt opposition to his views was much stronger than support; few of those who read books then were likely to go as far as he in attacking the status quo.

Yet it is significant that nonrevolutionary pillars of the established system, like economists Garnier, Droz, and Adolphe Blanqui, praised Proudhon. Their degree of receptivity would be difficult to comprehend unless elsewhere opposition to his ideas was mixed with some admiration as well. Consequently, the *mémoires* on property should have been profoundly unsettling to many, for Proudhon said, in essence, that there was grave contradiction between their ideals and the reality of contemporary life, and that this would not be ended simply by reestablishing the Republic. This might explain better than anything else why there was so great a furor over these tracts. Men trying to justify shaken convictions often feel most intensely a need to refute critics.

Of necessity this conclusion is conjectural, but there is much more solid reason to insist upon the heterogeneity and fluidity of political ideas at this time, denying the utility of speaking simply in terms of bourgeois ideology. Not until the advent of another revolution in 1848 did Proudhon complete his critique of existing conceptions of the revolutionary tradition. When he did this, it had great impact. If we are to understand the developing texture of French political ideas and attitudes, and his role in these changes, then we need to have thus refined our perceptions of the complex conditions in which this happened.

four: Intermediate Years, 1842-47

Destruam et aedificabo [I demolished and I shall build].
—Epigraph to Proudhon's *Philosophie de la misère*

WHEN SENSATION OVER the *mémoires* on property died down, Proudhon's life took on an aspect of relative calm, which lasted until the Revolution of 1848 swept him up and thrust him into public life once more. These were years in which he tried out ideas, methodology, system. He sought solutions to problems he had raised earlier, but the immediate results of his labors were not impressive in comparison to most of his other work. They were trial efforts which, although themselves weak, made possible sorties in greater strength later, less encumbered by excess intellectual baggage.

Proudhon had pressing personal concerns that must often have engaged more of his attention than did his intellectual pursuits. He had to earn a living and was burdened by debts and concern for his parents, by then old and in need of his support. His printing business remained moribund, and he could obtain none of the positions often open to French men of letters. He was, for instance, refused employment which he sought as an archivist or official's secretary in the municipal and prefectural administrations in Besançon. In January, 1843, the printing business was sold at a large loss. During the following years he was able to do little more with his debts than pay the interest. On the eve of the 1848 Revolution he owed approximately ten thousand francs—equivalent to roughly five thousand dollars.

A few months after disposing of the print shop Proudhon obtained a job in Lyon with Gauthier Frères, a firm engaged in shipping on inland waterways. Proudhon was a managerial factotum with considerable responsibility, and he appears to have performed much valuable work for the firm, particularly as an *avocat-conseil*. In this capacity he represented the company in court actions, writing elaborate briefs for the purpose.

His work caused him to travel frequently, taking him throughout a large part of eastern France and to Paris. He enjoyed this, for he did not like Lyon, a city already blighted by burgeoning industrialization and in any event too large and commercial for Proudhon's small-town provincial tastes.

The experience gained in this job was to be important for him because it made him familiar with aspects of contemporary life that he would scarcely have known in his capacities as writer or printer. Work and travel for a transport company gave him extensive and varied acquaintance with business affairs and the legal system's practices. It is clear from his later writing that this practical experience did much to inform his thought. Indeed, the extent to which he would make detailed examinations of commercial problems sometimes contrasts strangely with his unfailing dislike for the existing economic system and its rationale and for bourgeois morality. Proudhon's intellectual approach gives his writing a semblance of "objective detachment," but this impression is frequently dissipated by his apparent conviction that the world which the bourgeoisie upholds is fundamentally evil.

While this belief did not then lead him into an actively revolutionary role, it does seem that he had close contacts with industrial workers in Lyon; he may have had some relationship with secret revolutionary groups there.[1] In 1834 there had been a workers' insurrection in Lyon, which had been ruthlessly suppressed by Louis-Philippe's government. Bitter memories of this remained; there were

1. See A. Bertrand, *Proudhon et les Lyonnais* (Paris, 1904).

strong revolutionary undercurrents in the city, which was exceptionally industrialized for the France of this period.

The Gauthiers were Proudhon's patrons as well as his employers; he was a friend of the family. They liked and respected him and allowed him to devote a substantial portion of his time to his own study and writing. Both business trips and his own interests brought him to Paris frequently, although most of the time he remained in Lyon, or elsewhere in the provinces on business trips.

Proudhon read very extensively and eclectically in these years, as can be seen from the reading notes in his *carnets*. He concentrated on philosophy and economics, and he also had many opportunities to discuss these subjects with other intellectuals in Paris. He became acquainted personally with a number of liberal economists. Much of the material in the books he wrote during this period should be seen as his response to debates in the intellectual circles he frequented when in Paris.

He was constantly devising projects for things to do and write, but few of them were realized. There were several for newspapers, including one to be coeditor of a paper for Etienne Cabet, the author of a scheme for a socialist utopia, *Voyage en Icarie* (1840). He could reach no satisfactory agreement with Cabet. A final newspaper project was developed by Proudhon with others during 1847. After much difficulty in obtaining funds, this paper began publication shortly after the beginning of the Revolution of 1848.

The work for Gauthier Frères did keep him busy for prolonged periods, leaving him without sufficient leisure to work on all the projects which occurred to him. Many were never more than ideas that came to him as responses to his reading and daily events. Some of his intellectual activity was concentrated on the development of a science of society, and his conclusions on the subject he presented to a not especially eager public in *De la Création de l'ordre dans l'humanité*,[2] published in September, 1843, and in the *Système des contradictions économiques*, published in October, 1846, and often referred to by its subtitle, the *Philosophie de la misère*.[3]

2. *De la Création de l'ordre dans l'humanité, ou principes d'organisation politique; Oeuv.*, V.

3. *Oeuv.*, I, 2 vols. He also published two minor pieces in these years: "Le Miserere, ou la pénitence d'un roi," *Revue indépendante*, XIX (March, 1845), 203–29; published separately (Paris, 1849); *Oeuv.*, XV, 139–73. "De la Concurrence

Proudhon became increasingly unhappy about his job with the Gauthiers. Commerce itself he found distasteful; any role in it could not have been comfortable for a man who professed opinions such as his. More important still, the patronage of the Gauthiers was onerous to so proud a man, and he had not the time he wanted for his study and writing. After trying for some time to arrange with them a genuinely part-time employment, acting as their Paris agent, Proudhon left the firm and Lyon in November, 1847. On December 15, two months before the Revolution, he returned to Paris permanently, living there the rest of his life, except for four years of exile in Brussels and a brief period in a provincial prison.

At this time Proudhon's mother, to whom he had been very much devoted, died. His father had died in the previous year. While their deaths upset him profoundly—particularly that of his mother—this new lack of dependents eased his financial burdens and made his income from Gauthier Frères less important. He could hope to live on his salary as editor of the planned newspaper. At last Proudhon was independent and free to pursue the course of life he wished.

The matter of greatest interest in Proudhon's life during these years is his brief acquaintance with Karl Marx, beginning in 1844.[4] Apparently the two men were friendly at this time, but later Marx engaged in energetic polemics against Proudhon and wrote one of his major works, *La Misère de la philosophie*, as an attack upon him. This antagonism, originating in personal and ideological differences, was played out in the internal conflicts of socialist organizations, where Marx's chief opponents were followers of Proudhon or of men with similar ideas, like Bakunin. The French anarchist died in January, 1865, just after the foundation of the First Socialist International, and he had little part in the controversy himself. This conflict between anarchists and Marxists contributed to the early demise of the First International and continued to plague the socialist and labor movements long afterward.

Given these circumstances, the issue of the two men's relation-

---

entre les chemins de fer et les voies navigables," *Journal des économistes*, XI (May, 1845), 157–202; published separately (Paris, 1845, 1848); *Oeuv. (Lacroix)*, II.

4. Much of the following discussion of the two men was published in somewhat different form as "Marx and Proudhon: A Reappraisal of Their Relationship," *The Historian*, XXIX, 3 (May, 1967), 409–30; reproduced by permission of the editor.

ship and possible influence on each other has been the subject of numerous investigations and has become a basis of partisan polemic as well as an object of interest to scholars. Proudhon's more outspoken supporters have claimed that Marx acquired many of his most important ideas from the anarchist.[5] The concepts most often claimed as due to the latter are surplus value, historical materialism, and the class struggle. Proudhon has been supposed to be either the originator of these notions [6] or the stimulus responsible for Marx's conception of them.[7] The Frenchman has also been held responsible for the young Marx's "conversion" to socialism.[8] On the other hand, the German claimed to have taught Hegel to Proudhon—an explanation of the latter's peculiar "dialectic" method which has of course been accepted by Marxists.[9] A few writers have also thought that Proudhon may have been somewhat influenced by Marx on the issue of historical materialism.[10] An English historian, having examined the whole question and finding what he believed are close similarities in texts he quoted from each, concluded that they probably learned much from each other.[11]

Although the breadth of the gap between the final theoretical

5. The most sustained argument for this claim is by Arthur Mülberger, *Zur Kenntnis des Marxismus* (Stuttgart, 1894), 19–34.

6. Ibid.; Jeanne Duprat, *Proudhon—sociologue et moraliste* (Paris, 1929), 288–96; Karl Diehl, *P.-J. Proudhon—Seine Lehre und sein Leben* (Halle and Jena, 1888–96), I, 63; II, 301–7; Edouard Droz, *P.-J. Proudhon* (Paris, 1909), 15–19, 88–89; David Koigen, *Zur Vorgeschichte des modern philosophischen Sozialismus in Deutschland* (Bern, 1901), 256; Arthur Desjardins, *P.-J. Proudhon* (Paris, 1896), I, iv–v.

7. George Adler, *Die Grundlagen der Karl Marx'schen Kritik der bestehenden Volkswirtschaft* (Tübingen, 1887), 169–201; W. Pickles, "Marx and Proudhon," *Politica*, III (1938), 247–48; Pierre Haubtmann, *Marx et Proudhon: Leurs Rapports personnels, 1844–1847* (Paris, 1947), 39.

8. Pickles, "Marx and Proudhon," 241 et passim; George Adler, "Der Anfang der Marxschen Sozialtheorie," *Festgabe für Adolf Wagner* (Leipzig, 1905), 10; Emil Hammacher, *Das Philosophisch-ökonomische System des Marxismus* (Leipzig, 1909), 62–63, 79–86, et passim.

9. Karl Marx, "Uber P.-J. Proudhon. Brief an J. B. von Schweitzer," in Karl Marx and Friedrich Engels, *Werke* (Berlin, 1958–67), XVI, 25–32. Some non-Marxists have also taken Marx at his word (Droz, *Proudhon*, 139). Djacir Menezes treats questions of connections between Proudhon, Marx, and Hegel in his *Proudhon, Hegel e a dialética* (Rio de Janeiro, 1966). I cannot read the book, which is written in Portuguese, but it appears to consider the influences of one writer on another to be much more important than I think warranted.

10. Haubtmann, *Marx et Proudhon*, 24, 44–45; Pickles, "Marx and Proudhon," 250.

11. Pickles, "Marx and Proudhon," 260.

positions of the two men seems plain enough, there are some points at which their writings appear similar. Moreover, their differences were exaggerated by Marx for polemical purposes. These elements of similarity have contributed to the debate over mutual influence, although some scholars have insisted that any similarities in their ideas are less important than their differences in temperament, class background,[12] and ideological position.[13] However, Georges Sorel and his articulate disciple, Edouard Berth, believing that the ideas of Marx and Proudhon were compatible, derived a syndicalist philosophy from them.[14]

The following tries to achieve a balanced assessment amidst all this disparate opinion, while correcting important errors in and omissions of factual evidence found in many of the relevant books and articles. The conclusion developed here is that the differences between the two men were too great for them to influence each other significantly. A common interest in socialism and the philosophy of Hegel brought them together briefly, but that was in reality a rather vague basis for close intellectual bonds. They had little else.

Paris in the mid-1840's was a lodestone for German socialists, attracted by her revolutionary tradition, relative freedom, and celebrated socialist writers. Often they had been encouraged to leave Germany by unfriendly police. Many Germans gathered in Paris, and Marx joined them there in November, 1843. He planned with Arnold Ruge to found and edit a new journal, the *Deutsche-Französische Jahrbücher;* they tried to gain the collaboration of French socialists in this venture but were unable to do so. The only issue of the review appeared in March, 1844, with just one non-German contributor: Mikhail Bakunin.

The Germans were preoccupied with sectarian controversies

12. Edouard Dolléans, "Le Rencontre de Proudhon et de Marx (1843–1847)," *Revue d'histoire moderne*, XI (January–February, 1936), 15–26.

13. Maurice Bourguin, "Des Rapports entre Proudhon et Karl Marx," *Revue d'économie politique*, March, 1893; reprinted in *Le Contrat social*, IX, 2 (March–April, 1965), 105; Armand Cuvillier, "Marx et Proudhon," in his *Hommes et idéologies de 1840* (Paris, 1956), 163–226.

14. Georges Sorel, "Exegèses proudhoniennes," in his *Matériaux d'une théorie du prolétariat* (Paris, 1921), 415–49; Edouard Berth, "Proudhon, Marx, Georges Sorel," in his *Guerre des états ou guerre des classes* (Paris, 1924), 154–96; and "Proudhon et Marx," in his *Du "Capital" aux "Reflexions sur la violence"* (Paris, 1932), 69–168.

over idealist philosophy about which French socialists knew little and cared less. Furthermore, these Germans were usually insistently atheistic, coming as they did from a philosophical milieu of left Hegelianism and Feuerbach's ideas of an anthropomorphic God. Among French socialists some form of religious or pseudo-religious sentiment was common, and militant opposition to religion in all forms was not. In France "rejection of religion" primarily meant anticlericalism and deviation from Catholic orthodoxy; in any case, the abstractions of modern metaphysics had little or no pertinence for a French socialist's attitudes toward religion. There were other reasons for the nonparticipation of the French in this new journal, but their great differences from the Germans in philosophic approach seems to have been the most fundamental bar to collaboration.

A partial exception was Proudhon. Since he was agnostic as well as anticlerical, German atheism did not repel him as it did many other French socialists. While he was in the main ignorant of the intricacies of left Hegelian controversy, he was fascinated by what he knew or thought he knew of German idealism. His reputation among socialists had been established by his *mémoires* on property, which Marx would soon praise extravagantly in *Die Heilige Familie* (1845).[15]

Apparently Marx and Ruge wanted Proudhon's collaboration for their review. Ruge gave Marx the task of contacting Proudhon, but the latter was unavailable, being in Lyon preoccupied with his studies and writing and very active in his work for Gauthier Frères. He was in Paris briefly in the spring of 1844, but he and Marx probably did not meet until shortly after he returned to Paris for a prolonged stay that September.

The outlooks and interests of the two men were in reality quite different, as subsequent developments were to prove, but initially their superficially common concerns brought them together. On the one hand Proudhon was, as suggested above, receptive to German philosophy and presumably eager to discuss it. On the other, Marx apparently had at that time much admiration for Proudhon and his ideas. After all, Proudhon was celebrated and Marx's senior by nine years, while the German was just another little-known

15. See above, pp. 45, 48.

intellectual in exile. Their mutual belief in the primacy of economic relationships was a good initial foundation for their acquaintance, although the very different way they regarded this primacy would soon divide them irreconcilably. In these months economics was a principal subject in their conversations, according to the later comment of Friedrich Engels: ". . . in Paris the two of them often discussed economic questions the whole night long." [16]

One can learn almost nothing from Proudhon about his association with Marx. He did not mention Marx at all in works written for publication. He wrote two letters to him and mentioned him just twice elsewhere in his published correspondence; his *carnets* include only four mentions of Marx, the first not until 1847, and none of the four revealing much. During the period when the two men were seeing each other in Paris, Proudhon made few if any entries in his *carnets*.[17]

Marx, on the other hand, wrote a few days after Proudhon's death:

> During my stay in Paris, 1844, I entered into a personal relationship with Proudhon. I mention it here because I am somewhat to blame for his "sophistication," as the English call the falsification of goods. During long, often overnight debates I infected him to his great harm with Hegelianism, which because of his ignorance of the German language he could not study in the usual way. What I began Herr Karl Grün continued after my expulsion from Paris. As a teacher of German philosophy he also had the advantage over me that he understood nothing of it himself.[18]

W. Pickles has expressed doubt that the two men knew each other well, suggesting that there is no corroboration for Marx's reference to intimate acquaintance.[19] However, Pickles ignores the testimony of Engels quoted above and attaches significance to the failure of others, particularly Arnold Ruge and Alexander Herzen, to mention the supposed association. To argue thus from the lack

16. Friedrich Engels, "Vorwart zur ersten deutschen Ausgabe *Das Elend der Philosophie*," in Marx and Engels, *Werke*, IV, 558.

17. There are a few undated pages which may have been written at any time between June, 1844, and February, 1845. None have anything to do with Marx.

18. Marx, "Uber P.-J. Proudhon . . . ," 27; first published in *Der Social-Demokrat*, nos. 16–18 (February 1, 3, & 5, 1865).

19. Pickles, "Marx and Proudhon," 240–41.

of evidence is unconvincing, particularly when Herzen had not yet emigrated from Russia at the time in question. Granting that nothing in Proudhon's writings suggests close acquaintance, the same can be said with respect to other men whom he definitely knew well. Engels's comment, written after the death of his collaborator, could have been based on false claims by Marx; but in the absence of other evidence there is no good reason for doubting these statements of Engels and his mentor.

Marx's remarks about "infecting" the Frenchman with Hegelianism helped to create a controversy. From whom did Proudhon learn about Hegel's philosophy? Claims have been advanced for Marx, for Grün, and for Mikhail Bakunin as well.[20] By his own testimony Proudhon has not read Hegel; indeed, he knew no German. Except for his work on aesthetics, none of Hegel's writing was translated into French until after Proudhon's death. Yet Proudhon fancied that he knew Hegel well and that he had carried the Hegelian mode of philosophy to new heights of perfection and final successful application to the scientific understanding of society.[21] He felt that Hegel's philosophy was one of the most important influences on his thought. "My true masters," he said in August, 1848, "I mean those who have caused fruitful ideas to be born in me, number three: first the Bible, then Adam Smith, and finally Hegel." [22]

The content of Proudhon's works makes it apparent that his appraisal is not valid, particularly with respect to Hegel. Nevertheless, his reiterated pretensions led many to take them more seriously than is warranted, and they stimulated the controversy over the responsibility for his initiation into the Hegelian mystery.

The belief that Karl Grün taught Hegelianism to Proudhon does not seem to have originated with Marx's remarks in the passage quoted above but in an article written in 1848 by Saint-Réné Taillandier,[23] whose mistaken translation of a comment by Grün was

20. Droz, *Proudhon*, 139–41, suggests all three. Henri du Lubac discusses the matter of Grün's supposed influence and cites many who have alleged it (*The Un-Marxian Socialist*, trans. R. E. Scantlebury [London, 1948], 133–35).

21. Letter to Bergmann, January 19, 1845, *Corresp.*, II, 176.

22. Conversation with Proudhon reported by J.-A. Langlois, "P.-J. Proudhon: Sa Vie et son oeuvre," *Corresp.*, I, xxii.

23. Saint-Réné Taillandier, "L'Athéisme allemand et le socialisme français: M. Charles Grün et M. Proudhon," *Revue des deux mondes*, XXIV (October 15, 1848), 301.

followed by later writers. Actually, in the passage Taillandier misquoted, Grün had written that he confined his instruction of Proudhon to Feuerbach and related German critical philosophy. He stated that Proudhon already understood Hegel perfectly,[24] a judgment which lends credence to Marx's low opinion of Grün's own comprehension.

Grün, whom Marx despised, probably arrived in Paris and met Proudhon around October, 1844; he was expelled from France by the police in April, 1847. Proudhon suspected Marx's friends Heine and Weill of responsibility for this expulsion and may have thought Marx was also involved.[25] Marx himself had been expelled and left for Brussels on February 1, 1845. He and Proudhon never met again.

Shortly before coming to Paris Grün had been converted to the philosophy of Feuerbach by Moses Hess, and he intended to play the role of Feuerbach's apostle in France. He felt that Proudhon was in effect a disciple of Feuerbach's humanism without knowing it, and thus he tried to enlighten him on the subject.

However, the claim of Grün to have been Proudhon's *Privatdocent* in the passage referred to above excited the Frenchman to say with irritation in a letter to Marx that he had learned nothing whatever from Grün.[26] Though the latter probably did limit his "education" of Proudhon to Feuerbach and related current criticism, it is unlikely to have had significant effect. While Proudhon's notions of anthropomorphism in religion bear some resemblance to Feuerbach's, they predate the friendship with Grün and show no obvious change after having met the German apostle. The Frenchman's entire intellectual approach differs so greatly from Feuerbach's that the latter could have had little effect on him. In fact, Proudhon directly attacked the thought of Feuerbach as wholly inadequate.[27] In any event, the evidence does not warrant the conclusion that Grün taught him much about Hegel.

24. Karl Grün, *Die sociale Bewegung in Frankreich und Belgien* (Darmstadt, 1845), 404; quoted in C.-A. Sainte-Beuve, *P.-J. Proudhon, sa vie et sa correspondance, 1838–1848* (Paris, 1872), 209–11. Sainte-Beuve's correction of Taillandier's mistake was ignored by a number of later writers.

25. *Carnets*, IV, 162.

26. Letter to Marx, May 17, 1846, *Corresp.*, II, 201.

27. E.g., *Oeuv.*, I, vol. i, 388–98. In 1864 Proudhon read two of Feuerbach's major works then just published in French translation, *L'Essence du Christianisme*

Mikhail Bakunin is also supposed to have played some part in Proudhon's Hegelian education. The two men first met at about the same time that the latter made the acquaintance of Marx. The Russian tried to enlighten his French friend by preaching Hegel to him, as he had earlier with the Moscow intelligentsia. His understanding of Hegel seems to have been shallow, but he was a magnificent speaker with an overwhelmingly engaging personality. Whether a missionary for Hegelianism or anarchism, whether philosophically sound or dubious, this remarkable Russian was a powerful and influential figure wherever he wandered. Alexander Herzen's memoirs give the following anecdote about incidents which took place several years later.

> Until then I had seen very little of Proudhon; I had met him twice at the lodgings of Bakunin, with whom he was very intimate. Bakunin was living at that time with Adolf Reihel in an extremely modest lodging at the other side of the Seine in the Rue de Bourgogne. Proudhon often went there to listen to Reihel's Beethoven and Bakunin's Hegel: the philosophical discussions lasted longer than the symphonies. They reminded me of the famous all-night arguments of Bakunin with Khomyakov at Chaadayev's and at Madame Yelagin's, also over Hegel. In 1847 Karl Vogt, who also lived in the Rue de Bourgogne, and often visited Reihel and Bakunin, was bored one evening with listening to the endless discussions on phenomenology, and went home to bed. Next morning he went round for Reihel, for they were to go to the Jardin des Plantes together; he was surprised to hear conversation in Bakunin's study at that early hour. He opened the door—Proudhon and Bakunin were sitting in the same places before the burnt-out embers in the fireplace, finishing in a brief summing-up the argument begun overnight.[28]

While the night-long discussions between Marx and Proudhon may have been similar to this one, it is hard to imagine that they were as convivial or intimate.

Actually, neither Proudhon's German friends nor Bakunin intro-

---

and *La Religion*. His marginal notes in these volumes are reproduced in Pierre Haubtmann, *P.-J. Proudhon, genèse d'un antithéiste* (Paris and Tours, 1969), 247–58.

28. Alexander Herzen, *My Past and Thoughts*, trans. Constance Garnett, revised by Humphrey Higgens (London, 1968), II, 812.

duced him to Hegel. In *Qu'est-ce que la propriété?* (1840) he attempted to employ the Hegelian dialectic technique at one point; in his correspondence he mentioned Hegel as early as 1840 and discussed him at length in 1842.[29] During the following years his conception of Hegel and a pseudo-Hegelian dialectic played an important role in his thought and writing. While he could not read the German's works, a number of commentaries on and critiques of them had appeared in French,[30] and Proudhon derived an elementary and apparently faulty conception of Hegelian philosophy from these—a conception which was not much improved by Marx or Bakunin.

Proudhon's "dialectic" derives more from the ideas of Charles Fourier and Immanuel Kant (he did read Kant in translation) and from his own mind than it does from Hegel, the books about him, or the conversations with Marx, Bakunin, and Grün. Marx was fair in saying that Proudhon had only the language, not the dialectic of Hegel. The truth of the matter would appear to be that Proudhon built his "dialectic" philosophy while affected by a number of influences, with Hegelianism a very minor one.[31] Having for the most part fixed his concepts, he was made further aware of the ideas of Hegel by Marx and others. These ideas were too alien to him and he was too resistant to any persuasion or conversion for him to be much affected by the preaching of Hegelianism. However, he believed he discovered a close relation between his thought and Hegel's; no doubt this pleased him and encouraged him in his Hegelian pretensions. At the time he and Marx were having their discussions, he wrote:

> I cannot yet judge the kinship between my metaphysics and the logic of Hegel, since I have never read Hegel; but I am persuaded

29. *Oeuv.*, IV, 324–25; *Corresp.*, I, 248; II, 47. A letter to Tissot in *Corresp.*, II, 230–32, dated December 13, 1839, and discussing Hegel, is cited by several writers to indicate a still earlier acquaintance. This date clearly is an error: it should be 1846, as the contents of the letter show.

30. For these sources, see Armand Cuvillier's introduction to *Oeuv.*, V, 19–20, and Cuvillier's "Marx et Proudhon," 165–66.

31. While developing his dialectic method, Proudhon stated that he had constructed this system at a time when he had scarcely *heard* of Hegel (*Oeuv.*, V, 212). Although the evidence does not permit accepting this disclaimer at its face value, Proudhon's method must have been devised when he *knew* virtually nothing of Hegel.

that it is his logic that I am going to employ in my next work; now, this logic is only a particular case or, if you wish, the simplest case of my own.[32]

The whole controversy over Hegelian influence on Proudhon is a fine example of scholars brewing a tempest in a teapot. Proudhon's view of society is one of dynamic balance and interaction between opposing interests and groups. His conception includes ideas, ill developed but important to him, of historical movement through a mechanism of interactions. Thus his philosophy can be called dialectical and analogous to those of Marx and Hegel.

Nevertheless, his dialectic, described below, is markedly different from that of either German. For Marx and Hegel, "dialectic" is the logic of reality and the mode of relation between the terms of their ontological and phenomenological systems. Proudhon tries to develop a comparable system, but ultimately he has just a vision of society as a dynamic entity, without a systematic conception of an inner logic of reality and social interaction. The profound difference between Proudhon and the two German philosophers should be obvious from an intelligent reading of the three men, but the superficial similarities can be misleading.

When Marx left Paris after just a few months' acquaintance with Proudhon, he had not yet turned against the anarchist. Shortly before his departure he had written high praise of the Frenchman in a section of *Die Heilige Familie*, published in March, 1845. For the time being Marx regarded Proudhon as the best of French socialists.

Both men dreamed of an international association of socialists. The subject appears often in Proudhon's *carnets*, especially from 1845 to 1847. Despite his light regard for the leaders of French socialism and his polemics against them, he was quite serious about wanting to unite them and apparently had few misgivings about doctrinal differences interfering.

It is possible that the two men talked in Paris about an international association or about a renewed attempt to establish a Franco-German socialist review. In May, 1846, Marx wrote to Proudhon from Brussels explaining that he had often meant to write before and apologizing for not doing so. He invited his participation

32. Letter to Bergmann, January 19, 1845, *Corresp.*, II, 176.

in a sort of international committee of correspondence organized by himself with Engels and Philippe Gigot. The proposal envisioned extensive communication and cooperation between German, French, and English socialists.[33]

The project was a reasonable one, amicably presented. However, the letter had a postscript, probably composed by Marx,[34] which violently denounced Proudhon's friend Grün as "a swindler, a kind of charlatan who would like to deal in modern ideas" and plainly attempted to provoke enmity toward him. This addition could not have encouraged acquiescence by Proudhon.

His reply was polite in tone, but reserved in substance. He agreed that the proposed correspondence would be useful and that he would participate, but he said that he lacked the time to contribute much or often. He then went on to express "reservations" that amounted to severe criticism of Marx.

> First, while my ideas regarding organization and realization are at the moment completely fixed, at least with respect to principles, I believe that it is my duty, and the duty of every socialist, to maintain a critical or doubting stance for some time yet. In short, like the public I profess an almost absolute anti-dogmatism in economics.
>
> Let us search together, if you wish, for the laws of society, the mode of their realization, and the steps we may follow to discover them. But, for God's sake! after having demolished all a priori dogmatism, we must not dream of indoctrinating the people in our turn. Let us not fall into the contradiction of your compatriot Martin Luther who, having overturned Catholic theology, at once set about founding a Protestant theology, with much recourse to excommunications and anathemas. For three centuries Germany has concerned itself only with destroying Luther's botch; let us not by making a new mess carve out a new task for the human race. I applaud with all my heart your idea of bringing all opinions to light; let us have a good and honest polemic. Let us give the world an example of wise and foresighted tolerance and not, be-

33. Marx's letter and Proudhon's reply are reproduced in an appendix to *Oeuv.*, VII, 432–37. The letter signed by Marx is written in another hand, possibly Gigot's. It was probably copied from Marx's original because his writing was difficult to read.

34. This postscript was signed by Gigot and has been taken to be his composition but is more likely to be Marx's. For a discussion see the editor's introduction to Marx's *La Misère de la philosophie* (Paris, 1950), xxiin.

cause we are at the head of a movement, make ourselves the leaders of a new intolerance, not pose as apostles of a new religion, be it the religion of logic, the religion of reason. Let us accept, encourage all protestations; let us stigmatize all exclusions, all mysticism; let us never consider a question exhausted, and when we have used our final argument let us begin again if necessary, with eloquence and irony. On this condition I shall join your association with pleasure, otherwise, no!

. . . Perhaps you still hold the opinion that no reform is possible at present without a *coup de main*, without what once was called a revolution, and is plainly just a shock. I understand and excuse this opinion, which I would willingly discuss, having long shared it myself, but I confess that my most recent studies have caused me to give it up completely. I believe that we do not need that to succeed, and consequently we ought not to suggest *revolutionary* action as the means of social reform, because this supposed means would be quite simply an appeal to force, to arbitrariness, in short, a contradiction. . . . I prefer to have Property burn little by little, rather than give it new strength by making of proprietors another Saint Bartholomew's Day massacre.

. . . That, my dear philosopher, is where I am, for the moment; should I be mistaken and receive a caning from you I shall submit to it with good grace, while awaiting my revenge. I should tell you in passing that such seems to me to be the feelings of the French working class also. Our proletarians are so thirsty for knowledge that we would be ill received by them if we gave them only blood to drink. In short, it would in my opinion be a bad policy to speak in terms of extermination; sufficiently rigorous means will come— the people do not need any exhortation for that.

The letter goes on to "regret" divisions in German socialism, of which the attack on Grün is taken as proof, and to defend Grün and urge Marx to reconcile himself to him.

Proudhon did not remain as certain as he indicates here about revolution and reform, but his position on the issue is never close to Marx's. This and his condemnation of dogmatism would have angered the German and made plain to him that the division between the two men could never be bridged; the anarchist would have to be an ideological foe with whom there could be no cooperation and all. Although Proudhon sent Marx a copy of his *Philosophie de la misère* when it was published the following fall, as far as is known there was no communication between the two men after that.[35]

Karl Grün had for some time been preaching Proudhon's ideas in socialist circles. Engels saw that he had achieved success in this effort among German workers in Paris, of whom there were a large number. Already opposed to Grün's advocacy of Feuerbach, Marx must not have liked to see him adding to the influence of a possible rival in socialist politics. Marx waged a vendetta against Grün, of which the bitter postscript to his letter to Proudhon is just one example. Daniel Halévy has suggested that this postscript attack on Grün was deliberately calculated to divide Proudhon from him in order to stop Grün's advocacy of Proudhonism.[36]

Sending the *Philosophie de la misère* to Marx for criticism was not the most felicitous way for Proudhon to propagate his ideas. Even if Marx had not been personally antagonistic already, he would still have found the book's contents far from his own ideas. As Proudhon himself later admitted, this work had many faults, despite its sometimes eloquent rhetoric and occasional penetrating insights. Marx could only have had contempt for its weak points, as well as for those that diverged from his own views.

He determined to make the book the object of general derision; though he did not immediately succeed in this, eventually Proudhon came to be known best in the terms of Marx's judgment made in his *La Misère de la philosophie*, also known as *Anti-Proudhon*. Marx feared that Proudhon's book would mislead the masses, or, to put it less generously, he feared that Proudhon might gain the ascendancy that he himself wanted in any socialist movement. However one rates the question of possible personal jealousy, clearly Marx sincerely thought it necessary to block the propagation of what he believed to be grave error. Since Proudhon's writing style was impressively powerful and he was already a celebrity, the danger he represented was especially serious.

In December Marx wrote a lengthy letter criticizing the *Philosophie de la misère* to Pavel Annenkov, a Russian exile and liberal who

35. Apparently Proudhon wrote Marx a long letter shortly before the book's issue, announcing its forthcoming publication and asking for his criticism, but the letter seems not to have been preserved (Marx, "Uber P.-J. Proudhon . . . ," 27).

36. Daniel Halévy, "Proudhon d'après ses carnets inédits," *Hier et demain*, no. 9, (1944), 40–42.

was well acquainted with Bakunin, Herzen, and many others on the left. This judgment is severe enough,[37] but the book he worked on during that winter was to be his public statement and would cut much more deeply. Temperate and reserved criticism was never one of Marx's practices, but this polemic is especially thorough and vitriolic. He spared little in attempting to destroy Proudhon's reputation.

La Misère de la philosophie was published in Paris and Brussels in the summer of 1847, its title a clever parody of Proudhon's. In his *avant-propos* Marx adroitly damns Proudhon at the outset.

> M. Proudhon has the misfortune of being singularly misjudged in Europe. In France, he has the right to be a poor economist because he passes as a good German philosopher. In Germany, he has the right to be a poor philosopher because he passes as one of the strongest French economists. We, in our capacity as both German and economist, wanted to protest against this double error.[38]

Marx tries to demonstrate here that Proudhon is wholly incapable of abstract thought, that he understands neither Hegel's philosophy nor Ricardo's economics, that his idealism is hopelessly out of touch with reality, that his economic concepts are quite fallacious, that his individualism and his ideas of reform and revolution are gravely dangerous misconceptions, and that he does not comprehend the historical process. The criticism is often justified—or at least Marx develops his divergent ideas more compellingly than the anarchist had in many respects, especially in economic and historical theory. The book is a skillful though cruel polemic, a declaration that Proudhon's thought is far worse than useless.

This assault is so brutal that it may well have served to arouse more sympathy for Proudhon than rejection of his ideas. Very few copies were sold. Marx's initial attempt to form an international socialist organization was not at first successful, but when one was established, anarchists (many of them followers of Proudhon) came close to dominating it—just the turn of events that *La Misère*

37. Karl Marx, "Lettre à Annenkof sur Proudhon," *Mouvement socialiste,* XXXIII (1923), 141–54. In German translation in Marx and Engels, *Werke,* IV, 547–57.
38. Marx, *La Misère de la philosophie,* 25.

de la philosophie was intended to preclude. Only when Marx's later work and political activity gained him ascendancy did this book help to bring about the virtual eclipse of Proudhon's influence.

In the years after 1847 Proudhon's name appears repeatedly, but in hostile reference, in the works and correspondence of Marx and Engels. The judgment of Proudhon made by Marx just after the former's death [39] was moderated only by being less vitriolic, even though it was a kind of funeral tribute intended for publication. Marx was a man who nurtured hate for opponents, and his hostility to Proudhon seems to have been all the hotter because of the formidable character of the opposition. Writing about the London Conference of the International Workingmen's Association in September, 1865, a Proudhonist delegate there, E. E. Fribourg, said that Marx had told him then "how he had sworn a profound hate for P. J. Proudhon for his anticommunist opinions; how in response to a chapter of this philosopher: *La Philosophie de la Misère*, he had victoriously responded with his book Das Capital [*sic*], chapters of the Poverties of philosophy." [40]

Proudhon remained singularly silent in the face of the attacks, despite his usual readiness to join in polemical controversy. His marginal notes in his copy of *La Misère de la philosophie* have been preserved.[41] They reject some of Marx's statements and accept others or comment that he, Proudhon, had really said the same thing. These are the only specific replies to the criticism that the anarchist is known to have written. There is just one comment on the attack in his published correspondence: "I received at the same time the libel of one doctor Marx, the Poverties of philosophy, in response to the Philosophy of poverty. It is a tissue of scurrilous

39. The letter to von Schweitzer quoted above, p. 89.
40. E. E. Fribourg, *L'Association international des travailleurs* (Paris, 1871), 46. The oddities of expression in this passage are in the original French. *Das Kapital* had not yet been published at the time of this alleged incident.
41. These notes are printed with the corresponding portions of Marx's text in *Oeuv.*, I, vol. ii, 415–23. They are inserted integrally in Marx's text in *La Misère de la philosophie* (Paris, 1950), and the Pléiade edition of the same, Karl Marx, *Oeuvres* (Paris, 1965), I, 1–136. In his *De l'Aliénation à la jouissance* (Paris, 1957), 312–23, Pierre Naville gives close, incisive consideration to these marginalia and to Marx's critique. Naville's comparison of Marx and Proudhon on pp. 291–355 of this book is in some respects unique and excellent, though I think he sometimes views the anarchist too narrowly.

remarks, calumnies, falsifications, and plagiarism." ("One doctor Marx" seems a contemptuous way to refer to someone so well known to him.)

In 1851 he did write with distaste of Marx, Ruge, and Grün as the presumed leaders of German socialism, calling their manifestoes empty and hare-brained. His *carnets* contain a few minor comments. After having read Marx's attack he interjected in his *carnet* that Marx is the "tapeworm of socialism." Shortly afterward he included Marx in a list of critics of his *Philosophie de la misère*. Near the end of 1847 he mentioned Marx in an outburst against Jews, apparently inspired by suspected intrigues against himself and Grün by German Jewish emigrés. In 1848, in a list of proposed articles for his newspaper, *Le Peuple*, Proudhon included "Dr. Marx," [42] but no such item was published.

There are several possible explanations for Proudhon's surprising silence. The best is that he lacked the time to compose a thorough counterattack, for the next months and years were the busiest of his life. Still, one may ask why a reply was not sufficiently urgent for him to take the time from other activities. Possibly he recognized sufficient validity in Marx's criticism for him to be less eager to respond to insults, for Proudhon later admitted the weakness of his *Philosophie de la misère*. He may also have been reluctant to join in a brawl. Finally, it could have occurred to him that a published rejoinder to Marx would only give attention to an obscure book by an obscure author. After all, the *Philosophie de la misère* was translated into German almost immediately, Marx's *La Misère de la philosophie* not until nearly four decades later.

The question of influence of Marx and Proudhon on each other, like many such questions, cannot be answered with precision. Both had formed their dialectical concepts before coming into contact with one another, and there is no reason to believe that any further development of the dialectic of either man resulted from their relationship. The late, distinguished sociologist, Georges Gurvitch, wrote lengthy and provocative comparisons of their ideas, especially their dialectics; his analysis suggests that the "new wave" of socialist humanism may find in Proudhon's work a fruitful com-

---

42. Letter to Guillamin, September 19, 1847, *Corresp.*, II, 267–68; Letter to Edmund, August 28, 1851, *Corresp.*, IV, 92–93; *Carnets*, V, 109; VI, 110, 178, 316.

plement to the Hegelian and early Marxist writings to which so much attention is now being given.[43] But, although there is some affinity between Proudhon's dialectic and that of the young Marx, this is significant only when drawn out of the original context. The use each made of his dialectic renders any affinity unimportant by comparison with the differences, as far as the two men themselves and their followers were concerned.

Aside from the subject of dialectic philosophy, evidence indicating influence of one on the other is too meager for confident conclusions. It is necessary to evaluate influence in the light of each man's whole philosophy. Some have suggested that Marx's concept of economic materialism affected the French anarchist; in support they cite a letter written by the latter at the time he was seeing the German,[44] as well as some other, scattered instances of similar nature.

Here Proudhon places unusual stress on the fundamental importance of determining facts about actual material conditions and avoiding reliance on moral norms as sole standards of judgment. However, this is only a variation in emphasis from his regular position. He consistently emphasizes the essential importance of objective conditions for any judgments about social relations and action. But "objective conditions" must be understood just because they are the context in which moral principle is actually to be realized. For him, principle is incomplete without social science, but really is prior to it.

This puts Proudhon in opposition to two other common approaches. On the one hand he is insisting that moral norms can

43. Georges Gurvitch, "Proudhon et Marx," in *L'Actualité de Proudhon*, ed. Centre National d'Etudes des Problèmes de Sociologie et d'Economie Européennes (Brussels, 1967), 89–97, and in *Cahiers internationaux de sociologie*, XL (1966), 7–16; *Dialectique et sociologie* (Paris, 1962), 73–156; *Pour le centenaire de la mort de Pierre-Joseph Proudhon*, mimeographed Cours Public de la Sorbonne, 1963–64 (Paris: Centre de Documentation Universitaire [1964]), 8 et passim; *Proudhon* (Paris, 1965), 15–70; *Les Fondateurs français de la sociologie contemporaine: II. Proudhon*, mimeographed Cours Public de la Sorbonne, 1952–53 (Paris: C. D. U. [1955]), 30–48; *L'Idée du droit social* (Paris, 1929), 327–406. A far-reaching and incisive comparison of the two men's ideas is developed by Pierre Ansart in his excellent *Sociologie de Proudhon* (Paris, 1967), esp. Ch. 6, "Théorie et pratique révolutionnaire"; and in his *Marx et l'anarchisme* (Paris, 1969), 1–17, 141–325, 359–539. The latter Ansart book is a comparison of Marx with Proudhon and Saint-Simon only.

44. See p. 86.

neither be defined in abstraction from actual conditions nor be made effective merely by acts of will. Their meaning and the ways of making them effective have to be discovered in the real nature of society. Here he is contradicting what he later will attack as the "absolutism" of reason and of State and Church.

On the other hand, he opposes those who through expediency, fatalism, or high regard for tradition and stability would let objective conditions themselves be the primary determinants of the social order. For him, if existing conditions conflict with ideals, then of course the former must be changed, by deliberate action. In this he contradicts not only conservatives and pragmatic politicians, but also most of those who have attempted to develop a social science.

It is here that his perspective is very different from that of Marx. The latter also is a moralist with ideals he wants realized through revolutionary social change. Nevertheless, his ideals are not explicitly made primary criteria. They function through shaping the way he perceives things, but his systematic social science is supposed to be entirely objective in its basis. Only material conditions and the social relations they engender can determine the way men act. Whatever place moral values may deserve, they can have no decisive role in understanding social change or contributing to its process.

Such an approach was too alien to Proudhon's for him to have comprehended it, much less to have been significantly influenced by it. Neither could he recognize that objective relationships might have the profound effects on human thought and action that Marx believed them to have.

Marx's materialism and determinism could never have been meaningful for him. While the former drew conclusions from them similar at a number of points to Proudhon's, the Frenchman was unable to regard the relevant problems in anything like the other's philosophical framework. Even if he had fully understood Marx's dialectic (which he probably did not), he would have rejected the other's view of history as something foreign to his whole way of thinking. He could have had some sympathy for Marx's views on alienation resulting from labor; in fact, he did consider the problem—but in a different way. He could not think about it in anything like the terms of Marx. Likewise, he attacked capitalism as vigorously as did the German, but in doing so their patterns of thought were very different, although they sometimes ended by making much the same conclusions.

While Proudhon, like Marx, sought revolutionary change, he was skeptical about the process of revolution itself. Not only did he see no historical necessity for it ever to occur; he was afraid that violent revolution would not substantially advance the cause of justice, whatever new socio-political order it established. Thinking of the revolutionary events in France of 1789–99 and 1830, and later those of 1848, he believed that revolution would become perverted into a travesty of its intended form. Successful revolution, if possible at all, could result only from the evolutionary transformation of the moral character and philosophy of all men. Though he sometimes hoped sudden revolts could contribute positively though partially to such a transformation, the Marxist dialectic of revolution could be no more acceptable to him than his evolutionary approach and moralism could be to Marx.

As was usual for him when he read, Proudhon did not study German metaphysics in order to understand it on its own terms; he saw there only what he thought he could fit to his own essentially different preconceptions. In consequence, he had no real comprehension of German philosophy. He was capable of understanding neither Marx's ideas nor the German metaphysics which gave them birth.

With regard to Proudhon's supposed influence on Marx, it is known from Marx's writing and correspondence before 1846 that he had read and admired the French anarchist until then. It is reasonable to presume that the latter had a limited and indefinable effect on the formation of his basic outlook; so undoubtedly did a number of other writers, none of whom could be called Marx's preceptor. The claim that he owed key concepts to Proudhon cannot be accepted. Most of the more obvious similarities between their views are superficial; comparison of texts indicating such similarities takes their ideas out of context, ignoring important differences. While the two men shared some elements of belief, these elements fitted into their mature systems very differently. Many of these shared elements were part of the common intellectual currency of contemporary socialism. Where the anarchist's ideas were unique, they were generally odious to Marx.

Marx liked Proudhon's *Qu'est-ce que la propriété?* and praised it even in the otherwise condemnatory letter written just after the anarchist's death. The book has been credited with making Marx's thought more radical; since he praised it so highly, the work could have been more important here than other contemporary writing, much of which also contributed to the maturing of the young German's ideas. That is all that can be said for Proudhon's influence on Marx. To suggest that he derived or stole ideas from Proudhon gives unwarranted importance to the latter. Ideas like those in question do not spring to life uniquely and independently in the mind of one man, even a Marx or a Proudhon; they arise repeatedly in variant forms among different men who breathe in the same intellectual atmosphere.

After their break the German rejected Proudhon as a mere petit bourgeois publicist. As we have suggested, actually he was not bourgeois in background or sympathies. However, in the other's point of view the considerations we emphasized were not recognized as relevant. Proudhon's attitudes, especially his extreme individualism, were regarded by the German as essentially bourgeois in character. For purposes of polemic, Marx may have made his former acquaintance more of a devil than even his standards required, but he could not have seen in the French anarchist a congenial ally under any circumstances. His antipathy was a necessary consequence of their divergent outlooks and needed no personal contact to precipitate it.

The personal relationship of the two men was a transitory one. Marx was attracted to Proudhon by the latter's early writings, at a time when his own ideas were not yet fully developed and the glamour of the celebrated Proudhon could appeal to him. His ideas at the time may have had a certain affinity with the anarchist's, but any such connection would soon be far outweighed by other concepts of the evolving Marxist system. Proudhon was interested in German philosophy and so was drawn to the emigré briefly. When they became well acquainted with each other, they must have discovered that their personalities were far too different for friendship to grow and their ideas too different for an intellectual or political alliance. The Frenchman probably could have remained on amicable terms had not the other attacked him, but close associates they could never be.

There was no real common ground between the two men and little basis for either to influence the other substantially. In the final analysis, it must be recognized that the abyss between Proudhon and Marx was too broad for there to be much interaction across it.

Proudhon's two major books in these years, the *Système des contradictions économiques* and *De la Création de l'ordre dans l'humanité*, suffer by comparison with his later work, though some have thought his methodological efforts here important. I do not, but his attempts in these works are revealing. Not only do they show the process of his developing thought, but thereby they make more easily comprehensible the character of his mature philosophy. Because the latter is complex but not very well ordered, the insights to be gained here are welcome, and will be applied more fully in later chapters.

Were Proudhon more concerned with the study of society for the sake of the science itself, his system and method might be technically stronger, but he does not have the appropriate interests or frame of mind to be a rigorous scientist. He seeks a social science just so that man might gain the mastery over himself that he has been gaining over nature. This should be *self*-mastery, with social harmony and justice built upon individual liberty. Science would not seek to be the instrument for control of social interaction, with a basis in the mastery of man over man.

Proudhon's understanding of what constitutes "science" is not very clear. In his time scientific method had been well developed in practice, but no one had yet analyzed the essentials of the method as fully as was needed for further innovative work. Like most of those in the intellectual tradition stemming from the French Enlightenment, Proudhon is very much impressed with natural science's powers of discovery. He is especially drawn to the taxonomical accomplishments of biology, which do *not* rely on controlled experiment and mathematical analysis, as do developments in the physical sciences. He consciously tries to do the same kind of thing for social science.

The elements of this taxonomy are to be discovered through the observation of social structure in historical development: "the experience of the past is the science of the future." [45] These elements cannot be comprehended independently, but only when put together in a synthesis. To make the synthesis Proudhon tries at this time to adapt the "serial method" of Fourier, using it in combination with his own version of dialectic philosophy. While both methods claim an empirical basis in the study of historical process, in fact he concentrates more on contemporary society, with his interpretation of the past based more on that of the present than the other way around.

Though he does not truly derive his philosophy from the study of history, his conception of humanity's growth through time is vital to his theory of society.[46] The conception is one of man *making himself* through the course of history in a succession of stages. The stress on mankind's active role in the process is essential; Proudhon rejects both fatalism and any idea that history is made by exceptional men or by God.

His efforts at developing a systematic method turn upon determination of the mechanism by which these historical stages succeed each other. This would simultaneously define the essential character of social dynamics in any particular stage. In *Création de l'ordre* he takes notions of an ordered series of connected developments from Fourier, together with an idea of "antinomy" (contradiction) which comes from his reading of Kant, but differs from the German's conception. By these he describes a process of historical movement through the interaction of contradictory opposites. This method he further refines in the *Système des contradictions économiques*, with a pseudo-Hegelian dialectic employed to complete the theory.

Proudhon's method is not an effective one. Many of his thoughts about contradiction in society are astute, but he is not able to integrate them into a complete system. His knowledge both of

45. *Oeuv.*, V, 357.
46. See Ch. 10 for a fuller discussion of this.

science's methodological requirements and of empirical data is too limited. Marx's dialectical and historical materialism is similar in approach though not in execution, but he knows better what a systematic social science should be. Although it has its own faults, the German's theory is far more compelling—as a system.

While this system and method of Proudhon are weak, he eventually becomes enough aware of their shortcomings not to persist in their use, although their echoes appear from time to time. However, elements of the thought that goes into this effort at system-building do remain important for him. He says that men must go through the experience of successive historical stages in order to realize how better to order their lives. They must know through actual experience all the varieties of injustice and contradictory absurdities possible in social relations if they are to understand fully what really is required for justice. Any particular social structure entails its own peculiar forms of injustice and absurd contradiction, and it does not develop substantially different ones without becoming qualitatively different: a new set of conditions defines a new stage. Thus historical change is a succession of significant stages to be passed if progress is to be realized.

This reflects Proudhon's conviction that society is a dynamic, constantly changing entity. The change as he conceives it is not merely that of gradual evolution, or growth like an organism's, where each new form is very like the one preceding and stems directly from it. Rather, a society changes by becoming quite another thing than it was—a dialectic of historical stages. This is one reason he rejects not only conservatism and conventional progressivism, but also the utopias of contemporary socialists. Their utopias are conceived as final, ideal forms, to remain fixed in basic structure if not in detail. To Proudhon this is no less static than the absolutism of monarchs and Church, and scarcely less likely to prevent continuing human self-actualization.

His view of man making himself throughout history is significant because it adds dimension to his individualism. The ideal of freedom to strive and grow can be conceived in terms of merely private desires, or in the typical terms of liberal humanism, that mankind develops through the achievements of free individuals. Proudhon's vision builds upon the latter, seeing the growth still more as a collective, social process, the joint product of the efforts of all individuals rather than a select number.

> [Proudhon was reaffirming the old notion] that "man makes himself," that out of the common efforts of mankind, out of the struggles and collaborations among men, largely without design, intent, or self-consciousness, come the institutions, beliefs, and all that goes to make up civilization, purely human creations which humanity adds to what nature and/or God has made.[47]

He speaks of society as a "living being" whose existence is manifested by "the concert and intimate solidarity of its members." [48] Society has its own identity distinct from that of individuals, because it is what they can be only collectively. Yet its being is not beyond that of individuals, not something with its own demands and capacity to make them what they are, as it is in the social metaphors of conservative organicism. Moreover, society's vitality can be assured only if individuals are free, for only then can there be realization of their natures and hence of society's.

> Social science is the reasoned and systematic understanding, not of what *has been* in society, nor of what *will be*, but of what it IS in its whole life, that is, its totality of successive manifestations, for it is only thus that there can be reason and system. Social science must embrace the order of humanity, not only in such or such period of its duration, nor in some of its elements, but in all its principles and in the integrality of its urgent needs. . . . Such must be the science of all living and progressive reality; such incontestably is social science.[49]

47. Aaron Noland, "History and Humanity: The Proudhonian Vision," in *The Uses of History*, ed. Hayden V. White (Detroit, 1968), 69ff. As Noland indicates, Proudhon's conception is strongly reminiscent of Vico's. In particular, the Frenchman's preoccupation with philology in his early writings reminds us of Vico's thought. Proudhon read and admired him (letter to Michelet, April 11, 1851, *Corresp.*, IV, 365), but I cannot tell if he had read Vico when writing of philology himself. Michelet's translation of Vico's *New Science* was published in 1827, but in his published work Proudhon did not mention Vico until the *premier mémoire* (*Oeuv.*, IV, 333).

48. *Oeuv.*, I, vol. i, 123. He also uses the phrases "homme collectif" and "personne collectif," and he emphasizes the reality of "la personnalité de l'homme collectif" throughout his work.

49. Ibid., 73.

Society is not only a vital being, it is "the essential environment for the unfolding and realization of purely human, individual goals."[50] Knowing this environment means understanding the intricate web of social relationships and the forces of the collectivities and individuals constituting society. Proudhon is very conscious of how diverse are its elements and how varied the relations between them. A scientific approach typically (though not necessarily) would attempt to reduce connections between elements to rather mechanical terms, the stuff of precise analysis, as would the practical political leader. Proudhon cannot admit such a mechanical treatment. For him, social relationships have all the vitality of society and the men who make it. But the essential qualities of living things are not usually precise or regular. They defy attempts at mechanical analysis which seek to identify and exactly describe the regular. By reducing men to their universal terms, science tends to eliminate the idiosyncratic qualities that give beings their vitality.

Proudhon does not fully recognize how much his preoccupation with the vital being of society and its elements may interfere with his efforts in scientific analysis. With his notion of "serial order" he seeks to integrate distinct elements into a coherent synthesis, discovering a "unity in the multiplicity" of individuals and relations which is the order of society. This "synthesis" is quite artificial, claiming that it integrates without really doing so. Given his views of the separate elements, it could hardly be otherwise. His artificial construct serves principally to underline his conviction that individual and social concerns have a natural unity. Yet his pursuit of a method makes clear how definitely he believes that the bases of social order are to be discovered in what man makes of himself, rather than conceived in abstraction and imposed through authority. Re-creation of that order into better forms can be knowing and intelligent, but it must be spontaneous and self-directed by the whole being of society.

Although Proudhon's conception of science is deficient, he has strong convictions about what is wrong with the social science of others. In his time *the* social science was political economy (economics), and liberal economic thought was dominant, with virtu-

50. Aaron Noland, "Proudhon: Socialist as Social Scientist," *American Journal of Economics and Sociology,* XXVI (July, 1967), 319.

ally unquestioned authority. It was in effect a single "school," with variations in detail to be sure, but adopting uniform fundamental assumptions and analytic theses.

Both in order to challenge orthodox liberal economics, and because of his belief that economic relationships are central to the order of society, in this period he concentrates his writing on what he thinks to be the chief issues of political economy. He criticizes other socialists for lack of attention to economic questions and attacks liberal economists for lacking concern about "social problems"—those of justice in society.

He condemns political economy for the unfeeling quality of its analyses, its reduction of vital human activities and needs to laws and quantities. Even if a conventional economist expresses concern for the misery of the many, he does not let it interfere with his calculation, but merely anticipates the possibility of eventual improvement through deliberate, astute, and industrious application of economic knowledge. Factors in the calculation may be manipulated, but not changed altogether. Proudhon opposes the very "objectivity" political economy seeks, not only because he thinks it immoral, but also because he believes it to preclude achievement of adequate knowledge: it omits too many of the qualities of a "living" society.

Moreover, Proudhon attacks orthodox economists for failure to recognize the extent and gravity of conflict in economic relationships, and socialists for not realizing how difficult conflict is to eliminate. Believing that it can neither be eliminated or ignored, he writes that "the life of man is a tissue of contradictions." Man himself is a tissue of contradictions, his essential qualities an ensemble of opposites, good and bad.[51]

Economic liberals think conflict through commercial competition is healthy, without seeing many of the pernicious consequences. Those that are seen they accept fatalistically, or they hope for their elimination through evolutionary progress. They do not admit that there are evils that can be eradicated only through the total reorganization of society. Socialists seek the latter, but they are so

---

51. *Oeuv.*, I, vol. ii, 87; vol. i, 370–71. He repeatedly pursues this theme with great eloquence.

blinded through inadequate understanding of the dynamics of society that they think conflict can be altogether eliminated.

Proudhon, on the other hand, thinks that inevitable differences in ideas and interests of individuals and groups make conflict natural and unavoidable. What men need is balance between opposing forces, a dynamic equilibrium—flexible and changing but always remaining at or near balance. This requires that the opposed forces be equal in strength, with differences settled by means other than contests of power. Proudhon's ideal is individualistic but not egoistic, because it insists upon the fundamental necessity of universal equality.

The injustices inherent in the present social structure are, he thinks, bound up in systematic contradictions between different features of the economy. Based upon free competition, it encourages the growth of monopoly. With production growth requiring increased consumption, the system accentuates impoverishment. There are moral contradictions: between wealth and the misery it is built upon, between the employer's increasing power and the intensified subordination of the worker, between a landlord's idleness and the hard labor of his tenant. For Proudhon the list can be multiplied almost endlessly.

He feels that these contradictions are essential to the character of the existing economy. But they are not the elements of a stable economic system, for they are constituted by conditions of antagonistic and unequal strife. Those who suffer in these conditions must struggle whenever there is opportunity to reverse the imbalances which afflict them. The resulting contests of strength have to be destructive and morally corrupting; they prevent achievement of a stable order.

Such contradictions cannot be resolved except through destruction or complete transformation of the opposed terms: the oppositions are inherent in existing conditions, which cannot be significantly altered without becoming qualitatively different. A lasting reconciliation or mean between the opposites cannot be achieved. Yet the constant renewal and change wrought by the transformation of contradictions makes possible the movement vital to society. Thus the "system of economic contradictions" is unjust but essential for progress toward future justice.

Certainly in its outlines Proudhon's theory resembles the dialectic of Marx, but the anarchist has only a vision of dialectic conflict and movement without precise ideas of the system's logic and mechanism. It does not matter; for the anarchist's own philosophy, his vision is enough.

He thinks of his work as investigations in economic science, but his interests and ideas fall more naturally in the area we call sociology. (The word "sociology" had been introduced some years earlier by Comte, but it did not then have wide currency.) Proudhon's sociology is far from that of Comte or the positivism to which he helped give birth. Still, the anarchist seeks knowledge of a kind which can only be called sociological. The scope of sociology should be broad enough to include him.[52]

Proudhon's difficulty in developing a social science reflects a conception of the endeavor which has often misled others. He thinks of science as the discovery of conclusive truths, like those believed to have been precisely and finally defined by a Newton. This attitude involves an expectation that social science can have an instrumental power comparable to that which natural science has found through application in technology. (Proudhon never has any illusions, however, about how difficult it can be to get people to accept and apply social science discoveries, even though many eagerly welcome innovation introduced by natural science.)

While this faith in the potential of science has been common enough, it is not justified by what the study of society has actually accomplished or is ever likely to achieve. For Proudhon such expectations are especially doubtful, and not just because of the technical weaknesses in his own method. He is not able to conceive clearly the relationship between his ideals, conclusions drawn from social studies, and the objects of study themselves. Neither does he recognize the importance for science of clarifying this relationship.

His difficulty is not just the familiar one of letting values detract from objectivity, nor that of refusing to admit the validity of con-

52. In addition to the contributions of Ansart, Noland, and Gurvitch already cited in this chapter, see C. Bouglé, *La Sociologie de Proudhon* (Paris, 1911). Bouglé's claiming Proudhon for the ranks of sociologists aroused heated opposition, but the claim appears to be beyond dispute now, notwithstanding the anarchist's failings as a scientist.

clusions which conflict with principles to which he is absolutely committed. He *is* absolutely committed to principles like universal equality, but their definitions and practical implications are supposed to depend on actual social conditions. As society changes, so too must any understanding of the real meaning of ideals. In this sense we might say that his idealism is empirical in its elaboration, but its roots do not lie in experience alone. He does comment, in a marginal note in his copy of Marx's *Misère de la philosophie*, that he has never claimed "that *principles* are anything but the *intellectual representation*, not the *generating cause*, of facts." [53] Proudhon does not, however, consistently keep to the notion here suggested, that objective evidence is prior to ideas of principle.

Although his ideals are conceived in terms of experience, they are supposed to be compelling because of their moral excellence, and not just because they are "scientific" representations of fact, which indeed they are not. At the same time the elaborations of his ideals are inseparable from propositions intended as scientific and objective. Thus his notions of virtue ultimately are his decisive criteria, and these notions have no real objective foundation. He *intends* it to be thus: the positivist dream of value-free objectivity has no meaning for him. He is distinguished from others who would discover a science of society by his conscious placement of priority in issues of virtue, and from conventional normative philosophers by his refusal to consider norms as anything but continually changing statements of right derived from knowledge of actual social relationships.

Proudhon's moralism is realized in his sociology, yet he does not comply with some of the most hallowed canons of the sociological craft today. He cannot understand the requirements of sound scientific method, and his approach is too much colored by his values.

But are these canons sufficient, sophisticated though they may be? Even though Proudhon's sociology is seriously deficient in many ways, I think his approach is more realistic in important respects, as well as more attractive ethically.

In the first place, no social science is unaffected by the personal values and prejudices of the scientist. The degree of detachment achieved in physical science is impossible in the study of society.

53. *Oeuv.*, I, vol. ii, 418.

One's beliefs about man and society are better recognized and proclaimed openly than submerged in a pretense of neutrality. If beliefs are made explicit, some species of truth is more nearly attained, even though the dream of absolute objectivity is surrendered. A century after Proudhon's death such observations are hardly unusual—but, unfortunately, they lack general acceptance.

More important, however, is the issue of *systematic* interpretation of society. By its definition—*ordered* knowledge—"science" aims for systematic, total understanding. There is no question that Proudhon makes valid conclusions about *some* features of society: a critic can only say he does not know how even to begin development of a complete system.

Yet man and society are far too complex and too irregularly variable for systematic study and interpretation to achieve anything remotely approaching complete or fully integrated knowledge. Scientific investigations can achieve important though partial understanding, with many of the positive virtues of system and objectivity. Nevertheless, the undeniable strengths of a science blind us to its very great limitations.

Not only does any systematic body of social science lay claim to greater explanatory power and knowledge than the complexity of man permits, but also the system tends to exclude or derogate alternative and supplementary avenues to understanding. As Proudhon said in one of his last books, nothing is so inflexible as a system. Even a scientific proposition quite limited in scope is by its nature exclusive, for in saying one thing quite definitely it implicitly denies alternatives. If truth were so unique, men would not find such power in the creative vision of novelists, playwrights, poets, painters.

Proudhon was a rationalist, not an imaginative artist, and in some intellectual ways he was more detached from life's actuality than the least sensitive of artists. Yet he lived all his life among ordinary people, and he knew and felt what they felt. He knew the violence and crudity of their passions as well as the misery, frustration, and degradation in social conditions that helped engender and perpetuate these passions. His interest in the "philosophie de la misère" was neither philanthropic nor academic.

Outrage over injustice can be a healthy emotion. If a reasoning man is moved by outrage, then he is less likely to be beguiled by the intellectually satisfying products of a rational process which robs the real of its reality by abstracting from it only a select part of the whole. When Proudhon expresses himself, it comes as much from the gut as from the cerebrum. This may be bad "science," but his sociology gains its real power thereby. After 1847 he continues to develop his sociology, but with little of the artificial efforts in systematic methodology of these "intermediate years." Such efforts are not compatible with his perspective, and his philosophy benefits from his having turned away from them.

In their different ways Proudhon and Marx both call into question the usual assumptions concerning the real nature of scientific knowledge. Whether determined empirically or purely through reflection, "truth" has been assumed to have a conclusive definition that makes it superior to the vagaries of particular phenomena. The very purpose of science is to abstract the matter of thought from the chaotic flux of existence into a realm of being where order and regularity are discerned and chaos becomes intelligible through generalization and the definition of laws. Knowledge thus determined becomes the basis by which intelligent men conduct their lives, and the means by which the race can fundamentally alter the conditions of existence.

Despite wide variations in the epistemological theory underlying them, conceptions of science have involved a quite definite dichotomy between concrete existence and the abstractions which are the principal material of knowledge. Marx tries to eliminate this division, insisting that our ideas can have no definition or truth independent of particular phenomena, that the existential world is always in a process of fundamental change, and that knowledge itself is thus necessarily inconclusive, requiring alteration with the flux of phenomena. Moreover, phenomena cannot be taken in isolation from each other; they must be considered a concrete unity, understood through integration into a totality of related elements—both the elements and the whole the products of a definite historical process. Dialectical materialism is the means by which concrete phenomena are so conceived.

The novelty of Marx's approach may be obscure, especially in view of his vigorous assertion of a systematic analysis of society, a "science" soon transformed into usually rigid dogma by his epigones. Nevertheless, it is the approach to knowledge—dialectical materialism—on which he insists, rather than the particular theses thereby developed; this method is supposed to keep our thought firmly within concrete existence. On this Georg Lukács has written:

> Let us assume for the sake of argument that recent research had disproved once and for all every one of Marx's individual theses. Even if this were to be proved, every serious "orthodox" Marxist would still be able to accept all such modern findings without reservation and hence dismiss all of Marx's theses *in toto*—without having to renounce his orthodoxy for a single moment. Orthodox Marxism, therefore, does not imply the uncritical acceptance of the results of Marx's investigations. It is not the "belief" in this or that thesis, nor the exegesis of a "sacred" book. On the contrary, orthodoxy refers exclusively to *method*.[54]

In his quest for a method of social science and in his assumption of transcendent, determinant moral principles Proudhon is adopting the conventional approach to knowledge that Marx attempts to replace. Nevertheless, the former's failure to develop a method reflects a perception of reality akin to that of his German antagonist: he cannot accept the sort of abstraction from existence involved in the generalizations and laws of social science.

Anarchism insists on the uniqueness of each individual and of each relationship between individuals and groups; this insistence is the basis of anarchist rejection of normative prescriptions and of government through law. It can also be seen as expressing an urge to remain "within concrete existence"—the phrase used in reference to Marx. Despite his appeal to transcendent principles, Proudhon thus moves toward rejection of any "knowledge" distinct from particular phenomena. Though his thoughts here are relatively inchoate, later he will give them more definite form when he repudiates what he calls "absolutism," in his *De la Justice dans la révolution et dans l'Eglise*.

In 1845 Marx wrote that we must understand reality as "sensuous

---

54. Georg Lukács, "What Is Orthodox Marxism?" (1919), in his *History and Class Consciousness*, trans. Rodney Livingstone (London, 1971), 1. Lukács's essay develops more fully much of what I try to suggest here about Marx.

human activity" in which we are necessarily involved; abstract contemplation and objective detachment are neither possible nor desirable. "The philosophers have only *interpreted* the world, the point is to *change* it."[55]

More than a call to revolution, this much-quoted dictum encapsulates an urgent sense of the immediacy of the human condition and the need to keep social thought in intimate contact with that condition. Marx translates this sensibility into dialectical materialism; Proudhon conveys it through his attacks on illusions that pass for social science and jurisprudence, and through the eloquence of his outrage at what man suffers without effective demurral by conventional thought.

There is an important point to be drawn from this comparison of the two men, though I shall here only sketch it briefly. While neither repudiates altogether what "science" was thought to be, they both make significant departures. In this they anticipate a reaction against established modes of reasoning that becomes increasingly apparent from the end of the nineteenth century onward. Most often spoken of as a revolt against positivism, or even a revolt against reason, the reaction is more general and rather different in its import than these phrases suggest.

In the arts and philosophy we find highly negative responses to what I have here called a dichotomy between concrete existence and the abstractions of conventional knowledge. This may be regarded as a rejection of science itself, but we also find something comparable in the natural and social sciences, for there generalizations and laws come to be regarded less as conclusive truths than as convenient ways of expressing observed relationships. The relationships include the observer as well as the objects observed, and these expressions can change with the observer's own standpoint as well as with the discovery of additional phenomena.

Thus, as knowledge more often is thought to be relative to the situation of the knowing subject, and all generalizations to be tentative and subject to change, human existence and knowledge become less distinct from one another. "Knowledge" itself may come

55. Karl Marx, "Theses on Feuerbach," in Karl Marx and Friedrich Engels, *The German Ideology*, trans. S. Ryanzanskaya (Moscow, 1964; London, 1965), 645–47.

to extend beyond what once were thought to be its limits, those constituted by ordered reason.

Proudhon's philosophy enjoyed a renaissance among French intellectuals early in this century; there is reason to suppose that this revival was a consequence of dissatisfaction with the conventional uses of reason, and especially with the forms of practice these uses prescribed. Though this supposition is uncertain, the revival of Marx's humanism has more clearly occurred in conjunction with comparable dissatisfaction. Hence it is possible to say that the future impact of both men will depend in large measure on the further development of this "dissatisfaction," for their anticipation of it can remove their theories from the dustbin of the archaic.

five: Proudhon in the Revolution of 1848

I am like the salamander, I live in fire. Abandoned, betrayed, proscribed, execrated by everyone, I resist everyone. . . .
The people, who look upon me henceforth as their sole representative, come to me en masse. They swear only by me or against me.

I dream of a society where I shall be guillotined as a conservative.[1]

THE FRENCH REVOLUTION of 1848 drew Proudhon into a new life. Not only did he become important in the revolutionary politics of the Second Republic, but his ideas, old and new, won the attention of a much larger audience. Far too radical to exercise substantial power in the republican government, he nevertheless acquired during the Republic's brief history the public stature which was to give him a lasting place of prominence in the history of the French Left.

The *mémoires* on property had gained him notoriety, but the attention paid him was largely transitory. Although the *mémoires*

1. Letter to Maguet, August 16, 1848, *Corresp.*, II, 344; Proudhon quoted by C.-A. Sainte-Beuve in his *P.-J. Proudhon, sa vie et sa correspondance, 1838–1848* (Paris, 1872), 342. Published literature on Proudhon's role in the Revolution is very extensive. Recent studies of particular value are Edouard Dolléans and J.-L. Puech, *Proudhon et la révolution de 1848* (Paris, 1948); Edouard Dolléans, *Proudhon* (Paris, 1948); and Daniel Halévy, *Le Mariage de Proudhon* (Paris, 1955).

remained important for those interested in socialism, Proudhon was known mainly for his slogan, "Property is theft."

Relatively few noticed his new books. Prominent socialists like Pierre Leroux, Victor Considérant, and Louis Blanc had little to do with him. Those who still paid some attention to him, such as Lorenz von Stein, Karl Grün, Karl Marx, and Mikhail Bakunin, were a minority of outsiders. Proudhon's *Création de l'ordre* was a disaster. Virtually no one read it.

His *Système des contradictions économiques* did not achieve the distinction he had hoped for it. Its methodology may not have deserved acclaim, but its critique of contemporary ideas of political economy and socialism was most powerful; it should have held great interest for the men of ideas it attacked. Apparently it did not. Daniel Halévy has searched through the journals and newspapers of the time and found only silence with regard to the book, except for one article in Emile de Girardin's popular newspaper, *La Presse*.[2] (Girardin, a moderate republican, was usually sympathetic to Proudhon, although frequently in disagreement with him.) The *Création de l'ordre* had been abstract and abstruse and had not earned readers; Proudhon deliberately made the *Système des contradictions économiques* concrete and very much to the point of contemporary intellectual controversy. It won him new adherents, young unknowns like Georges Duchêne, Alfred Darimon, and Amédée-Jérôme Langlois, who were his close associates thereafter —and it helped to win him the opposition of another young unknown, Karl Marx. But Proudhon had hoped and expected that the book would gain him the ear and respect of the more distinguished French men of letters. He was deeply disappointed and disgusted with a France which cared little for ideas as radical as his.

His situation changed very rapidly during the Revolution. He wrote new books and reprinted his old ones; they sold quickly and were widely read. He served in the National Assembly; there he became the focus of the scorn and fear of the bourgeoisie and conservatives alarmed by the popular "extremism" expressed in the bloody insurrection of June, 1848. He directed a very radical newspaper which sometimes attained a daily sale of forty to fifty thousand copies, quite large for the time. On days when the paper

2. Halévy, *Le Mariage de Proudhon*, 22ff.

printed lead articles by Proudhon, circulation doubled and newspaper vendors commanded premium prices for copies.[3] He initiated
and directed an unsound but popular project for "the solution of
the social problem" through the organization of banking and exchange without charge of interest or profit. He so chivvied the
government that finally he was imprisoned. And, when nearly
forty-one years old, after decades as a confirmed bachelor, he
married.

The constitutional monarchy of King Louis-Philippe crumbled
in January and February, 1848, in a general and intense wave of
contempt for its fumbling inefficacy and corruption. Proudhon, in
Paris, remained apart from the meetings of protest which were leading to revolution. Contemptuous of the regime himself, he did not
believe the French were yet prepared to constitute anything substantially better. He kept to his studies; a project for a popular
newspaper prepared with his collaboration hung fire for want of
money required by the state, to be held as a security bond guaran-
teeing the paper's "good behavior."

On February 23 and 24, insurrection broke out and barricades
were erected in the streets of Paris. Louis-Philippe abdicated, and
the Second Republic of France was proclaimed. Proudhon wrote:
"I did my part of the work, although I had disapproved at first.
. . . But when I saw the battle joined, I didn't want to abandon
friends; I was at the barricade to carry stones, and I set the type
for the first republican proclamation issued by *La Reforme* [a republican newspaper]. Once victory was won, I returned home and
go out no more."[4] In the midst of tumult he wandered about,
watching the struggle on the streets and the devastation of the
Palais des Tuileries, but he did not rejoice in the collapse of the
regime he despised.

He sympathized with the popular revolutionary sentiment and
admired the workers who made the revolution in the streets. With
the urge to revolt he had no quarrel—but the revolution had to go
somewhere to be worthwhile, and that depended on its leaders, the
politicians and writers who had been giving voice to the opposition.

3. An editorial notice in the paper published just after his most sensational
articles recognized and condemned premium prices charged by vendors during
the past three or four days (*Le Peuple*, no. 72 [January 29, 1849], 1).
4. Letter to Huguenet, March 15, 1848, *Corresp.*, II, 291.

Among them virtually none inspired any hope or admiration in Proudhon. "The worker is worth more than his leaders," he wrote the day after the revolutionary climax.

> The Republic is placed under the tutelage of *honnêtes gens* and blowhards of the greatest strength but with a rare lack of ability. The twenty-fourth of February was made without an idea; it is a question of giving direction to the movement, and already I see it lose itself in the emptiness of words.
>
> There are no ideas at all in their heads; people are uneasy, but henceforth the mess is inextricable.
>
> It is a mob of lawyers and writers, each more ignorant than the others, who are going to contend for power. I have nothing to do in that. . . .[5]

Certainly the leaders in the Revolution had ideas, but they were without exception ideas which Proudhon had examined and found wanting.[6] None desired the kind of revolution he sought; none knew the changes society really needed; none were responsive to the actual desires of the people. Writing in his *carnet* on February 25 of the frenetic activity of those forming a new republican regime, Proudhon commented,

> All that is a sham; revolution fabricated from memories. The French nation is a nation of comedians.
>
> "25 resolute men have put a whole army to flight."—(Démocratie pacifique [Victor Considérant's newspaper]).
>
> The humbuggery begins.
>
> It's the sound of liberty for all peoples?! [7]

Disgusted with the trend of events and having no standing with the new leaders, Proudhon withdrew to his study for a time, writing acid comments on the situation in letters, his *carnet*, and a man-

---

5. Letter to Maurice, February 25, 1848, *Corresp.*, II, 282, 280; *Carnets*, February 24, 1848, VI, 225. *Honnêtes gens* ("men of good will") is a phrase from the 1789 Revolution, and has a strongly derogatory connotation.

6. Letters to the electors of the *département* of Doubs (April 3, 1848) and the economist Michel Chevalier (April 14, 1848) are contemporary summary statements of his rejection of ideas of liberal economists and socialists. He is particularly anxious to dissociate himself from Louis Blanc, whose proposals for the organization of labor were then the most important socialist program (*Corresp.*, II, 299–304, 321–25).

7. *Carnets*, VI, 229.

uscript on the "solution of the social problem." While thus engaged
he was visited by a group of printers—they were armed, in good
revolutionary fashion—who sought his collaboration and leadership
in a revolutionary newspaper, *Le Répresentant du peuple*. He received them and their project warmly and urged upon them his
scheme for solving the social problem; they were much impressed.

One, Joseph Mairet, later recalled the scene: "Wearing sabots,
settled at his work table, occupied like Archimedes during the seige
of Syracuse in searching for a fulcrum with which to lift up the
old world. . . ." [8] It is fitting that Proudhon, disregarded by leaders both liberal and socialist, should have been called to action,
sabots and all, by a formation of armed printers—the kind of company he was more at home with than either bourgeois republicans
or the proletarians of the new industrial enterprises.

The intellectual printer soon reentered the arena, becoming increasingly active and vocal. He acted partly in hope of making
something for the people of the opportunity, partly from an excess
of enthusiasm inspired by the high-flying popular hopes for a better
world. As an irrepressible gadfly attacking sharply in all directions,
he became the *homme terrible* of the Revolution and the *bête noire*
of the "men of good will" who were its principal leaders.

Proudhon's intense engagement in revolutionary politics followed
several paths simultaneously. Though these activities were involved
with one another, they are reviewed here separately for the sake of
clarity: his radical schemes for supplanting the existing financial
and monetary systems, his role in the republican Assembly, and his
popular journalism. In addition to their immediate impact on French
politics, these activities (especially the journalism) mark major steps
in the development of the anarchist's thought.

At the end of March, 1848, Proudhon completed his *De la Solution du problème social*,[9] the first of a flood of pamphlets, articles,
and speeches he produced in rapid succession during the course of
a year. By mid-1849 his imprisonment and the government's sup-

8. Quoted in Halévy, *Le Mariage de Proudhon*, 117.
9. (Paris, 1848); in *Oeuv.* (*Lacroix*), VI. This title includes three distinct
pieces: "Solution du problème social," "La Démocratie," and "L'Organisation du
crédit et de la circulation." The last one also appeared separately (Paris, 1848,
1849). Much of the space here, especially in the first of the three, is used to
develop a most remarkable attack on democracy.

pression of radical political activity had led him to change his pace, with longer works supplanting the articles. Like his later efforts in the republican period, this book developed a far-ranging and probing critique of the revolution and its leading figures, his attack cutting deeply into the substance of attitudes and ideas then current.

Simultaneously he introduced in this piece his own remedy for the "social problem." Proudhon employed this expression to refer to the material impoverishment and other evils suffered by the masses; these ills he thought resulted mainly from privilege and inequality in social organization, with political forms scarcely relevant. Thus he used the term "social problem" to distinguish these evils from matters of electoral suffrage and the constitution of government. Proudhon thought the "social problem" to be the fundamental one, rather than political questions; he regarded as a delusion the usual republican assumption that reconstitution of the political system was itself both the necessary and the sufficient condition for solution of all significant problems of society.

While his overall conception of the social problem and its solution was always much broader than the scheme here offered, Proudhon at this time thought he had discovered a panacea—or at least a major restorative elixir—in a unique plan for gratuitous credit and exchange. Although he had nurtured the idea at least since 1845 (when he wrote of it in his *carnet*),[10] and expressed high hopes for it, he broached the subject publicly only in 1848. Apparently he felt that it then had a chance of success for the first time. His scheme was an original one, differing substantially from superficially similar plans, like the "labor notes" idea of Robert Owen and the British cooperative movement, which have sought to remedy social ills by reform of commercial exchange.[11]

Proudhon's conception of his plan varied—or at least his explanations of it did—so that there are many inconsistencies and obscure

10. *Carnets*, I, 74ff.

11. An excellent, concise explanation of Proudhon's plan, with a critique and comparison to analogous schemes, is given by Charles Gide and Charles Rist, *A History of Economic Doctrines*, trans. R. Richards, 2nd English ed. (London, 1948), 314–26. More extensive treatment may be found in W. Oualid, "Proudhon banquier," *Proudhon et notre temps*, ed. Amis de Proudhon (Paris, 1920); and Marc Aucuy, *Les Systèmes socialistes d'échange* (Paris, 1908), Ch. 2. Proudhon's mutual-credit ideas have also been the subject of at least five doctoral dissertations: see the bibliography under Labrusse, Langelutke, Mattfeldt, Schumacher, and Stakitch.

points. However, his basic intent is clear: to combine producers in a program of mutual financial cooperation so that they can operate in commerce without paying interest to owners of capital, who he believes make no contribution to production. A special bank would provide credit and loans without charge, enabling the independent producer to enjoy the whole product of his labor, without part of it being drained away by the idle capitalist. The bank would issue "exchange notes" which could circulate as money. The notes would represent commodities already produced and delivered or promised for delivery by adherents of the bank. These notes would come to be circulated universally and exchanged like cash in commercial transactions. Thus both circulating and fixed capital could be obtained gratuitously. (There would actually be a small charge by the bank, in the form of a discount on the notes issued, to cover administrative costs.)

It is assumed here that "goods exchange for goods," as in the formula of J.-B. Say, doing so equitably and freely if only the evil effects of unearned income and the unnecessary intermediary, gold, are eliminated. The prices of goods would be determined wholly by the cost of production, which itself is determined solely by the amount of labor involved. Under the plan a worker can labor on what he wills, easily obtaining his equipment through free loans; he can exchange the products of his labor freely and simply for the products he consumes. The whole of his labor is equitably converted into goods for consumption by himself and his family.

The scheme is supposed to eliminate completely all economic inequality and thereby eliminate social inequality and injustice. The struggle between men, between the weak and the strong, would end. Since the purpose of government is to regulate this struggle, the need for government would end, and government could disappear.

Unfortunately, the whole scheme rests on a misunderstanding of the actual functioning of exchange, banking, and capital. In conventional economic practice, currency in the form of bank or government treasury notes depends for its real value on public confidence in the solvency of the issuing institution. If the note is a claim to goods belonging to a bank's clients, then confidence in the solvency and good faith of the clientele is required. Even with the best of intentions on the part of all involved, neither the client's solvency nor the ready marketability of the commodities claimed can be guaranteed. The confidence needed for their exchange notes is neither merited nor likely to be attained. In any event their circulation would be limited mainly to the bank's customers, and even they could easily be driven to defection from the free-exchange system by depreciation of circulating notes resulting from insolvency of the clientele.

Banks do issue bills of exchange, which are widely used in commerce. But the discounts they charge are not merely interest levies, as Proudhon believes. People ordinarily find immediate possession of cash more desirable than obligations for future payment, especially when the promised payment is to be in goods whose future value or marketability is uncertain. Thus the discount amounts to charging a premium for something of immediate tangible value, which is taken as preferable to a promise for the future.

Proudhon might reply to such criticisms by saying that, if people kept their promises faithfully and values were set only by quantities of labor expended in production, it should be possible to eliminate interest and discount while maintaining confidence in the value of instruments of exchange. However, if ever achieved, this situation would require and result from moral reform; creating his exchange banks would not be sufficient to produce the needed changes in popular morality.

Furthermore, like many schemes for achieving more fluid circulation, Proudhon's plan has little thought for the problems of accomplishing increases of social wealth (in the form of permanent goods—like machinery and homes) comparable in scale to the multiplication of circulation instruments. His scheme is better addressed to the exchange of consumption goods than to questions of the savings needed for the accumulation of capital, which makes possible extension of the productive base and economic growth. Both conventional economic theory and experience suggest that his exchange system would result in inflation of interest rates and prices, because of the scarcity of capital relative to notes in circulation.

The mutual-banking idea is not altogether without virtue. The public which places its confidence and savings in a bank is its true guarantor, with the capital provided by stockholders of private banks only a secondary factor.[12] Thus the mutual or cooperative credit society is a practical banking institution which can provide the public with lower credit rates, higher interest on savings, or both; such mutual banks were strange to France in 1848, although of course they are thriving in many places now.

In brief, Proudhon's ideas on exchange and gratuitous credit are largely mistaken. His scheme could not serve as a panacea or the chief instrument for initiating the solution of the social problem. If it were to be practicable, it would only be as a result of or in conjunction with other major social changes which would have to be introduced by different means. The concentration on mutual credit and exchange by Proudhon and many under his influence was a largely fruitless diversion.

Still, the plan is instructive in what it reveals about the mind of its author. While others in 1848 sought to improve society by re-constituting the political system (as had the Montagnards of an earlier French revolution), or by instituting programs of collective action, either on a national scale (the workshops of Louis Blanc) or in special communities (the Fourierism of Victor Considérant), Proudhon tried to erect his utopia on a foundation of individuals acting independently but with collaboration for reciprocal benefit. For him individual freedom was the first essential of economic as well as political liberty. They were inextricably bound together.

Economic liberty enjoyed and practiced unequally had wrought limitless injustice. Only when economic liberty was combined with economic equality could there be a free and equal society in which political changes could attain fruition. Only then did revolution become real, did the slogan, "Liberté, égalité, fraternité!" become anything but words.

Though Proudhon had high hopes for his scheme, he was not monomaniacal about it. Nevertheless, if the free-credit plan were not implemented successfully, he could see no immediate opportunity for the 1848 Revolution to become more than a vast delusion. The exchange bank offered the one hope of an *easy* solution; there were no others. While he varied his ideas on how best to

12. The preceding criticisms of Proudhon's financial ideas are based on those made by Gide and Rist, *History of Economic Doctrines,* 314–26.

form a system of gratuitous credit and exchange, he believed some such system to be necessary for economic equality and, hence, for true revolutionary accomplishment. The failure of his People's Bank increased his skepticism about the nation's prospects. France seemed ready only for small changes that altered very little and did not begin to match the promises of the Revolution and its leaders.

The exchange-bank plan appears hopelessly naïve in retrospect, but in 1848 and 1849 it aroused great interest and enthusiasm. In May, 1848, a host of leading figures in republican and socialist circles met to organize a "Banque d'Echange," with Proudhon as president. Included were the editors of sixteen newspapers, well-known economists, Assembly deputies, businessmen, ordinary workers, and most of the prominent socialists.[13] This project never got past the organizational stage, but a similar bank, the Banque du Peuple, went into operation under Proudhon's direction at the end of January, 1849. In April, when it appeared that Proudhon would soon be in prison for his published attacks on President Bonaparte, the bank was closed and liquidated, with Proudhon assuming personal responsibility for bank deficits. Ostensibly the bank was closed because he could not direct it from prison and because the forces of reaction had made its operation too difficult. Plainly it had not been a success—except, perhaps, in a moral or political sense. It claimed 13,267 adherents, quite a respectable number, but had collected only 17,933 francs in receipts. It had incurred 8,147 francs, 85 centimes expenses, and the costs mounted fifty francs each day.[14] Proudhon could at least be consoled by knowing that, after the liquidation, sympathizers contributed to help defray the deficit.

Much more important than the People's Bank was Proudhon's work as a radical journalist, which had a powerful impact on his Parisian readers and served as a major step in the evolution of his ideas. On April 1, 1848, *Le Représentant du peuple* commenced publication, with Proudhon named editor shortly afterward. This

13. Lists of those involved are in *Le Représentant du peuple*, May 18 and June 6, 1848.

14. *Le Peuple*, no. 144 (April 12, 1849), nos. 147–49 (April 15–17, 1849), no. 140 (April 8, 1849). No. 123 (March 22, 1849) claims 10,307 adherents, most of them workers, and gives an elaborate table of the numbers of adherents in the different trades and professions. The largest group is the tailors, with 1,291 adherents.

was the first of four journals with which he was associated, each with "people" in its name and each in turn suppressed.[15]

One of his first articles was titled "Qu'est-ce que la propriété?" From the beginning he used the journal as an instrument of combat, lashing out at his opponents. He contributed major articles every two or three days to the paper and its successors,[16] and *Le Représentant du peuple* carried Proudhonian slogans at the head of page one:

> What is the producer? Nothing! —What must he be? Everything!
>
> What is the capitalist? Everything! —What must he be? Nothing!

Newspapers played a major role in the period of the 1848 Revolution. Many of the leading political figures had their own organs and from these tribunes were able to exert unusual influence. Some stepped from pre-revolutionary journalism to important roles in the republican government. Socialists, however, were unable to exert much influence *in* the government, especially after the insurrection of June, 1848. They wielded what political strength they

15. Specimen numbers were printed on February 27 and 28. (A specimen number for a weekly paper, called *Le Peuple,* had been published by Proudhon and friends early in 1847.) Last issue, August 21, 1848. Proudhon, true to his ideas about representative democracy, objected to the name of the paper, preferring simply *Le Peuple.*

16. His articles are collected in *Oeuv.* (*Lacroix*), VI and XVII–XIX. The collection includes nearly all the articles signed by Proudhon and a few unsigned ones. Deleted are several articles and parts of articles which are harshly critical of Louis-Napoleon, for the Lacroix edition was published during the Second Empire. The deleted articles have been reprinted in *Oeuv.,* VII; several other volumes of the Rivière edition reprint some of the more important articles besides these. Twenty-six of Proudhon's 1848 articles were reprinted as his *Idées révolutionnaires,* introduced by Alfred Darimon (Paris, 1849). Deleted articles are so indicated in the *Oeuv.* (*Lacroix*) (by lines of dots), but some articles signed by Proudhon are omitted there, without indication or obvious reason, and have not been reprinted elsewhere: "La République et la coalition, troisième article: Organisation de la résistance," *Le Peuple,* no. 192 (May 30, 1849), 1; "De l'Influence du travail sur la moralisation de la famille," *Le Peuple,* no. 197 supplément (June 4 and 11, 1849), 5–6; and a letter to the editor, *La Voix du peuple,* no. 8 (October 8, 1849), 2. Presumably there was other material by Proudhon in the newspapers which he did not sign, but the editors of *Oeuv.* (*Lacroix*) worked with him on the papers and should have known of and included any significant unsigned articles by him.

had chiefly by means of their popular pamphlets and newspapers. Louis Blanc had *La Organisation du travail;* Victor Considérant, *La Démocratie pacifique;* Etienne Cabet, *Le Populaire;* Pierre Leroux and George Sand, *La Vraie république;* François-Vincent Raspail, *L'Ami du peuple;* Félicité de Lamennais, *Le Peuple constituant;* and there were many others, as a host of newspapers sprang up, seeking the ear of the people.

Proudhon was a poor orator and neither inclined nor able to be a political organizer. He would form or lead no political party; he would stir very few in street gatherings or the National Assembly —but as a political journalist he was brilliant. It was in this role that he made his mark in the history of the Revolution.

> . . . he was certainly a new kind of socialist, harder and shrewder than the others. He had denounced the sentimental rhetoric of the radicals, their senseless imitation of the first Jacobins. . . . Before June, 1848, while the workers could still hope that the promises made to them would be kept, they preferred to listen to Cabet or Louis Blanc; or, if they felt aggressive, they could learn from Blanqui that only a little courage would destroy the system that oppressed them. But Blanqui was now in prison and the clubs were quite discredited. In their present mood, bitter and disillusioned, the workers turned to Proudhon. He had attacked the leaders they no longer trusted, he made them no easy promises and he was obstinate in their defense. Proudhon was a man of the people, the only great socialist leader of the century who was one.
> . . . The French workers, after the June disaster, were in a mood to listen to home truths. Proudhon's roughness and cynicism suited them; and behind his manner they could sense the hatred of injustice, the contempt for power, the obstinate resolve never to be flattered or conciliated, the conviction that, however great the disaster, the fight must be renewed—all the emotions and beliefs (and there were others less good) that lay at the heart of the French working-class revolutionary movement.[17]

Except for Proudhon, Blanqui, and their allies, socialism and its leaders were thoroughly discredited in 1848, as was the Jacobinism born of the first French Revolution and cherished by many workers until 1848. Proudhon replaced Robespierre and Louis Blanc in

17. John Plamenatz, *The Revolutionary Movement in France, 1815–1871* (London, 1952), 79.

the hearts of discontented urban workers. He did not intend this, was uncomfortable about it, and did not take advantage of the opportunity his popularity offered to form a mass movement and become a demagogue or conspirator. Rather, he continued articulating his ideas and ideals as before; but now he did so to a larger and more attentive audience, among the hostile middle-class as well as a receptive working class.

Le Représentant du peuple suspended publication voluntarily on June 26 and 27, during the insurrection of the Parisian workers, and was suspended by the government from July 9 to August 10. On August 21 it was suppressed altogether. In October it was replaced by a new paper, *Le Peuple*, with much the same staff. Proudhon had not controlled the first paper, but he was editor-in-chief and director of *Le Peuple*, and it was entirely his organ.[18] He made it still more combative than its predecessor. In addition to the slogans of *Le Représentant du peuple*, the front-page head proclaimed:

Division of functions. Indivisibility of powers.
No more taxes.
No more usury.
No more poverty.
Work for all.
Family for all.
Property for all.

The newspaper's manifesto,[19] written by Proudhon, established *Le Peuple* in the most radical possible opposition to the middle-class Republic, short of open advocacy of insurrection. Proudhon consistently defended the *right* of the people to revolt, but he did not advocate immediate insurrection at any time. This was consistent with his conviction that the prospects of achieving a genuinely productive revolution were very poor. After June, 1848, advocacy of insurrection would have brought swift repression by

18. Specimen number dated "Septembre." Issued weekly until no. 6 (November 23, 1848); daily, including Sundays, thereafter, with supplements on Mondays. Final issue, no. 206, June 13, 1849. After the issue of December 10, 1848, *Le Peuple* gave Proudhon's name as editor-in-chief, but no longer as director also.
19. "Manifeste du *Peuple*," *Le Peuple*, numéro spécimen, September, 1848, 1–2. *Oeuv.*, VII, 392–98.

the government, but the evidence indicates that Proudhon was quite unrestrained by fear of prosecution.

Proudhon and his associates assumed the role of spokesmen of the people, whom the Revolution had viciously injured and betrayed. The betrayers had constituted the government, and virtually all its actions were opposed and attacked daily in the pages of *Le Peuple*.

Proudhon opposed the division of power—and thus of the sovereignty of the people—between a president and a legislative assembly, as provided in the Second Republic's constitution, which was drawn up in the fall of 1848.[20] When the presidency was instituted, he identified Louis-Napoleon Bonaparte as the most undesirable candidate and the one most likely to win election to the office. *Le Peuple*'s editorial policy was directed toward attempting to defeat Bonaparte, rather than supporting anyone else.[21]

After Bonaparte's election Proudhon published a series of bitter attacks upon him. Two of these articles resulted in the prosecution and conviction of Proudhon for "excitation of hate and scorn" against the government of the Republic, attacking the constitution, and attacking the rights and authority of the President. (*Le Peuple* was able to reprint these articles with impunity: they were read into the trial record by Proudhon's prosecutor, and *Le Peuple* simply reprinted these portions of the official record!) [22]

20. "La Constitution et la presidence," *Le Peuple*, no. 2 (October, 1848), 2. *Oeuv. (Lacroix)*, XVII, 151–56.

21. *Le Peuple* supported the revolutionary socialist Raspail's candidacy on the grounds that: (1) no one should be president, and abstention from the election was best in principle (initially Proudhon advocated abstention); (2) still, one should vote for *someone*, to reduce Bonaparte's chances; (3) Ledru-Rollin, the candidate of left republicans and many socialists, had no chance at all of victory; and (4) if you had to vote for a loser, Raspail was preferable to Ledru-Rollin. Proudhon's refusal to support Ledru-Rollin helped win him the enmity of many others on the left, as did other instances of his habit of seeing issues very differently than did his putative allies. His idiosyncratic positions resulted in a fist fight and a duel with Félix Pyat, in which no one was hurt; he refused a challenge to another duel, with Charles Delescluze. As Proudhon had expected, Bonaparte won easily and Ledru-Rollin received relatively few votes: Bonaparte, 74.25% (55% in Paris); Cavaignac, 19.5% (30%); Ledru-Rollin, 5% (9%); Raspail, 0.5% (5%).

22. "La Guerre," *Le Peuple*, no. 69 (January 26, 1849), 1–2; "Le Président de la république est responsable," *La Peuple*, no. 70 (January 27, 1849), 2. The former's first part is in *Oeuv. (Lacroix)*, XVII, 255–57. The portion deleted there is in *Oeuv.*, VII, 413–15. The entire second article is in *Oeuv.*, VII, 415–18. Most of "La Guerre" was written by someone other than Proudhon (possibly Alfred Darimon), but he assumed full responsibility for it (charges against Proudhon

Proudhon received a heavy fine and a three-year prison sentence. He fled to Belgium but returned to Paris almost immediately, feeling that exile would be more unbearable than prison.[23] After a week in hiding in Paris he was discovered and imprisoned in early June, 1849. He served the full three years. A week after his imprisonment an insurrectionary attempt, in which neither he nor his paper had any direct part, resulted in *Le Peuple*'s final suppression.

The conditions of confinement for political prisoners were not very restrictive. Proudhon was able to continue his writing and publication with few impediments, and to leave the prison on day-furlough frequently. (He even married and fathered a child while a prisoner.) A successor to *Le Peuple* commenced publication in October, 1849. Proudhon was a frequent contributor to the new paper, *La Voix du peuple*, but as a prisoner could not be an editor. He wrote that *"Le Peuple* was a journal of combat . . . *Le Voix du peuple* will be a journal of discussion."* [24] From the point of view of Proudhon and his friends, the forces of reaction had secured their controlling position so well that a "journal of combat" could no longer influence the course of events—and the state would not permit one to exist. However, the staff of the paper was too sharply hostile to Bonaparte to restrain itself for long, and *La Voix du peuple* became combative in its turn, with the result that it too was suppressed in May, 1850.

Proudhon himself was temporarily sequestered in a different prison, his privileges removed after he made violent attacks on Bonaparte in February, 1850.[25] After being acquitted of new charges and volunteering a promise to publish no more inflammatory articles, he was returned to his former situation of frequent access to family and friends.

La Voix du peuple was succeeded in June by yet another news-

---

reported in *Le Moniteur universel*, June 2, 1849, p. 1965). *Le Peuple*'s reproduction of these portions of the record are in no. 130 (March 29, 1849), 1–4.

23. Proudhon's objection to exile seems to have been due mainly to his reluctance to leave the center of events; however, he may also have been anxious to return to the woman he was to marry at the end of 1849.

24. *Le Voix du peuple*, no. 1 (October 1, 1849), 1. Specimen number, September 25, 1849. Publication daily, including Sundays, continued until no. 223, May 14, 1850.

25. "Au Président de la république.—le socialisme reconnaissant," "Vive l'empereur," nos. 124, 127 (February 2 and 5, 1850); *Oeuv.*, X, 347–58.

paper, *Le Peuple de 1850*,[26] to which Proudhon made a few contributions. After thirty-three infrequently published issues, this final journalistic enterprise went the way of its predecessors in October, 1850.

Most of Proudhon's writing for these four newspapers belongs in the category of topical political journalism. As such, its chief significance lies in its immediate influence on the newspaper's readers, which was discussed briefly above. However, many of his articles were more general statements of ideas relevant to current controversy. They assume the proportions of substantial expressions of Proudhon's social and political theory, although the concepts are developed more fully in later books. As a stage in the evolution of his theory, his career as a journalist is important, for it is the period in which his anarchist ideas reach the mature form analyzed in the next two chapters.

He was active in the politics of the republic in other ways also, despite his criticism of *political* revolution in general. Partly through infection with the enthusiasm of popular revolutionary spirit, partly in an attempt to salvage something from the debris, he was drawn into an active political role.

As a politician, Proudhon was included in the diverse group labeled socialists, although he was nearly as critical of many of his colleagues—like Louis Blanc and Victor Considérant—as he was of the center and right-wing factions. Daniel Halévy's definition of "socialist" in this context is very apt: "The word *socialist,* of recent usage [in 1848], then designated all those who put the social order, as distinguished from the political order, in the first rank of their preoccupations." [27] However, unlike most other socialists then, Proudhon was convinced that the political changes involved in the Revolution offered little promise for socialism.

Blanc and others expected that the Revolutionary government could and would effect social revolution through state action; they placed their hopes above all in "national workshops," state-sponsored enterprises intended to end unemployment and ultimately to supplant capitalist industrial production. The provisional government did institute such a program soon after the February Revo-

26. *Le Peuple de 1850*, nos. 1–33, June 15, 1850, to October 13, 1850.
27. Daniel Halévy, *Le Mariage de Proudhon* (Paris, 1955), 22.

lution, although its actual form was a perversion of the socialist plan as originated by Louis Blanc. The national workshops as developed were a fiasco; the government dissolved them on June 21, 1848, thereby precipitating the bloody insurrection of the "June Days."

The workshop debacle was popularly regarded as the decisive failure of "state socialism," although in fact Louis Blanc's ideas had not been give a fair trial. Proudhon's frequent declarations that political action could not effect real social change gained great weight from popular disillusionment with Blanc's approach and with the leadership of socialists who promised that revolutionary politics would win the people bread as well as votes. In addition, many of the socialist leaders were in prison or exile after the June Days; Proudhon was one of the few prominent socialist leaders at large in Paris. However, after the June Days there was little opportunity for any socialist to play a widely influential role in politics. Socialism appealed to few besides urban workers, who were a small minority of the French population. Only their potential as an overwhelming Parisian insurrectionary force gave the workers political power, power which they had frequently used—but after the June Days the government was very much willing and able to suppress any revolt they might attempt. Therefore socialists, as spokesmen only of a powerless minority, could not sway the course of politics; they became pariahs, except in the working-class quarters of a few cities.

It might be supposed that other poor people might have found socialist ideas attractive; in particular, one might expect that there would be large numbers of peasants and artisans with little or no property, to whom Proudhon would be most appealing. Individualism is, after all, dear to the hearts of the French. However, provincial Frenchmen were for the most part too suspicious of the Parisian metropolis, too suspicious of supposed threats by socialists to individual independence, and too suspicious of change to be attracted even to Proudhon's socialism.[28] Farmers, enjoying the bene-

28. However, in later years a major portion of the Proudhonian anarchists whose identities are known came not from the advanced industrial centers but from among the provincial clock- and watchmakers of Proudhon's native region: Besançon, the Jura, and the canton of Geneva. (See my comments in Chs. 2 and 13 on the appeal of anarchism to pre-industrial workers.)

fits of the very wide redistribution of land during the first French Revolution, remained basically a conservative force during the nineteenth century.

Although Proudhon was not a participant in the events leading up to the February Revolution or in those immediately afterwards, he soon was recognized as one of the leading socialists. Actually, the socialists were unable to enter very far into the corridors of power at any time, but before the June Days they were a force to be reckoned with. In the first months of the Revolution political conditions were unsettled nearly to the point of chaos, and socialists could hope to carry the Revolution much further than it ever went. The heady and tumultuous atmosphere of Paris in the first French Revolution was felt once more, and anything could be hoped for—until June. On May 15 a crowd burst into the chamber of the National Assembly, attempting to force the Revolution far to the left; such invasions of the Assembly had achieved their purpose before, but this one did not succeed. One invader attempted to proclaim a new socialist government: his list of members of the new government included Proudhon.[29]

Proudhon had unsuccessfully sought election to the National Assembly in April from the *département* of Doubs, whose center was his home town of Besançon. While he was not very popular in provincial Besançon, he easily won election to the Assembly from the *département* of the Seine (Paris) in the beginning of June. Louis-Napoleon Bonaparte was elected at the same time. One of Proudhon's first actions in the Assembly was to vote against seating him. Most of the votes for Proudhon were cast in working-class districts of Paris—a fact which stands in contrast to the claims of some Marxists, who have said he was representative only of the *petite bourgeoisie*.

After his conviction in 1849 for attacking President Bonaparte, he could no longer serve (nor did he wish to serve any longer) in an Assembly to which he was so opposed. However, associates induced him to run again anyway in 1849, and he was elected with

29. The others were Cabet, Blanc, Leroux, Raspail, Considérant, Barbès, and Blanqui (*Le Moniteur universel*, May 16, 1848, p. 1061). There were other lists, prepared in the event the *coup de main* succeeded, which include most of the same names, but not Proudhon's (Raymond Postgate, *Revolution from 1789 to 1906* [New York, 1962], 207, 209).

100,897 votes, 23,000 more than he had received in 1848. Since he had been proscribed, the election was not valid. Soon afterward he declined to run in another district. He refused again fifteen years later. Proudhon had had enough of parliamentary action.

Named in June, 1848, as a member of the Assembly's finance committee, Proudhon threw himself into parliamentary work with great energy. He was especially active in this committee, though a survey of the transcripts of Assembly debates published in *Le Moniteur universel,* the official gazette, shows that Proudhon rose to speak on the Assembly floor on very few occasions. As a poor orator facing a hostile audience there may not have been much point in his doing so. After the June Days he was very much alone in the Assembly, and he felt the futility of attempting oratory. Increasingly he lost taste for his role there and preferred the tribune he created with his pen. He was, however, usually present in the Assembly at voting roll-calls. Generally he seems to have been a conscientious but ineffectual representative of his electors, the Parisian workers.

As an elected deputy in the Assembly he was in an impossible position, almost tragically so. He opposed the idea of representative government and the political system of which election made him a part. Yet he felt compelled to work *within* the system he despised in order that there be someone to fight there on behalf of "the people." However, while the lack of influence of the urban working-class in the middle-class government was the reason Proudhon attempted to be a workers' spokesman in the Assembly, that lack of influence also meant that Proudhon was unable to be effectual there. He could not serve his people in the Assembly—and he could hardly serve them better outside it.

In the Assembly he became isolated from the people he sought to represent; later he bitterly condemned himself for this.[30] At first he spent all his waking hours hard at labor in the Assembly. He remained ignorant both of the intrigues within the government and of rising discontent and anger among the workers. The June Days caught him by surprise, out of touch with his people, and not comprehending the nature of the conflict, which at first he thought to be a display of political factionalism.

30. *Les Confessions d'un révolutionnaire, Oeuv.,* VII, 168–70.

The June Days were the "revolution of despair" [31] of the Parisian workers, angry that the February Revolution, which only they had made possible, had promised them everything and given them nothing but votes—which gained them no bread—and the unhappy trial of the national workshops, which had now been abolished. They marched chanting "Bread or lead," and fought desperately for four days against the army and the National Guard. A large proportion (perhaps 50,000) of the Parisian workers fought; for a time they held the eastern part of Paris. In the end they were crushed—some 1,460 lives were lost, and the rebels were cruelly treated by the victors. Political reaction followed and, while the Republic survived for a few years more, the Revolution of 1848 had ended.

Proudhon saw the street fighting but was not a part of it. He became ashamed of his blindness to the workers' needs and despair. In his *mea culpa* he wrote, "No, Monsieur Sénard [the Assembly president], I was not a coward in June, as you have said in insulting me in front of the Assembly; I was, like you and so many others, an imbecile." [32]

His experience in June gave Proudhon an additional (and for him very important) objection to representative government: the demands of parliamentary work on the time and energy of representatives of the people isolate them from their constituents and make them ignorant of their needs and desires. The representatives become part of a special society in the seat of government, aware of and concerned primarily with this political elite and its affairs, instead of with the larger society outside the corridors of power. Unresponsive to the people, the government becomes in effect an oligarchy, usurping the sovereignty of the people. Representative democracy can be neither representative nor democratic.

Although not involved in the street fighting, Proudhon was accused of complicity and was regarded as most deeply responsible for it. One of the few immediately available objects of antagonism of the "forces of reaction" after the June Days (other left-wing

31. The phrase is Priscilla Robertson's, in her *Revolutions of 1848* (Princeton, 1952).
32. *Oeuv.*, VII, 169.

leaders being in prison or exile), Proudhon was treated to endless invective and hostile calumny. He was the *bête noire* of the angry and frightened victors: the middle class of Paris, who feared the workers' mob, and the provincials, who feared Paris.

This was clearly evident when the Assembly heard Proudhon's most important speech there. On July 11, 1848, he had presented to the finance committee a proposal to impose a "tax" on all rents and interest, with one-sixth of their total returned to those paying them and another sixth taken by the State. The government would use its portion to finance free credit facilities and to reduce other taxes. The result would be increased production and consumption (by lowering producers' costs and prices and by leaving consumers with more to spend), with consequent ultimate benefit to proprietors on whom the new tax is imposed, as well as to others.

Though for Proudhon the proposal seems relatively modest, its implications were quite radical—and were denounced as such in a scathing attack by Adolphe Thiers, who reported on the proposition to the Assembly for the finance committee. The conservative statesman correctly perceived that Proudhon intended the ultimate abolition of rents and interest, and thereby to subvert and destroy the existing social structure. Thiers adroitly assaulted both this revolutionary purpose and the truly dubious financial calculations of Proudhon's plan.

The latter responded with a very long Assembly address which could have been eloquent at many points had it not been merely read from a prepared text, a practice not then usually well received.[33] The audience was bound to be hostile and unwilling to consider the proposition seriously, so Proudhon's position was an absurd one—a situation of which he probably was well aware. In speaking under these conditions his purpose seems to have been deliberate effrontery: to provoke responses that would make starkly

---

33. Proudhon's proposition, Thiers's report, the former's speech in response, and a record of the attendant uproar were printed in a number of places at the time, and are in *Oeuv.*, X, 343–406. A transcript of discussions of the proposition in the finance committee is in the Archives Nationales (Chambre des Deputés, C. 278); resumé in *Oeuv.*, VII, 27–31. The episode is discussed by Proudhon in his *Confessions*, *Oeuv.*, VII, 191–214, and by Daniel Halévy, ibid., 26–37, and in his *Le Mariage de Proudhon*, 168–82.

clear how little the reactionary Assembly was willing to address itself to French society's most urgent needs.

The speech's reception was most extraordinary. Proudhon directly declared his radical intent to transform the social order, declaring the Revolution of February to have been the beginning of a profound *social* revolution, not just a limited alteration of political forms and personnel. As he recognized, after the June insurrection his Assembly colleagues would accept only these restricted political changes, discarding even those minor social reforms discussed by some republicans before.

To Proudhon's solitary socialist declamation the Assembly responded with frequent, and eventually continuous, hostile remarks, laughter, and angrily shouted rejoinders. He was able to go on only because the presiding officer, Armand Marrast, vigorously insisted on his right to do so. At one point Proudhon's remarks appeared to suggest forcible expropriation of proprietors, and many members broke in furiously:

CITIZEN PROUDHON: [My remark] signifies that in case of refusal we ourselves will proceed with the liquidation without you. (*Violent murmurs.*)

NUMEROUS VOICES: Who, *you?* who is you? . . . (*Agitation.*)

CITIZEN ERNEST DE GIRARDIN: Are you alluding to the guillotine? (*Noise. —Various interpellations are addressed to the speaker from several sides.*)

CITIZEN PRESIDENT: I ask everyone to be quiet. The speaker has the floor in order to explain his ideas.

CITIZEN PROUDHON: When I used the two pronouns *you* and *we*, it is obvious that, at that moment, I was identifying myself, *me*, with the *proletariat* and I was identifying yourselves, *you*, with the *bourgeois class.* (*New exclamations.*)

CITIZEN DE SAINT-PRIEST: This is social warfare!

A MEMBER: This is the twenty-third of June at the rostrum?

SEVERAL VOICES: Let him speak. —Listen! Listen! [34]

34. *Oeuv.*, X, 370. Proudhon later expressed regret over his outburst here, mainly because, he said, no one should pose as spokesman for the proletariat (*Oeuv.*, VII, 204). Despite this disclaimer, the outburst certainly reflects his actual feelings.

In the end, a resolution to prohibit publication of the speech in *Le Moniteur*, the official gazette, was offered but rejected as a threat to freedom of the press. The following resolution was proposed, with variations, by a host of members.

The National Assembly,
Considering that the proposition of Citizen Proudhon is an odious attack on the principles of public morality; that it violates property, that it encourages denunciation; that it appeals to the worst passions;
    Considering that the speaker has slandered the Revolution of February, 1848, while claiming to make it accessory to the theories he had developed,
    [Rejects his proposition and] passes on to the order of the day.[35]

The resolution was approved, 693 votes to two (Proudhon's and that of a socialist worker, Greppo), and the Assembly rose for dinner at 7:15. The surest sign that the deputies had been urgently disturbed by Proudhon is that they had remained so long—through his three-hour speech—in order to vote against him.

He writes of the hostility toward him from this time on as having been intensely bitter and widespread;[36] similar comments by others and the numerous contemporary published attacks on him support this claim. While he may nevertheless be exaggerating, it must have been important for him that he *felt* there was so much antagonism. Despite his distaste for leadership, under such circumstances he was bound to feel himself a proletarian tribune declaring the people's just cause in the face of an increasingly vicious enemy, the reactionary middle and upper classes.

If he was a poor tribune in the Assembly, he earned bourgeois hatred by his journalism. Perhaps, however, the calming of Frenchmen's emotions with the passage of time, and his own imprisonment a year later, made him once more seem the critical intellectual who could not be very dangerous. In prison he began writing the books which represented for him the product of his revolutionary experience. During the weeks just after his imprisonment he composed

35. *Oeuv.*, X, 406.
36. *Oeuv.*, VII, 202ff.

his *Confessions d'un révolutionnaire*,[37] a scathing and bitter analysis of revolution in France from 1789 to 1849. Sainte-Beuve, writing as a literary critic and one who had lived through the 1848 Revolution, called the *Confessions* Proudhon's best work, although as an expression of Proudhon's theory it holds less interest than some of his other books. For students of revolution it remains one of the most important books to come out of the explosion which shook much of Europe in 1848.

Continuing the development of the themes emphasized in the *Confessions* and in his articles and pamphlets of 1848–49, he produced the *Idée générale de la révolution au XIXe siècle*.[38] Written in prison and published in July, 1851, this book was the culmination of Proudhon's work of the past dozen years. His anarchism had appeared even in the first works on grammar and on the celebration of the Sabbath, had assumed defined form in his *mémoires* on property, and had been extended in scope in his essays of the mid-1840's. When confronted with the present realities of revolution in 1848 he developed his anarchism into full-blown theory, most notably in *De la Solution du problème social*,[39] his *Confessions*, "Qu'est-ce que le gouvernement, qu'est-ce que le Dieu?"[40] and the "Polémique contre Louis Blanc et Pierre Leroux."[41] The last of these formed a link between the *Confessions* and the *Idée générale*. In a way, all that Proudhon had done before was but the foundation for the *Idée générale de la révolution au XIXe siècle* and a preparation for him to conceive it.

This date must remain a solemn one in my moral and intellectual life. I have signed the press order for the last sheet of my book,

37. *Les Confessions d'un révolutionnaire pour servir à l'histoire de la révolution de février* (Paris, 1849). Published simultaneously in different formats but with identical texts by *La Voix du peuple* and Garnier Frères, the latter edition dated 1850, though printed in 1849. In 1851, Garnier published a revised, augmented edition, marked as the third one, though actually the second. This edition, with variorum from the first, *Oeuv.*, VII.

38. (Paris, 1851); *Oeuv.*, II. The first edition of 3,000 copies was sold out in a month and a second edition immediately printed. The revised edition of the *Confessions* followed in October, 1851.

39. (Paris, 1848); *Oeuv.* (*Lacroix*), VI. See above, pp. 123ff.

40. *La Voix du peuple*, no. 36 (November 5, 1849), 1–2. Used as a preface to the revised edition of the *Confessions* (*Oeuv.*, VII, 57–64).

41. *Oeuv.*, II, 353–459; this is the Rivière edition's title for a series of ten articles published in *La Voix du peuple*, November 25, 1849, to January 28, 1850. The

P.-J. Proudhon as a National Assembly deputy in 1848, from a lithograph by
H. Jannin. *Photo Bibliothèque Nationale, Paris.*

Gustave Courbet, "Proudhon and His Family," *original version*. A scene of 1853 painted in 1865, after the anarchist's death.

Gustave Courbet, "Proudhon and His Family," *existing version*, in the Petit-Palais, Paris. Redone by the artist after the painting was severely criticized at the 1865 Salon. *Photographie Giraudon.*

"M. Proudhon Making Just Redistribution of Social Wealth —'Monsieur is rich and goes in a carriage. . . . Monsieur is poor and goes on foot. . . . Henceforth you shall both go in wheelbarrows.'" By Cham, in *Le Charivari*, September 28, 1848.

"Saint Proudhon Preaching Proudhonism. —'Go in peace, oh my brother, much will be forgiven you because you have envied the property of others so much.'" By Cham, in *Le Charivari*, October 2, 1848.

"The Socialist Siren. —'Gallant noncoms, good peasants, come to me! . . . I've always had you in my heart!' —'We've heard that tune before! Heard it before! You'll have to make another sort of music for us!'" By Cham, in *Le Charivari*, March 23, 1849.

"Thanks to the superiority of his doctrines, Citizen Proudhon carries the flag of socialism high and proud, and marches with great steps along the new road, followed by the entire people whom he has succeeded in convincing.' —(Taken from a socialist newspaper.)" By Cham, in *Le Charivari*, April 5, 1849.

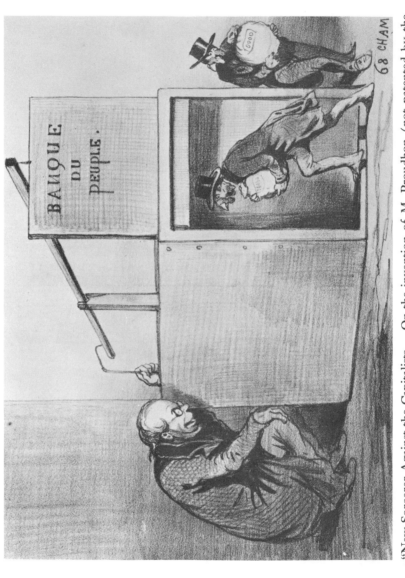

"New Sorcerer Against the Capitalists. —On the invention of M. Proudhon (not patented by the government)." By Cham, in *Le Charivari*, February 27, 1849.

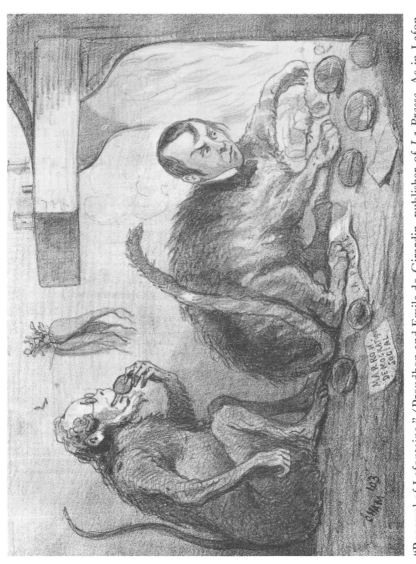

"Renewal of Lafontaine." (Proudhon and Emile de Girardin, publisher of *La Presse*. As in Lafontaine's fable, Girardin is pulling Proudhon's chestnuts out of the fire, including one labeled "Social democratic chestnut.") By Cham, in *Le Charivari*, July 30, 1849.

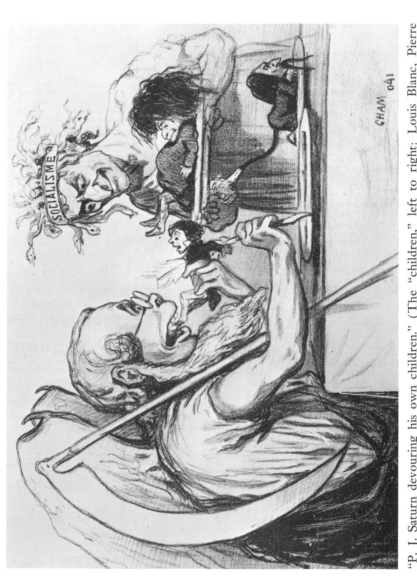

"P. J. Saturn devouring his own children." (The "children," left to right: Louis Blanc, Pierre Leroux, and Victor Considérant.) By Cham, in *Le Charivari*, January 24, 1850.

"Gendarme, don't let him out! See here, look how he's taken care of us! This man was most offensive socially, always beating up his friends. It's probably for that that the government has put him in solitary! That'll give our wounds time to heal!" (Left to right are Louis Blanc, Pierre Leroux, and Victor Considérant. The sign reads, "Citizen Proudhon is in solitary confinement.") By Charles Vernier, in *Le Charivari*, February 20, 1850.

"The terrible Red Beard hanging up Frédéric Bastiat, his latest victim, in his collection of curiosities." (Other victims, left to right: Pierre Leroux, Victor Considérant, and Louis Blanc.) By Cham, in *Le Charivari*, April 5, 1850.

"The Confessions of a Revolutionary." (Emile de Girardin is on the left, and Adolphe Thiers above Proudhon.) By Charles Vernier, in *Le Charivari*, December 4, 1849.

"Just let me see you playing again with those rascally little swells!" (Proudhon and Emile de Girardin. The sign reads, "Proudhon. Democratic weaning with its social consequences.") By Cham, in *Le Charivari*, March 22, 1850.

"Père Molé bringing a New Year's gift to Little Thiers." By Honoré Daumier, in *Le Charivari*, January 15, 1850.

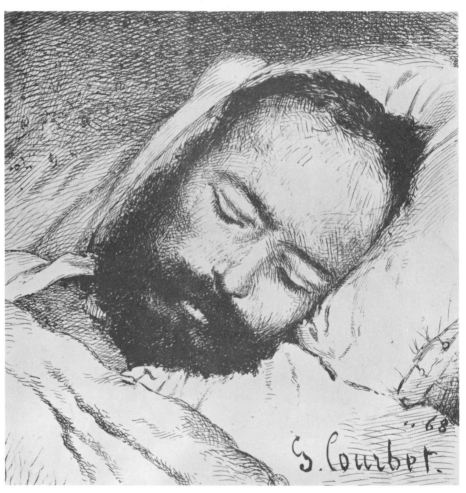

Gustave Courbet, portrait of Proudhon on his deathbed. Lithograph rendered in 1868.

Idée générale de la révolution au 19ᵉ siècle, and in signing this order I have broken definitively with the theological idea already so
much shaken by me in chapter VIII of my *Contradictions.* This
scission, expurgation, equation, or whatever you will, is not made
without a certain rending of the heart, some murmur of conscience, the strongest that I have felt in my life. It is true indeed . . .
that conversions, returns by the soul to possession of itself, are not
made without a great effort and a great sadness.[42]

Before 1848 Proudhon had sought in quite radical fashion to discover the nature of social justice and evils of the existing society
and polity; yet in a significant sense his work had been that of detached intellectual inquiry, for all its passions. It had been revolutionary in its conclusions, but his thought had not been intimately
involved in the actuality of revolution and its peculiar demands.
He had not really made use of past revolutionary experience, much
less felt directly what could happen to a society in upheaval.

Being part of an actual revolution, truncated and uncertain as
its course was, gave much to Proudhon's thought. Not only did
events provide stimulus for rapid development of his ideas and material to give them flesh, but also the 1848 Revolution forced him
to assess his entire philosophy in terms of a refreshed and more
realistic view of France's revolutionary experience through six
decades.

It has all too often been the habit of men of ideas, Frenchmen
especially, to give their abstractions a far greater reality than the
original experiences from which the ideas had been drawn. With
ideas taking on life and images assuming solid substance, men could
and often would fight with frightening intensity for the most foolish figments.

Proudhon could never escape this failing himself, but he could
suspend belief in phantoms enough to recognize much of his contemporaries' foolishness about their society and its recent history,

---

first two were published with "Qu'est-ce que le gouvernement . . ." as *Actes de
la revolution* (Paris, 1849).

42. *Carnets,* July 10, 1851, IX, 98ff. Here he means "theological" literally, and
speaks of human progress as made wholly by man, not God. A number of other
articles written by Proudhon in 1848 and 1849 are significant for the development
of his anarchism. Many are reprinted in his *Idées révolutionnaires* (Paris, 1849),
and a few in *Oeuv.,* II and VII. For a discussion of the more nearly complete collection of his articles in *Oeuv. (Lacroix),* see note 14 above.

and to perceive the delusions of republican renewal in 1848. His departure from the by then hallowed traditions of the 1789 Revolution and liberal republicanism made possible the maturing of his theory. It gave to his anarchism a force and a base in real human experience that was lacking in the thought of earlier radical critics. Thus his response to the 1848 Revolution and to the whole revolutionary tradition since 1789 is central to his later and most important writing.

six: The Revolutionary Tradition

> All these popularity hunters, mountebanks of revolution, have for
> their oracle Robespierre, the eternal denunciator, with the empty
> brains and the viper's fang.[1]

SPECTERS OF THE PAST often loom large in the lives of men long
after they might better have been exorcised, or at least laid to rest
with the bodies from which they sprang. In France the principal
specter has been the memory of the Revolution of 1789. Frenchmen's images of the Revolution may not have corresponded faithfully to the reality of the original, but these images have profoundly
shaped their attitudes toward the public life of their contemporary
worlds.

If one traces the outlines of these images and relates them to post-
Revolutionary French history, he finds that the year 1848 assumes
a central position. The experiences of that year so deeply affected
people's attitudes that it became the major watershed in French
revolutionary history. Proudhon's own attitudes and ideas should
be regarded in light of the more general revolutionary tradition.

Although the revolution which began in 1789 may be said to
have ended with the Thermidorean reaction of 1794, with Napoleon's assumption of power in 1799, or with the Bourbon Restora-

1. *Idée générale* . . . , *Oeuv.*, II, 233.

tion in 1815, such suggested terminal points are more formal than real. It is convenient for the historian to delimit the revolutionary period, but the reverses suffered at these junctures could not be sufficient to terminate a process with the momentum that the Revolution had gathered.

Under the restored Bourbon monarchy France was a far different country than it had been in 1789; most of the more important changes wrought by the Revolution and Napoleon's Empire had been too firmly consolidated to be reversed. Intervening experience had put immeasurable distance between the *ancien régime* and the restoration reign of Louis XVIII.

The gap between 1788 and 1816 was more than a matter of changes in governmental forms and the political roles of the throne and the three estates, in law, in feudal privileges, in land tenure, in the status of the Church, in the relative positions of the social classes, in any and all of the explicit issues over which the conflict had been joined. More of the old world had passed away than the institutions and customs challenged by the revolutionaries. So many features of the old life had been altered that the whole character of existence was different for most Frenchmen. In a way they were all somewhat like an aristocratic emigré returned in 1815, after a quarter-century of exile, to his ancestral home. Whatever his material fortunes might be, whether or not the ancient château and the lands around it had survived unscathed, for him the kingdom of Louis XVIII could be very little like that of Louis XVI.

The deliberate substantive changes of the Revolution had been advocated and initiated or rejected and attacked in the name of Reason. Ideas had been as much a part of the struggle as guns and guillotines. When the shooting had stopped, the ideas lived on. As dissonant as were the voices sounding ideas, each man could find some party or faction to call his own, and its ideas remained valid and important for him. In thinking rationally about public affairs the French continued to use the philosophies of the Revolution or of its antagonists; their concepts and attitudes were shaped by the battle of ideas occasioned by the Revolution.

The Revolution lived on in influential ideas and in institutions, like land tenure and the legal code, which shaped the character of everyday life. However, in considering the endurance of the Revolution there are less tangible factors not so readily defined but in some ways more significant. If men had ideas, plans, and policies shaped by the Revolution, far more did they have emotions, memories, images in which the Revolution loomed large. Passions remained hot and the slogan "Liberté, Egalité, Fraternité!" still had powerful evocative force long after Thermidor. Memories of the "glorious French Revolution" remained, more altered by prolonged emotional regard than dimmed by the passage of years. On the popular level, tales of the Revolution's events passed into folklore and family history, its dreams into myth more real and moving than mere fantasy. People grew up with the Revolution as an intimate part of their culture; for older ones it was a very personal part of their own pasts.

On an intellectual level, nonrational responses to the Revolutionary heritage played a much larger role in forming "rational" positions than men determined to be reasonable would have liked to admit. At all levels the categories of discourse and political position, the language and modes of expression, and the issues of dispute in public life were set by the Revolution. The promise of a better future dreamed of by many was a recapitulation of the visions of men of the Revolution. The black future dreaded by others would be a return to what they thought fearful in the Revolution. Often the same individuals extracted both promise and terror from their images of the Revolution.

There were many positions taken on public affairs by nineteenth-century Frenchmen; each one was shaped, even determined, by how its adherents had come to terms with the Revolution. If the problems and challenges which France faced in the nineteenth century were in some respects novel, her responses to them were not basically so. In time this too changed; even a nation so burdened by its past as France does not remain static. Yet the change was slow; the Revolution of 1789 still plays a major role in the French imagination and intellect.

The most direct result of this in the nineteenth century was that there were many Frenchmen who sought to renew the Revolution, to complete the process of "liberation" it had begun. For some of these (though not all) this meant completing what they thought Robespierre's Montagnards had begun and Thermidor interrupted

and partially reversed. Assuming that revolution should be a resumption of an old process rather than an initiation of a new one
made a critical difference in revolutionary expectations, tone, and
action. That something substantially different from what the past
offered might be required by the contemporary situation seems to
have been little suspected. While novel concepts for the reordering
of society were formulated by socialists and economists, even they
were too closely bound by the past to regard revolution in essentially fresh ways. Most of all, the popular imagination was so caught
up by the revolutionary tradition that it had no motivation to alter
the tradition's pattern.

Revolution came again in 1830, but too little was substantially
altered and too little conclusively decided for the revolutionary
tradition to be significantly affected. The renewal of revolution in
1848 was another matter; changes were more substantial and the
experience more traumatic and prolonged. Expectations were great,
but for many they were not fulfilled. The middle classes consolidated their position still further, but for other revolutionary hope-
fuls 1848 and its sequels brought little but disillusionment and despair.

The key steps of the 1789 Revolution were reenacted, although
with the faster tempo of 1848 some were omitted. Rebellion rose
against an unsatisfactory king. Although not specifically republican
initially, the rebellion soon resulted in termination of the monarchy
and establishment of a republic, with a predominantly middle-class
government and legislative body. The popular left threatened the
moderate middle-class elements and, in the bloody June Days, the
course of the revolution was reversed, as it had been in Thermidor
of the year II. Radical forces were suppressed and the hope of popular democracy snuffed out. Finally another Bonaparte appeared
to become chief of state, then to replace the republic with an empire and democracy with the dictates of a "liberal" messiah. The
bourgeoisie profited by the change; the rural peasantry was largely
unaffected, and the rapidly growing urban lower classes were left
chiefly with the myth of renewed national grandeur to sustain
them. While those who rested their hopes on the promise of revolutionary renewal were disillusioned, those who dreaded it had
their fears eased.

To the popular imagination the 1848 Revolution's most significant innovation was the national workshops scheme inspired by Louis Blanc. Regarded by many as a renewal of Jacobin radicalism, the workshops were an especially bright hope, yet they were proving unequal to the task they sought to accomplish when closed by the government. It had not been the sort of program which Blanc had advocated, but however unfair the trial, his approach was discredited—and in some ways this was the most bitter disillusionment of all.

For many all hopes for revolution had been bound up in their much-cherished Jacobin tradition and their expectations for a return to the politics of the Jacobins, or, more particularly, the Montagnards. Because the workshops were thought to be the best plan of revived Jacobinism, their failure seemed to repudiate the tradition, for their collapse had been due to their inefficacy as well as to conservative opposition.

The debacle of 1848 destroyed illusions and discredited much of the revolutionary tradition, but it did not stifle the urge for revolution. It did force radical intellectuals to reformulate their ideas, and thus it became a dividing point in intellectual history. It marked the beginning of deep changes in the revolutionary impulse and tradition, in its popular as well as its intellectual forms.

Alexander Herzen, whose reflections on the 1848 Revolution are among the most profound contemporary commentaries on this or any crisis, called his essays a protest "against an obsolete, slavish and spurious set of ideas, against absurd idols, which belong to another age and which linger on meaninglessly among us, a nuisance to some, a terror to others." On the morrow of the June Days he wrote, "Paris has grown old, and youthful dreams no longer become her."[2] His indictment of the republicans is a sorrowful epitaph for a lost dream.

> I was sorry for them because of the sincerity of their delusions, their honest belief in what could never be, their ardent faith as pure and as unreal as the chivalry of Don Quixote. I was sorry for

2. Alexander Herzen, *From the Other Shore*, trans. from Russian (London & New York, 1956), 3, 53. The first excerpt is from the introduction written by Herzen in 1855 for the first published Russian edition, the second from a section dated Paris, July 27, 1848.

them as a doctor might be sorry for a man who does not suspect the terrible disease within his breast. What moral suffering these men are preparing for themselves! They will fight like heroes, they will work all their lives and achieve nothing. They will give their blood, their strength, their lives, and when they grow old they will see that nothing has come of their labours, that they did not do what was wanted. They will die with a bitter disillusion in man, who is not really to blame, or—still worse, they will lapse back into childhood and will, as now, every day expect some enormous change, the establishment of *their* republic—mistaking the agonies of death for the pains of birth.

The Republic, as *they* conceive it, is an unrealizable abstraction, the fruit of theoretical reflections, the apotheosis of the existing state organization, the transfiguration of *what already exists;* their republic is the last dream, the poetic delirium of the old world. There is an element of prophecy in this delirium, but it is a prophecy concerning life beyond the grave, life in some future epoch. That is what they cannot understand, these men of the past, who for all their revolutionary temper, remain tied to the old world, body and soul. They imagine that this decrepit world can, like Ulysses, regain its youth, unaware that the realization of one fraction of their republic would kill it instantly. They do not see that nothing could be more violently incompatible than their ideal and the existing order, that the one must die for the other to live. They cannot abandon the old forms; they regard them as eternal boundaries—that is why their ideal only bears the name and colour of the future, but in essence belongs to the world of the past and does not repudiate it.[3]

Although Herzen admired Proudhon and later was his friend, he probably arrived at these conclusions quite independently of any influence by the Frenchman. However, Herzen's remarks represent very well the spirit and substance of Proudhon's own reaction to the Revolution, although even Proudhon did not express himself so eloquently.

3. Ibid., 56–57. Dated Champs-Elysées, October 1, 1848. It should be noted that, despite the close relationship between Herzen and Proudhon and between their ideas, Herzen differed substantially from Proudhon in his overall ideological position. As is suggested here, Herzen concluded that Western Europe was too irremediably corrupt and too chained by convolutions of its heritage for revolution to be successfully concluded there. He looked to his native Russia as the nation of the future and of the revolution's triumph.

The principles which guided the transformation of the French polity in the years just after 1789 had been—or seemed—radical enough then. Considerable change was wrought; much more was promised, if not accomplished. Prospects for human advance seemed unbounded. Great enthusiasm was aroused; hope grew in many a man who had known little of it. Thermidor denied the realization of the hopes of many, but it did not shatter an enduring dream containing these hopes.

The Revolution had many different meanings to men afterward, but whatever they thought and felt, they *believed*. The Revolution had inspired faith—a faith complete with idols, saints, and devils. Yet were the aspirations and needs consonant with the articles of faith? For those to whom the 1848 revolutionary renewal brought not reaffirmation of faith but its disintegration, the articles of faith were a delusion. For them the credos of the 1789 Revolution, however radical they may have been in eighteenth-century French society, proved inadequate—and hence insufficiently radical—for coping with society's ills in the middle of the nineteenth century.

The numbers of those whose aspirations were denied by the Second Republic and Empire, especially urban workers, were growing as industrial revolution came to France. For them and the intellectuals who spoke for them the experiences of 1848 were bewildering and largely unforeseen. Almost none had suspected that their faith might be outmoded. Herzen did, but he spoke only to a small Russian audience. Proudhon did—and in this lay the basis for his influence.

If the Jacobin Republic was, as Herzen put it, "an unrealizable abstraction . . . the apotheosis of the existing state organization, the transfiguration of *what already exists*," then a new credo had to be adopted. New revolutionary paths should be followed which would lead not to a transfiguration of the old society, but to a wholly new one. The next revolution could not be another reenactment of the first. For many the Revolution which began in 1789 finally ended with the June Days of 1848. It was thus that the revolutionary movement began to strike off in new directions after 1848.

So powerful a tradition as that of the original Revolution could not be utterly destroyed by the experience of 1848, but the effects and nature of that tradition could not be the same afterward. Here we are concerned primarily with the consequences of the tradition for popular and intellectual revolutionary attitudes and movements. The aspirations of the French middle classes were frustrated far less than those of the urban lower classes by the failures of the First and Second Republics, and they were fortified far more by the Republics' successes. Their versions of the national dream were thus quite different and were not so shaken by the events following the Revolution of February, 1848.

There was little reason after 1848 for profound discontent among the bourgeoisie or among much of the rural farming population, except that some wanted a republican government rather than the Second Empire—a desire fulfilled in 1871. They neither needed nor wanted further revolution. For them the French Revolution could be and was simply a proud heritage, a myth embodying patriotism and middle-class ideals.

The urban lower classes, who by their numbers and violence had given the Revolution its strength, had been largely cheated of their victories. Although much of the rural population benefited from land redistribution and the abolition of feudal dues in the 1789 Revolution, and in consequence became more conservative, the urban workers still had plentiful motivation to be revolutionary, while their numbers and misery increased rapidly as France industrialized. They and the intellectuals who were their spokesmen constituted the revolutionary movement after 1848; that year's events were very influential for them.

While emphasizing the shifts in revolutionary ideas produced by the 1848 experience, I cannot claim that there were no novel ideas before then or that the 1848 catastrophe brought sudden and total disaffection from the traditional revolutionary faith. The discontinuity could hardly be so sharp. However, the relevant intellectual concepts before 1848 are more noteworthy here for their affinity with the kinds of thought characteristic of the 1789 Revolution than for specific differences with the latter's ideology. (It is this affinity which Herzen condemns as obsolete; he has no quarrel with the revolutionary intent.) Moreover, intellectual criticisms of the Revolutionary credo had little effect on the popular imagination until events, which reached a climax in 1848, shattered the faith. Afterward, novel ideas could be more influential than they could when the old credo was untarnished, and intellectual approaches to revolution were increasingly independent of the old tradition.

However valid and valuable the revolutionary intellectual tradition may actually have been for the reconstruction of the French nation, Proudhon was as disgusted with it as Herzen, while the rational basis of his distaste was more deeply rooted and more thoroughly developed. It was in this spirit that he reacted so negatively to the initiation of the revolution in February, 1848. ("There are no ideas at all in their heads. . . . It is a mob of lawyers and writers, each more ignorant than the others, who are going to contend for power.") [4] Proudhon's antagonism toward the ideas of the Revolution animated his efforts in revolutionary journalism and gave them much of their power. His *Confessions* are an extended and devastating attack on the entire tradition of the Revolution, striking at the protagonists of each stage, from 1789 to 1849. While his natural and constant enemies are those who seek to preserve the status quo, many of his most bitter words are reserved for those who have contributed to upsetting it: republicans of the Jacobin tradition and, above all, Rousseau and Robespierre. "All these popularity hunters ['the continuators of Jacobinism'], mountebanks of revolution, have taken for their oracle Robespierre, the eternal denunciator, with the empty brains and the viper's fang. . . ." [5]

Revolution in France had always failed to produce the kind of change Proudhon hoped for. The Revolution had been betrayed, and the ones most responsible for its betrayal were those who represented it, who sat on the Mountain in the Republican Assemblies and failed to make something of real value of the opportunities available.

A revolution must always face the opposition of those who would preserve the status quo or even restore an earlier state of affairs. These elements seek to block or divert the course of the revolution. But many of its advocates may at some point seek to thwart its further development toward still more radical goals. This has been the great difficulty of many revolutions: the revolutionaries have

4. See above, p. 122.
5. *Oeuv.*, II, 233.

widely differing goals, the ultimate objectives of some more noxious to others than the pre-revolutionary situation itself. As the revolution progresses, it reaches a point where a sizable bloc of its supporters break away, saying, "This far and no farther." The moderate republicans had in effect made this conclusion in the spring of 1848, once the republic had been reestablished. The split may even come to be a matter of pushing back to some earlier stage which the revolution had rushed headlong through and beyond. This happened in the Thermidorean reaction of 1794, and a similar development might be said to have occurred after the June Days of 1848.

Proudhon recognizes and deplores these divisive elements in the revolutionary process; his condemnation is directed in large part at those revolutionaries who would not carry the process far enough. As many others have done, he attacks the Revolution for doing too little to bring all rights and benefits to everyone equally, and too little to end the misery of the poorest and most numerous classes. Though the poor furnished the necessary force, the bourgeois leaders of each of the revolutions have halted the process when they have secured their own rights and advantages, lest they lose their gains through egalitarian leveling.

Having finally recognized the differences between middle- and lower-class revolutionary goals, after 1848 rebels associated with the working class increasingly dissociated themselves from bourgeois republicanism. In contributing to this departure, Proudhon condemns the bourgeoisie for the *mode* of their revolutionary efforts as well as their selfish pursuit of private and class interests.

For him the failure of France's revolutions to produce wider benefits has resulted directly from preoccupation with securing constitutional change and merely political rights. By their very nature these political goals cannot introduce the major social change which is necessary. Although they may accomplish a securing of bourgeois privilege, they do little to touch society's most fundamental problems.

The dream of the Revolution, however, has been a vision of a universal humanism foreseeing much more profound developments. Proudhon thinks the means suggested for fulfilling this dream are doomed to be virtually fruitless, that they are compounded of fraud and self-deception. He attributes this to a misbegotten political tradition stemming from Jean-Jacques Rousseau, whom he makes the target of some of his most bitter and cutting attacks.

> We say . . . that, to the shame of the XVIIIth century and ours, the *Social Contract* of Rousseau, the chief work of oratorical jugglery, has been admired, lauded to the skies, regarded as the roll of public liberties. Members of the Constituent Assembly, Girondins, Jacobins, Cordeliers, all took it as their oracle. It served as text for the Constitution of 93, declared absurd by its own authors. Still today this book inspires the most zealous reformers of political and social science. The cadaver of the author, which the people will drag to Montfaucon [a notorious site of public executions] the day they understand the meaning of those words, Liberty, Justice, Morality, Reason, Society, Order, reposes glorious and venerated in the catacombs of the Pantheon, where there will never enter one of those honest laborers who nourish their poor families with their blood, while the profound geniuses they adore send, in their wanton passion, their bastards to the alms-house.
> All aberration of public conscience carries with it its own penalty. The vogue for Rousseau has cost France more gold, more blood, more shame, than the detested reign of the three famous courtesans, Cotillon I, Cotillon II, Cotillon III (la Châteauroux, la Pompadour, and la Du Barry), made her expend. Our native land, which never suffered except from the influence of foreigners, owes to Rousseau the bloody struggles and the deceptions of 93.[6]

Demolition of this "vogue for Rousseau" plays an important role in Proudhon's *Confessions* and *Idée générale de la révolution:* he develops much of his critique of the Revolution and of government through making his assaults on the Genevan.

Proudhon's representation of the other's theory is a caricature. Rousseau's ideas are not as far from his own as he says.[7] His attacks on Rousseau are best understood just as his repudiation of the in-

---

6. *Oeuv.*, II, 194–95.

7. For a fine discussion of Proudhon's response to Rousseau, see Aaron Noland, "Proudhon and Rousseau," *Journal of the History of Ideas*, XXVII, 1 (January–March, 1967), 33–54. Also see Silvia Rota Ghibaudi, *Proudhon e Rousseau* (Milan, 1965); Edouard Loüys, "Pierre-Joseph Proudhon et Jean-Jacques Rousseau," unpublished thesis, 1955, Bibliothèque de l'Université de Paris (Sorbonne). While I have found Proudhon's reaction against Rousseau more revealing than his debt to the Genevan, that debt is a major one and merits more attention than I could find place for here.

tellectual heritage of the 1789 Revolution. Rousseau had contributed to this tradition, and it ordinarily was thought of as Rousseauean, despite the substantial elements there which were not due
to him. French republicans, especially those whose position stemmed
from the Montagnards of the First Republic, found in this "Rousseauean tradition" the rational basis of their politics. Since latter-day
Montagnards claimed support from the lower classes, to Proudhon
they and the Rousseauean tradition were still more dangerous and
deceitful than a republicanism that excluded plebeians. The tradition as he saw it regards the problems of man and society in the
following way.

Man is obliged to live in society and forms a system of government to regulate this society. Every man is endowed by nature with
certain rights which can be protected from the encroachment of
others only by the means of a political system superimposed upon
the social structure to control and prevent antisocial behavior. The
rational necessity of social and political organization justifies its
existence. Political relationships have the form of a contract between men to protect their interests through collective action.
However, such an agreement does not sanction the abridgment of
natural human rights, for it is meant specifically to guarantee them.
Thus governments and laws that deny rights are tyrannical and
should be changed, by revolution if need be. Proudhon thinks that
any regime must deny human rights, but Rousseaueans believe that
a proper government will only limit the willful and antisocial exercise of rights, without threatening the rights themselves.

The Rousseuean tradition has, he believes, restricted itself to concern for the exercise of rights only in political and legal contexts.
The right of equality is seen only as a requirement that all men
should be treated identically by law. The most extreme interpretation is that in the ideal situation all should have equal opportunity
to participate in the process of government. The right of liberty
is understood as a matter of freedom from certain restrictions, as on
expression of ideas or on commerce, and freedom from arbitrary
rule by a monarchy or oligarchy able to exercise its will without
limitation of law or constitution. The right of security is understood
as a guarantee against physical injury or the theft of property.

Rousseau's disciples believe that securing these rights is the fundamental task of the Revolution; whatever else is required by society can best be gained within a political system thus reconstituted. However, they do not think of these rights as entailing anywhere near as much as does Proudhon. To him, equal political and legal rights are almost useless if economic conditions are fundamentally unequal. Security is more than protection of what is already possessed; it is opportunity to work, to escape poverty through work justly compensated, and to enjoy the whole product of one's labor. Liberty is freedom from any power exerted over you, whether that of the state or of private persons and institutions.

He is convinced that denial of these rights is fundamentally due to the iniquity of the existing social and economic structure, with political tyranny a symptom rather than a cause. Neither political change nor the economic growth which liberals expect it to promote can secure human rights, unless the social and economic structure is wholly reconstituted upon a very different and just foundation. Republicans have not sought this sort of *social* revolution, nor do they want any fundamental social changes beyond those needed to complete the elimination of feudalism. Consequently Proudhon scorns the political focus even of radical republicans; their preoccupation with politics and their narrow social perspective are scarcely less pernicious than the attitudes of others less sensitive to the misery of the masses.

The abolition of the Bourbon monarchy in the Revolution of 1789 was, according to him, more than a political change: it was the abolition of feudalism, a socioeconomic system as well as a political one. The feudal structure was an organization of society for war, originating in times of chronic violence. Such a military society had long been outmoded. The new regime established principles of liberty and equality, and had it followed the rational consequences of these principles, it should have reconstituted society for the better organization of labor, in place of the former organization for military strength. It should not have been a matter simply of forming a new government but of establishing an "industrial regime"—reconstituting society in order to permit the free organization of labor on a more natural and just basis, promoting both productivity and equality. Here Proudhon clearly is writing under Saint-Simonian influence. The phrase he employs is "le régime égalitaire ou industriel." The concept of "le régime industriel" is the essence of Saint-Simonism; "égalitaire" represents Proudhon's modification of Saint-Simonism, whose ideas he does not follow very far.

The Revolution did not proceed in this way, however; the revolutionaries failed to set out upon their proper mission. All activity was in partisan politics; ideas were political ones. Political theorists Rousseau and Montesquieu took the place of economists Smith and Quesnay.

> . . . it had to follow that the new society, scarcely conceived, remained in the embryonic state. Instead of its economy developing according to its law, the society languished in constitutionalism, its life a perpetual contradiction. In place of its own proper order, it offered everywhere systematic corruption and legal poverty. In short, power, the expression of this society, reproducing in its institution with scrupulous fidelity the antinomy of principles, found itself always fighting the nation, and the nation had to strike at power without cease.

Thus it has been ever since, with everyone distracted from the real problems and their possible solutions by the sterile disputes of politics, which can in the end produce nothing but a reconstitution of tyranny and prolongation of the exploitation of man by man.

> It is necessary, however, to convince ourselves that outside the parliamentary sphere, which is as sterile as it is absorbing, is another one, incomparably more vast, where our destinies are made sport of. Above these political phantoms there are the phenomena of the social economy, which through their harmony or discordance produce all the good and evil of societies.[8]

In thus shifting emphasis from primarily political questions to what he refers to as "the social problem" Proudhon is doing much the same thing all contemporary socialists did. As was noted earlier, this shifted emphasis defined "socialism" at that time. But he differs from other socialists in the way he understands politics, and in the role assigned to it. Although plans for utopian communities by such men as Fourier and Cabet lay outside the ordinary political realm, most socialists in 1848 sought to implement their schemes by means

8. *Oeuv.*, II, 126–28.

of political instruments. Many hoped to use the legislative and executive machinery of the Second Republic to effect social change, both for reforms of limited import and for introduction of socialism itself.

The outstanding instance was the Luxembourg Commission, established by the Republic's Provisional Assembly early in 1848 in order to devise solutions for problems of poverty and unemployment. The Commission, under the direction of Louis Blanc, did not succeed in accomplishing anything of genuine substance. Its deliberations and proposals were not impressive, and in any event thanks to bourgeois and provincial opposition it lacked the political weight needed to make its work fruitful.

In the failures of Blanc and other socialists in politics, including the frustration of his own efforts in the Assembly, Proudhon finds support for his conclusion that government will not solve social problems. At best it will only offer very limited relief from the consequences of social injustice. Ultimately he concludes that the necessary social revolution cannot be fully achieved as long as government exists in any form.

Proudhon shares many of the assumptions of the republican democrats and socialists he attacks. Like them he is a child of the Revolution, as well as its critic. But he sees a very different logic in these common beliefs, and thereby draws from them his own rational conclusions.

His critique of Rousseauean notions of social contract reveals how his conception of the proper foundations of social organization differs from that of ordinary democrats. Conventionally social contract is regarded as agreement to the constitution of a *system* for regulation of social intercourse. This system is thought of as political and legal; social contract serves as the justification of government. This assumes that government and law are the only effective means of social regulation and the preservation of order and harmony. The problem men must solve is how best to constitute political power and to make and administer law.

This Proudhon regards as totally and mischievously fallacious; for him the problem is not how to constitute political power, but how to eliminate it. The social contract need not and should not be political. The political conception of social contract supposes that the "general will" of society, exercised through the medium of government, is substituted for the conflicting wills of individuals. It is presumed that if the individual accepts the way in which the law is made—assenting to the social contract—then he can accept the laws themselves, deferring in his judgment to that of the whole social body, as expressed in the law. This adaptation of individual wills to some collective decision creates the "general will" of society.

Proudhon rejects the whole notion of general will; he can regard individuals deferring to the collectivity in this way only as loss of vital liberty. He denies that there can be any expression of volition which comprehends within it all the disparate wills of individuals. The democratic ideal is based on the assumption that it is possible to do just this; Proudhon sees in government only the denial and frustration of individual will. For him rule by the general will reduces to a transfiguration of the tyranny of the faceless, hostile State of old.

Thus stated, his complaint may seem only an exaggerated expression of what democrats freely agree to: that in submitting to the general will, individuals often are required to accept what they do not personally want. However, they say that the prevailing of the general will should result in the greatest good for the greatest number and, by means of majority rule, the conflict between individual and general wills should be minimized. General participation in the process of law-making and government, with free debate and consequent compromise of opposing views, should further reduce differences, preserving the essence of liberty. However, Proudhon cannot accept this; his criticism is more radical than simple objection to the relation of individual and general wills. He believes that the concept of general will is itself a delusory fiction, together with all the associated justification of democratic government. Only individual will has any reality.

Proudhon's critique here is more than just an individualist's antagonism toward the subordination of the individual to the collectivity. His vision of the character of society itself differs from that of the Rousseauean tradition, and this is essential for his approach to politics.

Rousseau believes that society as it has developed is depraved.

Corrupt society has corrupted man; if human corruption is to be eliminated, then society itself must first be purified. He assumes that this is to be accomplished by the reconstruction of the political and legal system, together with the extension of knowledge and education.

Rousseau's is an idea common in Enlightenment philosophy and assumed, often without explicit consideration, in the theories of the revolutionary tradition. Before the Enlightenment the Christian belief in the depravity of man and the attribution of human misfortunes to the consequences of human sinfulness were the commonplace bases of political philosophy. The new philosophy rejected these assumptions, transforming the basic questions of the human condition from those of personal morality and divine will to those of social institutions and the prescriptions of universal rational truth. The source of evil is no longer within man: the "problem of man" has become the "problem of society."

Proudhon essentially accepts the transformation made by Enlightenment rationalism, together with many of its assumptions, but he does so with some major deviations from the ideology of the Rousseauean tradition. He does not assert that man could be good if only he were not corrupted by depraved society, nor does he believe in Christian notions of original sin, the inevitability of human sinfulness, or divine origin of human misfortune.[9] For him, although man can become good, he is deeply flawed at present. While only a restructuring of society will make moral regeneration possible, deliberate voluntary effort by every individual is essential both to moral regeneration and to successful conclusion of social reconstruction.

Not only does Proudhon deny that social reconstruction and solution of the social problem can be accomplished by political instrumentalities. He also believes that the approach to reconciliation of social conflict taken by Rousseauean theory is completely wrong. In seeking to regulate social conflict by political institutions, it is assumed that society has a collective being whose existence is made concrete in these institutions. The state represents the collective

9. This matter is treated at length in the *Système des contradictions économiques, Oeuv.*, I, vol. i, 349–98; this is the chapter referred to in the passage quoted above, p. 143.

being of society; the will of the state should be the general will of the collective being.

Involved in this conception of collective being is a supposition that conflict between individuals with sharply disparate interests must be overcome. Some conflict can be acceptable, as in commercial competition, if opponents exercise self-control. However, more often it will be necessary, because ultimately more advantageous to all, for conflicting individual interests to be deferred to the higher requirements of the collective. Dissonance is to be reduced to the vanishing point by smoothing over and blurring the conflicts. Their significance will diminish as pursuit of collective interests progressively eliminates the sources of conflict, decreases their influence, or controls and finally removes them through restriction and suppression. In order for social order to be maintained, many individual urges and interests must be submerged in the life and will of the whole. Society can be made good by removing or repressing whatever gives occasion for dissonance.

It is apparent from the sociology in his *Contradictions économiques* and *Création de l'ordre* that Proudhon does think of society as a being *sui generis,* distinct from the individuals who compose it. However, this distinctive being is just the manifestation of those individual human qualities which find definition only in collective life. He refuses to personify the collective being. Society's needs do not supersede those of individuals: the requirements of the whole are just those of the parts. There is no general will, but only that of individuals.

Thus Proudhon reacts negatively against conventional conceptions of society, especially the virtual personification of it in Rousseauean notions of collective being and general will. Regulation of the collectivity by means of government seeks to control and eliminate conflict and difference: diversity is the serpent in the Garden of Eden. For the anarchist this is tyranny through the forcible imposition of uniformity.

He believes that differences between people are too essential to human nature for the elimination or restriction of diversity's effects to be either possible or desirable. Social order can be achieved only through acceptance of the diversity of individuals, and accommodation to difference rather than control of it.

As we have seen, Proudhon is convinced that attitudes of others toward social conflict are no more realistic than they are just. Most would repress the irrepressible while fatalistically accepting some conflict as unavoidable though noxious. With unwarranted optimism many expect significant conflict to disappear with technological and economic development and the reformation of the polity, but without fundamental change in the social structure. Others have an essentially pessimistic view of man and his future; they would use both imperative authority and the powers afforded by new knowledge to make conflict and its fruits more bearable, yet not to alter its foundations. All of them misunderstand or ignore the most severe problems of social and economic inequality and the clashes between men it gives rise to.

Proudhon's socialist contemporaries better recognize the gravity and extent of social problems and the necessity of confronting them. Nevertheless, he thinks other socialists are wrong because they expect to eliminate clashes of personal interests by eliminating their sources, which are thought of as due wholly to social injustice. Conflict would be replaced by the harmony of a community of interests, the "collective being" in new, more egalitarian clothes.

Since he emphasizes that it is natural for men to differ, and that individual desires and interests would not be submerged in those of the whole, he cannot accept the plans of other socialists for reorganization of society. Their schemes would still force subordination of the individual to an unreal abstraction, the collective. A true commonweal or community of interests can be achieved, but only if conflict is recognized as normal.

Reorganization of society must be executed through elimination of those elements which render conflicts between men unequal, enabling some to overpower the rest. Proudhon's goal is not a static utopia or one progressing while in a continually conflict-free condition, but a state of dynamic equilibrium, flexible, changing, yet basically stable. Rather than uniformity there should be order in diversity through the balancing of different wills and interests against each other.

While conflicting interests and wills are to be balanced rather than eliminated, Proudhon does think that aggravated antagonism between men can be avoided, if relationships between men are just. For him disturbance of social order is the result of injustice which transforms normal differences between men into occasions for injury and disorder.

Although Proudhon's approach here differs from most contemporary views, many of his notions about conflict and dynamic society are compatible with more conventional ideas. However, he says that essential features of the existing society or utopian ones must inevitably cause the kind of aggravated antagonism that cannot be justified. This makes him radically different, a social revolutionary and an anarchist.

Like others, he thinks that order in society and protection of man's rights can be achieved through "social contract," but he does not conceive of it as did Rousseau or Locke. Unlike theirs, his social contract is not the basis of government, but a mode of human relationships which is to be realized only by the total abolition of government.

Proudhon specifies that contracts are mutual agreements between individuals with differing interests and an expectation that each party to the contract will benefit from it. Alternatively, they are such agreements between groups, the members of each group having common interests with respect to the terms of the contract.

This should be the character of a social contract, where men acting as individuals and treated as individuals freely enter into contractual relationships with each other, negotiating them anew in each fresh situation. Thereby they voluntarily undertake obligations to each other, for mutual benefit. They are not bound by rules, laws, or agreements made by and for other men. They are not compelled to undertake the obligations, nor are they constrained to accept terms unfavorable to themselves.

"The social contract must add to the well-being and liberty of each citizen." If one party is subordinated or exploited by another, or is deceived or ignorant about the nature of the terms, it is not a contract but a fraud. "The social contract must be freely debated, consented to individually, and signed, *manu propria*, by all those participating in it." [10] Everyone must be included in making any

10. *Oeuv.*, II, 189. Proudhon's mature conception of social contract in a just society is examined below in Ch. 11.

arrangements affecting him. If exclusive, the contract is no longer social, but special and relative.

In contrast, the usual conceptions of social contract do not require deliberate and explicit consent by every man on every occasion, although the desirability of this consent may be admitted. Requirements such as Proudhon's cannot actually be adhered to if there is to be any government or collective authority. In practice, authority must act despite objections from some citizens, since universal consent to its every action cannot be obtained. Instead, "social contract" plays the role of a convenient figment justifying the political system and requirements of political obligation and obedience to law. According to this conception, citizens and their government should have obligations to each other and derive benefits thereby as if there were actually a contract specifying these relationships. Then the justice of a political system can best be evaluated in terms of how well it conforms to such a hypothetical contract.

People do not ordinarily offer their explicit consent to these arrangements. Rather, by their acceptance of the regime their "tacit consent" is assumed. If a government's rule is just, truly rational men should accept it. An individual can withdraw consent by leaving the society for another; a society withdraws consent by replacing the government with another.

Yet in reality withdrawal of consent in these ways is not usually possible. The notion of tacit consent itself is vague and vulnerable to criticism. In justifying government through use of the social-contract conception, one speaks of what must actually be explicit consent. Then to transfer this justification to conditions where consent is supposed to be essentially tacit is to engage in very dubious reasoning. To remedy this apparent fault, democrats seek a basis of explicit, active consent through citizen participation in government.

Democratic rule does not secure universal consent to every act of government, but according to theory this should not matter. Fully rational men ought to accept the acts of a just government, even when they have not actually been consulted or when they doubt the wisdom of particular acts. If they have consented to the process by which the government operates and have either participated directly in making its decisions or chosen others who do, then they should be confident that the rule is just. Each rational citizen should recognize that his particular interests have been considered in the making of decisions, and that, though fulfillment of his own needs may be deferred to those of others, he benefits equally from the advancement of the good of the whole. Thus the basis of democratic government is supposed to be the confidence of citizens in the political system, obtained through their active involvement in it and their expectation of joint benefit, rather than through universal explicit consent.

Proudhon insists that this confidence can never be merited. In claiming that confidence, government offers a promise which is only a sham.

> Oh, man in your individuality! Can it be that you have rotted in this baseness for sixty centuries? You call yourself pure and sacred, but you are only the whore, the sucker, the goat of your servants, your monks, and your mercenary soldiers. You know this and you endure it! To be GOVERNED is to be kept under surveillance, inspected, spied upon, bossed, law-ridden, regulated, penned in, indoctrinated, preached at, registered, evaluated, appraised, censured, ordered about, by creatures who have neither the right, nor the knowledge, nor the virtue to do so. To be GOVERNED is to be at each operation, at each transaction, at each movement, marked down, recorded, inventoried, priced, stamped, measured, numbered, assessed, licensed, authorized, sanctioned, endorsed, reprimanded, obstructed, reformed, rebuked, chastised. It is, under the pretense of public benefit and in the name of the general interest, to be requisitioned, drilled, fleeced, exploited, monopolized, extorted, squeezed, hoaxed, robbed; then at the slightest resistance, the first word of complaint, to be squelched, corrected, vilified, bullied, hounded, tormented, bludgeoned, disarmed, strangled, imprisoned, shot down, judged, condemned, deported, sacrificed, sold, betrayed, and to top it off, ridiculed, made a fool of, outraged, dishonored. That's government, that's its justice, that's its morality! And to think that there are democrats among us who claim that there is some good in government—socialists who support this infamy in the name of Liberty, Equality, and Fraternity—

proletarians who proclaim their candidacy for the Presidency of the Republic! Hypocrisy! [11]

This conveys the spirit of Proudhon's case against government. His substantive arguments are expressed with more restraint, but their import is equivalent.

11. Ibid., 344.

seven: Anarchism

MISCELLANEOUS EVENTS

A traveler arriving from the United States has sworn to us that Proudhon is living in Philadelphia, and that the celebrated revolutionary, in order to utilize his spare time, has made himself a teacher of music. He teaches harmony. It was high time, after having preached discord so much. On the evidence of the communication given us we take the liberty of telling the maestro some hard truths.

In-fernal utopian without a god or soul,
Re-trograde windbag with a worn-out system,
Mi-racle of impudence in this deluded century,
Par-tial to the rogues for whom you make demands,
Sun-whose light is kind to thieves,
The-land would know your baneful worth,
If-every man with mettle told you hard truths.[1]

[In the original, a play on words is made. "Tell hard truths" translates an idiom, *chanter une gamme,* which literally is "sing a scale." The separated first syllables on the successive lines of the verse make up the musical scale.]

" 'To FIND A FORM of association which defends and protects, with the whole common force, the person and goods of each associate . . .' This is the fundamental problem for which the Social Contract gives the solution." To this statement of Rousseau, Proudhon responds:

1. Newspaper clipping pasted by Proudhon in his *Carnet,* December, 1852, X, 45. Notation in his hand: "Courrier de Marseille 26 9ᵇʳᵉ [November] no. 2832." Proudhon never left Europe.

Yes, indeed these are the conditions of the social pact, *as far as the protection and defense of goods and the person are concerned.* But as for the mode of acquisition and transmission of goods, for exchange, for the value and price of products, for education, for that multitude of relationships which for better or worse establishes man in perpetual society with his fellows, of all this Rousseau says not a word: his theory is of the most perfect insignificance.[2]

By emphasizing this "multitude of relationships" Proudhon focuses on the differentiation and unique individuality of men in society. The ideas of government he opposes have to assume that there is a large measure of uniformity among men and their relationships. This is done whenever "society," "the people," "the nation," or "the collective being" is spoken of as a unitary whole. Because of its claim to universal application, the rule of law rests upon a presumption that the body politic does have such a unitary and integral character.

Proudhon is willing to speak of a collective being only if the differences within it are fully and constantly recognized. For him there can be unity in diversity, but not a homogeneous unity. The potential unity of a society is a matter of *spirit* (the bonds between men resulting from feelings of sociability) and of *mutual dependence* (bonds resulting from need for joint action and for exchange of service and products).

These bonds, though real and vital, cannot be translated into the kind of definite, concrete terms required by the prescriptive authority of political institutions. The relationships are too varied and too rapidly changing, and they too often rest upon indefinite sentiments like friendship, special sympathy for neighbors, or love for family and home. And, even if the potential rationality of all men should provide a basis for universalism, irrational passions are also natural to man and cannot be neglected or suppressed.

Thus collective being cannot be regarded as having unique qualities and needs or its own unitary reason and will, for it represents a sum whose parts are too highly differentiated. Proudhon is convinced that the elements of universality in mankind must always

2. J.-J. Rousseau, *Du Contrat social,* in *The Political Writings of Rousseau,* ed. C. E. Vaughan (Oxford, 1962), II, 32. Rousseau's first draft of this passage has "the institution of the State" in the place of "the social contract" (ibid., note 2). *Oeuv.,* II, 191. Proudhon refers here to Rousseau's statement, which he quotes.

be too limited in scope to permit the just prescription of systematic, universal rules for the regulation of human conduct.

This lies at the heart of all his arguments against government, just as belief in an integral collectivity must underlie any positive conception of government. While Proudhon's anarchism embraces much more than attacks on the rational grounds of political institutions, many of his most original and incisive ideas are developed from this critique of assumptions about collective being. To illustrate his perspective more fully, one of his major statements of it should be quoted at length. The passage is from a polemic against two of his most prominent socialist adversaries, Louis Blanc and Pierre Leroux.

> What is the State? . . . The State is the EXTERIOR constitution of society's dominion.
>
> By this exterior constitution of their own power and sovereignty, the people do not govern themselves: instead one or a few individuals, by elective or hereditary title, are charged with governing them, administering their affairs, dealing and compromising in their name—in a word, performing all the acts of a father of a family, guardian, manager or agent, provided with a general, absolute and irrevocable power of attorney.
>
> This external constitution of collective dominion—which the Greeks called *arche*—sovereignty, authority, government, rests on the hypothesis that a people, whose collective being we call society, cannot govern itself, think, act or express itself in ways analogous to those of beings endowed with individual personality. It supposes that they must be represented by one or several individuals who, by whatever right, are deemed the depositories of the people's will and their agents. According to this hypothesis it is impossible for collective power, which essentially belongs to the mass, to express itself and act directly, without intermediary organs expressly constituted and insinuated for that purpose. It seems, we say—and this explains the constitution of the State in all its varieties and species—that the collective being, society, being only a creature of the imagination, can be rendered perceptible only by monarchical incarnation, aristocratic usurpation, or democratic mandate. Consequently, its own and personal manifestation is wholly denied to it.
>
> Now, it is precisely this notion of collective being, its life, action, unity, individuality, personality—for society is a person, as

all humanity is a person—it is this notion of the collective human being [as only imaginary] that we deny here. Likewise, we deny the State and government, and we reject from economically revolutionized society all constitution of popular power outside and above the mass, by hereditary royalty, feudal institutions, or democratic delegation.

We insist, on the contrary, that the people, the society, the mass, can and must govern itself, think, act, rise, and stop like a man, manifest itself finally in its physical, intellectual, and moral individuality, without the aid of all the interpreters who formerly were despots, who now are aristocrats, and who at one time or another have been sham delegates, sycophants or servants of the mob, whom we call purely and simply popular agitators, *demagogues*.

In brief, we deny government and the State because we affirm what founders of States have never believed, the personality and the autonomy of the masses.

We assert moreover that any State constitution has no other goal than to lead society to this state of autonomy; that the different forms of States, from absolute monarchy to representative *democracy*, are only intermediate positions, illogical and unstable, serving turn by turn as transitions or stages in liberty, and forming the steps of the political scale with whose aid societies ascend in conscience and possession of their own selves.

We assert, finally, that this *anarchy*, which as is now seen expresses the highest degree of liberty and order which humanity can attain, is the true formula of the Republic, the goal toward which we urged the February Revolution, so that there is contradiction between the Republic and government, between universal suffrage and the State.[3]

This represents one face of Proudhon's anarchism, his belief that no institution can speak or act for the whole of society. This is a basic article of faith which he buttresses with elaborate criticism of the various ways political theorists say government can act as the true embodiment of society.

Yet he does not think that the people of a society can act as one for themselves, either. There can be no concrete, unitary expres-

3. "Résistance à la révolution" (second article), *La Voix du peuple*, no. 64 (December 3, 1849); *Oeuv.*, II, 367–69. In speaking of "the People" Proudhon consistently uses singular verbs, pronouns, and adjectives; in my translations I use both singular and plural forms, according to variations in meaning and common English usage.

sion of the people simply because of their diversity. This denial of a definable popular will provides the basis of much of his attack on democracy, and especially on those democrats who would maximize active popular participation in government.

Thus he says that the people "can and must govern itself," yet goes on to assert that they cannot act as one. The apparent contradiction disappears when we recognize that for him collective action and self-governance emerge only from the separate acts of individuals and small groups. He thinks that ideas of a more coherent people are just illusory abstractions from perceptions of separate action. Suppositions that there is a single joint will and decision to act in deliberate accord have no basis in reality.

> I ask then, like Rousseau: If the People has spoken, why have I heard nothing?
>
> You point out to me this astonishing revolution in which I too have taken part—whose legitimacy I myself have proven, whose idea I have brought to the fore. And you say to me: There is the People!
>
> But in the first place, I have seen only a tumultuous crowd without awareness of the ideas that made it act, without any comprehension of the revolution brought about by its hands. Then what I have called the logic of the People could well be nothing but recognition of past events, all the more so since once it is all over and everyone agrees on their significance, opinions are divided anew as to the consequences. The revolution over, the People says nothing! . . .
>
> In principle then, I admit that the People exists, that it is sovereign, that it is predicated in the consciousness of the masses. But nothing yet has proven to me that it can perform an overt act of sovereignty, that an explicit revelation of the People is possible. For, in view of the dominance of prejudices, of the contradiction of ideas and interests, of the variability of opinion, and of the impulsiveness of the multitude, I shall always ask what establishes the authenticity and legitimacy of such a revelation—and this is what democracy cannot answer.[4]

The People is an abstraction which does not think; it does not reason; it does not decide; it does not will. The People must be

---

4. *Solution du problème social, Oeuv. (Lacroix)*, VI, 37, 46. In this tract Proudhon elaborates on this theme with exceptional eloquence.

thought of as numbers of reasoning individuals, not as a single entity making decisions which the state executes. The People does not govern; only individuals do. There is no general will, for there is no general mind to do the willing. Government is always *outside* the society and imposed upon it. No matter how government is constituted, its will is always something other than the wills of the citizens, and their wills must thereby be subordinated, their liberty diminished.

Such extreme individualism may appear antisocial, but his is not. Instead, he argues that the institutions created to regulate social intercourse are themselves antisocial because they are totally alien to society. He thinks that Rousseauean ideas about the corruption of man by a depraved society lead logically to a conclusion that man should be isolated from society as much as possible. This would be a sort of individualism, and may suggest the controlling spirit of the individualism, or egoism, of commercial practice.

Proudhon does not want the individual isolated from society at all; he seeks to alter the character of social relationships, thereby both liberating the individual and fully integrating him into society. Society "corrupts" when its elements are opposed in hostility to one another. With equitable relationships, antagonized divisions can disappear and society can become as it should be, the natural medium in which man fulfills himself.

Proudhon's contemporaries concentrate on the qualities that individuals and groups are supposed to have in common. When differences are plain, as between different levels of wealth and social status, they emphasize or assume uniformity of interests and attitudes within social groups—classes—of large size. In order to find a basis for conscious unity and systematic theory they distinguish elements of universality, trying to discover or create patterns of homogeneity so that they can render coherent apparent diversity.

In contrast, Proudhon considers society as an intricate web of highly differentiated personal relationships. Social behavior is essentially a matter of unique and independent acts of distinct, spontaneous individual wills, in a context of intimate interdependency. In manifold social relationships elements of universality cannot constitute unity or identity: common elements are always accompanied by unique ones.

Proudhon emphasizes the complexity and variety of social relationships much more than most in his time did, but others did not ignore it. While sociology and allied sciences were then relatively primitive, they were aware of many of society's qualities of complexity. Their theories often were quite complicated, as they tried to take man's variability into account. In particular, Fourier, whose thought could have influenced Proudhon in this regard, tried in marvelously elaborate ways to analyze human variety and to provide for it in his utopian plans.

The anarchist, however, thinks we must act with the unique as primary determinant, while the others believe that intelligent action has to rest on knowledge of the general. He would have us treat each encounter between men as novel, while they would treat it as a particular instance of what happens regularly. Thus they would regulate conduct with normative prescriptions, while he would leave men autonomous, regulating their own behavior through individual conscience and voluntary mutual agreement.

Proudhon recalls concepts of Roman law by distinguishing between "distributive" and "commutative" justice. In his definition, the former is based on laws prescribed and enforced by governing institutions, the latter on voluntary conventions for exchange of goods and services. Commutative conventions are his idea of true social contracts. Laws should be agreements serving to regularize the processes of exchange, not the imposed rules of an imperative authority. Thus conceived, law assumes the form of reciprocal guarantees, undertaken anew in each contract.

There can also be some few laws which are normative rules, but they must also be conventional in basis, not prescriptive. Thus, for instance, men may agree that homicide or rape is never justifiable, or that vehicles shall always travel on the right-hand side of the road. They should not prescribe and enforce laws specifying how any violation of these standards should be treated. Even where agreement to norms is universal, each departure from the standard is made unique by its particular circumstances, and justice cannot be rendered through enforcement of universal prescriptions.

Both in its origin in Roman law and its relevance to existing forms of commercial exchange, Proudhon's idea of commutative justice bears connotations of petit bourgeois business probity. An imputation of petit bourgeois perspective here would be mistaken, however. His ideas of exchange relationships are derived from very different considerations and set in a context quite alien to any system of belief appropriate to customary business enterprise.

However, "commerce" is an important part of Proudhon's outlook, for his conception of the exchange process is more than a concern for the preservation of individuality and natural social relationships. To him, labor is the very center of individual and social existence, and the exchange of goods and services the circulation of lifeblood. Thus the most vital social relationships are "commercial"; social revolution's purpose must be to transform the exploitive commerce of today into transactions for equal, reciprocal benefit.[5]

Proudhon's anti-statist critique of political institutions can seem just a libertarian individualism divorced from any economic vision. Many have drawn conclusions to this effect from selective reading of a few of his books, especially the *Idée générale*. However, his conceptions of economic and political justice form a closely integrated whole, as his ideas about commutative conventions demonstrate.

More broadly inclusive, though, is his attitude toward Jacobinism and the revolutionary tradition more generally. In condemning them for concentrating on political issues, he recognizes that many republicans want to "solve the social problem" as well. Proudhon attacks them because he believes that political reconstruction cannot be separated from social and economic reconstruction.

His principal criticisms of government then go on to argue that none of the forms of political reconstruction which have been attempted or envisaged can prove satisfactory, for they actually prevent necessary social change. No form of imperative authority is compatible with the requirements of social and economic justice.

Reacting against an almost universal belief in government as the only possible guarantor of order, Proudhon scorns the idea that government is a necessity and only its abuse an evil. He says that, in assuming that this idea is true, men resist governments and revolt against them—only to end by an act of faith in government, sub-

5. His schemes for mutual banking represent a concrete application of this line of thought.

mitting to its power once it has been altered in its outer form. Yet alterations such as the establishment of constitutional limitations on the State's authority are only illusory, hypocritical modifications: in its essence the authority remains absolute and therefore tyrannical.

Authority is the fundamental principle of any government: impose genuinely significant constraints upon it, and there is no government. Political authority justifies itself by claiming to be the sole means of preserving order. This assumes that antagonism between people is natural, and that they must be restrained by powerful authority for order to be maintained. Such restraint is the basic activity of any government, no matter how constituted.

These political assumptions appear to Proudhon to represent humanity as naturally and permanently savage, with the masses presumed to be morally and intellectually inert and unchanging. He, on the other hand, believes that men are capable of both moral and intellectual growth, while imposed authority can never force them to be good, or even to be merely obedient to its requirements. Men can be good only by their own efforts, and they can succeed if unimpeded by the restraints and antagonisms of an unjust society.

Proudhon thinks that people are now too divided, too egoistic, and too often controlled by nonrational or falsely reasoned motivations for them to govern themselves. In this he is much more pessimistic than democrats, who assume that people will participate in a democratic polity with the needed measure of rationality. Nevertheless, because of his greater expectations for human moral and intellectual growth, his vision is ultimately more optimistic than that of any who suppose that government control must always be necessary.

Government, he believes, has served a necessary function in the past, for it helped mankind to progress when individual capacities for self-governance were still less developed than now. Nevertheless, if man's progressive development is to continue and his potential be fulfilled, government must be supplanted. Merely altering its form is insufficient, since this can make no essential change in the barriers it maintains.

> The Constitution of the State supposes besides, with regard to its object, that antagonism or a state of war is the essential and indelible condition of humanity, necessitating intervention between

the *weak* and the *strong* by a coercive force which puts an end to the combat, by means of general oppression. We maintain that the State's mission in this regard is finished; that, through the division of labor, industrial solidarity, the taste of well-being, and equal distribution of capital and revenue, liberty and justice gain guarantees more sure than all those religion and the State have ever offered.[6]

Under present conditions the rich are strong and the poor weak, and the inevitable antagonism between them is the most serious source of social disorder. Government does not use its coercive powers to restore and preserve the order thus disturbed, but to protect the rich and join them in oppression of their victims. However popular its origin, the State is always the servant of the wealthier classes, the scraps of service it yields to the rest standing for little in comparison to what it takes from them. A democratic regime might avoid this initially, but it inevitably will become increasingly exclusive, for the wealthier citizens are best able to claim the preference of the State and soon will control it. However egalitarian its origin, government naturally tends toward a reinforcement of special privilege. Preserving order comes to be just a matter of protecting property—and on this basis there can be no true order: ". . . the history of governments is the martyrology of the proletariat." [7]

In his newspaper articles and *Confessions*, Proudhon frequently reiterated attacks on the State as the exclusive preserve of the rich. This provoked vigorous response from socialists and some nonsocialist republicans, who maintained that their plans for democratic rule would ensure equal protection and service for all. He in turn replied with some of his best polemics, among them the series of articles attacking Louis Blanc and Pierre Leroux from which was drawn the long excerpt quoted earlier in this chapter.

His *Idée générale de la révolution* develops the response to these critics into a systematic effort to demonstrate that, even in the best possible form (democracy), government cannot be what its advocates intend. This line of argument, much of it found in a section of the fourth *étude* called the "General Critique of the Idea of Authority," is one of the most distinctive elements of Proudhon's

6. *Oeuv.*, II, 380.
7. Ibid., 184.

anarchism. He writes in direct reply to radical democratic schemes of four men: Emile de Girardin, who proposed a "simplified government" with universal suffrage; Moritz Rittinghausen and Victor Considérant—"direct legislation"; and A.-A. Ledru-Rollin—"direct government." [8]

Proudhon's method is to reduce to absurdity the idea of government by distinguishing, then demolishing in turn, five successively more "liberal" forms: absolute rule, constitutional monarchy, universal suffrage, direct legislation, and direct government. He deliberately discards the categories traditionally employed in such comparisons—monarchy, aristocracy, and democracy. His identification of categories is just a methodical device, for he thinks that the most significant features of government are universal characteristics, whatever the form of constitution. Taxonomies of government types so often employed in political theory only classify differences he believes to be illusory or of no real consequence.

In his schema he represents absolute authority as the "purest, most rational, energetic, and honest form of government and the least immoral and painful." If government's primary purpose and justification is the maintenance of social order, then it should reasonably follow that the stronger government is the more perfect government. Regimes with restricted authority are less able to compel obedience, but no better able to reconcile the social discord which justifies imperative authority in the first place.

Proudhon's contentions here are vulnerable to counterattack: a democratic regime may secure greater obedience through the citizens' confidence in it than absolute government can through simple compulsion or respect for a monarch. Such criticisms would not bother Proudhon, however, for he speaks thus of absolute government only as a step in arguing that, no matter how exercised, authority is effectively absolute in any government. It can suppress but not eliminate destructive antagonism. Being oppressed, the people will always end by seeing the State as their enemy. If ever obtained, confidence must dissipate and compulsion remain as the

8. As is often the case, Proudhon misrepresents the ideas of others while arguing against them. The following discussion takes these men's ideas as in his version of them.

chief instrument of the State. Since this only aggravates discord, the process of government inevitably is self-defeating.

> At all events, men of power, here is what is said by the Producer, the proletarian, the slave, those whom you aim to make work for you: I ask neither the wealth nor the work of anyone, and I am not ready to suffer the fruit of my labor being pilfered by others. I too want order, as much and more as those who disturb it with their sham government; but I want it as a result of my will, a condition of my labor and a law of my reason. I will never submit to its coming from an alien will and imposing servitude and sacrifice on me as prior conditions.[9]

Even though sovereignty may be said to be the whole people's, political authority in fact is always exercised by a relatively small number. They may be a king and his ministers or the executive of a democracy but, whether they hold it by their own right or by delegation, authority is theirs to exercise. The people are not coherent enough, even if otherwise able, to wield it directly themselves. Those who do wield authority have their own conceptions of how government's purposes can best be fulfilled, and many of those whom they rule must inevitably differ from them. This is no way to reconcile divergent wills. There can be no true self-government: the wills of most men will be frustrated and their liberty denied in any political system.

Authority is the power to make and enforce laws, which themselves define and order government's system of regulation. Laws serve both to direct the conduct of those governed and to specify the extent and limits of the rulers' power. Lawmakers are confronted by innumerable different individuals and interests, with infinitely varied relationships between them and unlimited potential for antagonism. In order to contend with all this, the laws are multiplied in number and complexity, applying more and more widely. Sometimes it is said that by keeping the laws simple and few in number, they can be made just—but this simplicity is impossible when the human relationships to be regulated are so manifold and complex. Then even in a democracy every citizen will have reason to be

9. Ibid., 203.

dissatisfied and even profoundly aggrieved with much of the law and its execution.

Democratic theory maintains that dissatisfaction with some particular laws need not cause disaffection, since citizens should remain bound to the State and the law by their participation in the political system and their consequent confidence in its process. Even when he might have preferred an alternative measure, a citizen actively involved in the system can accept his fellows' contrary judgments, because his own views and needs have been weighed in making the decision.

Proudhon has to reject this line of argument, since he contends that the State is necessarily an alien and hostile force that can neither merit nor secure such faith. Though this is the fundamental thesis of his anarchism, he also goes to considerable effort to demonstrate how little a citizen in a democracy really has an opportunity to affect the making and administration of laws. If citizens do not even participate in this process indirectly, then democracy's claims to justification lack validity, and there is no more reason to say a man is free, or bound in allegiance to the State and its laws, in a democratic system than in one of absolute monarchy.

> I am ready to negotiate, but I want no laws. I recognize none of them. I protest against every order where a power is pleased to pretend it necessary to impose on my free will. Laws! People know what they are and what they are worth. Cobwebs for the powerful and rich, chains that no sword can break for the little ones and the poor, fishing nets stretched between the hands of Government.[10]

Political theorists may say that the whole people ought by right to rule but, even as they make this claim for popular sovereignty in theory, they find reason to place the main responsibility for governance elsewhere. Against this Proudhon contends that only the actual exercise of authority matters, not some abstract notion about where sovereignty resides. He develops this theme through examination of constitutional monarchy, which he considers to be primarily an attempt to curb the corruption of power and abuse of authority which can occur when the king is absolute. Constitutionalists may say that a monarchy thus limited is based

10. Ibid., 205.

on popular sovereignty, arguing that the people and the throne share in the exercise of authority because the monarch regularly consults with his subjects, or at least with the most notable of their number. Thereby government and the people remain in communion, while the nation benefits by having the final decision reserved to the deliberate wisdom and undivided judgment of the throne.

But "consultation with subjects" is a fiction, for the throne is not bound by such a process, exercising its authority independent of the wishes of those who must obey it. The monarchy is limited only by laws the people did not make themselves; its authority is absolute with respect to the mass of the population which has no active part in wielding power.

Proudhon's point is that a democracy is essentially the same. Between absolute monarchy and the most radical democracy there are only variations in the portion of the citizens supposed to participate and in the degree of their involvement. But the variations are delusory and the participation meaningless, because the authority is always wielded by someone else. Whether a monarch "consults" or officials stand periodically for election, it makes no real difference. Each form of government from absolute monarchy to democracy can be no more than an illogical and unstable position, a transitional stage in progression toward full autonomy for individuals within society.

In denying that variations in citizen participation can matter, Proudhon asks why number should offer a more rational, authentic, or moral basis than faith or force. Why should the ballot be more sure than tradition or heredity? Is rule by force of the strongest any more a usurpation of human rights than rule by number? What is number anyway—what does it prove, what is it worth? What relation is there between the opinion of voters and truth, between their opinions and what is right?

Why, he demands, should I submit the matters of closest concern to me and my family to the arbitrary decision of an assembly of strangers who do not know or understand me? What guarantee does the assembly make to me? "Why would I make on its authority this enormous, irreparable sacrifice, to accept what it decides by itself as the expression of my will, the just measure of my rights?"

When this assembly, after debates to which I was not party, imposes on me its decision as law, at the point of the bayonet, how am I a part of a sovereign whole?[11]

One premise of theories of popular sovereignty is the supposition that men with power in the State hold their authority by delegation from the people. This presumes that these delegates are able to know what are the best interests and the desires of the people they govern. Proudhon is convinced, however, that those with authority are too distant in background and outlook from most of the populace.

His entire experience of parliamentary government has been of assemblies dominated by bourgeois deputies. Even if middle- and upper-class deputies are (as they are supposed to be) the most capable members of the society, he cannot believe that they are able to understand the true interests of the masses and represent them adequately. Reason and his experience, especially that as a deputy in the Assembly himself, tell him otherwise.

So far even universal suffrage has not produced a government free from attachment to special class and economic interests. Proudhon thinks that any parliamentary government is most likely to be a bourgeois one, and that the bourgeoisie can never rule disinterestedly. Not only can they neither understand nor care much about the needs of the lower classes but, more important, bourgeois and lower-class interests are fundamentally and irrevocably opposed. The middle class can truly serve those beneath them only at an impossible cost in self-sacrifice.

However, even a genuinely popular government, including many members of the lower classes, would be too distant from the people. Proudhon had been dismayed by his own experience in June, 1848, when he was so busy with his work in the Assembly that he lost touch with his Parisian working-class constituents. If even he became separated from the people, what of others in government whose ties with the people are less close than his?

Government business is an engrossing affair for those directly involved in it. The halls of government are a world apart in themselves. The mechanisms and devices of politics and those of administration become so involved that concern for them replaces original

11. Ibid., 209.

concerns directly related to the needs and desires of the people. Though animated by lively intelligence and sincere desire to serve the people, the men who hold authority in their hands use it while quite separate from the people they govern.

Government, if it is to have any hope of adequately handling the complex problems it confronts, should be conducted by the ablest and most honest men in the society.[12] This may be reasonable, but, Proudhon suggests, this only replaces the aristocracy of birth with an aristocracy of talent. Saint-Simon found this more desirable because he thought that disinterested, fully rational administration could solve all problems; Proudhon, of course, thinks this a delusion. He objects to Saint-Simon and to democracy because he is sure that this new aristocracy ultimately will be just as foreign to the masses as was the old one.

Moreover, the government need not be one of talent for an artificial aristocracy to be created. Power constitutes privilege, and authority elevates its possessors above the masses. Every factor increases the separation of the rulers from those ruled. Only a small portion of the population can serve in government, since most are needed to get on with productive labor. Thus with any kind of government there is an alien, privileged ruling class, even if in a democracy its membership is not fixed or exclusive. "In short, since hierarchy is the primary condition of governments, democracy is a chimera."

Universal suffrage is no panacea. The whole population can choose representatives and officials just as badly as a select electorate does. There is nothing magic about the judgment of the multitude. "I do not believe at all, for good reason, in this divinatory intuition of the multitude, which would allow it to discern at first glance the merit and honor of the candidates." [13] Men are often elected as a result of the influence of passions, prejudices, personal antagonism—anything but reason. Proudhon characterizes the bulk of the elections since February, 1848, particularly the election of Louis-Napoleon Bonaparte to the presidency, as examples of how badly the people choose rulers.

12. The ancient Athenian practice of changing officials frequently and selecting them by lot was not seriously considered by Proudhon or his contemporaries.
13. *Solution du problème social, Oeuv. (Lacroix)*, VI, 66; *Oeuv.*, II, 210.

It is evident from the passion with which Proudhon criticizes the electoral experience of the Second Republic that much of the force with which he rejects democracy results from his disgust with the way it has worked since the 1848 Revolution began. At the beginning of the Revolution he condemns democracy on theoretical grounds in the *Solution du problème social*, but he is still hopeful that democratic institutions can be employed temporarily to good effect. After 1848 he has no use for the democratic republic at all: ". . . universal suffrage, imperative mandate, responsibility of representatives, the system defining legal capacity, in the end all that is infantile: I would not entrust my labor, my leisure, my fortune, nor risk a hair on my head to defend them." [14] These words sum up the sentiments of many of the urban workers and their allies after 1848, suggesting why the revolutionary movement in France takes on a different character in the years that follow.

Proudhon would reject democracy even if these defects could be overlooked or overcome, for he believes that it does not and cannot accomplish what it claims as its principal virtue: the participation of citizens in government and rule by consent of the governed. The ideal of democracy could be very nearly realized in ancient Greece, where productive labor was largely performed by slaves; but it is not possible now, when free workers cannot be spared from production to occupy themselves with government. It is patently false to say that universal suffrage makes all citizens a part of government.

Even the elected representatives do not actually handle the direction of public affairs. Instead, it is the ministers, their appointees, and the professional civil servants. Authority is delegated to and exercised by particular individuals; *they* are the government, not the people. Men surrender to government their own affairs and make their own judgments.

Above all else, citizens in a democracy are supposed to participate in making the laws. Justice is supposed to follow if the system for making the laws is just and the laws are issued with the consent of the governed. But the citizens do not approve the laws; they only vote for representatives who do this for them. The representatives, once elected, can do as they please. Thus democracy is absolutism:

14. *Oeuv.*, II, 214.

in essence the power of the representatives is as total and unchecked as that of an absolute monarchy. The fact that the persons with this power are changed more frequently and through the mechanism of elections does not alter this essential quality, as far as Proudhon is concerned.

He does not seriously consider the possibility that representatives may feel a sense of obligation or compulsion to adhere to the will of their constituents, as a matter of duty or of desire to maintain potential strength at the polls. The French had not by 1851 had enough experience with the practical operations of politics in a democracy to make balanced judgments about it. Indeed, what Proudhon had observed inclined him to believe that the representatives would for the most part follow the direction of the ministry passively, leaving real control of the legislative process in the hands of a very few men. More important, his conviction that deputies cannot know their constituents and that there is no collective will does not permit him to accept the possibility that representative government can be responsive to the will of the electorate, whatever the exigencies of politics may be.

A few of Proudhon's contemporaries, notably Rittinghausen with his *La Législation directe par le peuple ou la véritable démocratie*,[15] attempted to eliminate the alleged defects of representative democracy by proposing that all legislative decisions be made by the direct vote of the entire body of citizens. The justification of representative legislative institutions is that there are too many citizens for effective deliberation and decision by all of them, and that most of them have not the time or qualifications for legislative work themselves. Agreeing with Proudhon that representative legislation is not just, proponents of "direct legislation" contend that such a process can be conducted effectively. Proudhon rejects their proposals—but not primarily because they might be impractical.

He asserts that his major objections to democratic government apply equally well to democracy with direct legislation in place of representative processes. It still makes uniform and impersonal law. The deliberative assembly still decides with one voice, whatever its number and portion of the citizenry, and whatever its degree

15. (Paris: Librairie Phalanstérienne, 1850).

of agreement, making rules which govern all men in their diversity uniformly.

One of the greatest "absurdities" of both the elective and the legislative processes remains, whatever the system. A plurality as small as that of one vote can prevail. Parliamentary and elective institutions are supposed to be justified by their claim to determine the will of the electorate—but how can they make this claim when the electorate is so divided that the victorious faction is little larger than the losing one? In many instances the victorious faction may be a distinct minority of the total of those eligible to vote. A law is supposed to be just when it is decided by a democratic vote, yet in a close vote the switch of just one voter or the addition of absentees may alter the decision. How can a proposed norm be made "right" or "wrong" by pluralities of just a few votes out of many? What gives that magic rightness to any plurality?

The trouble lies in the false conception, present in all democratic thought, of the nature of popular sovereignty. "What M. Rittinghausen looks for, without saying so, is the general, collective, synthetic, indivisible Thought, in a word the Thought of the People, considered not as a multitude, nor as an imaginary being, but as a superior and living existence." [16] Rittinghausen seeks to approximate rule by the "general will" of society more closely through direct legislation than can be done with votes by representatives. Here once more is the notion of Rousseau's general will which Proudhon has rejected so emphatically. The entire virtue of the direct legislation theory, in his view, lies in its claim to offer a better means of expressing a general will which does not really exist.

This theory of direct legislation not only takes the People as a real personality with individuality, essence, thought, and will, but also assumes that the will and thought of the People is discovered by the process of voting. Decisions agreed to by a majority should command all because they represent the will of the People. Here Proudhon attacks the concept of the collective will from a somewhat different direction, questioning democrats' understanding of the meaning of popular sovereignty, which assumes such special importance in the advocacy of direct legislation. He asks how, if some disagree with the majority decision, they can be a part of People

16. *Oeuv.*, II, 216.

when the collective will is not theirs. He insists that the People is one and indivisible, not a majority and minority—but it is also a collection of individuals, not a personal being in itself. When a majority prevails, you do not have sovereignty of the People, but only that of a portion who constitute a special group. In other words, Proudhon believes that it is logically nonsensical to say that a part equals the whole, and he believes that every theory of popular government rests on this fallacious assumption. The whole must include all its parts and, since they are all different, the sum can have only descriptive and symbolic significance.

Proudhon refers to Rousseau's dictum, "It is against the natural order that the greater number govern and the smaller be governed." [17] On this he himself insists, but he also maintains that democracy cannot avoid introducing the "tyranny of the majority," since the Rousseauean general will is a delusory fiction. More precisely, the trouble is the tyranny of the prevailing faction, for it is possible, especially in a representative democracy, that a minority faction will prevail.

Popular sovereignty can never be exercised through uniform laws, because there is never a single will of the People to agree to them. Popular sovereignty is essential to liberty, but democracy cannot be the vehicle for the exercise of this sovereignty and is only another arbitrary system for establishing authority over the People. The sole value of democracy is as preparation for anarchy, where popular sovereignty can truly be realized as the sovereignty of persons, but not of the collective People.

His concern with principle here comes down finally to his concentration upon individual liberty and making it possible for each man to decide for himself all matters which concern him. The principle of majority rule is unacceptable simply because each man who disagrees with the prevailing faction is compelled to act against his own will. Even if a man agrees with a law when it is enacted, should he change his mind later he is still compelled by it. If he misunderstands the law and supports it although it is contrary to his interests, he is still compelled by it, even if he later recognizes his mistake. If he is disfranchised or otherwise excluded from the

17. *Du Contrat social,* III, iv; in *The Political Writings of Rousseau,* ed. Vaughan, II, 73. Proudhon's quotation of this (*Oeuv.,* II, 227) is inaccurate.

law-making process, as some always are, he is still compelled to obey the law. If the law was enacted before he was born or before he came of age, he is still compelled by it. Government can never be carried out by the consent of the governed: even at best, each of its acts will only be agreeable to some of those governed some of the time.

Proudhon argues that the system of direct legislation cannot fulfill its purpose even if you were to accept the concept of popular sovereignty assumed by advocates of the system. In a large population opinion is almost infinitely diverse. Even where there can be wide agreement to certain propositions or acts, the shades of opinion within the umbrella of agreement are still quite varied. This means that there is no way of learning by induction what precisely "general opinion" really is. All that can be done is to offer propositions to the population, to which they answer yes or no. It is not the people who poses the questions, but the government and its chiefs. The people can say no to an obnoxious proposition, but they cannot say what they do want unless the government chooses something to which they can assent. Rittinghausen says that for direct legislation to be practicable, the people cannot pose questions themselves or amend the propositions offered. Then his proposed system rests on the false presumption that the questions asked of the people will always be just the right ones, phrased in precisely the right way, and understood by the people in the way intended.

The final case which Proudhon examines is that of "direct government." As proposed by Ledru-Rollin,[18] to whom Proudhon is responding, all general issues would be decided by the entire citizenry, while matters of detail would be decided and executed by State institutions. Proudhon contends that this would take government still further away from the people and that it is wrong to call such a system "direct" government. As with the system of "direct legislation," most of whose faults this scheme shares, the real power and authority would be in the hands of those who handle the "details." It is only through decision and execution on matters of detail that the general decisions of the people have any practical effect.

18. In his *Du Gouvernement direct du peuple* and *Plus de président, plus de représentant!* (both, Paris, 1851).

The same criticism is applicable to any government and serves to underline a defect of democracy which is often ignored: that however sound the popular base of legislation, its virtues can be undermined in the process of execution, particularly when most of the government administrative staff is not directly responsible to the electorate.

However, such criticism of Ledru-Rollin's scheme suggests to Proudhon a corrective: "direct government" in which all powers, decisions, and acts—legislative, executive, and judicial—remain in the hands of the People. All of them participate directly in all the business of government. But this is impossible, both because the sheer numbers of citizens make such a system unworkable and because it is essential for most of the population to occupy itself with producing the necessities of life. Yet the logic of democratic theory leads inevitably to the conclusion that only by such a direct government can the People be truly "self-governing," in the sense of the word intended by democrats. Thus direct government is the final "reduction to absurdity of the idea of government."

> Direct legislation, direct government, simplified government, old lies that they would try in vain to rejuvenate. Direct or indirect, simple or composite, the government of the people will always be the fleecing of the people. It is always man who has command over man, brute force which decides questions in place of the justice which alone can resolve them, perverse ambition which makes a stepladder for itself out of devotion and credulity.[19]

In addition to his main arguments based on justice and right, Proudhon has a number of other complaints against government. It is a grossly inefficient and wasteful machine, all the more so as it is made larger, and especially so as it is increasingly centralized. Inefficiency and waste aside, the work of government is not truly productive, so that governmental expenses become a gross burden on those whose labor is productive and thus socially useful. In one sense this criticism is like the one Proudhon makes against absentee landlords: they tax the producers without contributing anything of value themselves. Just as he cannot conceive of capital as having a productive function, he does not think of government as being

19. *Oeuv.*, II, 199.

productive through its facilitation of productive operations and its various social services.

As a native of a province with a long-smoldering resentment against the heavily centralized government of France, Proudhon is especially sensitive to the possible faults of centralization and "big government." He calculates that most of the expenses of the French government result from the cost of keeping the machine running, with relatively little remaining for public services.

Not only is the large, centralized government wasteful, but it is also a vast, impersonal structure unable to cope effectively with all the myriad detailed problems which confront it and with all the variations in different local situations. Officials are arbitrary, unfeeling, incompetent, and grasping; courts administer a sad substitute even for that species of justice which they are supposed to uphold; the laws make up a crazy quilt that covers only the wrong things and provides a living for an army of small men—pettifogging attorneys—who seek to draw something coherent or at least profitable from the mess. Corruption in government is virtually inescapable, and this corruption is not only odious for its own sake, but also further increases the wasteful expenses of the state. The more the government extends its public services, the worse are the waste, inefficiency, and corruption.

Despite his rationalism and faith in the potential power of scientific knowledge, Proudhon is skeptical about the ability of men to deal with social problems rationally—this above all in the context of government, but also, generally, in any situation. Soon after the Revolution of February, 1848, he speaks of "The Republic transformed into a doctrinaire democracy; empiricism and utopia taking the place of ideas and making the People into material for experiments; little men, little ideas, little speeches; mediocrity, prejudice, doubt, and soon, perhaps, anger." [20]

In the 1848 Revolution he has witnessed the tragic fumbling of men who, despite their good intentions and considerable intellectual abilities, failed to translate their ideals and ideas into a polity which suited either them or the people. The problems are so big, so complex, and men's abilities so limited. If solutions are to be found at

20. *Oeuv.* (*Lacroix*), VI, 19.

all, how can they be found except in the simple man-to-man relations of Proudhon's suggested contract society?

He is still more skeptical about man's using what abilities he does have wisely and dispassionately. Dogmatism particularly bothers him, and not merely because it may represent insistence on ideas with which he disagrees. Repeatedly he accuses his democratic contemporaries of dogmatism; he is as much distressed by their inflexibility as by the supposed error of their ideas. Experience in 1848 proved how very difficult it can be to translate their ideas into action, yet they seem little willing or able to adapt their ideas to the apparent exigencies of practical situations.

The problem as Proudhon perceives it is more than just a matter of blind inflexibility. He attributes great importance to those passions and divisions of men which arise from their insistence on ideas and opinions, the absolute *need to be right*. This insistence can often go beyond considerations of simple self-interest and ambition. It makes of politics and government a mockery of what they are supposed to be.

He is deeply conscious of what he believes to be the very limited virtue of men, their greed, passion, irrationality, violence, and hypocrisy. Because of men's limitations Proudhon cannot trust them to govern others, but his fear, or skepticism, is concerned with more than the faults of those in authority.

He is unequivocally devoted to the ideal of popular sovereignty (though his understanding of the ideal is idiosyncratic), but he does not idolize or idealize the People. They are just men to him, individuals with all faults conceivable. Blind egoism, violent and destructive instincts, ignorance and impatience—all are common human traits which social planners must recognize. "Man is a tyrant or slave through will before he is thus through fortune; the heart of the proletarian is like that of a rich man, a sewer of bubbling sensuality, a furnace of base debauchery and deception." [21]

Unless men's faults are glossed over, there is insufficient basis for faith in the exercise of popular sovereignty through procedures of democratic government. There is little reason to suppose popular government will be wiser and more just than any other, even if its claim to power should be superior. Such a faith in popular govern-

21. *Oeuv.*, I, vol. i, 356.

ment Proudhon regrets as part of the dogmatism of democracy.

Furthermore, although he regards revolution as legitimate, necessary, and inevitable, he is very skeptical about the possibilities of a felicitous outcome for any actual revolution. In February, 1848, he lamented a revolution born without fertile ideas, but he feels that something more than ideas was lacking. As long as men are no better, revolution is all too likely to follow a disastrous course, as it did in 1848. If the people prevail where they failed to do so in June, then the outcome is little likely to be much better. In 1863, with 1848 and more than a decade of Louis-Napoleon Bonaparte's reign behind him, Proudhon wrote:

> The people, through the same fact of their inferiority and their distress, will always form the army of liberty and progress. Labor is republican by nature: the contrary would imply contradiction. But, by reason of their ignorance, their primitive instincts, the violence of their needs, the impatience of their desires, the people are inclined to summary forms of authority. They do not seek legal guarantees, of which they have no idea and whose power they do not comprehend. Nor is it a machinery, a poising of forces, which they make for themselves, but a chief in whose word they trust, whose intentions are known to them, and who is devoted to their interests. To this chief they give unlimited authority, an irresistible power. The people, regarding as just all that they judge to be useful, seeing that they are the people, make a mockery of formalities and in no case do they impose conditions on the depositories of power. Ever ready for suspicion and calumny, but incapable of methodical discussion, they have definitive belief only in the human will, hope only in the man, confidence only in his creatures, *in principibus, in filiis hominum*. They expect nothing from principles, which alone can save them. They have no religion of ideas.

Here Proudhon's approach shows a marked departure from the progressivist conceptions of the Enlightenment and contemporary socialism.[22] The ideal of progress was that of the moral and intellectual improvement of man through the combination of extending knowledge, improving material conditions, and enlightenment through education. Following this notion of progress quite closely,

22. *Du Principe fédératif, Oeuv.*, XV, 301. The following has been suggested in part by James Joll, *The Anarchists* (London, 1964), 67ff.

Saint-Simon, Fourier, and the other utopian socialists thought to improve man's nature by changing his environment. Indeed, the whole of the revolutionary tradition was based on the presumption that changing his environment is sufficient for the complete reformation of human morality, although socialist and nonsocialist conceptions of the process differ substantially. Fourier actually claimed that the whole nature of man, even his physical abilities, would be greatly altered by the reconstitution of society into his cooperative phalansteries. Marx continues this approach, despite the very different way he uses it, when he insists that not only the standards of morality, but modes of human conduct themselves are conditioned entirely by material circumstances. He too expects that change in environment is both necessary and sufficient for man to become good.

All in their own ways are reiterating Rousseau's contention, which Proudhon rejects, that man was not bad originally but has been corrupted by life in society. Proudhon's view is that man and existing society basically are neither good nor bad, but each at present has bad qualities. "Man is by nature a sinner, that is to say, not essentially a *wrongdoer* (*malfaisant*) but, rather, *wrongly made* (*malfait*), and his destiny is perpetually to re-create in himself his ideal." [23]

If man is "wrongly made," existing social conditions contribute greatly to making him so—but man the sinner also prevents the social conditions from being any better. It is *necessary*, but not *sufficient*, to change the conditions and organization of society in order to change man's moral character. Reform of society has to be based upon a moral reform of each individual resulting from his own voluntary efforts. The function of leadership in social revolution must first of all be to guide individuals in moral reform.

> Man is good [the socialists say], but it is necessary to *disinterest* him in evil in order for him to abstain from it. Man is good, but it is necessary to *interest* him in the good for him to practice it. For if the interest of his passions brings him to evil, he will do evil, and if this same interest leaves him indifferent to the good, he will not do good. And the society will have no right to reproach him

23. *Oeuv.*, I, vol. i, 372.

for having listened to his passions, because it was up to society to lead him away from his passions.[24]

Reason and irrationality are both natural to man, but the latter is now the more fully realized in his nature, and rationality the potential quality on which future hopes must rest. It is not enough to teach him how to act with full rationality: the social conditions in which men live must be more conducive to rational thought and conduct than to passionate, thoughtless, and immoral acts. Morality, social justice, and the use of reason have to grow together, interdependently, as increasingly there is cause for rational men to see moral conduct and the pursuit of self-interest as identical. This is possible only when men can work together instead of at war with one another.

Thus revolution is necessary to change the unequal and antagonistic relations of existing society, but to be successful revolution must do much more than overturn the old order. In its preparation, execution, and sequels, the revolution must concentrate on leading mankind along the path of increasing rationality and sense of sociability.

Proudhon's skepticism and fears about the revolutionary activities of his contemporaries stem from his conviction that they will do little to discover that path or lead men in its direction. Then revolution can only release the passions of the opposed sides, with force predominating and establishing a new tyranny, as it did in 1848. When violence is the chief agency of change, irrationality prevails over reason. This belief, together with his hostility toward dogmatism, led Proudhon to respond coolly to Marx's proposal for collaboration in 1846. ". . . we ought not to admit revolutionary action as the means of social reform, for this supposed means would be simply an appeal to force, to the arbitrary, in short, a contradiction."[25]

Proudhon's attitude toward violent revolution is always ambivalent, for he knows that it will be difficult, if not impossible, to achieve peaceably the revolutionary transformation he wants. He thinks it all too likely that the misery of the exploited people will lead them to armed revolt far greater in scale than even that of the

24. Ibid., 360.
25. Letter to Marx, May 17, 1846, *Oeuv.,* VII, 435.

June Days, and far more terrible in its consequences. Writing in 1851 of the chief contemporary advocate of violent revolutionary action, he says in a letter to a friend:

> What! you do not understand that Blanqui is the incarnation of popular vengeance, that he is, like Marat, one of the hideous but unfortunately logical, necessary faces of the Revolution! You will strike the enemy, you in the fire of indignation; Blanqui will exterminate him in the coldness of his calculations. . . . Have pity then on stupid and ferocious humans, but have no thought for God's justice. Today neither you, nor I, nor anyone are capable of anything any longer against the force of things. The reaction has willed it: we are carried on toward catastrophe, toward vengeance. Already people are no longer concerned with ideas; already, having a few luminous, fecund principles of social economy, they believe they know the rest, and in all quarters revolutionary impatience accuses the theorists. Blanqui will have his hour, it is useless to deny it. It would be imprudent, and nearly unjust, to put obstacles in the way. What will follow, without doubt, will be the dissolution of France, if not as a nation at least as a State. But the fall of the French State will drag down with it all the European States: passing through the bacchanale of sects, parties, factions, collapses, civil wars, proscriptions, we shall arrive, after trial upon trial, at the pure and simple practice of liberty.
>
> As for me, I shall continue to serve my contemporaries and humanity with the fruit of my studies; but, I cannot hide it, I dream of standing aside, for human reason at this moment is in full eclipse, and I do not feel in myself the strength to struggle with passion against the passions.[26]

Convinced of the justice of popular complaints, he cannot condemn vengeful and rebellious impulses although he thinks them most likely to result in disaster for the people themselves. He asserts the *right* of revolt and even on occasion advocates active revolt by the masses. Advocacy of this sort, found mainly in his newspaper articles of 1848 and 1849, is partly attributable to momentary passions and flights of rhetoric, but he is never immune to the romance and esprit of revolutionary militancy, a tradition he has been immersed in since his early childhood in a Jacobin family.

His ambivalence results from more than a conflict between heart

26. Letter to Langlois, August 14, 1851, *Corresp.,* IV, 83ff.

and head, however. On the one hand he does not think cataclysmic revolution can achieve a happy outcome. At best it may help to prepare more positive, substantial changes; he is dubious even about that. Moreover, although he cannot condemn as evil popular impulses to strike out at oppressors and overwhelm them, such self-defeating, irrational conduct is just the kind of behavior he wants men to become able to forego.

Yet, despite good reason for rejecting violent revolution, on the other hand what alternative is there? Proudhon does not think that the ruling classes will voluntarily surrender their privileges to embrace true equality, or that economic growth will eliminate the basic problems of inequality. He believes that the bourgeoisie will resist any substantive progressive change in social relationships, and that they have the power to make their resistance effective should the people pursue a moderate course in pressing their claims for justice. Likewise, he does not think constitutional changes or other political reforms can help, or that political justice is possible without social revolution. Finally, he sees grave social conflict as the inescapable consequence of injustice, and expects that these irreconcilable antagonisms must make the existing order unstable.

Revolutionary change in the present situation appears inevitable to him, and a violent, disastrous course for this process seems by far the most likely prospect. If such is to be the course of future development, how can there ever be a solution of the social problem?

In 1851 Proudhon had no answer. His reflections on past revolutionary experience had by then enabled him to complete the powerful anarchist critique he had begun a dozen years before. He had the elements of a conception of what forms the just society should take, but as yet he had little notion of how to realize his ideal. In his remaining years he would complete his constructive theory, a vision of what the just society must be. He would also develop a theory of how men can proceed from their present condition to one of justice; but by the very nature of his vision their ability to follow the path he identified would always remain doubtful.

eight: Proudhon in the Second Empire

> I am more convinced than ever that there is no place for me in this world, and I regard myself as in a state of perpetual insurrection against the order of things.[1]

WHEN LOUIS-NAPOLEON BONAPARTE executed his successful *coup d'état* on December 2, 1851, Proudhon was serving a prison sentence for published attacks on him three years before. In the intervening time the prisoner had frequently expressed his disdain for Bonaparte. Indeed, his unbroken fierce opposition to the great Emperor's nephew extended back to the latter's first major entry into politics; when he was elected to the National Assembly in May, 1848, as a deputy himself Proudhon voted not to seat him. After Bonaparte was installed as President at the end of that year, Proudhon was able to see quite clearly how he was proceeding to secure popular support while destroying organized opposition. Later, expecting a restoration of the Empire, the prisoner had the nerve to say so in print, and in consequence was sequestered in the fortress of Doullens for a time, until acquitted in a trial court of new charges which had been brought against him.[2]

---

1. Quoted in Erich Thier, "Marx et Proudhon," *Marxismusstudien,* Zweite Folge, ed. Iring Fetscher (Tübingen, 1957), 127. It is said to be from *Corresp.,* II, which includes letters from 1842 to 1849.

2. See p. 133.

Despite this, Proudhon was to be accused of collaboration with Bonapartism. His volume on the *coup d'état* and its consequences has been called an apologia for Bonaparte by Marx and a number of others, and many of Proudhon's French socialist comrades were shocked and angry at him because of the book. He was never "exonerated" of such charges in the eyes of many, and the compromise with power supposedly involved has been of haunting significance for French socialists, who so often in the years since have been subject to the opposed attractions of comparable compromises or unfaltering proletarian militancy. After De Gaulle's resumption of power in 1958, Georges Cogniot, a French Communist party leader, used Proudhon's history to attack De Gaulle and the socialists who acquiesced in his resumption of authority. Cogniot accomplished this with a pamphlet entitled "Proudhon et la démagogie bonapartiste: Un Socialiste en coquetterie avec le pouvoir personnel." [3]

The charges do not lack foundation. Proudhon's actions with respect to Bonapartism after the *coup d'état* were suspect. Yet his attitudes reflect not an affirmation of Bonapartism but a reasoned repudiation of the illusions of democracy in the past. Clarification of this requires a more detailed examination of his actions and ideas.

When Bonaparte first carried out his sudden *coup d'état* and a year later made himself Emperor, most of the outrage of intellectuals and politicians resulted from the overthrow of the Republic and, presumably, of democracy. Some wept more for having seen power or the potential for it wrested from their hands than for the demolition of democracy. Still, the Republican ideal was sacred to many, as a basis of liberal, constitutional, bourgeois government if not necessarily of universal popular sovereignty. Some more truly democratic republicans and socialists were upset because they regarded the *coup d'état* as a triumph for reactionary forces.

Proudhon, on the other hand, had long since repudiated the Republic, which had not in his eyes been democratic since the suppression of the people in the June Days. Government had been just the factional struggle of bourgeois parties whose only interest in the masses had been to keep them under firm control. Even the electoral suffrage had been greatly narrowed by the National Assembly, in May, 1850. The year before Proudhon had written in

3. (Paris: Editions Sociales, 1958.)

his *Confessions* that France had elected Bonaparte President because she was tired of party politics; [4] even then Proudhon foresaw a moribund republic on its way to renewal of the Empire.

He had little esteem for political democracy in any form and thought that the people had yet to display a matured ability to participate in the political process responsibly and intelligently. With the privileged classes securely in control of both the political system and the economy, there was little hope for the improvement of the situation under the existing system. His position is clearly reflected in these notes written in his *carnet* just after the *coup d'état* and in response to it:

> To define the word *democracy*, no longer through government of the people, but through progressive *emanicipation of the people*. The day when people are completely emancipated, there will no longer be any government.
>
> . . . Liberty! The free man is the one who is pure of heart and reason, the true Gnostic. The people are beasts of burden, whose whole business is to drink, eat, sleep and make love: they care little for anything else. For my part I have never been democracy's dupe, and it is too clear that my socialism has justice for its point of departure, not the sovereignty of the mass, the competence of the people. But even in that, I fear that I am too advanced; there is no justice for those who are incapable of receiving it. [5]

Democratic government may be desirable if it represents a forward step toward genuine emancipation, but the Second Republic did not fit this description. What then might make such progress possible? Finding nothing in the complexion of the existing political situation that could make positive contributions to social progress, Proudhon sought to provide guidance to the popular cause himself, intellectually though not as a political activist. The following he wrote in his *carnet* just before the *coup d'état:*

> . . . I declare that, if I am devoted to the unfortunate class, I am neither its obsequious servant, its plaything, nor its slave; I regard myself as one of its tutors, and I try to enlighten and instruct it. If it has no need of my services, then I retire; we listen to what it will say. Speak, people; speak, proletarians.

4. *Oeuv.*, VII, 277.
5. December 9, 1851, *Carnets*, IX, 232, 233.

My goal, very clear: I believe, I say it without difficulty, that no progress at all is possible as long as it remains the affair of the former democratic party and the old republican bands.[6]

Thus the crisis of December, 1851, was for him an occasion for reshaping his thoughts about how to make the best of a situation which had always been poor. Though Bonapartism was no solution, relatively speaking it might be better than the bourgeois republic, if it offered a better chance of movement in the direction of still distant emancipation.

In the developing position of Proudhon with respect to the Second Empire we see him trying to determine the optimum immediate response for a repressed people to make toward an authority it cannot yet displace. Though not actually like the reformism of moderate socialists in the Third Republic, both the moderation of many of his political recommendations and his initial, half-positive reaction to Bonaparte's seizure of power did clash with his radically revolutionary ideals.

This can be explained only by his skepticism about republic, political democracy, the People, and revolution. His political thought is developed at three levels. On the first he is mainly concerned with what may best be done to improve the immediate condition of the masses—given their limited present strength and resources—and at the same time to prepare for progress toward a new situation where their eventual emancipation at last becomes possible. At the second level he is trying to develop patterns of organization and action, particularly for a workers' movement, which though still within a State system can actually lead to genuine, if partial emancipation—although the forms envisaged are still not ideal. At the ultimate level he deals with the ideal forms themselves.

The ultimate ideals may appear to prohibit some of the conclusions of his "first level" reasoning. Actually, it is because his ideals are so far from being realized that he can find no good in recent political history and looks for some relief in an authoritarian system basically obnoxious to him. Radical ideals lead him to reject political practices he has already found wanting and to grasp for a new tactic for temporary use.

6. November 23, 1851, ibid., 214.

The principal difficulty in disentangling the strands of Proudhon's thought in the period of the Empire is that he shifts freely from one level of reasoning to another. What may be explicable as a response to an immediate political problem conflicts with other ideas if taken as a general principle. Since he does not always make it clear how far an idea should be generalized, his work has to be read most judiciously. Only in his final books [7] do the different levels of his thought merge, as he evolves strategy and tactics for political action that are nothing other than implementation of his theoretical principles.

It *is* clear from his correspondence, *carnets,* and posthumously published manuscripts, if not from his finished books, that he never altered his contempt for Louis-Napoleon and that he did not welcome the *coup d'état.* On the morning of December 2, 1851, Proudhon secured permission to go out from his Paris prison, on parole for the day. He wandered through the capital, observing the population and seeking out friends. More sorrowful than outraged, he lamented the blindness of his democratic friends and the passivity with which most people accepted the *coup.* (This reaction is reflected in the *carnet* note of December 9 quoted above.) Napoleon he called "knave," "usurper," "brigand," and other choice epithets. His most colorful characterization appears in the *carnet* for October 31, 1852.

> People assert that Louis-Napoleon is so exhausted with a surfeit of women and of all life that he can no longer retain his excrement, that his bowels are perpetually loose. His breeches are always fouled with s . . . and in his erotic orgies the most infamous filth serves to perfume his voluptuous pleasures.
>
> This man, seen and examined plainly, is ill built and has an ugly physique. Very short, with legs placed awry, *culletant et torticulant* as Rabelais says, his face ignoble, its sides grossly unequal and ill-balanced, one eye higher than the other, his forehead without majesty or intelligence and his eyes lifeless. Upon seeing him for the first time in 1848, I felt the confused sentiment that I had before me a man in whom modesty was dead, or rather did not exist, like that prostitute of Martial who did not remember ever having been chaste. This confused revelation of instinct was translated into

7. *Du Principe fédératif, Contradictions politiques,* and *De la Capacité politique des classes ouvrières.*

the pamphlet I wrote in 1848, at the end of November, where I painted him as a monster of lewdness who one day would seize the Republic with [four bandits?] and violate it between their hands.[8]

Apparently Proudhon was not fond of his Emperor-to-be. Indeed, the malice displayed in this remarkable sketch is most unusual for him. Later remarks in his *carnets* and letters show the opinion unchanged. However, he had a different attitude toward the Emperor's first cousin, Jerome. Called Prince Napoleon,[9] Jerome was heir to the throne until the birth of the only son of Napoleon III in March, 1856, and was the Bonapartist pretender after the son's death in 1879. Young and politically liberal, he professed admiration for Proudhon, and was even thought to have opposed the *coup d'état*. He and Proudhon exchanged letters and met on about a dozen occasions. The latter hoped to make something of the Prince's liberalism and admiration for him. Through Jerome he might get the Imperial government to make some meaningful reforms. He sought no aid for himself from the Prince, and even refused it when offered.

Proudhon's main effort here was a proposal for the national Exposition of 1855, of which Jerome was the chief director.[10] The proposal sought to develop the Exposition into a foundation of social reforms, chiefly through a revival of Proudhon's gratuitous credit and exchange scheme. Nothing came of his project or of his connections with Prince Napoleon. Although Jerome was an object of hope to enough men for the term "Jeromist" to have been coined to describe them, his liberal and democratic ideas appear to

8. *Carnets*, IX, 473. "Culletant et torticulant" might be approximated by "ass-wagging and contorting." The words, which are distinctively Rabelaisian, occur in a passage where Rabelais attacks clerics for hurting people through mischievous deceit, and presumably Proudhon employs the allusion to suggest the same about Bonaparte (*Gargantua et Pantagruel*, Bk. II, Ch. 34).

9. 1822–91. The second son of Jerome Bonaparte (1784–1860)—brother of Emperor Napoleon I and the one-time King of Westphalia—Prince Napoleon was first named Napoleon Joseph Charles Paul, but he assumed the name Jerome upon the death of his older brother, Jerome Napoleon Charles, in 1847. A half-brother and his son also bore the name Jerome, as did Prince Napoleon's own eldest son. Prince Napoleon was also called "Plon-Plon," supposedly derived from "Plomb-Plomb" or "Craint-plomb" (Fears-lead), a nickname said to have been given him by his soldiers in the Crimea. When one is a nephew of the great Napoleon I and does not even have a name of his own, the Crimean War might be a bit of a trial.

10. *Projet d'exposition perpétuelle;* written in the summer of 1853, first published posthumously in 1866, with the *Théorie de la propriété. Oeuv.*, IX, 299–384.

have been too radical for him to have exercised much influence in the government. The chief significance of Proudhon's flirtation with him is that it constitutes an additional indication of how for a time the anarchist did think it possible for the Bonaparte government to be persuaded that there were advantages in making genuine social reforms.

At first he thought the initiative for change might come from Louis-Napoleon himself, since for all his faults Bonaparte did have a past history of liberalism and had even taken part in a revolutionary insurrection in Italy two decades before. He did rely on popular support and he was imitating his emperor uncle, who had been a reformer as well as an authoritarian ruler. With this in mind Proudhon wrote *La Révolution sociale démontrée par le coup d'état du deux décembre*, published in Paris in July, 1852.[11] While hardly an unqualified affirmation of Bonapartism, it gained him a reputation as a supporter of that cause. Yet even as he composed this book he was having misgivings, which were expressed in his letters. By the autumn of 1852, he had no more hope for the Prince-President, soon to be Emperor Napoleon III. He transferred his hopes to Jerome, now thinking that through him the Empire might yet become the agency of advancement toward social revolution. After 1855 Proudhon no longer looked to the regime for anything positive, and his previous dalliance with "revolutionary Caesarism" embarrassed him, so that in 1863 through the course of another topical tract he felt compelled to justify and apologize for his earlier position.[12]

There is much more that can be said in response to his critics, in order to demonstrate finally that his record on Bonapartism is not "disreputable," but this has been done already by Georges Duveau and Edouard Dolléans.[13] Neither is it useful here to follow in detail the arguments of *La Révolution sociale*, though others have focused on them,[14] since its main theses represent a position

11. *Oeuv.*, IX.

12. *Les Démocrates assermentés et les réfractaires; Oeuv.*, XIII, 31–92. This tract is further discussed below.

13. In their joint introduction to *La Révolution sociale, Oeuv.*, IX, 7–103; Dolléans's *Proudhon* (Paris, 1948), 201–27 et passim; and Duveau's introduction to *Les Démocrates assermentés . . . , Oeuv.*, XIII, 2–30.

14. Particularly those who have wanted to regard Proudhon as a proto-fascist, or as a prop for right-wing groups like the Action Française.

soon discarded. However, when examined in a suitably wide perspective, much of the book does prove illuminating.

Proudhon, no less than others on the left, recognized and attacked the reactionary elements in Bonapartism and its conservative supporters. Because of his antipathy toward authority he could find no other virtue in the imperial system than the possibility of its facilitating transition to a libertarian regime. For this reason it is foolish or disingenuous to put him in a class with fascist ideologues.[15]

Initially he thought important the dynamic and revolutionary elements in the Bonapartist tradition. After all, the first Empire had been the chief agency for securing the victories of the Revolution of 1789 in France and for extending them to other parts of Europe. Ambivalent though his attitude toward the Revolutionary heritage was, Proudhon did in general regard the changes wrought as progressive steps away from traditional feudalism.

At this time he was developing his ideas about progress, writing the *Philosophie du progrès* during 1851. (It was not published until two years later.) But here the relation between the grand structure of historical progress and its immediate manifestations is not well defined and probably was not clear to him then, though he seems less uncertain in later works. In a letter of 1850 or 1851 he speaks of progress as "the eternal advance of revolutionary ideas; in a word, the philosophy [or "physiology"] of reforms." He writes, ". . . if the truth is that which *is*, it is still more that which is BECOMING." In attacking the way reforms are now wrought, he refers to "the absolutism of the principles and the slowness of applications."[16]

15. As did J. Salwyn Schapiro, in his "Pierre-Joseph Proudhon, Harbinger of Fascism," *American Historical Review*, L (1945), 714–37, and his *Liberalism and the Challenge of Facism* (New York, 1949), 332–69. Incomplete pieces by Proudhon on the Emperors Napoleon were published posthumously. Though fragmentary, these passages reveal a wholly negative view of Bonapartism. *Napoléon Ier* and *Napoléon III*, ed. Clément Rochel (Paris, 1898 and 1900). Schapiro's article provoked a response which is one of the best essays ever written on Proudhon: Nicola Chiaromonte, "P.-J. Proudhon: An Uncomfortable Thinker," *Politics*, III (January, 1946), 27–29.

16. Letter to Marc Dufraisse, June 2, 1850, *Corresp.*, III, 290. Inexplicably, this same letter, fourteen pages long in print, is repeated with the date October 15, 1851, in *Corresp.*, IV, 106–19. The second version substitutes "physiologie" for "philosophie" (des réformes). Proudhon's philosophy of progress is discussed below in Ch. 10, "Historical Perspective."

Progress is thus the actualization of revolutionary ideas—but whether this process is inevitable and whether it goes on continually or intermittently are important points on which Proudhon is not consistent in his various statements. It would seem, however, that he generally regards such progress as ultimately inevitable, but presently slow, irregular, and subject to reversal.

Insofar as he thinks of present developments in the historical perspective of long-term progressive movement, his notions about immediate political practice become more readily explicable. In the overall structure of man's historical experience, the fundamental dynamic factors are not governmental forms or laws, which themselves are really of accidental nature with only limited relative significance.

Thus he cares little about the *form* of government if it is authoritarian, which he believes all governments have been. In this sense Jacobin power in the first Republic offered little improvement over the *ancien régime*, although in bringing emancipation closer the Republic was a more positive development. However, the Republic merited little credit for the steps made toward emancipation; it was instead a manifestation and effect of dynamic forces which were historically responsible for the progress made.[17]

Constitutions and governments succeed each other with little real change. As far as Proudhon is concerned the basic tenets of the bourgeois political system are fixed, while most contested political issues—constitutions, dynastics, presidencies, dictatorships, legislative power, executive or ministerial responsibility—are merely questions of form incidental to the preservation of more fundamental principles and privileges.[18] Here his theory resembles that of Marx, but the latter is more deliberate and insistent in his exposition of the matter, generalizes further with it, and goes on to conclusions about the class struggle and the revolutionary process which are not as clearly defined by Proudhon.

The anarchist believes that class conflict resulting from economic

17. At one point he suggests that the only time since 1789 when a freer government was being built in France was the period from the convocation of the Estates General to the expulsion of the Girondins from the Convention in mid-1793. Since then the exercise of power by government has subordinated freedom and the healthy growth of society (*La Révolution sociale, Oeuv.,* IX, 134).

18. *De la Capacité politique, Oeuv.,* III, 261.

iniquity makes governments necessarily unstable, but he does not have Marx's vision of inexorable movement thereby to victorious proletarian revolution. Proudhon does, however, see a perpetual movement—"autokinesis" he calls it—in government and in social life, involving innumerable successive changes of constitution.[19] While this autokinesis can result some day in genuine revolution, the weakness of popular forces and their failure to adhere to the revolutionary cause with intelligence and wisdom make the immediate prospect of meaningful change a poor one. People, fatigued by political maneuver and intrigue, may well come to rest passively with absolute government, or await and welcome ambitious demagogues and the reaction of conservatives. It is here that Proudhon at first thinks it possible for Louis-Napoleon Bonaparte to be preferable to the bourgeois republic or to either a legitimist or Orleanist restoration of monarchy.

The country is unwilling to move backward, but there is doubt, suspicion, and even fear of the Revolution, among poor people as well as with the privileged. Bonaparte's advantage lies in his intermediate position between the two extremes of revolution and reaction. At the same time he affirms the ameliorative and liberal purposes of the Revolution while protecting the conservatives. Proudhon calls it a "bilateral and contradictory solution, but logical however, in view of the state of opinion. Circumstances render it almost inevitable." [20]

Besides forestalling real retrogression in consequence of popular fatigue and fear, Bonaparte may give effect to the socialist idea, more because of his pivotal role than because of any desire to do so. Though Proudhon soon discards this hope, it is significant that he believes a bad government may yield positive results despite itself. Forces including popular and revolutionary ones press upon even the strongest dictator. Despite its repression and tyranny, a regime which must rely on force and massive popular support will be obliged, as Robespierre was, to undertake the purification of society.

Proudhon was adapting the concept of "revolutionary Caesarism," the notion of a regime whose dictator, relying for power

19. *Contradictions politiques, Oeuv.,* XIII, 205–34.
20. *La Révolution sociale, Oeuv.,* IX, 285.

on popular support, introduces measures which ostensibly benefit the people, and sometimes do so in fact. Thinking the Republic's Assembly unwilling to improve the condition of plebeians, Proudhon was at first ready for a trial of Louis-Napoleon as Caesar— or better still, Caesarism with a different emperor, perhaps Jerome Bonaparte. After repudiating Caesarism, Proudhon remained interested in the main premise of his own version of the concept.

This premise is that the State can stimulate the growth of society in many ways, while not necessarily controlling that growth. Indeed, the proper role of any state is to legislate, institute, initiate —and then to leave the execution of what it has started to local communities and individuals. It cannot stimulate growth effectively if it is a vast, anonymous company organized to do everything, which instead of aiding and serving citizens and communities dispossesses and stifles them.[21]

On occasion, as in his *Projet d'exposition perpétuelle*, he suggests that the State take the initiative to establish a thriving system of gratuitous credit, although the State is only to start the system, not to operate it indefinitely. Proudhon's proposal of the State as stimulus is a bit surprising in view of his anarchist opposition to all government, and especially of his strictures against Louis Blanc and the Luxembourg Commission, who also sought to have the State initiate socialist programs. In his hopes for Bonapartism, and again in his last book, *De la Capacité politique des classes ouvrières*, he approaches a positive view of government power without embracing it, as indeed he could not.

The attraction to government as a major stimulus to social growth probably stems from the heritage of the *philosophes*, for most of whom enlightened despotism was a favorite form of rule. The despot was to be initiator and guide, but not the main agency of action or a rigid controller. Though largely rejected in nineteenth-century liberalism, in conventional American politics today the idea has come into its own. The State provides stimulus, especially in the form of funds, but private and local community interests are supposed to continue and complete the work. State socialism under centralized control represents a different alternative, but the tendency in socialist countries seems to have been in

21. *Du Principe fédératif, Oeuv.*, XIV, 329.

the direction of State as stimulus also. It would appear then that some such notion is likely to arise when there is suspicion of both egoism and State authority, and may do so in a variety of political contexts. Proudhon's views of this type should be regarded in the light of this general observation, while remembering that his "first level" appraisals of practical politics should not be mistaken for "third level" declarations of fundamental philosophy.

Proudhon had almost welcomed imprisonment in 1849 because it gave him leisure to study and write—and it let him cut expenses so that he might pay some of his debts with income from the writing (although he then imprudently assumed the responsibilities of matrimony). While imprisoned he wrote his *Confessions*, the *Idée générale de la révolution*, and the *Philosophie du progrès*, as well as articles contributed to *La Voix du peuple*, some of which were published separately as pamphlets.

After his release in June, 1852, he continued writing at a rapid pace, producing in his remaining years much of his best work despite chronic, occasionally disabling ill health together with difficulties and distractions stemming from continual poverty. Though he felt heavily burdened by these problems and those of mankind, Proudhon was sustained by a happy family life and warm relations with friends. At the end of 1855 he wrote:

> For three years . . . I have worked on my complete transformation.
> From 1839 to 1852, I had what is called my period *of criticism*. . . . I gather the materials of new studies and prepare to begin soon a new period that I shall call, if you will, my *positive* or constructive period. It will last as long as the first, thirteen to fourteen years.[22]

Although he died only nine years later, with much of his work incomplete, the "positive period" was a fruitful one. After a few minor topical books, he published in 1858 his greatest and longest composition, *De la Justice dans la révolution et dans l'Eglise*.[23] Here he elaborates his mature philosophy; his subsequent books serve as

22. Letter to Micaud, December 25, 1855, *Corresp.*, VI, 285ff.
23. A much-revised and enlarged edition appeared in 1860. The Rivière edition, *Oeuv.*, XII, is in four volumes and includes the later additions, with variorum notes.

addenda, corollaries, and applications of *De la Justice*. The book was offensive to both the State and the Church, and five days after its publication its seizure was ordered, although thousands of copies were sold anyway. Shortly afterward its author was tried and condemned to the maximum sentence of three years in prison and a fine of four thousand francs. Rather than go to jail again, Proudhon chose to leave France in July, 1858, for Belgium and indefinite exile.[24]

The change of environment helped him to gain fresh perspective and attracted his attention to events outside France. Exile thus provided him creative stimulus, more solitude, and time to write. He experienced some difficulty in completing compositions once begun, and he left quite a few unfinished manuscripts at the time of his death. His problems in completing these projects resulted in part from competing interests or changes in his ideas, but there were protracted periods when he was able to do little or no work at all. Physical illness must have contributed to this, but he seems also to have suffered from intermittent emotional depression, although indications of this are inconclusive. Despondency may have interfered with his work. After his prosecution for *De la Justice* he had some difficulty in finding French firms to publish his books, although at least two publishers offered to guarantee him large sums for his works, if he would moderate his writing enough to avoid dangers of further criminal proceedings and to keep from frightening away buyers for the books. He refused the offers despite his acute poverty. His many problems, while hindering him severely, did not prevent his writing and publishing the most important of what he had left to say.

With the perspective gained through living outside France, he turned much of his attention after 1858 to international politics, with five books resulting in part or entirely from this concern.[25]

24. In Brussels he wrote a book responding to the attacks on him for *De la Justice: La Justice poursuivie par l'Eglise* (Brussels, 1858); *Oeuv.*, XII.

25. *La Guerre et la paix* (Paris, 1861), 2 vols.; *La Fédération et l'unité en Italie* (Paris, 1862); *Du Principe fédératif* (Paris, 1863); *Si les traités de 1815 ont cessé d'exister* (Paris, 1863); and *Nouvelles Observations sur l'unité italienne* (Paris, 1865). He also wrote much of a planned book on Poland; the unpublished, incomplete manuscript is in the Proudhon family archives. While *La Guerre et la paix* is thought by some a most important contribution to the study of international politics, I think it necessary to disregard this aspect here, for its significance in the present context is peripheral.

These caused even more misunderstanding and outraged attacks on Proudhon than had his qualified espousal of Caesarism in *La Révolution sociale*. On these later issues, however, Proudhon was perfectly clear and consistent, the misunderstanding hardly his fault, and the outrage a response to "heresy."

He was much aroused and disturbed by the Crimean War and even more by the wars for the unification of Italy which began in 1859. In both the Crimean and Italian conflicts Napoleon III introduced French armies, in large part as adventures to gain personal and national glory in martial imitation of Napoleon I. In 1861 another French adventure was begun in Mexico.

Proudhon despised power politics, adventurism, military intervention in the affairs of other countries, and the rule of peoples by foreign powers. He recognized and condemned Bonaparte's use of chauvinism and the pursuit of national glory to secure popular support and divert attention from faults and inertia in domestic affairs.[26] Here Proudhon differed little from many of those ordinarily receptive to his views, but his criticisms did arouse the anger of patriots of several sorts.

His condemnation of war and nationalism proved more far-reaching than just this, however, and almost everybody found something in it to attack. In 1861 he published *La Guerre et la paix, recherches sur le principe et la constitution du droit des gens*.[27] The book begins with lyrical praise of war as the chief mechanism of social change and basis of law, but ends by condemning war without reservation. Shocked at the first part, his friends were dismayed, indignant, uncomprehending; some may not have read the reversal in the second part. Proudhon had to write to some of them in order to explain his method, where the praise of war at the beginning serves to set the stage for his conclusion that war is obsolete.

It is difficult to see how his purpose and overall conception could have been mistaken by any who read the whole book with

26. For a time he thought it possible for nationalistic adventurism to prepare the people for social change, but he soon came to believe that it would only lead them to exchange liberty for glory.

27. Leo Tolstoy visited him as he was finishing the book. It appears that Proudhon and his work much impressed the Russian, who may have titled his novel, *War and Peace*, with the other's book in mind. Tolstoy scholars are uncertain about this.

care. However, in addition to his contemporaries who disliked the encomium for war, much later there were intellectuals who took the encomium seriously and drew from it a mystique of violence. This was not as great an abuse of the original as was much of the nonsense written about Proudhon, although it was a distortion of his ideas. His tribute to war and to force is more than a device of rhetorical method; it is intended seriously but is also tied indissolubly to a final reprobation of all war.

To complicate the matter further, *La Guerre et la paix* also drew criticism for its pacific conclusions, from those convinced that war can be necessary and just in the cause of *la patrie*, or of the revolution. While Proudhon never altogether overcame his ambivalence about insurrections, rejection of violent revolution was dominant in his thought and pacifism more natural than bellicosity. In condemning violent insurrection he was set apart once more from the mainstream of the developing revolutionary socialist movement, although his repudiation of international wars suited the movement's later temper. His recognition of a reality including a class struggle escapable only through a revolution likely to be violent would not make his departure less problematical for socialist militants.

The heresy probably causing the most difficulty in these last years of his lifetime was his repudiation of nationalism, especially his rejection of contemporary movements for national independence and unification. Italy most attracted his attention, but Germany was also being unified, the peoples of the multinational Austrian and Turkish empires were restive, and nationalism was increasingly intense throughout Europe in both disputed territory and integral nation states. The 1863 attempt of Poland to break away from Russian rule was important to him as well, but it came after he had already established his position on national independence movements.

Proudhon was not devoid of patriotic sentiment, though he did not often express it. One instance where he did is his conclusion to *La Révolution sociale*, which is an eloquent lyric of love for France, for all its faults the best hope of the cause of liberty. This is a familiar refrain in the tradition of the French Revolution. It was thought that French culture, the Republican ideals of *liberté, egalité*, and *fraternité*, and French armies would be the agency for the liberation of humanity; with this vision the nation had fought for more than two decades following the outbreak of war in 1792. Since then this Franco-centric dream had remained an essential part of the Revolutionary heritage, one of those least subject to questioning by the heirs.

From this heritage Proudhon had discarded much, but not this. Knowing very little of other cultures, he could not appreciate what potential for self-liberation existed outside France, and there was still little in historical experience or in revolutionary literature to alter the common belief in French leadership of the revolutionary cause.

However, nationalism in many parts of Europe, though stimulated by the French Revolution and its ideals, and often involving combination with liberal aspirations, had become something of another color than the original. If independent, unified, and even dominant national identity and sovereignty required devaluing or discarding the Declaration of the Rights of Man, then the new nationalists were ready to do so, and some would not accept liberal premises under any circumstances.

They put nationalism above all else, or combined it with a conservative absolutism of Church and State. This Proudhon could never accept, of course, and it was chiefly for this reason that he was so critical of contemporary nationalism. "Nothing, not even the safety of my native land, could make me sacrifice justice." [28]

While the relevance of this to aggressive chauvinism and the nationalism of reactionaries is plain enough, Proudhon also had in mind ostensibly more liberal and just national causes. Italian unification was a cause popular among French and Belgian democrats, and the Polish rebellion perhaps even more so. Proudhon opposed both causes, provoking a storm of abuse from liberal newspapers and intellectuals.

He contended that the national movements in Italy and Poland were not the liberating forces they were supposed to be. The Polish rebellion he identified as the affair of aristocratic landowners whose victory, if won, would benefit themselves but not the Polish people. As for Italy, he believed that its unification likewise was destined to benefit only the privileged. He thought little of most of its leaders, scorning even Mazzini and Garibaldi, the heroes of liberals all

28. *Du Principe fédératif, Oeuv.*, XIV, 416.

over Europe. To his mind few of the leaders were devoted to liberty and equality, and those who were had chosen methods that would not bring closer the realization of these ideals.

One Italian leader he did like was Giuseppi Ferrari, a philosopher, historian, Turin politician, and important opponent of Cavour, the chief builder of Italian unity. The link between Ferrari and the French anarchist is easy to perceive: the former opposed an Italy unified under a centralized monarchy, which was the goal of Cavour, and instead advocated a loose Italian federation compatible with Proudhon's own federative principles.[29] In a letter to Ferrari the other stated his attitude toward the Italian movement; while more exaggerated in form than his public writing, it expresses the idea of the latter.

> I believe that Italy's so-called liberal party is composed only of bourgeois *atheists*, businessmen, traders, avid for the powers and goods of the clergy, worthies depending, in short, on all the bourgeoisies of France, England, Belgium, Germany; races of exploiters, man-eaters, whose preponderance in the nineteenth century constitutes the corruption of the epoch and would determine the irremediable decadence of the human species, if we, men of the Revolution, were not there to prevent it.[30]

The lines following continue in a like vein.

If nationalism were part of a politics of true, egalitarian democracy, Proudhon's strictures would be far less severe, but he would still reject nationalism except for a recognition of common cultural identity with virtually no political implications. As an anarchist opponent of central government, he cannot, of course, accept the ideals of nation statehood and unqualified, unitary national sovereignty. In part as a response to contemporary nationalist movements, Proudhon wrote his *Du Principe fédératif*, in which he proposed a decentralized "mutualist" federation in place of the sovereign national government.

In September, 1862, articles by him in a Brussels weekly, *L'Office*

---

29. Proudhon was first attracted to Ferrari's work in 1842, when the Italian's writing was primarily in history and philosophy, his advocacy of federative principles yet to come. (Letters to Bergmann, February 8 and May 9, 1842, *Corresp.*, II, 14, 35.)

30. Letter to Ferrari, November 7, 1859, *Corresp.*, IX, 224ff.

de publicité,[31] were the occasion of a near-vicious furor. Writing in these articles about Italian unification, Proudhon spoke ironically and was taken literally as advocating annexation of Belgium by France. The supposition that he could seriously mean this was ridiculous, but nationalism is often thus, and Belgians were hypersensitive in their condition of recent independence and potential danger from imperial France.

A large number of liberal Belgian newspapers attacked him as an annexationist; at the height of the controversy, on September 16, a crowd gathered outside Proudhon's house in Ixelles, a Brussels suburb. They carried the Belgian flag, sang the national anthem, "La Brabançonne," and shouted out below his windows, "Vive la Belgique! A bas les annexionnistes!" The next day Proudhon departed for Paris, an amnesty having permitted him to end his exile after four years. He left behind angry Belgians who demonstrated once again, calling forth police barricades and a proclamation to avert rioting.[32]

Proudhon's idiosyncratic views of certain issues frequently outraged possible allies. Patriots and republicans were not the only ones thus alienated—feminists found still more in his writing to infuriate them. While attacks on Proudhon often resulted from misconception of his ideas, on feminism his position is unambiguously and extremely negative.

He regarded women as certainly and innately inferior to men, and once remarked that women could only be housewives or courtesans. Though active in an intellectual milieu where feminism was quite modish, Proudhon remained true to traditional, provincial attitudes about feminine roles and capacities. Likewise, he was extremely puritanical in his ideas about sexual conduct. He wrote at

---

31. "Mazzini et l'unité italienne," July 13, 1862; "Garibaldi et l'unité italienne," September 7, 1862. These were joined to a response to the Belgians and published as *La Fédération et l'unité en Italie* (Paris, 1862); *Oeuv.*, XIV.

32. Proudhon names Belgian papers attacking him in *La Fédération et l'unité*, *Oeuv.*, XIV, 190ff. The description of the demonstrations is from Edouard Dolléans, *Proudhon* (Paris, 1948), 420. French newspapers also responded with intense invective to his writings on Italian unity. Jean Bartier gives a very detailed account of Proudhon's Belgian period, including the furor at the end, in "Proudhon et la Belgique," *L'Actualité de Proudhon,* ed. Centre National d'Etude des Problèmes de Sociologie et d'Economie Européennes (Brussels, 1967), 169–227.

length developing these views and attacking contemporary feminists like George Sand and Daniel Stern.[33]

While he tries in these pieces to justify his negative opinion of feminine capacities, his arguments are quite specious, and his critics easily have the better of their debate. Proudhon's antifeminism contrasts sharply with his radical egalitarianism. A companion belief, his authoritarian conception of the family, seems equally to contradict his other ideas. This conception derives from his assumption that women and children are less capable than men and thus subject to the direction of the paterfamilias. Unlike many others with similar notions, Proudhon denies that there can be any analogy between the biological family and a larger society.

He does assign to the family a central social and moral role, however; his view is much larger than mere reflexive adherence to the traditional values of his provincial background. Proudhon's theory in this regard is examined in the next chapter, where it can be seen as a part of a plausible moral outlook, but it also needs to be understood in terms of his personal history.

Family life was always an intensely enriching experience for Proudhon. He was deeply attached to his parents and his brother Charles. The warmth of his regard for both his mother and his father is readily apparent in recollections of them scattered through his writings.

His own wife and children played an equally vital role for him, though he married late. While he does not seem to have been altogether continent before marriage, he was fundamentally a chaste man, self-consciously so, who sought and found in marriage not passion but family. Still less was his wife to be a companion in his vigorous intellectual and political life: that was a different sphere of activity, to which family life was a necessary but distinct complement.

Proudhon first met Euphrasie Piégard in February, 1847; they were married at the end of 1849, when he was nearly forty-one and

33. See especially the tenth and eleventh études of *De la Justice, Oeuv.,* VIII, vol. iv, 1–340, and *La Pornocratie, ou les femmes dans les temps modernes, Oeuvres posthumes* (Paris, 1865), in *Oeuv.,* XI, 303–469. The principal published reactions are works by Jenny d'Héricourt and Juliette Lambert, cited in the bibliography.

she, twenty-seven. Upon first seeing her, on the street, he was impressed by her modest demeanor and simplicity, which for him contrasted favorably with the manners more typically affected by Parisian girls. Even before introducing himself he seems to have determined that this was to be his wife. He had little difficulty winning the assent of the young woman and her family, despite his notoriety; no doubt at her age they welcomed the match.

Euphrasie was no beauty and she was ill educated, scarcely literate. But Proudhon did not like women with talents other than domestic ones, and he sought her hand without any amorous attraction. He had decided that it was time to start a family and with deliberation sought and wed a woman to join him in this. She was pregnant within weeks after they married.

But Proudhon did not regard his wife as either brood mare or kitchen drudge. For him a married couple became an androgynous unity, each of the pair contributing his or her unique and complementary qualities to the whole. His letters to Euphrasie during times of separation reveal deep affection for her.[34] At the same time he usually employed a somewhat formal manner in this correspondence, as the proper and rather stuffy husband writing to his unlettered wife. He wrote to her just of domestic affairs, touching on intellectual or political matters only when requesting a service of her, like conveying messages to his friends.

Naturally Proudhon was a most loving and beloved father, the ideal paterfamilias. Appropriately, the best-known portrait of the anarchist is *Proudhon and His Family*, painted by his friend Gustave Courbet and now in the Petit Palais in Paris. The picture shows Proudhon with his two daughters; originally Euphrasie was included, but the artist was dissatisfied with the representation of her, and painted her out. Euphrasie had declined to sit for the portrait and so was, as usual, self-effacing. In family life, as in much else, Proudhon's ideas clearly reflect the kind of man he was.

Despite his many quarrels with contemporaries, his ideas were widely popular. He was isolated by temperament and conviction from most conventional life and thought. No doubt many thought him dangerous and most others ignored him, but nevertheless his

34. *Lettres à sa femme* (Paris, 1950).

books sold very well. From mid-1848 until well after his death, workers in France and parts of Switzerland followed his lead more than any other's. Why? Though he was one of them in his origins, his critical skepticism and literary life set him apart. His ideas were appealing, no doubt, but usually expressed too intellectually for a proletarian audience, except in some of his newspaper articles years earlier.

Proudhon did not tailor his rhetoric in order to gain ascendancy in the nascent workers' movement. Few workers probably ever became familiar with his writing. It cannot be claimed then that there was widespread conversion of workers to his ideas. Rather, they must spontaneously have developed beliefs that were most aptly expressed in rational terms by Proudhon. This suggests that he had a sympathy with the workers' common point of view, or better, that it was his own—but this seems a bit odd. Not only was he isolated from men in general, but also he expressed repeatedly and sharply his disillusionment with the people. He had made it clear that he did not think mankind's past behavior encouraged optimism about what it might do in the future.

Yet there is no real conflict between a gloomy perception of human corruption and a love for man combined with hope for its moral, material, and spiritual salvation. The optimism of some progressivists, when alloyed with little or no recognition of human fallibility, is in a sense inhumane, because it sees not man himself but an incomplete reflection of him as the observer would like him to be. Proudhon's humanism is more genuine just because it is fully conscious of man's fallibility, without succumbing to the pessimism of the conservative. The following remarks express his attitude well:

> . . . since we are close to the new year, I hope that you begin this course again with a firm heart, virile resolution, a faithful love for humanity and a supreme disdain for the rabble.

> Craven and stupid humans! Rabble, foolish species! Oh! if I only had prospect of the deliverance of this vile multitude, I would be at the forefront of those who exploit it. But there is *right*, there is liberty, there is human dignity, there is the inviolability of our per-

sons, our minds, and our consciences; it is for this that I harden myself, and have no fear, I will not yield.[35]

Such comments, provoked primarily by disillusionment with the people, occur in the context of a more general vision of contemporary moral decadence. He had been judging the entire society in terms of essentially moral standards since his youth, and he increasingly found it defective. As the miseries of industrialization became more terrible, the complacency, indifference, and egoism of the bourgeoisie more insufferable, and the culture and regime of Second Empire France more corrupt, Proudhon's consciousness of and manifest disturbance with moral decadence throughout the society became more acute. It is a frequently recurring theme in both his public and his private writing, especially in his *De la Justice*, in its last *études* and supplementary notes added in the augmented 1860 edition. This is a typical example:

> More than once in the course of these Studies I have cited the diminution of well-being, in spite of the industrial creations which give luster to our epoch; the aversion for labor, the fever for luxury and pleasures, the general increase in the costs of production, which the perfection of human exploitation does not make up for at all; the frightful demoralization of the lower classes; the abandonment of family life, the development of libertinism, the enfeeblement of the races, manifested in so striking a manner by the decrease in height [presumably a reference to consequences of undernourishment]; the multiplication of crimes, robberies, bankruptcies, and suicides; the decadence of arts and letters, all the more astonishing as it is not related to incapacity of people: never have we seen so many able pens, so many artists trained in all the secrets of the trade; finally the discouragement of consciences who no longer believe in liberty and who ask themselves, like Brutus, if Justice is anything but a word.[36]

The intensity and universality of his moral consciousness was important for the maturation of Proudhon's philosophy. While his earlier work had certainly been wide in scope, its manner of focusing on the social problem somewhat circumscribed the extent of its

35. Letter to Micaud, December 25, 1855, *Corresp.*, VI, 287; Letter to J. Buzon, June 1, 1863 (the day after elections), *Corresp.*, XIII, 91.
36. *De la Justice, Oeuv.*, VIII, vol. iv, 453ff. Is it purely accidental that in modern Paris the Rue Proudhon leads into the Rue Taine?

moral vision. Finally, in *De la Justice* he went beyond these limits to comprehend and describe a complete moral universe. It is conditioned by his social concerns, his peculiar sociological theory, and his radical rebellion against received conventional beliefs. Yet his vision is a general one, encompassing more than revolutionary ideology. Its very breadth helps his conception to retain its force still today, when historical change has made the conditions of revolution very different than he knew.

In conceiving this moral universe, he prescribes the appropriate conditions for a just society and provides a historical perspective in which the steps of past and future progress toward this ideal are to be seen. Here his attention is concentrated, on the one hand, upon ideas, realization of which will make progress possible, and on the other upon the People, who must discover and know the ideas and act upon them for progress to occur. True progress cannot result from the ministrations or the enterprise of a privileged bourgeoisie and a paternalistic government. Progress must be a revolution, one genuinely based upon the people as a whole.

Thus, more deliberately than ever before in his writing, Proudhon in his last years concentrated upon the people and popular forces as the agency as well as the object of the revolutionary process. Their liberation and their moral regeneration are part of each other, even equivalent. In this context the development of Proudhon's attitudes about the workers' movement become clarified and clarifying.

After the June Days of 1848 and the repression of the militant workers he had developed his repudiation of the bourgeois, ostensibly democratic Republic, arguing this in his *Confessions* and the *Idée générale de la révolution*. Discouraged and forlorn over the powerlessness of the workers and the socialists who stood with them, in the 1848 presidential election he advocated voting for the socialist Raspail, primarily as a protest and also to reduce the chances for victory of Louis-Napoleon Bonaparte. In 1849, after expulsion from the Assembly, he did not want to stand for re-election. It would serve no good purpose, and he rejected the government on the basis of anarchist principle.

He still supported the cause of "social democracy," meaning by the term those socialists, radical republicans, and workers who were dedicated to establishing truly egalitarian democracy and to the solution of the social problem. While disagreeing on many subjects with most of his comrades in the cause and having little hope for salvation under any sort of government, he loved the cause and its broad social goals. Commitment to the objective of social revolution and egalitarian liberation could and should bind men to social democracy, despite wide differences in their views.

In 1852 elections Proudhon advocated participation in the voting and the taking of the oath of support for the regime by successful candidates. He did this despite the almost universally opposite position of other democrats, who thought it imperative to refuse such an admission of legitimacy to the usurper Bonaparte and to refuse cooperation with the reactionary forces who supported him. Proudhon, however, maintained that the supporters of democracy must not isolate themselves and close themselves into a sect alienated from the rest of the nation. A party of opposition would be valuable even if having little real power. He was led by tactical considerations, trying to find a basis for political viability in difficult circumstances. At the time he still thought it possible to turn the regime in the direction of reform.

By 1857 he had reversed this position, recommending abstention from elections and refusing requests from several constituencies that he offer himself as a candidate. In part this resulted from his conclusion that no meaningful social reforms would be forthcoming from the Bonapartist regime. More important, however, was the further evolution of his conception of a class struggle and its political consequences.

In the spring of 1863 elections were held for the national Corps Législatif. Although Napoleon's power was secure, there was a vocal opposition, composed mainly of Orleanists and republicans. They contested this election energetically, each faction trying to establish a position from which to advance to dominance when the Empire eventually folded—an event they thought not very far distant. If an end to the regime were in the offing, then Proudhon might reasonably have advocated voting for republican candidates in order to advance the cause of social democracy in the post-Imperial future, particularly to forestall victory then by forces hostile to the cause. He did in fact show rather accurate foresight into the manner and time-span of the Empire's decline, but he opposed support of republican candidates. On the eve of the elections he published a tract, *Les Démocrates assermentés et les réfractaires*,[37] advising the people to cast blank ballots.

Casting a blank ballot was "active abstention," explicitly signifying repudiation not only of the regime but of all those who, though in opposition, would swear loyalty to the Emperor. In concert with others, Proudhon sought to lead substantial numbers to active abstention in this manner. This effort and other similar ones achieved limited, although not insignificant, success. It was hoped that a sufficiently large protest vote might induce the regime to make changes in order to reduce disaffection, and that it would remove from the parliamentary opposition any claim to popular legitimization.

This represented a sharp contrast to his 1852 position, a contrast which he was at pains to explain in *Les Démocrates assermentés*, particularly since there he would no longer admit that the oath of allegiance could be permissible. In 1863 his negative appraisal of the opposition did not permit him to hope for progress through its victory, even in the event of a renewed establishment of the Republic.

Proudhon had always believed that with the existence of grave economic inequality class conflict would be fundamental in the society, the basic cause of its disorder and instability. Only in the last years of his career and in the context of the election-abstention question did he develop his ideas on the class struggle into a clear, definite, and complete conceptual structure. Finally he came to believe that the cleavage between the bourgeois and plebeian classes was completely unbridgeable and could be transcended only through the determined efforts of plebeians acting as a class to rise out of their inferior status. (While making sociological distinctions between different elements of the lower classes, especially between urban workers and peasants, and using a number of different words to denote the members of the lower classes, Proudhon thinks "plebeian" the most useful term. For him it denotes all of those who are poor and regularly subject to economic exploitation, regardless of the type of work.)

37. (Paris, 1863), in *Oeuv.*, XIII, 1–92.

He maintains that since 1789 all parties have been in coalition against the plebeian, with the political system basically the same: governmental concentration and "economic anarchy" (a term he frequently uses to describe unbridled free enterprise).[38] This constitutes the bourgeois order; the opposition has always been a part of it, serving as a foil to the prevailing faction but definitely not as its enemy. Always the opposition has remained faithful to caste and the system of the bourgeois order. It can never act in the true interests of the plebeians, because bourgeois and plebeian interests inevitably conflict, and the opposition will not betray its own caste.

Thus Proudhon calls upon the working class to break away from the tutelage of the bourgeoisie and to act exclusively by and for itself. His protest against such tutelage is strong, a reproof of contemporary proletarian attitudes.

> . . . there exist in the Democracy of workers, and in good number, educated persons capable of holding the pen as well as of handling words, knowing affairs, twenty times more capable, and especially more worthy, of representing [that Democracy] than the lawyers, journalists, writers, pedants, intriguers and adventurers to whom it throws away its suffrage, and it rejects them! It does not want them for its agents! The Democracy [of workers] has a horror of truly democratic candidates! It takes pride in giving itself for chiefs individuals who have an aristocratic color! Does it think to ennoble itself thereby? How is it, after all, if the people are ready for sovereignty, that they hide themselves behind their ex-tutors, that they lower their eyes like young girls before those who pay their wages, and that, when set belatedly to express their opinions and make acts of will, they only know how to follow the tracks of their former patrons and repeat their maxims? [39]

In February, 1864, a group of workers issued a political declaration, known as the Manifesto of the Sixty because it bore sixty workers' signatures, which was to become a major step in the development of an independent, self-conscious French proletarian movement.[40] The manifesto seems to have been inspired in large part by Proudhon's *Les Démocrates assermentés*. Its principal

38. *De la Capacité politique, Oeuv.*, III, 241ff.
39. Ibid., 87ff.
40. The manifesto is reprinted in *Oeuv.*, III, 409–17.

author probably was Henri Tolain, a worker himself, a promoter of workers' candidacies a year earlier, and soon afterward a founder of the First Socialist International, then a Proudhonist delegate to it. In the next decade he was a deputy and senator for Paris.

The manifesto was a radical document proposing and defining the conditions for a militant, separate workers' political movement. In most respects its position was like Proudhon's, but it advocated having workers stand as candidates in elections. Proudhon responded at length to the manifesto in an open letter written in March, 1864.[41]

He supports most of the manifesto, approving the idea of having workers stand as candidates of the proletariat specifically, not merely as citizens who happen to be workers. However, his support is for the proletarian identification and for the idea of proletarian political self-consciousness, not for the candidacy itself. He insists that the candidacy will hurt the workers' cause, for it is impossible to cooperate with the enemy, even in so limited a way as participating in his elections. Again he urges abstention.

In reiterating his insistence on abstention, he is not just saying that one should decline to lie down with the devil. He also is asserting that the enemy controls everything, including the press, and thus it can only be degrading and fruitless to attempt to engage in politics. He did not stop with this negative conclusion, however, but went on to work out a further analysis of the conditions and prospects of a popularly based political movement.

Through the summer of 1864, Proudhon wrote the first part of such an analysis, the *Contradictions politiques,* a book which was never finished and was first published only in 1870.[42] Here he examines the conditions of the class struggle and of the political problems of a workers' movement. The final and consummating part of his analysis is *De la Capacité politique des classes ouvrières,*[43] one of the most important of all his books. In conjunction with *Du Principe fédératif* it constitutes Proudhon's final statement of the appropriate course for men to take in order to create a just society.

Having rejected the people's engagement in bourgeois politics, he

41. "Lettre aux ouvriers en vue des élections de 1864," *Oeuv.,* XIII, 305-26.
42. (Paris, 1870), *Oeuvres posthumes,* VI; in *Oeuv.,* XIII, 105-303.
43. (Paris, 1865); in *Oeuv.,* III.

suggests that they have not yet succeeded in achieving a separate identity. In consequence they are not yet able either to affect the course of government or to bring about its revolutionary change. To achieve this vital separate identity the people will have to make major changes in their whole outlook and their patterns of behavior. The requisite changes in morals, ideas, and customs should be part of, result from, and make possible the adoption of mutualist ideals and forms of social relationships. He envisages this as a dynamic process and directly relevant to the immediate practical problems of proletarian politics and organization of labor.

In fact, the relevance of Proudhon's final vision to these problems was to be demonstrated in subsequent years by the extent to which the practice of the French workers' movement followed his recommendations, although not for the most part doing so consciously. Even after the eclipse of Proudhonist leaders following the disaster of the Paris Commune of 1871, the actual temper of the movement at the level of the rank and file often seems to have been closer to Proudhon's point of view than to those of the new Marxist leaders. In this sense he was indeed a genuine ideologue of the people.

During 1864 the respiratory and cardiac ailments which had long plagued Proudhon became increasingly acute. He was unable to attend the London meetings which established the First Socialist International in the fall. As the year's end approached, he became too weak to write; his last letters he dictated to his daughter Catherine. He remained intellectually alert and eager to finish the most important of his numerous incomplete manuscripts, *De la Capacité politique*. In his last days he told his friend Gustave Chaudey in complete detail what he intended for the concluding chapter and for revision of the rest, which was already in printer's proof. Chaudey wrote the final chapter according to these instructions after the other's death.

Proudhon died on January 19, 1865, at the age of fifty-six. The years of his birth and death were the same as those of Abraham Lincoln. A few days earlier the curé of the local parish came to his home, but Proudhon refused to see him. "This man does his duty," he said, "but let him know I have no need of his ministry."

He turned to his wife and said to her, "It is from you that I ask absolution." [44]

He was buried in Passy, the quarter of Paris where he had lived since returning from Belgium. Thousands of workers and other friends and admirers were present. The movement of the funeral cortege to the cemetery was interrupted by the sudden arrival of a large unit of soldiers with drums beating. The crowd called out, "Silence! Respect the dead!" and the troops stopped. Then the crowd shouted, "Beat the salute!" and the drummers did so, to the consternation of the colonel commanding, who had given no orders. After receiving explanations from members of the family, the officer commanded his troops to resume their march, and as they passed he saluted the bier with his sword. Then the funeral procession continued on to the Passy cemetery. [45]

It was a fitting conclusion to the anarchist's life.

44. Anecdote from an obituary by L. Legault in *L'Avenir national,* excerpted, with other obituaries, by D. Alph in *Le Figaro,* XII, 1037 (January 22, 1865), 2.

45. This anecdote is given by Jacques Bourgeat in his *Proudhon: Père du socialisme français* (Paris, 1949), 213ff. The story was authenticated for him by Proudhon's daughter Catherine, who lived until 1947.

nine: Justice

What is the fundamental, organic, regulatory, sovereign principle of societies; the principle which, subordinating all others, governs, protects, restrains, chastises the rebellious elements, in case there is need for suppression? Is it love, force, necessity, or hygiene? There are systems and schools for all these affirmations.

This principle, according to me, is Justice.

What is Justice?—The essence of humanity.

What has it been since the beginning of the world?—Almost nothing.

What must it be?—Everything.

PROUDHON HAD ASKED the "What is . . . ?" question in many different forms and places since first inquiring, "What is property?" This formulation, from *De la Justice,* is in effect the final query, subsuming all others within its universality.[1] Justice was always the master concept of his philosophy; he had clearly specified it as such in *Qu'est-ce que la propriété?*, where he wrote:

Justice is the central star which governs society, the pole on which the political world turns, the principle and rule of all transactions. Nothing is done among men except by virtue of *right;* nothing without the invocation of justice. Justice is not the work

1. *De la Justice, Oeuv.,* VIII, vol. i, 280. Other uses of the formula are cited above, pp. 43, 129.

of law at all; on the contrary, law is never anything but a declaration and application of the *just*, in all circumstances where men can find their interests related. Then if the idea that we form for ourselves of the just and of right be ill determined, if it be incomplete or even false, it is evident that all our legislative applications would be wicked, our institutions vicious, our politics erroneous: consequently, there would be disorder and social evil.[2]

That had been more a declaration of commitment than an analytic statement. It was the intimation of a point of view, but not yet a complete philosophy. What was justice for him when he wrote this? *Egalité* and *liberté* conceived more broadly than by the men of the Jacobin clubs a half century before. *Fraternité*, also thought of differently, but less clearly than the other two. Justice was also the foundation of law, but he had then done more to perceive what law ought not to be than to see what best to do in order that law might be just.

In the two decades intervening between the preceding statements about justice, his ideas on the subject had been developing. He had tried to invent a science of society to discover the way men could achieve the goal of justice. Finding his explorations in science and system unsatisfying, he had then been plunged into direct political involvement, in 1848 and after. His experience grew as another decade passed, and so did the extent of his philosophical explorations. The elements had long been there in his intellect and in his spirit. Now he brought all together and built upon them to create *De la Justice dans la révolution et dans l'Eglise.* The critical faculties formerly exercised to destroy received ideas now became an integral aspect of a constructive moral and social philosophy, as well as the basis for it. The epigraph of his *Philosophie de la misère*, "I have destroyed and I shall build," was now fulfilled.

> Man, by virtue of the reason with which he is endowed, has the faculty of feeling his dignity in the person of a fellow man as in his own person, of affirming himself as individual and as species simultaneously.
>
> . . . JUSTICE is the product of this faculty: it is *respect, spontaneously felt and reciprocally guaranteed, for human dignity, in*

2. *Oeuv.,* IV, 144.

*whatever person and whatever circumstance it finds itself jeopar-
dized, and at whatever risk its defense exposes us to.*

. . . From the definition of Justice are deduced those of *right*
and of *duty*.

Right is for each one the faculty of requiring of others respect
for the human dignity in his person;—duty, the obligation for
each one to respect this dignity in another.

. . . From the identity of reason in all men, and of the feeling
of respect which brings them to maintain their mutual dignity at
any price, results equality in front of Justice.[3]

This statement gives *subjective* meaning to a concept of justice,
for it defines the subjective attitudes of the just man, but *objective*
content is absent. We are not told here what objective forms human society must take for it to be just. Therefore Proudhon goes
on to give such objectivity to his conception, and to redefine justice
in its multiple particular objective aspects.

His conception of justice is not, of course, wholly novel. The
definitions of justice by many others before him closely resemble
his—or at least they propose recognition of human dignity as vital
to justice if not its sole defining condition.[4] However, his own conception does have distinctive features which differentiate it from
comparable views.

A legist might define justice primarily as a matter of a rigorous,
objective application of laws. This leads, however, to our asking
what is the source and the basis or rationale of the laws. In traditional terms the source would be the prevailing authority, usually
divine will as stated by officials of the governing ecclesiastical and
secular institutions. Alternatively, the source would be Reason—
an authority no less compelling, but an internal one, unlike the
external power of God and King. Further, external authority may
rely in part on reason, as was usual in the Church, and expect rational men to find its authority all the more compelling because of
its rationality.

Whatever the source, the primary laws are derived from standards of morality, as either applications or generalized normative
statements of them. Thus moral standards are the basis of law,

3. *Oeuv.*, VIII, vol. i, 423.
4. Proudhon discusses a number of writers in this regard; *Oeuv.*, VIII, vol. i,
427–33.

either directly or through their role in determining the judgments of lawmakers about the norms they enact. Justice then is a matter of implementing moral standards through the establishment of normative regulation, ordinarily enforced by institutional means.

However, the original moral standards are primarily those of *individual* conduct. Moral norms and moral responsibility traditionally are conceived as matters concerning the individual in himself and in relation to the Divine. Even with standards having social content, like the injunction of Christian charity, attention focuses upon individual sin and virtue.

Proudhon's moralism differs. Justice is not the application of moral rules; it is itself the fundamental moral standard. For him, morality is social: this basic standard is defined solely as a matter of the relation between the individual and the rest of mankind. Despite Proudhon's concentration on the individual, in his demand for right moral action he regards one's conduct as having moral significance only in its social consequences and relations.

Moreover, he recognizes no external authority as source of any norm. The rules a man lives by must be entirely internal in origin, stemming from his rational faculties. In no other way will men act morally; they must freely recognize and accept moral norms through rational conviction, and not be forced to accept them through obedience to the dicta of others.

Explicitly adapting theological terminology, Proudhon writes that justice is "*Logos*, the common soul of humanity, incarnate in each one of us." Elsewhere he says, "Justice is not at all a commandment decreed by a superior authority to an inferior being . . . justice is immanent in the human soul; it is the soul's foundation, constituting its highest power and its supreme dignity." [5]

The conception of *Logos*, or Divine Spirit, as universally immanent within all men is an important theme in Christian theology, though it is not always stressed in this way. Proudhon's ideas of justice as *Logos* and as "spontaneous respect for human dignity" correspond closely to the conceptions of God and love found in the thought of a number of heretical and Protestant mystics, although it is unlikely that he was acquainted with their writings. The affinity is intriguing, though, especially in view of his continu-

5. *Oeuv.*, VIII, vol. i, 415; VI, 127.

ing interest in the origins of religion, particularly Christianity, which parallels the desires of these mystics to return to a primitive Christian faith, divested of dogma, idolatry, and ecclesiastical authority.

Proudhon's distaste for the Church is similar, but more bitter. With his jaundiced anticlericalism and restricted knowledge of the varieties of Christian thought, he cannot find in religious faith, however molded, a means of expressing his yearnings. Moreover, his economic and political concerns direct him to a perspective which is secular in tone and temper, whatever affinities it may have to religious beliefs.

His idea of the internal, rational origin of morality and justice leads to more than a rejection of external authority. Like his Enlightenment predecessors, Proudhon believes that rationality is the essence of human identity and that all men are equal just because they *can* reason, regardless of how effectively they use their faculties. Emphasizing as he does both this universal rationality and the necessity for each man to recognize it in every other, Proudhon's approach bears egalitarian implications even more strongly than did conceptions of the *philosophes*. His egalitarianism, always quite radical in its conclusions, becomes more profound in this context.

Perhaps most important is the way his approach concentrates on the development of a genuine social morality by each individual thinking and acting for himself. This distinguishes Proudhon from many other socialists who concentrate so much upon social dynamics that they lack his conception of individual responsibility for these dynamics. Despite his attention to the forms and institutions of social organization, he is convinced that all depends ultimately on individuals' responses to social demands upon them. Individual morality and social structure are interdependent, but the former is the more basic and vital determinant.

Obviously this has bearing on his condemnation of the use of political means to solve social problems. It also leads to his rejection of explanations of moral corruption which suggest that only changes in bad institutions are needed to bring about thorough moral regeneration. For this reason he suspects utopian schemes even before considering the possibilities of the suppression of individual liberty in a collectivist or other utopian community.

Starting with the basic notion of reciprocal respect for individual dignity and rights, Proudhon goes on to define economic justice in terms of reciprocal exchange of goods and services on a basis of equality and mutual benefit.

> *Reciprocity of respect,* such is the principle of personal right;
> *Reciprocity of service,* such is the principle of real and economic right. The second is an application of the first: from there the expression of which I have availed myself, application of Justice to political economy.
>
> Justice does not create economic facts . . . it does not disregard them; it does not misrepresent them for its own use; it does not impose alien laws on them. It is limited to ascertaining their variable and antinomic nature; in this antinomy it seizes upon a law of equilibrium, and from this law of equilibrium, similar to itself, it makes a practical principle, a general truth for society, an obligation.

Here he develops further his criticism of the theses of liberal political economy, which he attacks for refusal to count moral values as relevant to its analyses and judgments. Political economy is not a science, indifferent as it is to the just and unjust, counting merely the quantifiable; it is just a collection of scraps and undifferentiated matter. Only Justice, through its formula of reciprocity and equilibrium, can reestablish order, create unity, and bring to the variability and contradiction of phenomena a rational foundation of law and constancy.[6]

The facts of economic and social life are by their very nature indeterminant, variable, contradictory. The operative forces are perpetually in conflict. Rigid expressions of law and broad generalizations cannot adequately describe the indeterminant and contradictory, and thus no true science can be based merely on the analysis of facts. Proudhon's own approach is one of striking equations between opposites in which the two sides can vary as independent entities, finding levels for balance and reciprocity. He believes that this makes the facts and forces of economic life susceptible of intellectual definition and order. "Justice" is thus the

6. *Oeuv.,* VIII, vol. ii, 149. "Antinomy" is a term adopted long before by Proudhon while under Kantian influence, and is used imprecisely by him to denote contradiction and opposition of forces.

pattern of analysis that makes life intelligible as well as being the basic moral code.

"Science" and "morality" are for him virtually identical faces of the ever-extensible complex of ideas called "justice." Justice, true moral sense, and science are all the rational regard of the human life situation, making it intelligible, and ultimately perfectible by means of its intelligibility.

Combining as he does affirmation of rationalism with repudiation of inflexible systematic thought, Proudhon devotes much of *De la Justice* to attacks upon "absolutism." The first enemy is absolutism of ideas. From absolute idea systems come absolute institutions, above all the authoritarian Church and State.

What he means by the "absolute" remains obscure, because he employs the term in varied ways and without great precision. He does not reject the possibility of certainty and universality in ideas: justice is certain and universal. But the idea of justice is perpetually modifiable in its particulars and application; it is at once certain and flexible. The absolute to be rejected is the dogmatic idea which comprehends and includes all and from which law is derived in abstraction from the actuality of the human condition.[7] In the first instance the absolute idea thus rejected is that of God in his infinite and all-powerful universality. For Proudhon God must remain "the eternal X." If he be more than the *Logos* immanent in man, he is unknowable and without discernible effect on life.

Of more general significance is Proudhon's rejection of "absolutism" in worldly matters, where the word takes on the broadest connotations. In social relations absolutism is inordinate emphasis upon individual will and interests—demanding, unrelenting egoism. This is absolute because it disregards the relative: other men's needs and rights in relation to one's own personal desires.

In science and philosophy, absolutism is first of all dogmatic thought, but it is more besides. It is thinking characterized by total abstraction from actual life and by concentration on generalizations that simplify and make regular that which is complex and varied. Such conceptions are figments and fantasies which should

7. Georges Guy-Grand suggests that Proudhon is here adopting Kantian doctrines about the relativity of knowledge. Probably his rejection of the absolute in ideas can be better understood through recalling Kant's conceptions (Introduction to *De la Justice*, *Oeuv.*, VIII, vol. i, 69ff.).

be devoid of true relevance to reality, except that they are utilized by institutions of authority as the bases and instruments of oppression. A priori reasoning, especially as employed in theology and speculative secular philosophy, is thus repudiated by Proudhon, but so too is the bulk of positivist thinking in social science, especially in political economy. Ideas must be based on facts and phenomena, but never abstracted from them altogether or disconnected from moral values.

In rejecting absolutism in ideas, he does not advocate a wholly relativistic approach, which he attacks as futile Pyrrhonist skepticism. Ideas can achieve certitude and generality, but in both qualities they improve and expand as they comprehend and express more truly and completely the reality of things and phenomena, and they must change as the material of experience changes. With such expanding certitude and relevance, ideas are essential to moral regeneration and to social revolution. It should be recalled how bitter Proudhon was in February, 1848, because he thought that the revolution then had been born without ideas to sustain it. The revolution must be based on ideas and the ideas popularized—and internalized popularly as the foundation of a sense of justice. In his criticisms of contemporary thought and its emptiness, his strictures are directed at popular concepts as well as at those of learned men. According to him, in France people have lost even a basic notion of standards of moral behavior. The just and unjust are for them only vague, indeterminant expressions of convention. He writes:

> The individual's reason will always be mixed with elements that are passional, egoistic, transcendental, in short, absolutist. This is observed in the movement of the multitude, national prejudices, hatred between peoples, so often embellished with the name of patriotism: all are things that are only individual absolutisms multiplied by the number of empty blockheads who express it.[8]

Humanity has long been the victim of ideas and institutions derived from such absolutist individual characteristics—but "collective reason" can destroy this system and replace it with practice based upon the equal and common quality of men. This collective reason results from the opposition of the ideas of individuals,

8. *Oeuv.*, VIII, vol. iii, 268.

whose particularistic conceptions regularly are absolutist. The resultant is produced through free and open discussion of individual points of view; with the interchange of ideas people can understand and reconcile differences. The clash of opinions leads to the "annulling" of incompatible points and, "considering only the product of the antagonistic terms to be real and legitimate, we come to synthetic ideas, very different, often even the inverse, of the conclusions of the *individual I*." [9]

The synthesis is collective reason which, freed of the absolutist elements of individual reason, can more nearly approach a true appraisal of the real relations between the elements of experience—and thus serves as a basis for both social and individual action. Collective reason is simultaneously superior to and dependent upon individual reason, for it is a composite of the independent thoughts of individuals. It cannot suppress their autonomous reasoning and can be meaningful only to the extent that each man reasons for himself freely. Collective reason must comprehend within itself *all* the differences between each one of us; if it includes only the positions taken by those strong enough to assert themselves above others, then the fatal absolutism remains.

Proudhon's conception of collective reason recalls Rousseau's general will, but the former is much more specifically defined. By avoiding the essential ambiguity of his predecessor's idea, Proudhon precludes the personification of the collective and abstraction from reality that he believes characteristic of Rousseauean theory.

Collective reason is another aspect of the universal spirit which itself is the recognition of true justice in the minds of all men. How is such a spirit to be developed when people are such egoistic and empty blockheads? It is here that we see that Proudhon's conception of social dynamics is not confined to the equalizing and balancing of elements. His ideal is a society with fundamental organic unity and solidarity, but this is not to be achieved through coercion and constraint, or through eliciting adherence to false symbols like the nation. It is certainly not to be achieved through a hierarchical ordering of mankind, as in the ideal of conservative organicism. Proudhon's is an ideal of unity by means of the voluntary, rational recognition of the justice and the personal advantages of solidarity

9. Ibid., 253.

based upon the mutual recognition of rights and interests in all social relations, with arrangements undertaken for reciprocal benefit.

Such solidarity is conceived as unity in diversity, a harmony achieved while preserving equality, individual liberty, and independence. The utopian character of this conception is immediately apparent, but Proudhon's skepticism about the moral and political conduct of the people should not be forgotten. Though he sees a way to realize his ideal, he is restrained in his hopes for its fulfillment.

Justice can be made real and people made to be just either through *external* pressures, including social ones, or by creating and developing the *internal* faculty in each man whereby he recognizes and appreciates the dignity of others as he does his own. Proudhon insists on the latter, although he recognizes the possible utility of social pressures—when noncoercive—in leading a man to form this faculty for himself.

Men develop this faculty as they acquire sympathetic understanding of their fellows, through constructive association with them. Moreover, collective reason is not simply what is left when elements of individual opinions in conflict cancel each other out. Rather, it is a new creation resulting from the interaction of opposed views and interests, the synthetic product of a dialectic which is at the very center of social relations. Thus through controversy mankind grows in self-mastery and moral stature, becoming more closely knit in the process.

Associative bonds develop within and between social groupings where men come together naturally, through propinquity and mutual need. The most important and compelling associations are those formed when men join in productive labor. Therefore collectivities of working men should be the principal schools for the growth of sympathetic understanding and the discovery of social solidarity and morality. This conclusion is the basis of Proudhon's fully matured theory of a working-class revolutionary movement, which will be examined later.

In speaking of man's developing collective reason, Proudhon opposes the *immanence* of the idea of justice to the *transcendence* of the Divine Being in the orthodox conception. The transcendent is external, authoritarian, and thereby suppresses individuality; it is inaccessible to the rational faculties. Thinking of God in this way, Proudhon makes religion, along with government, his main target in attacking the absolute and the injustice resulting from it.[10]

While obscure in some particulars, overall his attitudes toward religion are clear and unaltering, although the balance of emphasis changes. Always sharply anticlerical, under the Empire he becomes more intensely hostile to the Church because he is more perturbed than ever about the clergy's supposed efforts to suppress liberty. It is the Church as a major reactionary force, Catholic thought as absolute philosophy, and God as transcendent Being that Proudhon is fighting.

Although not affirming God's existence, he will not deny it either, for that would be to pronounce upon the unknowable. Thus he is not atheistic, but he is anti-theist, since he will not accept the transcendent God of established religion. He will not argue or speculate on the articles of religious faith, but he insists that they can neither be taken as elements of knowledge nor serve as premises of justice. He does retain a certain respect for the religious spirit and the force of faith, especially in its historical role. However, he believes that theology must be supplanted by secular philosophy and religious spirit by the human sense of justice.

For Proudhon the primary ethical content of Christianity is true, but religion is false. He accepts its moral precepts, but for different reasons. For progress to occur, independent reason must succeed myth and the absolute, facts succeed mystery and miracle, ideas succeed symbols, and human will and energy succeed divine providence. Quietism about present human misery results in part from undue attention to life after death, and it must be ended. So too must the denigration and demeaning of man because he is a sinner.

In sum, Proudhon believes that the Revolution and the Church are irreconcilably in opposition, and not just because of the reactionary political role of the clergy. The Church can be joined to the Revolution, subordinated to it, or eliminated. It must be the

10. For a thorough, able, and different examination of Proudhon's religious philosophy, see *Proudhon et christianisme* (Paris, 1945), by Henri du Lubac, a distinguished Jesuit philosopher. Many of Proudhon's pieces concerning religion are collected in *Ecrits sur la religion, Oeuv.*, XV.

last, for to transform religion as Proudhon would require is to abolish religion as he conceives of it.

The absolutist mind takes for its maxim authority; as the Church is to man's spirit, so is the State to his attitudes about relations with his fellows. The arbitrary, the necessary, the fatalism, and the transcendence in the Church have their precise correlates in the structure and the idea of the State. Proudhon matches his attacks on religion with strictures against the secular equivalents in politics, emphasizing parallels between their distinct but closely connected realms.

There are two standards for the regulation of human society: justice and *raison d'état*. By the one phrase *raison d'état* Proudhon connotes all that he has ever said in his anarchist criticism. It is absolutism and the arbitrary; it is every thought and act whereby men employ power to violate the natural rights of those subject to their authority. By *raison d'état* rulers "justify" acts which serve only the interests of the State and the privileged, doing nothing to serve the society on whose behalf government was constituted in the first place. "Justice, by the hypothesis of natural and social inequality . . . becomes a superfluity, an embarrassment for a power whose principle is necessity, whose means is force, whose goal is to prevent through force the revolt of poverty against privilege." [11]

All of the State's power originates solely in the citizenry; the State exists only to serve them, and it has no higher interest or prerogative. That is what government ought to be but never is: there is always *raison d'état*, even if the State should lay aside the service of special interest groups and its stewardship for a false, transcendent God. The interests of the State itself and its preoccupation with the problems it generates for itself preclude the fulfillment of its duty to the people. To fulfill the objectives of *raison d'état*, the State seeks to complete its "unity of power," subsuming all authority and denying both individuality and integral community. Thus the spirit of the absolute, unable to achieve culmination in the Church alone, reaches complete fruition in the idea and practice of the State.

11. *Oeuv.*, VIII, vol. ii, 178.

Given the IDEA of government, the *form* follows: these two terms are tied together, like the organization of the animal is to its destiny. We know what until now has been the form of States, according to the idea of the exploitation of man by man: despotic centralization, feudal hierarchy, an order of patricians with clienteles, democratic militarism, mercantile oligarchy, constitutional monarchy.[12]

Closely tied to Proudhon's criticism of Church and State is his rejection of the bourgeois system and its ideologies, especially liberal economics. Church, State, and the unequal, stratified economic order complement and support each other in the maintenance of fundamental, near universal injustice. He applies his conception of fatality and arbitrariness in absolute thought and rule to the bourgeois order also. Man's freedom has always been circumscribed by the fatality of nature—the natural forces beyond his control and often beyond the compass of his understanding. Yet man through his rational faculties can push back or break through limits imposed upon him by natural conditions: not only does he overcome many of them through developing technical expertise, but also he learns how to live with them and grow in freedom despite them, through intelligent reordering of his life and that of his society. For example, the division of labor in society manages through specialization to reduce the effect of limited natural strength and abilities.

Potentially, nothing which is really important for man should be impossible for him to achieve, but the bourgeois order rests on a denial of this premise, on the implicit conviction that the arbitrary in the present life cannot be escaped and that the bulk of humanity must bear the burden of unkind necessity. Conventional faith in progress does not negate this fatalism, for it accepts the burdens of the present even while deriving millenarian expectations from the promise of the future. That future is to be enriched by material accumulation achieved through enterprise, technology, and the extension of knowledge, but there is little vision of the structural and moral change that Proudhon thinks essential to genuine social, *human* progress.

So liberty remains denied and the misery of most of mankind accepted because it is supposed to be necessary in nature just now.

12. Ibid., 253ff.

Egoism, the doctrine that self-interest is the proper goal of all human actions, is accepted as the core of bourgeois ethics. If, in the face of hard necessity, little relief of human suffering can readily be gained through altruistic social concern, and the arbitrary displaces liberty for most men, then why should anyone be condemned if he seizes available opportunities to improve his own condition without regard to others? This kind of self-seeking fatalism is the heart of the bourgeois mentality which Proudhon criticizes.

Economic science rests on the same fatalistic assumptions, even if in its quietism it does not assert doctrines as dogmatically rigid as those of traditional Catholic theology. Economists presume that the economy is subject to certain laws of operation independent of the human will and thus of man's justice. Despite his technical mastery of much of nature, man must still struggle against the reason of things and even be engulfed by them. Moreover, in practice the needs of man and his society are subordinated to things and their management. Proudhon insists that the order of precedence should be just the opposite. He denies the suggestions of laissez faire economics that man cannot and should not interfere in the economic process, and that the laws of that process are definite and regular. Truth is to be found by discerning through observations the variations as well as the regularity of the economy, and by recognizing how human will affects the process. Thereby economic science can be used constructively for the common good rather than as the instrument of the rich. The science is not now in satisfactory conjunction with the needs of the society: then we have not yet arrived at the necessary first principles which must govern the acquisition, possession, and transmission of goods.

Liberal economists believe, he says, that the revolution was completed with the elimination of feudalism and the introduction of liberal economic policies, particularly those of laissez faire. He concludes that such beliefs imply that labor is not essentially human, but only an external necessity imposed by natural conditions. Nothing of labor is spontaneous, and its freedom is only what is left after the impositions; all labor is thus repugnant.

Proudhon rejects all these beliefs, insisting that labor is indeed essential to the life experience and should be fulfilling and liberating rather than onerous and enslaving. Then the function of economics is to make labor thus, not to accept the present morass while describing it and discovering ways for able, fortunate, or unscrupulous egoists to achieve comfort despite the unpleasantness of conditions. He calls for:

> Land for the one who cultivates it;
> Trade for the one who exercises it;
> Capital for the one who employs it;
> The product for the producer;
> The benefit of collective force for all those who work together, and wages adjusted according to participation . . .
> In two words, the fatality of nature redeemed by the liberty of man. . . .
> Either fatality and privilege, or liberty and equality: there is the dilemma. On the one side are paganism, despotism, the routine of peoples and all their history; on the other, science, right, the future, the infinite. It is necessary to choose, and first it is necessary to judge.[13]

The capitalist economy divides the society, making competition into civil war and "labor-saving" machinery into the instruments of destruction and death of the human spirit. When men meet as employer and worker, capitalist and wage-earner, proprietor and tenant, then they meet as opponents on a wholly unequal footing. Since they do not enter their transactions on an equitable basis, there is no justice—and no justification for the acts of the stronger party. Only power matters, power and the convictions of absolutist casuistry.

All of Proudhon's earlier condemnation of the bourgeoisie and capitalism are presented once more in *De la Justice;* now they are placed in this broader analytic framework of the structure of justice and its opposites. He repudiates the bourgeois system because of its profound economic and social injustice, but also because of its part in constituting the oppressive and absorbing central power of a hierarchical society, one headed by authoritarian institutions and directed by *raison d'état* and absolutist norms.

The liberal bourgeoisie thinks it escapes authority and enjoys liberty in free economic enterprise—but all it does is create eco-

13. Ibid., vol. iii, 16ff. Fulfillment of man through labor will be discussed in more detail in Ch. 11.

nomic anarchy, shredding the social fabric in the name of individualism. True individualism and viable, humane anarchism require social solidarity and mutualist reciprocity as complement and prerequisite if man is not to destroy himself. But the bourgeoisie cannot distinguish potentially destructive conflict from potentially constructive competition, and it has no principles, only interests. It thinks it escapes the arbitrary through the free play of market forces, but there is nothing more arbitrary than the values of the marketplace, bearing as they do no relation to real values, which are constituted only by labor. Ironically, when the bourgeoisie lets its political views and its vote be determined solely by the rise and fall of the marketplace, it exchanges the arbitrariness of King and Church for a new one no less confining.

In its preoccupation with material gain the bourgeoisie is content to accommodate itself to despotism. It seeks wealth above all, and most bourgeois have few political ambitions if government is hospitable to "free" enterprise and gives them a modicum of what passes for liberty. It does little to oppose State oppression of the people, but protests mightily at State interference in business affairs. The misery of the masses serves just to draw the bourgeoisie closer to the State, in their fear of insurrection and jacqueries.

> The bourgeois is the friend of order, in the sense that he fears uproar, agitation, demonstrations, overturned omnibuses, ripped up paving stones, breakage of street lamps. But the arbitrary in government, the confusion of powers, the parliamentary intrigues, the jumble of ideas, the twisting of laws, the abuse of majorities, the chaos in accounts, the general corruption, these scarcely move him. His soul is like the Bourse: the least uproar alarms him, while the annihilation of moral life has no effect on him.[14]

Proudhon's view of the bourgeoisie is a dual one, for while condemning the class as a whole and individuals in their roles as perpetrators of injustice, he expresses an understanding of the bourgeois as the unwitting victim of his own egoism and mistaken ideas and fears. The true villains in Proudhon's view are not individuals—save some particular ones in positions of authority—but the institutions, laws, and ideologies that systematize injustice. He can sym-

14. Ibid., 145.

pathize with human fallibility while rejecting what men have created in their error and amorality. Church, State, and capitalist economy are the highest expressions of the absolute: as such they are human creations, to be displaced by humane creations, but they are also abstractions with existence apart from their human creators and agents. That is why they must be destroyed, and it is the basis of their vulnerability as well.

This is so first of all because the impersonality of the sources of evil makes possible positive change in the mind and will of the men who exercise the power and without whom the system does not function. Probably more important is Proudhon's belief that the system, operating as it does with its own impersonal rationale, contains within itself the seeds of its own destruction. There are too many irreconcilable contradictions in the system, too many elements in destructive conflict, for it to achieve lasting stability.

Government is supposed to exist to maintain order: that is its primary rationale. The chronic ill health and instability of governments indicate that something is wrong, both with government itself and with the system it regulates. "And you ask where revolutions come from? From the exclusion of Justice from human transactions, the betrayal of the social economy to privilege, when it is not abandoned to chance." [15] Economic and social injustice are fundamental; government and the Church are the instruments for preserving, in the name of order, the system in which the injustice is perpetrated.

It is wrong to seek the causes of government's instability in its origins, forms, organization, and personnel, for these are more accidental than essential. What is necessary, Proudhon insists, is the examination of the spirit which animates government, its soul and its *idea*. If the idea is true, then the State should withstand all threats; if not, it must fall. Examined thus, the State must be seen as in irreconcilable opposition to Justice and right, indifferent to every moral idea. It is an instrument of force, relying on ideas of fatality and providence. Substituting the appearance of unity achieved through power for the organic unity to be achieved through genuine social solidarity, it oscillates from catastrophe to catastrophe.[16]

15. Ibid., vol. ii, 81.
16. Ibid., 169ff.

Based as it is on oppression, consecrated to the maintenance of inequality, the State is continually faced with revolt. It must be prepared to utilize force to suppress such resistance; ultimately this is self-destructive.

Instead of the State arising from the society, the reverse occurs, with the standards of society determined according to the idea and form of State power. Justice is conceived as an "emanation" of force, which is the very negation of justice. Real justice results from the equilibrium of forces; society's normal condition should be one of a distribution of powers whose dynamic interplay results in a balance without coercion and constraint. Thereby stable order can be constituted. Instead, the State, relying as it must on dominant coercive force, makes its "justice" only an attribute and function of authority, not a spirit inherent in the citizenry. They obey only because of the coercion: this cannot be a stable basis for order.

Proudhon believes that harmony or accord necessarily supposes terms in opposition, not an identity of terms, which would make "accord" meaningless. Divergent interests in conflict are natural to society; there is a foundation for resolution of conflicts in the simultaneously existing community of interests and in similar customs and beliefs. The prerequisite for social stability has to be the balanced opposition of divergent interests of various groups and individuals. This requires a meeting of the different interests on a basis of equality and flexibility, not of rigid hierarchy and attempts to dominate through superior power. If conflict is "resolved"—that is, suppressed—by dominance in place of equilibrium, then the weaker parties are not satisfied, having acquiesced only through constraint.

As long as they remain weaker, then a semblance of order can be maintained, but it is inherently unstable. Force which is not counterbalanced by equal force naturally varies in the margin of its superiority. Other groups coexist with the dominant one and may clash with it. The dissatisfied challenge their masters when able, or when desperate; where power alone rules, each element maneuvers to increase its own strength and to exercise it to achieve dominance in transactions with every other element. The "order" thus achieved is only a shifting complexion of forces jockeying for position. Such a society is in a normal state of war.

Every self-conscious being, whether an individual or a collectivity, is naturally sovereign simply because it is conscious of its own identity and interest. If that sovereignty is denied by some group or institution with the will and strength to make that denial practically effective, then conflict must result from this contradiction between potential and effective sovereignty.

"Sovereignty" in the sense thus used by Proudhon is equivalent to fundamental liberty. Authority and liberty are contradictory and consequently in perpetual struggle with each other. The principle of authority is essential to government, and there tends naturally to the development of hierarchy and the centralized unity of power. The consequent conflict with the principle of liberty leads to concessions without conciliation. The latter is not ultimately possible, because the two principles are mutually exclusive. As a result, political systems are a composite of these opposite principles. The opposition results in political movement—the eternally shifting forms and practice of government—because of the continual imbalance of power.

The ostensible forms of various governments are only ideals; actual constructs are more complex, combinations of often antithetical forms in a single constitution. Fidelity to principles exists solely in the ideal, and government is reduced finally to a hybrid and equivocal regime. "The arbitrary fatally entering into politics, corruption soon becomes the soul of power, and society is dragged, without rest or mercy, on the endless decline of revolutions." [17]

The emphasis in the preceding discussion on the political aspects of social conflict and instability does not correspond to the balance of emphasis in Proudhon's work. He is equally concerned with socioeconomic class stratification and the contradictions and conflicts arising between classes. However, this can be better treated in a different context, and will be examined more carefully in Chapter 12, "The Revolutionary Movement." Class struggle is not distinct from politics; political conflict both originates in class struggle and serves to perpetuate it.

Because Proudhon relies on an analysis which examines ideas and institutions in partial abstraction from the people behind them, his

17. *Du Principe fédératif, Oeuv.,* XIV, 307.

philosophy often appears separated from what he examines elsewhere as the "revolutionary movement" and the "social problem."
Nevertheless, he regards it all as integral and believes that the problems discussed in terms of "absolutism" and "fatality" can find resolution only in revolutionary social change, through translation into
practical terms which alone have direct popular immediacy. This
is the conclusion reached at the end of "Le Travail," the sixth étude
of *De la Justice*.

> Thus society is divided into profoundly different strata.
>
> The worker cries, with the Revolution: Justice, balance, libera-
> tion!
>
> The old world responds: Fatality, necessity, predestination, hier-
> archy!
>
> What will be the issue of the debate?
>
> For me there can be no doubt: *Credo in Revolutionnem*. But to
> a precise question a precise answer, and here is my conclusion:
>
> The worker will not join the conflict on the personal question:
> he still feels his dignity as man and citizen too little.
>
> He will not revolt for economic balance: *debit* and *credit* are
> terms too obscure for him, and stock speculation, like the lottery,
> scarcely displeases him.
>
> He will not take arms for political sovereignty: indifference in
> matters of government has seized him like everyone.
>
> Much less still will he protest against the bad education given
> him: it is contradictory to say that nothingness protests against
> itself. Only he who has learned much hungers for knowledge.
>
> The worker will rise for work: for him this question implies
> all the others.[18]

Labor is the vital force in man's existence; it is the means of maintaining life and of the fulfillment of the human spirit, and it is the
activity which establishes the patterns of social relationships. The
science of society, which Proudhon had sought through the mechanics of analytic methods, in his mature thought becomes a
nonrigorous yet penetrating apprehension of the dynamics of
collective groups. The most significant force integrating men into
collectivities is labor, and workers collectively must be the agency
of progressive social change. Thus his sociological concerns and his

18. *Oeuv.*, VIII, vol. iii, 116.

repudiation of bourgeois leadership combine to yield an ideology of proletarian revolution.

The links between the various strands of his thought are perceptible from the beginning, but the web is not easy to disentangle. He does not make a deliberate effort to tie it all together; *De la Justice* does the job best, but even there the connections between the elements are not laid out cogently and concisely. This vagueness in integrating a complex philosophy ought to disturb profoundly a more systematic mind than Proudhon's. As a means of gaining adherents the "scientific certainty" of Marxism was bound to have more appeal to generations devoted to scientific rationalism than was the equally rational (but relatively disorderly) philosophy of the French anarchist. Proudhon was vociferously opposed to system-building because he condemned its supposed inflexibility and dogmatism, but he might still have been more regular and orderly without being "absolutist." However, as G. D. H. Cole has remarked, no one could accuse Proudhon of having an orderly mind.[19] The discursiveness and prolixity of much of his writing should controvert anyone who tried to do so. One might say that Proudhon's intellect was not sufficiently acute or original to improve upon these shortcomings, but it is hard to insist upon this, for it might be said with equal or greater justification that he simply did not care to be more definite or orderly, and that his attitude is so well in keeping with his convictions that we should not complain, except to wish that he had been less prolix.

Proudhon repudiates system-building both in reaction against dogmatism and because of his insistence that social interactions are not regular in character. A pattern of regularity may be conceived in generalizations made in order to improve rational understanding, but these patterns are imposed on reality and not a part of it. Every transaction between men is unique, with its own particular conditions. Systematic ideologies and governments try to make a living reality of the generalized conclusions they reach through attempts to achieve rational comprehension, but the generalizations are only figments. Useful they may be, but attempts to force society into their molds can only be disastrous.

In reality society is ungovernable; trying to govern it engenders

19. *A History of Socialist Thought* (London, 1953–60), I, 201.

the resistance and the conflict of rival forces which constitute instability. If there is to be stable order, each man must voluntarily rule his own conduct, according to the principles of justice, which alone can command his allegiance. Thus for Proudhon total individual liberty is not only a matter of right but also is essential if there is to be an end to rebellion and civil war, both open and hidden.

If men are not to be governed by laws devised and enforced by institutional authority, then there must be another sort of rules to regulate individual conduct and commutative conventions between men. Proudhon speaks here of *droit*, whose English translation as "law" or "right" can be ambiguous. For him *droit* is a principle or rule—or a system of such principles, for the word can be either general or specific—defining what relationships between men should be. *Droit* ought to be determined by reason reflecting on the facts of social existence; in historical actuality it has often been established in other ways, and these alternative bases for *droit* must be supplanted by reason.

While *droit* at its most general is the principle that each man can claim respect of his personal dignity and worth from all his fellow men, in application what *droit* signifies becomes quite diverse. As might be expected from Proudhon's attitude toward "absolutism," he maintains that the meaning of justice and the rules of *droit* should be determined according to the merits of the situation at hand. Thus there are as many sorts of *droit* as there are matters to be judged and men judging. This is not a total ethical relativism, because general moral principles remain unchanged, but the general becomes relevant to practice only through interpretations that must be flexible in the face of always novel conditions. In this way Proudhon is able to make the great general statements that his rationalism and idealism naturally lead him to, without expressing himself with the finality and dogmatism he condemns in others.

Since *droit* based upon the exercise of rational faculties must serve as the foundation of stable order and every man should voluntarily govern his conduct according to this *droit*, it is vital that men grow in their use of reason. "Philosophy" is not for Proudhon just the speculative game of intellectuals nor an activity for moments of quiet contemplation; it is the very core of moral life and the basis and guide for all right action. "Thus man is moral to the extent that he obeys reason understood as such; he becomes all the more moral as, his reason extending further each day, he embraces its law with a more manly courage." [20]

People are not regularly rational or moral in their thought and conduct: still, Proudhon's often-expressed criticisms of popular behavior and his frequent gloom about the immediate prospects for progressive change do not reflect a corresponding cynicism about the actual possibilities of accomplishing this change. The moral and intellectual level of the people must be raised if justice is to be established. This is an educational process, but not just a matter of conventional schooling or even of insemination of ideas through various extrascholastic means. Such instruction can be invaluable, but the fundamental inner convictions about justice which are required are not likely to establish themselves just because people are told that they should believe. Men must arrive at these convictions through their own efforts and because justice appeals to their most basic needs and sentiments.

In believing that men can rise above selfish greed and irrational passion to do this, Proudhon reflects his essential optimism about human nature. He even says on a number of occasions that man's rationality and the truth of the idea of justice make its universal realization inevitable, but he does not confine himself to this utopian faith. He is not as naïve as Fourier, who expected the rational beauty of his system to convert all those needed to establish it, and who for years waited without avail at lunchtime each day for the arrival of a convert ready to advance the capital required to make a start.

To make possible the sought-for "conversion" of mankind and eventually to bring it about is the purpose of the revolutionary movement as Proudhon conceives of it. Little can be gained from revolution if man is not changed, but structural changes can make possible the needed moral and intellectual ones. The particular form that the anarchist wants the revolution to take and new forms of organization he seeks to create are not desirable solely because they

20. *Oeuv.*, VIII, vol. ii, 362. Jurisprudence is one of the aspects of Proudhon's thought which I have chosen to treat more briefly than it may deserve. For an extended discussion, see Georges Gurvitch, *L'Idée du droit social* (Paris, 1929), 327–406.

are more just in themselves. They are needed in order to provide the environment which will facilitate the growth of men's moral and intellectual faculties. Thus in the broadest sense the social revolution is to be the education of mankind.

In his final writing on the revolutionary movement and social organization, Proudhon emphasizes "organic" social solidarity and the related problems even more than the questions of individualism always so primary in his thought. This is not just because he believes social responsibility to be indissolubly tied to individual rights. As important is the recognition that only through the growth of social solidarity can man acquire an immanent spirit of justice.

Proudhon assumes that man tends naturally and spontaneously to develop society; the social is his natural state, not isolation and egoism or some dualistic combination of egoistic and social orientation. The flowering of innate social morality should be a natural development resulting from social experience.

Man comes to know justice when in collective existence he simultaneously and increasingly becomes aware of his own human dignity and that of his fellows. If this is to occur, then all others must recognize his dignity and worth; this requires that the society be truly egalitarian. Hence the need for revolution—and the need to prepare that revolution by the creation of a self-conscious workers' movement which can provide the egalitarian social setting in which workers can grow in confidence, dignity, and self-knowledge.

The initial practical basis for the recognition of equal reciprocity in human relations is that it should serve the requirements of self-interest. In any transaction a man can be expected to act in his own best interest, deciding in the case of an opposition of interests according to his weighing of relative gain and loss. Egalitarian reciprocity should serve his own interests best in the long run, and he can make the rightful choice for that reason whether or not it matters to him that the choice is just. But he may be mistaken in his calculations, and men have very often been thus.

The existence in him of a sentiment of sympathy for his fellows should be the factor leading him to prefer the just alternative to another offering greater apparent short-term advantage. Such benevolence can result from natural sociability; it increases with appreciation of the rational and spiritual value of justice. If this increasing appreciation is not to be reversed by disappointment in the fulfilling of self-interest, then the transactions must continue to be personally beneficial, as they will be only if the parties to each agreement meet on a basis of equality and mutual respect.

If men discover that acting thus increases their felicity as individuals, then their social sense will displace egoism and in time just conduct will become habitual, natural. In a sense altruistic justice then becomes a new sort of "egoism," for self-interest and social obligation come to be identical and are understood as such.

In this context Proudhon's definition of justice as reciprocal and spontaneous respect for human dignity becomes especially meaningful. When first offered, it appears simply to be a general definition well in accord with his preconceptions and widely useful in theoretical application. Now, however, we can see that such respect is the most basic condition necessary for realization of a society which is just according to any alternative definition he would find acceptable. Indeed, psychologically the requirement for mutual respect makes very good sense—remarkably so when one considers that Proudhon's perceptions of actual human psychology are hardly profound.

Here Proudhon's conception of the family can be seen as an integral part of his vision of fruitful human relationships. Although this conception employs assumptions about feminine inferiority and sexual morality that are scarcely more than traditionalist prejudices, it comprises much more than this and most of it could be justified without appeal to such beliefs.

In his view the family is the fundamental unit of society, its members naturally bound together by their care for biological relationship and by ties of intimacy, love, and a mutual dependency too inescapably profound to be regarded as a matter of voluntary contract. Husband and wife play different, complementary roles, together forming an androgynous whole with a character different from and superior to that of a solitary individual. Each accords to the other, and the children to their parents, a deep respect which arises from natural love and intimacy, and from an appreciation of the vital familial role each plays.

Thus a basis for social morality arises naturally in the family, and the latter becomes the effective core and foundation of moral life. Here youngsters receive their basic moral education, and from both instruction by their parents and the family experience itself they can acquire the basis of a moral perspective and inclination out of which justice in the larger society will evolve.

For Proudhon, then, the family constitutes the moral center of society and the necessary foundation of his vision of social renewal, altruism, and justice. Some of his peculiar notions about love and the family need to be regarded in this light. He is, for instance, willing to allow religion in the bosom of the family (or at least of its womenfolk), despite his hostility to the Church. Religion has been a primary basis of morality; though the Church's absolutism in morals has been a negative force, popular religious sentiment can provide some basis for morals until familial bonds and rationality replace it through their further development. Since women are intellectually inferior and more prone to religious sentiment, let them have their faith for now. Proudhon's own wife kept a crucifix in their room and taught religion to their children. He himself even wore a religious medal given him by an admirer, a practice that might have amazed the Catholic critics who thought him a terrible atheist.

Similarly, there is a rationale to Proudhon's puritanical view of sexuality, though none which explains the severity of his attitudes. Between husband and wife a chaste love without extremes of passion contributes to the growth of conjugal bonds and yields the offspring who complete the family. But sexuality in other contexts or intense passion in this one contributes nothing to the family and most often is a destructive and divisive factor in social relationships. Moreover, Proudhon says that chastity is required to establish a limit upon population growth, to forestall the disaster forecast by Malthus. Proudhon's injunction sounds very much like the contemporary bourgeois attitudes on chastity and on the dangerous proclivities of the lower classes to breed without self-control. However, he speaks here as one of the lower classes himself, quite without the note of reproof from a superior position characteristic of bourgeois pronouncements on the subject.

For Proudhon the family is not only the basis of social morality and moral education, but also the fundamental unit in the social structure. While other social relationships must be continuously subject to rearrangement on a deliberate and voluntary basis, within a family relations are quite differently established and cannot be so freely altered. Its head is not simply an individual acting on his own and in shifting combinations with others; he always has his family responsibilities. He involves his family with him whenever he joins in any combination or when he engages in transactions alone. One speaks of individuals as parties to social transactions, for men think and relate to each other as individuals, but actually behind most men are the families they head. Likewise, the father is the agent through whom the relation of the whole family to the rest of society is established.

Unlike many conservative theorists, Proudhon does not suppose that the requirement for paternal authority in the family indicates a corresponding need for paternalistic authority in the larger society. Not only does he reject the underlying assumption of popular inferiority corresponding to the inferiority of wife and children, but also he does not suppose that social relationships are comparable to the biological ties within the family. Like conservatives he speaks of organic unity in society, but unlike them he does not conceive of this organicism as a biological metaphor with organic society directly comparable in structure to individual organisms or families.

While he thinks the family is the basic social unit, he insistently refuses to take it as a prototype for social organization. This is also relevant to his rejection of utopian communism. He believes that proposed utopian schemes would extend to the whole community the family's subordination to paternal authority. No matter what the form, Proudhon rejects paternalism outside the family because it must always suppress liberty.

Saying that he regards the family as the basic unit of society can be misleading if it causes him to be classified with other theorists, such as de Bonald and Comte, who in various ways ascribe to the family the role of basic social unit. Proudhon's conception here is different from most of the others. He means that the individual does not act apart from his family role, but not that families are ordinarily the primary elements in social dynamics or organization.

Neither does he follow Rousseau's practice of focusing on the individual as an abstract unity whose interactions with others themselves constitute the major part of the functioning of society.

While individuals and families can often be the prime units in social interaction, the significant groups usually are larger. Of course, the ways individuals and families function in these larger combinations and the ways they relate to others within a group are most important, but society also has to be examined and understood in terms of these larger collectivities functioning as units. The memberships of such groups overlap and vary, but effectively they are the active elements in the dynamics of society.

His concern is with what he calls a "natural group," any grouping with natural affinities and common interests.

> Every time that men, followed by their wives and children, gather together in one place, join their homes and their cultures, develop diverse industries in their midst, create between themselves neighborly relations, and willy-nilly impose conditions of solidarity upon themselves, they form what I call a natural group. . . .
>
> Similar groups at a distance from one another can have common interests; and one imagines that they understand each other and associate, and through this engagement form a superior group. . . .[21]

These joint bodies can arrive at agreements or contracts on the basis of reciprocity, just as individuals may; they function as units and should engage in their transactions with the same sovereignty and equality as individuals must. On the other hand, the sovereignty of groups in their transactions with other groups ought not to give them claim to sovereignty over individual members. Each member must participate voluntarily as a free and independent being, or there will be generated the same antagonisms which divide existing societies and create conditions of struggle within them.

In short, the natural group is a society within society whose problems are like those of the whole, but whose solidarity is increased by its greater homogeneity. The mutual recognition of equal dignity vital to justice is more readily achieved because of the existence of natural affinities and a community of interests. Any man may be a part of a number of such natural unions; the re-

21. *Contradictions politiques, Oeuv.,* XIII, 237.

sulting links between groups should increase the opportunities to achieve just relations throughout society. It should be noted that only in this context does Proudhon think the cultural, ethnic, linguistic, and political affinities emphasized by contemporary nationalists to have practical importance of a positive nature.

Men in combination have a collective force greater than the sum of their individual capacities. That, it will be recalled, was a principal point of *Qu'est-ce que la propriété?*, which made the collective force of labor the center of an argument against exploitation of wage-earners and tenants by employers and property-owners. Bodies of men who work together in the same trade or under similar conditions are the most important natural groups in Proudhon's conception of the revolutionary movement. However, the joint power of collectivity is not confined to the collective force of labor. Any assemblage of people achieves increase of power through combination, and of course the larger group should achieve greater collective force—but there is a limiting factor: the disintegrative tendencies arising in large collectivities.

The State, since it ostensibly results from the union of all groups within the country's borders, might be considered a combination of superior order, with the greatest power of all. Indeed, through its monopoly of police and military forces it may be able to coerce any group in the country to obey its will, but its *social* power is doubtful, for it is not a natural group. The whole realm that it governs is too heterogeneous really to be one and too large for there to be sufficient bonds to keep it together. The cohesiveness of any collectivity is limited by and inversely proportional to its size. Proudhon gives as a universal generalization his conclusion that growth dissipates cohesive force, and this is as true of the polity as it is of the nonpolitical social group.

Altogether his libertarian views and his sociology fit together very neatly: liberty is more likely to be circumscribed and denied as the size of the principal sovereign body increases, and therefore this community should be small; the same conclusion follows from considerations of integrative and divisive social forces and the necessary conditions for promoting an immanent spirit of justice. In *Du Principe fédératif* Proudhon goes on to complete the sequence of reasoning, proposing that the centralized State be replaced by a system in which most of government's functions are performed by sovereign local communities, with larger combinations of communities acting in concert but with fewer functions as the size of the combinations increases.

If one recalls the thoughts on groups within the community presented in Rousseau's *Du Contrat social*, then Proudhon's approach to group dynamics may be rather surprising. Rousseau treats an individual's group affiliations as profoundly affecting his relationship to the larger community, but he still speaks mainly of individuals interacting rather than of collectivities. With Proudhon's individualist emphasis one might expect him to do the same, giving the most weight to men dealing with each other as individuals, though with their outlooks and interests reflecting their group affiliations. Of course, this would be the way a man actually experiences social intercourse in most instances. Proudhon writes mainly in these terms in his earlier works and still does quite often in his last ones. However, the weight of emphasis in this later analysis of society is given to the dynamics of groups acting as units.

While Proudhon's philosophy is enlarged rather than altered in his final years, this extension does place his previous ideas in a somewhat different perspective. He had started with the individual and his rights and worked from there; his concern was also a profoundly social one but in "solving the social problem" he thought primarily of achieving a balance of diverse individual rights and interests. However, men's selfishness, irrationality, and widespread immorality gave him much to think about, particularly after the experience of the 1848 Revolution and the subsequent political disasters. His ideas about the growth of an immanent spirit of justice result; these concepts, as developed in *De la Justice* and after, follow naturally from his previous individualism but are an addition. Individuals become just only through the effects on them of life in society; thereby social bonds become vital to the growth of the individual. In earlier work the object had been to remove from society those features that make it possible for men to do injustice to one another. Now there is the added goal of making society the agency that will cause men to become naturally just. From thinking of society primarily as the setting in which men meet, Proudhon has come to think of it as essential to man, nourishing him in his growth to intellectual and moral maturity.

In earlier discussions of social contract, Proudhon had defined it basically in terms of engagements agreed upon between individuals and between one man and his community. Now he extends his thinking to contracts between groups as well, always concluded on the basis of equitable mutual benefit. Here his concern is with transactions that involve joint interests, such as the hours and conditions of work for the employees of a factory or the need of two villages to build a bridge spanning the river passing between them. Individual interests within the factory labor force or either village are quite similar with regard to the respective problems at hand. All must act collectively to solve them, and their weight in any bargaining is determined by their joint strength. Thus it is the integral community of workers or villagers which is the effective unit in arriving at an agreement with factory management or neighboring village, even if individuals negotiate the transaction.

Such transactions and the obligations thereby undertaken are no less important than the social contracts involving individuals. Since collective identity and interests are the effective factors in these joint transactions, Proudhon has added reason to examine and emphasize the dynamics of groups taken as units.

However, the importance of groups does not mean that their interests supersede those of their members; the collective interests are just those which are common to all. The community cannot be regarded as a being with existence and requirements of its own, distinct from its constituent parts. If a member defers to the joint body, it must be because he spontaneously identifies his own felicity with that of the whole, not because of pressures upon him to submit "for the common good," or "for the good of our party/class/nation/city/company."

Most theorists have thought of collective unity as requiring a surrender of personal liberty, if only to reestablish it on a more secure if circumscribed basis. When they speak of solidarity, unity, and especially of organic relation, they usually do so while expressing or implying requirement for either a hierarchical ordering of the community or one in which individual independence is subordinated to demands imposed by the whole. Since Proudhon speaks so much of organic unity and solidarity, it is important to distinguish his views sharply from others which his phrases recall.

He seeks social unity, but it is always unity in diversity; solidarity must be achieved, but not at the cost of a loss of independence for the individual. Personal sovereignty and integral community not only are compatible; they are necessary for each other. Just as universal liberty cannot be achieved without unity and order, equally there can be no real unity without variety, plurality, divergence, and no stable order without conflict, contradiction, and antagonism. Liberty, unity, and order cannot be separated, and they can be realized only in a world in which difference is normal and accepted. Through a dynamic equilibrium of conflicting needs and forces, differences can be transcended to achieve unity, but they cannot and should not ever be eliminated or absorbed.

> What new generations require is a unity which expresses the soul of society: spiritual unity, intelligible order, which joins us together through all the powers of our consciousness and our reason, and nevertheless leaves us our free thought, free will, free heart. . . . What we need today is a unity which, adding to our liberties, grows in its turn and fortifies itself with these liberties themselves. . . .[22]

Proudhon's repeated use of phrases like "spiritual unity," "the soul of society," "collective reason," "immanent spirit of justice," and "*Logos*, the common soul of humanity enshrined in each of us" reminds us again that the links between his philosophy and Christian theology are substantial, although their significance may be uncertain. When writing of collective reason he even quotes Jesus speaking to his disciples:

> The organ of collective reason is the same as that of collective force: it is the working, instructing group; the industrial, skillful company; the academies, schools, municipalities; it is the national assembly, the club, the jury; in short, every union of men formed

---

22. *De la Capacité politique, Oeuv.,* III, 202. In a note here, Maxime Leroy points out that "unité spirituelle" is a Saint-Simonian idea.

for the discussion of ideas and the search for right: *For where two or three are gathered together in my name, there am I in the midst of them.*[23]

This scriptural quotation could indicate that Proudhon wished his readers to recall and transfer to this context Christian precepts. The apparent relation in his thought between Divine Spirit and the spirit of justice was discussed in the first part of this chapter. It is necessary to his philosophy that this spirit be regarded as wholly rational in its essential nature. The central conception here is that of *Logos*, the rational spirit and ordering principle of the universe in Aristotle's metaphysics and the Holy Spirit of Christian beliefs. In medieval theology the Aristotelian and the scriptural *Logos* merged.

Proudhon does not develop the idea of *Logos* very far, but he is close to Aristotle in thinking of a rational ordering principle, and his conception can be better understood in these terms. His problem, like that of Christianity, is to make this spirit consciously immanent in every man.

Although establishing this connection may help to clarify Proudhon's rather abstruse conception here, it is more important that it serve to underline how essential he believes rationality to be for the unifying spirit in society. Recognition of affinities with one's fellows, understanding of the potential benefits of equitable reciprocity, admission of one another's rights and dignity, all must be established through the use of each man's rational faculties.

Solidarity must be that of reasoning men, achieved *because* they are reasoning men. Proudhon does not want or think fruitful any bonds arising from common irrational sentiments. Passions, prejudices, customs, and opinions not founded on reason cannot serve as the basis of stable unions and moral growth. Furthermore, individuals must not make decisions for partisan reasons, just because they identify with a group; rather, they should identify with the group because they decide rationally that their cause is a common one.[24]

The goal of mankind should be a union of sentiments and reason,

23. The scriptural quotation is from Matthew 18:20; *Oeuv.*, VIII, vol. iii, 270.
24. Here Proudhon singles out chauvinism and voting by party loyalty, both of which he condemns as typical negative examples of collective response and action.

of will and philosophy, of action and science. Justice is to exist not merely in the ideas of moralists and legislators but as the substance of functional reality.

What now is this princely Idea, at the same time objective and subjective, real and formal, Idea of nature and humanity, of speculation and of sentiment, of logic and art, of politics and economics; reason practical and pure, which at the same time rules the worlds of creation and of philosophy, and upon which they construct the one and the other; Idea which, dualist by formula, nevertheless excludes all priority and all superiority, and embraces in its synthesis the real and the ideal?

It is the idea of *Right*, JUSTICE.[25]

The Idea of Justice has been the subject of this chapter; its practice is the concern of the three to follow.

25. *Oeuv.*, VIII, vol. i, 215.

ten: Historical Perspective

I speak for PROGRESS and, as the incarnation of Progress, for the reality of collective man and, as consequence of this reality, for an economic science: that is my socialism. Nothing more or less.[1]

INCREASING USE of rational faculties, growing appreciation of the dignity and worth of one's fellows, moral regeneration, revolution introducing major structural change into society and radically altering established norms: all of these themes envisage humanity in the process of movement. Indeed, Proudhon's whole philosophy denies stasis while embracing the dynamic. His attacks on intellectual absolutism, dogma, and inflexibility are reactions against the static mind, and anarchism his reaction against fixed organization of society. His dream is the liberation of every man from all the bonds that nature and other men impose upon him, and the transformation of society from a hostile environment which prevents man's being fully human, into an integral community which nurtures him in his growth to completeness of being and fulfillment of potential.

With change in men and ideas so critically important to him, it would be strange if Proudhon had no vision of the span and process of history in which these transformations are to occur. An idea of historical movement in the future is implicit in all such notions of

1. *Philosophie du progrès, Oeuv.,* XII, 79.

transformation, and even a critic of philosophical systems can hardly consider future process without conceiving it within a perspective of historical development, from the distant past through tortured present to the hopefully better future. Given the nature of his thought and the known influence on him of the intellectual heritage of the eighteenth-century *philosophes*, his historical vision has to be of some kind of progress through enlightenment.

Proudhon does have a philosophy of history, one developed at some length. Elements of such a philosophy appear frequently throughout his work. After his attempts at methodical system-building in the 1840's, his next major effort in philosophy of history is the *Philosophie du progrès*. This is not one of his better books, and the approach developed there is more adequately represented in revisions and reassertions appearing in later works. *De la Justice* provides the major statement of Proudhon's philosophy of history,[2] with *De la Capacité politique*, *Contradictions politiques*, and *Du Principe fédératif* its translation into philosophy of revolutionary practice.

La Guerre et la paix, which appeared the year after the revised and augmented edition of *De la Justice*, is more philosophy of history than anything else. However, although many of the ideas it presents have general importance for his philosophy, the peculiar view of history in *La Guerre* really seems to be little more than an awkward effort to provide a rationale for conclusions that he would have done better to offer and argue far differently.

As a philosopher of history Proudhon is not remarkable. If taken apart from the rest of his work this portion of his thought does not merit much interest; it is not particularly distinctive or even original. Perhaps *La Guerre et la paix* should be excepted from this observation, but the distinctive features here need further development if they are to constitute a theory of major importance. Proudhon does not carry on with the theory, for it would not suit his ideals or purposes; others have gone on, with some effect. Of these a few, like Georges Sorel, have done so under his influence.

2. In particular, the ninth *étude*, "Progrès et décadence," *Oeuv.*, VIII, vol. iii, 481–648. Proudhon developed his philosophy of history further in several works which he did not complete. The principle one, extensive notes for a universal history, is *Césarisme et christianisme*, ed. J.-A. Langlois (Paris, 1883), 2 vols.

Proudhon's philosophy of history does not have the grand sweep of vision of a Vico or a Condorcet. He lacks the knowledge and intuitive grasp of the reality of historical conditions that make his friend Michelet's work so powerful. Although he sees history in terms of social revolution, he is unable to develop a theory of the process comparable in analytic precision and force to Marx's dialectical materialism; his conception of revolution suffers significantly from this disability.

While Proudhon's philosophy of history is weak, it does form a significant part of the whole of his theory. His ideas not only suggest a historical perspective, they require one to be fully and coherently comprehended. Moreover, much of what he has to say about historical forces and movement can clarify other facets of his philosophy in ways additional to the establishing of relationships in time. Thus it is more fitting and useful to regard his conceptions of history as perspective rather than as a discrete philosophy of history.

La Guerre et la paix is a peculiar book. Early in the text Proudhon warns the reader that he will come to decide against "le *statu quo* guerrier," its institutions of militarism, its poetry and its customs.[3] But one might not expect this conclusion from the book's first half, which glorifies all of these. He is building a structure in order to demolish it, but not all that he says on behalf of war is supposed to be twaddle. It is often difficult to see how seriously he intends what he says, although this may not be very important unless one intends to call upon Proudhon to lend authority to one's own fondness for the romance of "l'esprit guerrier."

This difficulty in appraisal arises chiefly from the delight the man takes in pursuing arguments to extreme conclusions, squeezing all he can from rhetorical eloquence and the semblance of logic, with a fine disregard for ultimate plausibility and consistency with what he says elsewhere. If he can startle or irritate, he is pleased; contrived novelty and the riddles of contradiction are familiar devices in his work. In *La Guerre* he carries them to excess—but there is a more solid conceptual scheme there also.

The starting point is his observation that, however one judges

3. *Oeuv.*, VI, 49.

war in principle, historically it has been central to all human experience.

> War is divine, that is primordial, essential to life, to the production even of man and society. It has its seat in the depths of the consciousness, and embraces in its idea the universality of human relations. Through it are revealed and expressed, in the first days of history, our most elevated faculties: religion, justice, fine arts, social economy, politics, government, nobility, bourgeoisie, royalty, property. Through it in subsequent epochs customs are invigorated, nations are regenerated, States are balanced, progress is pursued, Justice establishes its empire, liberty finds its guarantees. Suppress, hypothetically, the idea of war and nothing past or present remains of the human race.[4]

The passage continues in a like vein, but this should be enough. Its extravagance is all too typical—but the extent of its claims for war's virtues and importance shows how Proudhon uses the word "war" idiosyncratically. Sometimes—but not always—by "war" he means *any* conflict between men. Since he regards conflict as the essence even of the ideal future society, it is plain that this notion of war can have wider significance than that indicated by the usual connotations of martial violence.

In saying that war is "primordial" Proudhon is trying to construct from his observations of past and present human experience a generally valid description of social conflict. His idiosyncratic use of the word is more than just a matter of including all sorts of struggle: he speaks of war as the exercise of *force*, its principle, its idea, and as the synthesis of opposed forces.

Historically, he says, force has been the primary foundation of *droit:* most of the principles that rule human life have been based not on reason but on the will of whomever has a preponderance of force. In particular, the hierarchical ordering of society and the exploitive relationships of economic inequality rest upon ability to exercise dominant force. As the foundation of *droit*, force has constituted the judicial order that has ruled mankind—and war is its code of procedure.

Proudhon takes this rather shaky argument and runs away with

---

4. From Proudhon's own summary of the first book, ibid., 23.

it, constructing a whole sociology of historical society based on force. The *droit* of force has been positive and useful; it should not be judged by the abuses of it. The expansive forces of collectivities, especially nations, have naturally tended to clash, finding battle as the only tribunal. This is the model of how a judicial order is constituted; from clashing forces in armed combat men go on to formulate principles to settle conflicts by tribunals of law, without military struggle. From the *droit* of force Proudhon deduces the whole gamut of *droits*. *Droit* derived from employment of force is not the ideal, but it has introduced the multitudes to the notion of *droit* itself. In this way it can lead to development of justice based on equality, respect, and reciprocal guarantees.

Since war is force at work it is thus constructive. It is all the more so because it effects or stimulates basic changes in the society; war is the chief factor in avoiding social stasis. "War" in the most inclusive of Proudhon's several usages seems to be intended here. Society is thus permanently at war through its internal conflicts. Every man is always at war—with nature, with other men, and with himself. Thus broadly defined, war is the basis of all that is dynamic in human existence.

Since he conceives it in this way, it is natural that Proudhon thinks "war" is important, but he runs on to glorify war with all the enthusiasm of a retired colonel holding his grandson on his knee and telling him tall stories. Here he returns—without so specifying—to the narrower meaning of "war" as violent armed combat between nations. The confusion of usages of the word is complete and unrecognized.

War's fundamental importance for all human experience is described in terms almost mystical in the form of expression. War is said to confer prestige, exalting the virile and courageous. Man under arms appears and feels himself greater than nature—more worthy, more proud, more capable of virtue and devotion. In making such claims, Proudhon reaches hard for arguments, many of which are much below his usual standards. He even contends that *l'esprit guerrier* is estimable because people, especially women, admire warriors more than ordinary men. If someone else had written that, he would have treated the claim with contempt.

For all that, Proudhon does not urge anyone to go to war or

engage in any violent action, not even in the cause of revolution. It was mentioned earlier how despicable he thought Napoleon III's search for martial glory to be. Ambivalent about the possibilities of violent revolution, he is attracted to it only because overcoming the entrenched power of the established order by pacific means so often seems impossible. Not only is he unwilling to recommend violent revolution, he does not even advocate violence in limited actions like trade-union strikes. Apparently there is less to his praise of *l'esprit guerrier* than meets the eye.

After nearly two hundred pages speaking of war in a positive manner, Proudhon trips the lever and the trap snaps shut. "Sublime and holy in its idea, war is horrible in its execution: as much as its theory elevates man, its practice dishonors him." [5] The forms which war actually takes do not correspond to its principle. There is little or none of the high morality and spiritualism of the idea of war in its practice. The reasons wars actually are fought are most often base; their methods are brutal and inhumane. War is no longer a judicial tribunal; its objective is extermination of the enemy, not a determination of whose principle shall rule.

Since nation states and *raison d'état* have little regard for spiritual niceties or those of *droit*, they can hardly serve to uphold the principle of war. More important, economic injustice ultimately is the root cause of modern wars, making it impossible for war to be purified. Social revolution is the only way to eliminate this corrupting cause, but it would also eliminate any need for war at all. Even heroism is finished: it may have served gloriously to initiate the reign of *droit*, but the free man cannot be ruled by heroics and heroes.[6] Moreover, the bestiality of war is dishonoring.

Proudhon's extended and eloquent criticism of war's brutality and destructive consequences could easily be excerpted and published as a pacifist tract today. Indeed, this could explain the use of the same title by Tolstoy, who was both pacifist and anarchist, and knew the Frenchman and his book. In addition to the condemnation of violence in warfare, Proudhon's other strictures against war relate to his remarks in *De la Justice* about conflict between

5. From his summary of the third book, ibid., 197.
6. In other works Proudhon severely condemns all admiration of heroes, especially Napoleon I.

forces without a balance of strength. Whatever the form of struggle, violent or not, such lack of balance results in perpetual instability. This has resulted in continual change and thus in the development of civilization, but unequal struggle cannot continue in a society of justice.

Not only is the contradiction between the practice and the idea of war complete, it is irremediable. Economic, social, and political inequality prevent the remedy even as they cause the instability which perpetuates war. The brutality and inhumanity of warfare add to the instability and thus to the impossibility of achieving a cure. What is needed is a transformation of war and its replacement by something else: Justice.

In summary (with many omissions), the following is the grand construct of a universal history in *La Guerre et la paix*. War has been the central element and dynamic factor in past experience. Force, the instrument of war, remains the basis of *droit* today. War and force can no longer serve man's needs. They are travesties of any ideals that may be called upon to justify them, and they bar men from further progress. We should recognize them for the vile, corrupt, inhumane, and self-destructive phenomena they are, and go on to embrace the cause of Justice. Only if mankind does this can progress continue and lasting peace be realized.

Stated thus simply—which Proudhon never does—this view of war and history fits into the rest of his philosophy well enough. The actual fit is less comfortable, since he pushes the themes of war and force too far for consistency with his pacific conclusions, too far to serve well the main purpose he must have intended in the first place: to clarify and make more persuasive the conceptions of justice and social revolution he advocates elsewhere. Proudhon has a personal demon which urges him to pursue any species of argument that occurs to him, letting himself be carried on in currents of reasoning and eloquence thus set in motion. The demon was hard at work when its victim wrote *La Guerre et la paix*. As an excuse for Proudhon it may be said that he was sick and depressed while writing it, and deeply perturbed by the wars of his lifetime— especially the civil wars of revolution.

To treat so lightly as we have ideas which others have taken to be most significant may seem cavalier, particularly when it is not possible to say definitely just how earnest Proudhon was in his praise of war. Nevertheless, the quality of his reasoning in the book is so far inferior to his usual standards and the resulting theory so weak that it is impossible to take very seriously his view of history here. Some similar conception may have genuine cogency, but Proudhon was not the man to advocate such a view. The frailty of his presentation of the theory and insights into his thought gained elsewhere are the chief reasons for judging this version of his philosophy of history to be little more than an ill-conceived attempt to make his ideas about justice more convincing.

If there were no more to *La Guerre et la paix* than what has already been mentioned, then the foregoing discussion would be of use mainly to show what it was that attracted those drawn to Proudhon's mystique of *l'esprit guerrier*. There is more, however. His repudiation of war is significant in itself and relatively cogent in its presentation. Nevertheless, his pacific conclusions are implicit in the rest of his writing, and their development here does not contribute very much to his philosophy, although they shed some light on his largely negative attitude toward revolutionary violence.

More important is what he has to say about the transformation of war, for this strengthens and adds to what he has said before about social dynamics. As brutal and inhumane as violent warfare has become, Proudhon is no less concerned with "war" in his wider sense of virulent civil struggle between unequally opposed elements of society. Even if martial violence is repudiated, its principle is perpetuated in this antagonism of forces in civil society.

The antagonisms are changed then only in form. The problems which underlie and give rise to the struggles remain the same: economic injustice and the passions it occasions. The bitterness and anger of the poor and exploited, the fear and hatred of the privileged who feel threatened by their victims: these are the materials from which internecine war, open or hidden, is created.[7] Moreover, however attenuated the intensity of antagonism, force remains the primary arbiter, and a trial of strength the usual tribunal. Legislation and legal institutions serve chiefly to formalize all this.

7. Proudhon often speaks of "class struggle" and "class war." He does not, however, conceive of it quite so literally as was common in later socialist thought, as a deadly struggle between irreconcilable foes, a fight to death or victory no less violent in its essence than conventional military combat. (See below, Ch. 12.)

Then the system must be changed altogether; the foundation of jurisprudence and the organization of economic forces have to be transformed for the ideas of war and *droit de force* to be repudiated in fact as well as in principle. "For Proudhon the meaning of history is clear. It is to go from the *droit* of force to the *droit* of labor, from absolutism to contract, from mysticism to science, from war to justice."

It should be remembered that he believes the opposition of forces to be normal and positive for society—if the forces meet on a basis of equity and if the parties involved act in the spirit of justice. "Force . . . only has *droit* if it is human, that is, intelligent, moral, and free." [8]

Proudhon's goal is not the total abolition of struggle but the elimination of its violence and the transformation of antagonisms from destructive to constructive ones. He objects to the usual understanding of peace which conceives of it merely as the negative of war. Such a conception envisages an equilibrium of forces which is basically static, unproductive, and incapable of leading to progressive social transformation. Usually such peace-seekers want only to maintain the *status quo*, organizing and maintaining political forces in essentially hierarchical structures. The antagonisms dividing men are only perpetuated then beneath a mask of inertia and absence of open combat—until this inherently unstable arrangement breaks down and war again results.

What Proudhon requires is an active, dynamic peace based on a structure of economic balance and social justice—not a compromise of the sort reached at the Congress of Vienna. There they achieved a balance—temporary and unstable—of political forces through recognition of interdependent interests, particularly the interest of each state in resisting foreign aggression and domestic rebellion and in preventing any rival from gaining dominant strength. But these were the interests of governments, not of peoples; the forces were those of states, not natural groups; the rationale was that of *raison d'état*, not justice.

Peace, he says, should have a positive reality, but we know its idea only in purely negative form, as the absence of struggle and

8. Georges Guy-Grand, referring to *La Guerre* in his introduction to *De la Justice, Oeuv.*, VIII, vol. i, 15; *Oeuv.*, VI, 187n.

destruction. Peace ought to have its own action, expression, life, and movement. In peace we can and must preserve the virtues of war.

Now we can see something more to his praise for *l'esprit guerrier* than flights of rhetoric and a feeble attempt to build a schema of the bad old world against which to oppose the merits of the new world of justice to come. *L'esprit guerrier* is intended to signify more than the virility and courage of a warrior people: it can also be a pacific spirit of a dynamic society of people striving forward with energy and fortitude, but without killing each other or coercively imposing their will on weaker victims. *L'esprit guerrier* does not require armed combat in order that it be preserved—there are other and better means of keeping humanity in productive, progressive struggle. The object is a society in a state of tension which is creative instead of destructive.

If each faculty, power, force, bears with it its own *droit*, then forces in man and in society must balance, not destroy each other. The *droit* of one cannot prejudice the *droit* of another, since they are not of the same nature, and they cannot meet in the same action. Quite the contrary, they can develop only through the aid they render each other reciprocally. What occasions rivalries and conflicts is that just now heterogeneous forces are joined and linked indissolubly in a single entity, as is seen in man with the conjunction of passions and faculties, in government with the conjunction of different powers, in society with the jumble of classes. On the other hand, just now a similar power is found divided between different entities, as is seen in commerce, industry, property, where multitudes of individuals fill exactly the same functions, seek the same advantage, exercise the same rights and privileges. Then it can happen either that the forces grouped together fight one another instead of preserving a just equilibrium among themselves, and one alone subordinates the others, or else that these divided forces neutralize each other through monopoly and anarchy. These results are inevitable when, under the influence of impetuous passions, the dignity of the individual, justice in the State, the feeling of solidarity in the corporate body, all come to weaken.

In a soul governing itself, in a well-ordered society, the forces struggle only a moment in order to recognize, register, confirm, and classify each other. . . . In the cities the corporate forces balance and produce general felicity through their just equilibrium. Thus the opposition of forces ends with their harmony. . . . All antagonism in which the forces destroy one another, instead of placing each other in equilibrium, is no longer war. It is a subversion, an anomaly.[9]

Constructive antagonism is the central, vital concept of *La Guerre et la paix*. The development of the conception is badly flawed by the remarkable lack of precision with which Proudhon uses the words denoting his key ideas, as well as by the poor overall quality of his arguments. "La guerre," "la force," "le droit," and "l'esprit guerrier" are used indiscriminately by him in a multitude of distinct senses which are not fully compatible with one another. His imprecision not only promotes confusion in readers, but also makes the whole theory needlessly obscure.

Probably he was vague in his own mind about the subject. There can be no doubt about what he was driving at, however: definition of the necessity for society to be genuinely dynamic in its very essence.

The need for dynamism is clearly stated in *De la Justice*, but not sufficiently developed there. *La Guerre et la paix* is important because it adds substantially to the conception of social dynamics offered in the earlier book. The idea of equilibrium there might mistakenly be thought to have the form of some quietly pleasant gentlemen's agreement, where the parties to the transaction make needed arrangements according to customary codes and then courteously go on their ways in their personal, private worlds, careful not to disturb any of the accepted normalcies of life. After all, Proudhon's requirements for respect of one another's dignity and internalized codes of conduct bear a resemblance to the bases of relationships between gentlemen, though without the latter's limited definition of coequals.

His idea of equilibrium is not like this, as *La Guerre et la paix* should make clear. The image of gentlemanly behavior is so unsuitable a representation of his viewpoint as to become almost ludicrous when one compares on the one hand a picture of gentlemen in a Pall Mall club determining who will pick up the luncheon tab,

9. *Oeuv.*, VI, 133ff.

and on the other a vision of village peasants debating plans for construction of a community irrigation system.

For Proudhon the desired social balance would be an ever-shifting complex of relationships continually renewed and revised as the needs of groups and individuals vary. Society would always be moving, changing, developing with all the vigor of a healthy young animal. Men would approach each other not only with respect and a strong sense of what is right, but also with energy and *élan;* they would approach adversity and the uncertainty of the future with courage. Man would live in a state of constructive tension that would excite and keep all from inertia, rather than that tension which produces only anxiety and fear. It would be a "brave new world" in the literal sense, rather than in the ironic one of Aldous Huxley.

Proudhon's conception of social equilibrium may also be erroneously confused with certain ideas about social and political pluralism frequently offered to explain democratic politics in the United States.[10] Both Proudhon and these pluralist notions stress natural conflict between opposed groups, each identified by the common interests or other vital qualities of its members. There are other points of superficial similarity, but the differences are quite substantial even without counting Proudhon's repudiation of government and capitalist economy. The groups spoken of in this kind of pluralist theory are too large and heterogeneous to be identified with Proudhon's "natural groups," except perhaps within small communities which pluralist theory has little reference to, and to a certain extent with professional and union organizations which, however, usually are more heterogeneous than Proudhon thought feasible. Pluralism speaks of relatively vast conglomerations like ethnic and religious blocs, professional and commercial associations, and large trade unions, in reference to the politics of big city, state, and national government. These groupings are expected to act as

10. Pluralist ideas referred to here are those suggested by James Madison and a number of nineteenth-century writers. In this simple form such notions are the common coin of American political discourse. However, there are more deep-seated similarities between Proudhon's conception and those of some others speaking of pluralism, especially certain British socialists.

units, as much for reasons of emotion, prejudice, and habit as for those of rational appraisal of problems at hand.

The real interests of individual members of these blocs may differ sharply on any particular question, but they are expected nevertheless to count their group identity as the primary determinant of their attitudes and actions. Each man is expected to continue to adhere to the group indefinitely, rather than only when its interests and his are similar. Decisions made by established leaders are supposed to matter far more in the relations between blocs than the independent judgments of individual members, with persuasive communication of these leadership decisions to rank and file more important than how well these decisions correspond to the initial mood and mind of the membership.

However, the preceding are "microscopic" observations about the relation of the individual to the bloc of which he nominally is a part. Practitioners of pluralist politics may recognize that the actual relationship is not as regular or predictable, but they believe that the theory is valid and invaluable for assessing the functions of blocs in "macroscopic" perspective. Here too the difference of the American pluralist conception from Proudhon's theory is profound. The political balance of conflicting blocs in a "pluralistic society" is not the balance in his ideal of justice at all. The former is supposed to be achieved between groups all struggling for increased advantage over competitors through more effective marshaling of strength, manipulation of instrumentalities, outwitting of rivals, and straightforward bargaining. Because no bloc ordinarily is able to achieve absolute dominance, each must act in concert with others: the coalitions and the bargaining between all parties which is necessary to maintain them produce the compromises which are supposed to serve the interests of all in the best possible way. In this fashion liberty is supposed to be guaranteed, since no one is likely to gain the kind of dominant power possible in a homogeneous society, except through compromise of his interests with those of all the heterogeneous factions on which his power must rely.

Here is a balance of hostile groups accepting compromise only because none can dominate altogether. There is little thought of equality, and power determines issues rather than an integral spirit of social unity and justice. Judged by Proudhon's standards the force employed is rarely humane, moral, or even intelligent. This is nothing but the civil war and *droit de force* which he says must be left behind us. The order that such pluralism is supposed to establish is unstable and bound to disintegrate—in view of urban conditions in the United States today, perhaps Proudhon has the better of the argument with proponents of pluralism.

Finally, although pluralism in American society is dynamic and keyed to change, Proudhon would have to regard it as essentially a system for maintaining the basic social structure while adjusting to those inevitable changes that do not pose a grave threat to the system itself. Its flexibility is limited and, if there should be a genuine need for more fundamental change, "pluralistic society" will try to contain and absorb the forces that press for it. Such a system is better able to contain these revolutionary forces than a polity of absolutism, but Proudhon would think its efforts bound to be futile in the ultimate decision.

Although *La Guerre et la paix* contributes to clarification of his theory of equilibrium and constructive conflict, it introduces another source of confusion between his ideas and those he despises. If one disregards the book's pacific conclusions, his mystique of war and *l'esprit guerrier* is very much like the views of many traditionalist ideologues. The impression of similarity is reinforced by Proudhon's liking for the simplicity and stalwart independence of peasants and their communities, his distaste for many of the characteristics of industrializing society, his complaints about moral corruption, and his ideal of organic unity.

Nineteenth-century writers reacting against the supposed evils of industrial, political, and social revolutions developed a romantic and usually conservative view of traditional society. They emphasized the organic harmony of rural life and the virtues of the unspoiled peasant while condemning modernization in most or all respects, especially with regard to urban moral degeneration and socially divisive industrialization. However, they did not take the moral faults of rural folk as seriously as did Proudhon, who thought them grave enough to require vast change in the countryside as well as in the city. Moreover, these proponents of organic unity usually had an ideal of hierarchical social structure, with the simple peasants protected by a paternalistic order of actual or surrogate noblesse, clergy, and magistracy. Of course this view is alien to Proudhon's.

This complex of traditionalist ideas generally glorified martial valor and patriotism, adopting these values from the aristocratic ethic, which was a major component of the entire outlook. The paeans of praise for virility and for military courage and self-sacrifice—though not the patriotism—are virtually identical to Proudhon's own encomium for war and self-sacrifice.

However, in its original and best-known form the whole complex of ideas is directed toward the past; its goal is the preservation and restoration of traditional social conditions and moral values. It stands in total opposition to all forms of modernization. Proudhon's desire for revolutionary renovation of the human condition is completely different. He does not esteem traditional values in their time-tested context; as with *l'esprit guerrier*, he wants only to adapt elements of past ethics and customary relations under wholly new conditions.

Nevertheless, Proudhon's idiosyncratic mystique provided a basis of affinity between him and conservative traditionalists who chose to minimize and ignore the differences between his views and theirs. A striking example of this was the formation of a "Cercle Proudhon" in December, 1911, by Charles Maurras, Georges Valois, Henri Lagrange, and others. Maurras was the chief ideologue of the ultra-conservative and nationalist Action Française, and the Cercle Proudhon was scarcely more than an arm of this, the major reactionary organization in France for many years. Before expiring at the beginning of World War I, the Cercle served to discuss and disseminate anti-democratic and traditionalist ideas, drawing quite selectively from Proudhon's writing for support. Presumably this was an effort to attract intellectuals who would have shunned more direct association with the Action Française. However, there were contemporaries of Maurras, most notably Georges Sorel, who were attracted by Proudhon's mystique and attacks on democracy, but remained closer to him in their ideas.[11]

Except perhaps in the Marxist caricature of Proudhon's individualism as the foolishness of a *petit bourgeois* mentality, his mystique

11. See the *Cahiers de Cercle Proudhon* (Paris), 6 numbers in 4 issues (1912), and one issue (1914). The Cercle Proudhon is discussed at length by Boris Souvarine in his "P.-J. Proudhon: Cent Ans après," *Le Contrat social*, IX, 2 (March–April, 1965), 86–94. More will be said about the matter in the last chapter.

in *La Guerre et la paix* may have suffered more abuse through distortion by others than any other aspect of his thought. For this the book itself must bear much of the responsibility.

While *La Guerre et la paix* gives us some insight into Proudhon's historical perspective, the book's scheme of civilization advancing by means of war does not adequately represent his outlook, which is a theory of progress in many ways like others of the Enlightenment intellectual tradition. He does not accept the common nineteenth-century belief in progress as primarily a matter of technological and economic advance, with resultant increase in material well-being; nor is he satisfied with the broader view which also encompasses progressive expansion of knowledge and education, and improvements in political constitutions to aid in securing the other gains.

As was indicated in previous discussion of Proudhon's concept of progress, he defines it in terms of the *revolutionary* movement of humanity, with this change marked by man's use of ideas. Progress is the "eternal march of revolutionary ideas," or more precisely, their actualization. To return to the language of *De la Justice*, progress is the negation of the absolute and all that results from it.

> Progress is the same thing as Justice and liberty considered first in their movement through the centuries, and second in their action on the faculties which obey them and which they modify by their advance, a synthetic entity unable to develop in one of its powers unless all the others participate in the movement.[12]

This is the work of man himself, not of some providential agency. Progress is synonymous with increase of liberty, as men emancipate themselves from fatality—from all external forces that would direct their lives, whether it be divine will, human authority, absolute ideas, natural forces, or the coercion and exploitation of the economic system.

Increase in ordered knowledge and apprehension of ideas are essential, but progress actually occurs as the new ideas become internalized by all men. Most important, the progressive function of ideas lies in their effects on the moral order—in their role in the

12. *Oeuv.*, VIII, vol. iii, 485.

realization of justice. Other functions of ideas, such as in gaining mastery over nature, are progressive only as they contribute to the development of the moral order.

The distinctive features of Proudhon's idea of progress are his moral emphasis and his thinking of revolution and progress as identical. By the latter he means, in the first place, that future progress cannot occur without revolutionary change of the existing social structure. However, this reflection of his responses to the 1848 Revolution and of his ideas about class struggle is also set in wider historical perspective. He concludes that in all times true progress has been essentially revolutionary in character, requiring changes too fundamental to occur simply by gradual variation of existing conditions through successive slight changes.

There is a certain confusion and lack of clarity here. It is possible to conceive of change which is revolutionary in overall character but proceeds continuously and at a gradual pace. However, such a conception becomes difficult to sustain if it is supposed that the elements changed cannot vary without becoming something else altogether. In this case, revolutionary progress proceeds in a succession of sudden breaks with the past. Proudhon suggests just this when he identifies progress with revolution, but his conception is not simply one of history moving by fits and starts. He also speaks of the growth of the awareness, knowledge, and morality of man as going on continuously. Humanity is always in movement, renewing itself and developing without end. In the long run this is revolutionary, but it is not a fitful process.

It is the "absolutist" elements which cannot change without becoming something else: intellectual fixations, the State, the Church, anyone whose great personal stake in preserving the *status quo* makes him unwilling to accept innovation. They do remain static while the rest of the human condition varies. Movement is restricted by their resistance; then they yield, and a step is marked in revolutionary progress.

Proudhon's definition of progress would be clarified if he had distinguished its continuous and discontinuous components more carefully than he has. Then we would have a relatively simple theory of humanity in continuous movement which is progressive in tendency. Discontinuities occur when resisting elements yield and are transformed. These breaks are prepared by the continuing development, and they mark the steps by which progress proceeds. The continuous process is gradual but revolutionary overall, while the sudden transformations are revolutionary by their very nature.

In theory this is fine. But what of the actual experience of discontinuity? Proudhon's dilemma is the problem of how the next major progressive step can take place without disaster. On the one hand, the forces resisting the desperately needed social revolution are so strong and so completely obdurate that no easy, gradual transition to a new world seems possible. Sudden, forcible revolutionary action to overthrow the existing order appears to be the only feasible course. But on the other hand, Proudhon believes such cataclysmic revolution most unlikely to produce the desired result, because of the uncontrollability of the process and its reliance on violent coercion. It would seem that at present progress cannot continue without the submission of forces that will yield only to revolutionary might, which itself will prevent progress. Perhaps this violent revolution would establish conditions in which eventual progress can more readily be realized, but this is a poor substitute for progressive revolution itself.

This dilemma is the source of the ambivalence about revolution which Proudhon never resolves. In his last books he does develop a possible way out. If we translate the ideas there into the terms of the present discussion, this possibility can be described in the following way. Through the organization of the proletariat an integral society within society can be formed in which the spirit of justice actually can be realized. This would be a continuous process of realization, because resisting elements would remain outside this inner society. Additional groups would adhere to the initially proletarian core as recognition of common interests and aspirations grew. These additions would include all the poor, rural as well as urban, and also the lower-middle classes as their disadvantages under industrial capitalism increase. Eventually their moral and physical strength would become great enough to overcome resistance to fundamental structural change in the whole society. The desired transformation could occur without violent revolution, because previous supporters of the *status quo* would either accede to the moral superiority of the innovators or acquiesce in admission of the futility of further resistance.

This is an alluring picture, but skepticism about seeing events actually develop in this way is hard to avoid. To better understand Proudhon's own doubts about such an outcome, it is helpful to examine some additional features of his historical perspective.

With any philosophy of progress one may ask whether the progression is supposed to go on in all times or only under certain conditions. Most Enlightenment *philosophes* believed that the Middle Ages had been static and progress had required the new modern, scientific rationalism and independence of thought in order to proceed. They had also been much concerned with the decline of ancient civilizations, taking their falls to represent breaks in human progress, or decadence.

Influenced as he is by this background, Proudhon is not definite on the question, but his notion of continual movement is more important to his perspective than his concern about decadence. Man's capacity for intellectual and moral self-development transcends unfavorable conditions. Together with his dynamic view of a society which is unstable and ever changing because of its lack of equilibrium, this means that he regards progress as unending, even though it develops in a series of jerky steps.

Such a view is significant, in part because it gives historical perspective to his opposition to conservative traditionalists and their notions of decadence. More important, the theory suggests optimism about the possibilities of contemporary social revolution, since the assumption that progressive process does not stop implies that social revolution is inevitable. However, the preparation of the revolution could go on indefinitely without achieving victory, and regardless of his theory about unbroken progress Proudhon is perpetually uncertain about the actual prospects of revolution.

He affects a denial of optimism, but more often than not he expresses views that would have to be called optimistic. This denial amounts to disclaiming banality while affirming recognition of the great obstacles to progress. Yet even in this he wavers, at some times boldly declaring his humanistic faith and at others seeing humanity as affected by irremediable moral aberration. The former is the necessary assumption of his entire philosophy, the latter a result of frequent moments of despair, most often appearing in his private correspondence and *carnets*. Thus his position can best be described as one of a faith in man and progress which is tempered by and sometimes submerged in his concern over human fallibility.

This temperate optimism takes the form of a conviction that, while human progress is unending, it is erratic. A typical expression of his attitude can be found in a long letter written just after the publication of his *Philosophie du progrès*. In this letter he tries to explain some points of the book which had bothered a reader.

> [Consideration of the facts proves] that first, the Revolution does not stop at all; second, that if the Revolution cannot be stopped there can be no decadence; third, that if, hypothetically, there were momentary eclipse of the moral sense of our country—which would be nothing extraordinary, as progress occurs only through oscillations—the necessity of things, that same necessity which at this moment humiliates us, ought soon to bring us to awareness of our dignity. . . .
>
> Yes, I repeat, society by itself is an incorruptible, indefectible thing; society always advances. They can kill it, by killing its members; they can weaken it by devastating it, tyrannizing it; they can retard it by decimation, by taking away its elite (its aristocracy) through which it lives and reducing it to the dust of the *multitude*. By itself, it always advances; it is always erect; it is, in its essence, valiant and pure; cowardice and corruption are its contrary; they are nonsociety. And it is for this that the crime of those who violate it, outrage it, obstruct it, is unpardonable.[13]

As indicated in the preceding passage, Proudhon often thinks of the erratic course of progress in terms of oscillation. Just as "oscillation" implies an alternation of positive and negative movement, he is concerned with the possibilities of retrograde movement, the reversal of progress. Here he vacillates: his theory would seem to preclude major retrogression, but it is difficult for him to deny its possibility, particularly with respect to the contemporary French situation. In his grand view of the past he vociferously denies that the historical decline of civilizations can be rightly represented as the decadence of peoples or retrograde movement, but his denials

13. Letter to Troessart, September 16, 1853, *Corresp.*, V, 247ff.

have a note of desperation about them. It seems as if he wants them to be true but lacks conviction. He says a true theory of progress must give an explanation of retrogression and decadence, but he does not succeed in doing this.

Although his uncertainties remain unresolved, Proudhon is firm about the attitude we ought to have toward progress and the revolutionary cause. Strive to advance the cause, or we may indeed retrogress—or at least stagnate, which amounts to virtually the same thing.

How much can deliberate striving affect the course of progress? Once more Proudhon's theory is not well enough defined, but the implications of what he says are fairly clear. Since progress results from the movement of all men, it is a phenomenon whose momentum is too great for it to be entirely controlled by deliberate acts. Revolutions cannot be dragged onto the stage; they come only when the massive change of mankind has prepared them. In this sense progress completely overshadows more transitory phenomena, and much that man has counted great and earth-shaking appears as accident when seen in the wider and more basic perspective.

However, Proudhon's conception is not a variation on the old theme of determinism. Progress can be affected by human will, for it is possible to accelerate or correct the direction of its motion. Its pace is almost infinitely variable, and it may stop, reverse, or be diverted into unwanted byways. Man cannot just sit back in complacent anticipation of continuing forward motion. The revolution may be inevitable, but its day could be indefinitely postponed.

Those devoted to the revolutionary cause must attempt to compress the time span of progress. Through human will the series of needed steps can be abbreviated and the intervals between them shortened. Negative movement can be reduced in extent and impact. The pace of change can be accelerated, if we have wisdom and determination—but it is making the effort that matters most, not the pace. Only from the effort itself can come the spirit which eventually will bring success, whatever the rate at which the movement appears to proceed now.

Man must make himself, through the deliberate efforts of each of us. There are no magic formulas whose applications by wise leaders will bring us all to the promised land, no certain laws of history determining the course we must follow. History has been an endless succession of forces clashing, establishing momentary equilibrium, then passing on to new groupings, new contests. By reflecting on this past dialectical movement of mankind, we can understand better what to do now, but we must do it by our own volition and conscience, with understanding of the novelty of the situations we confront. The true enemy is neither hostile ruling classes nor the natural world around us that technology strives against so mightily. Victory over ourselves is the real goal; somehow, Proudhon is sure, we will win.

Although his level of hopefulness varied in oscillative reaction to disappointing events and trends in contemporary society, positive humanism and optimistic expectation were far more typical of him than expressions of despair and unrelieved pessimism. Late in life he wrote while in one of his more mellow moods to a friend of his youth, recalling that distant time and his career since. In this letter we see revealed the nature of his faith and spirit.

> If everything only demonstrated to me that society has entered a crisis of regeneration, which will be long and perhaps terrible, I would believe in the irrevocable decadence and approaching end of civilization. But it is necessary to believe that we will emerge from it, precisely because our contemporaries are more dissolute and less intelligent than we were. The movement of history occurs by oscillations whose amplitude it is up to us to attenuate. Then let us work to make ourselves better, to think justly; let us seek frugality and flee sloth. With that we shall shorten the trial and be reborn superior to our fathers.[14]

He believes that, as humanity develops its goal of justice, it changes and grows in correspondence to mankind's own transformation and increasing potential. As each individual approaches his fellows and the spirit of justice, all are absorbed into one another in an ever more integral, organic whole, and society progresses and makes increasingly real the ideal of what man can be. Technically Proudhon's philosophy of history is defective at many points; in its relation to the actuality of contemporary conditions, he is uncertain

14. Letter to Milliet, November 2, 1862, *Corresp.*, XII, 222.

and sometimes vague. Nevertheless, his vision of human history is a noble one.[15]

15. The preceding gives only a partial analysis of Proudhon's philosophy of history. For a somewhat different and less selective treatment, see Aaron Noland, "History and Humanity: The Proudhonian Vision," in *The Uses of History*, ed. Hayden V. White (Detroit, 1968), 59-105.

eleven: Mutualism

What is Justice? the pact of liberty.

Two men encounter each other, their interests opposed. The debate is joined; then they come to terms: the first conquest of *droit*, the first establishment of Justice. A third arrives, then another, and so on indefinitely: the pact which binds the first two is extended to the newcomers; so many contracting parties, so many occasions for Justice. Then there is progress, progress in Justice of course, and consequently progress in liberty.[1]

No EXPRESSION of Proudhon's ideal of social relationships more characteristic than the one above could be cited. It is especially significant that this model for the foundation of justice begins with two individuals and goes on from their solitary transaction to encompass a whole society. The individualist focus and its extension to a general social theory is familiar to us from his earlier writings, and it forms the basis of the anarchist attack on government he elaborated while in prison after the 1848 Revolution.

Nevertheless, as expressed the model is incomplete. The vast numbers of people and the considerable size of relatively coherent groups interacting in modern society make the model seem as inadequate as an attempt to treat the mathematical analysis of gas kinetics as if no more than the simple mechanics of two-body col-

1. *De la Justice, Oeuv.*, VIII, vol. iii, 513.

lisions were involved. Yet the analysis of gas kinetics does start with two-body mechanics and goes on from its conditions and rules to development of methods for handling the more complex problems of the kinetics of colliding bodies whose number is limitless.

Likewise, while Proudhon uses a "two-body model" as a foundation and as the center of his orientation, he goes on to develop methods for handling the more complex problems of a large society. The theory first worked out in full in *De la Justice* provides a framework for doing this. Its view of society completes the anarchist, individualist critique laid out earlier and makes it possible to conceive how the values defined in that critique can be realized in practical application.

Total liberty for each individual and complete equality between all individuals are the primary criteria which determine Proudhon's anarchist outlook. In making this a truly *social* theory he recognizes as equally important the interdependence and social responsibility of all men. Thus anarchism's negative political analysis becomes a positive political and social synthesis that he calls "mutualism."

Society is an intricate structure whose members need each other and must constantly associate with each other in an infinite variety of ways. Even if a person tries to minimize social contact, like everyone else he must depend on countless others in the sphere of economic activity. Therefore the independence of the free man cannot be absolute: his liberty may be real enough, but its realization is bound up with the lives and liberty of others. If he is to be truly free, his participation in the life of society must always be voluntary and in accord with self-interest; his independence is to make his life himself, in conjunction with others, without being subject to decisions and requirements which he has no part in making and which are not freely acceptable to him.

Thus we have this fuller statement of the concept expressed in the passage just quoted.

> Two men encounter each other, recognize their dignity, ascertain the increased benefit which would result for both from their working in concert, and consequently guarantee each other equality, which amounts to saying, economy. There is the entire social system: an equation, and therefore a power of collectivity.
>
> Two families, two cities, two provinces, contract on the same

basis: there are always only two things, an equation and a power of collectivity. It would involve contradiction, violation of Justice, for there to be anything else.[2]

A balanced equation: that is the basis of social relationships which preserve the rights of the individual while achieving that joint strength of men working together. This "power of collectivity" is essential if people are to survive the dangers of nature and their own passions and violence, going on to the accomplishments of which only man, out of all living beings, is capable. Integral society is organic through the necessary interdependence of its component elements, but these parts must remain discrete, each with its own will and motion.

How is the balance struck? In what ways can the physical, intellectual, and economic capacities of mankind best be employed to establish lastingly viable social equilibrium? It cannot be simply a matter of eliminating economic exploitation and political tyranny. Some socialist schemes might permit more equitable economic relationships, but would they be just? Justice can no more be sacrificed for the sake of economic equality than it can exist without such equality. As we have already seen, Proudhon thinks political tyranny will be ended only when all institutions of government are abolished, not merely modified. Yet public order has to be maintained somehow if anarchy is to be more than dissonant, violent chaos.

So Proudhon must reconcile the requirements of liberty with those of public order, of economic equity with those of individualism, of autonomy for individuals and natural groups with those of integral community. A substitute for historical political systems is needed; whether the proposed system resulting from his struggle with those problems is a "government" or not is a moot point. His system is supposed to perform the useful functions of government but lacks enough of its usual key characteristics to be called anarchist. More significant is the point that with Proudhon for the first time "anarchy" has a positive meaning instead of denoting merely an absence of government.

The libertarian arguments emphasized in his earlier works form a vital prelude to the later writings, where the definition of justice

2. Ibid., 266.

is stated mainly in terms of equality. He believes that, if equality alone is the primary goal of a new social system, it is likely that the new society will be neither free nor just. Proudhon's frequent criticism of other socialists' theories centers upon his conviction that their routes to equality will *not* lead to liberty as well, and may even cut off movement in that direction.

If one recognizes the equal worth and rights of men but implements this recognition merely by maintaining throughout society a single level of status and wealth, assuring equal distribution of the fruits of production, then many social ills will be eliminated but the society will not be healthy. Conceivably, it might be free and orderly, but only if its elements are inert. Immobile, it vegetates without progress. Uniform and lacking the healthy conflict of a diverse population, without its social bonds constantly renewed through negotiation of fresh transactions, the society will stagnate and disintegrate. If this sort of egalitarian society is to maintain both unity and dynamism, then it must have direction and sources of energy. Likewise, there must be some means of coordinating the work of the collectivity for productive purposes. The agency that energizes and coordinates must be made up of men who inevitably assume the imperative power required for them to be effective. Whatever may be the limits and source of their authority, they will dominate the wills of all, subordinating them to the demands of the common good and swallowing all individual spontaneity.

Though economic equality might be preserved in such a society, there would be neither political equality nor liberty. Men can be equal without reduction to uniformity. If they can act as spontaneous, autonomous individuals animated and directed from within themselves, then there can be an egalitarian society which will live and grow. If individual identity is absorbed in the name of equality, then the society will perish.[3]

Although Proudhon objects to subordination of the individual

---

3. In Proudhon's usage, the word *communauté* almost always denotes the egalitarian socialist utopia, which he attacks in this fashion. The word most closely corresponding in English is "commune," used as in socialist discourse. In French, the *commune* is the usual local territorial division of government, and the word may denote just the administrative structure or the entire local community. There is no single word in Proudhon's vocabulary which corresponds closely to the English word "community."

to the community, he does want society to be organized into some kind of structured system. Moreover, while he fails to recognize how extensive the interdependence of discrete communities has to be in an industrialized society, he does not adopt the common utopian supposition that a small, integral community can be totally self-sufficient. This would permit him to take a relatively simple approach, just developing a pattern of organization for a collectivity of very limited extent, with its members sharing many common interests and having relatively few divisive problems. Instead of this he offers a plan for the organization of a society of any size, and ultimately for all of mankind.

His ideal system cannot be built around a central institution, whether that be a government with full administrative and judicial authority, or primarily a legislative body to provide a set of universal norms with which local communities can govern themselves. Universal laws administered locally could provide the structural framework for a coherent overall system whose elements are effectively compatible, but this would still not fulfill Proudhon's requirements. He has too many objections to universal laws and to all varieties of legislative process to agree to any government of law.

Even assuming that a constitution and a flexible legal philosophy could be devised which would satisfy most of these objections, it is impossible for a centralized system to be justified in his eyes. Unless the central institution has some authority, it is absurd to regard it as the center of social organization. Without authority it can be no more than a debating academy with hopes that its conclusions can be influential. The responsibility for maintaining the social order would lie elsewhere. If its lawmaking role is to be more substantial, then it must have authority to require observance of its laws.

If the central institution has enough authority for its lawmaking to be meaningful, then it is the State which Proudhon has so many reasons to reject. He is convinced that there is no way to limit State authority except by what amounts in actual effect to denying it altogether. The centralized State may permit local communities and individuals to exercise a substantial degree of autonomous initiative and power, but only that which it does not see fit to exercise itself at the moment. It can and does assume these functions and powers for itself when ready, and local autonomy exists only at the pleasure of the centralized State. There can be little effective resistance.

Although constitutional safeguards might avoid much of the danger of the State arrogating excessive power to itself, this does not alter the basic situation as Proudhon sees it. When it makes laws and exercises authority over an entire society, central government incorporates natural groups into an unnatural unity, with all the attendant ill consequences. The only natural unity is one achieved spontaneously, without the intervention of authority. Under central government equilibrium is impossible: State and society are doomed to irreconcilable destructive antagonism. Steps taken to preserve unity only increase discord. When the State intervenes in conflicts between groups within society, it disturbs and artificially modifies the natural relationships, often aggravating differences and preventing equitable settlement.

Whatever its constitution, Proudhon says, government develops toward centralization and the subordination of natural groups, upsetting equilibrium and generating civil strife. He reviews and rejects various palliatives suggested to remedy this: constitutional revision, municipal and provincial organization as a counterpoise to central authority, division of powers, collective sovereignty.[4] "Collective sovereignty" is an illusion: even though power be exercised in the name of the collectivity, it is still unitary and dominant, subordinating and absorbing the natural powers and identities of groups and individuals throughout the dominion. He also argues that the schemes for division of power envisaged by reformers stand in impossible contradiction to the very idea of government in any form.

The only sort of genuine separation of powers that Proudhon thinks feasible or just is that which confines to a minimum the functions of all institutions or governments which encompass within their purviews some numbers of diverse groups. The principal unit of "government" must be the natural community with its homogeneity of interests. These natural collectivities can employ federative arrangements for needed joint action, but the federations can have no substantive authority, acting only by mutual agreement.

4. *Contradictions politiques, Oeuv.,* XIII, 238-45.

Government is impossible, but a system of political organization is needed: Proudhon's solution is "federalism."

> . . . all known governments until this day are nonmatching frag-
> ments of the true social constitution, which is unique, the same
> for all people, and can be called *Federative Republic;* save for
> that there is neither liberty, *droit,* morals, nor good faith. . . . In
> short, this is what I call the *solution of the political problem.*[5]

In the usage of the English language, there is an important distinction ordinarily made between the words "federation" and "confederation." Both denote associations of states, groups, or even individuals in order to achieve some common purpose; usually the
words connote a permanent league or union. However, "federation" denotes an agreement whereby each party subordinates its
power to that of a central authority conducting the members' common affairs. A confederation is a union whose central body has
relatively little authority and whose members are virtually autonomous. The United States of America, before and after the introduction of the 1787 Constitution, is often offered as an example of the
two forms of association.

Proudhon does not recognize this distinction at all, using both
fédération and *confédération* (usually the former) to denote what
would be called a confederation in English. His definition:

> FEDERATION . . . is a convention by which one or several heads
> of family, one or several communities, one or several groups of
> communities or States, are obligated reciprocally and equally to-
> ward one another for one or several particular objects, whose
> burden is then the special and exclusive duty of the delegates to
> the federation.[6]

He also uses without distinction the words "convention" and
"contract." In both French and English "convention" often means
an agreement which, once concluded, is supposed to be accepted
tacitly and adhered to indefinitely without express reaffirmation,
until abrogated by joint declaration. It may even be obligatory
upon a dissenting minority. "Contract" more often signifies an ar-

5. Letter to Buzon, January 31, 1863, *Corresp.,* XII, 269. This was written just
after the completion of *Du Principe fédératif.*
6. *Du Principe fédératif, Oeuv.,* XIV, 318.

rangement which requires the continuing explicit agreement of the parties to it, or which binds them to it only for a specified term. It is contingent upon fulfillment of its conditions and transitory in duration, though perhaps repeatedly renewable. All those bound by the contract give their voluntary assent initially, even if thereafter they are not free to withdraw until after the specified term. As we saw earlier, whatever word he uses Proudhon definitely means a *contract* with the continuing express and voluntary concurrence of all parties. His demand for constant, deliberate assent by all citizens to all collective action underlies his entire criticism of government, and of the Rousseauean tradition.

He requires that the contracting parties each undertake obligations to one another (*contrat synallagmatique*), and that these reciprocal obligations be equivalent in value to each other (*contrat commutatif*).[7] The obligations of contracts are distinguished in his thinking from those of legal norms; contractual obligations are not imposed or legislated by a superior authority, and they are incurred individually rather than having the universal reference of norms. They do have a moral and rational force, however, and thus are compelling upon the contracting parties as long as the reason and sense of justice of each one requires it.

The character of the federative contract then is clear: it is "synallagmatic" and "commutative," and it guarantees to all parties their independent liberty and sovereignty, establishing no imperative federal authority. The obligations undertaken have real force, but only as long as each contractor is satisfied that the arrangement remains morally and rationally compelling. The purpose of the federation is the accomplishment of measures that will serve the common interests of members or permit them to reconcile conflicting interests so that each enjoys equivalent benefit.

Federative contract defines the relations between collectivities and between them and individuals acting alone. But for Proudhon collective entities have no being apart from that of the individuals who constitute them. He will not personify the political community; contracts are not arranged for the good of the abstracted collective, but for the people within it.

7. *Oeuv.*, XIV, 315ff. Proudhon uses the current *Code civil* to define forms of contract; he regularly employs some of its technical terms, of which these are two.

Corresponding in form to the federative contract and prerequisite to it is the social contract, by which the community assumes its identity and according to which it acts. This is not an arrangement between man and government, or between man and polity, but between man and man. Agreement between men becomes the basis for negotiating the requirements of their joint interests with those of other groups. Like all contracts, it should be contingent upon the continuing express assent of each party. Thus at all levels voluntary engagement and transaction on the basis of reciprocal, equivalent benefit should be the basis of all human relations.

> Then there exists a contract or constitution of society, given a priori through the forms of the consciousness, which are liberty, dignity, reason, Justice, and through the relationships of neighborhood and exchange which inevitably sustain individuals between them. This is the act through which men, forming themselves into groups, declare *ipso facto* the identity and solidarity of their respective dignities, recognize each other reciprocally and with the same sovereign claim, and bear guarantees for one another.[8]

Although his description of it is very detailed, Proudhon's political plan is simple, once his ideas about contract and existing governments are clearly understood. As the basic political grouping, or "state," the local community should have the characteristics which for him define a natural group. He does not consider carefully the problems for federative "government" which may be raised by local communities too divided to be called natural, or by natural groups too extended geographically to form compact local units. Proudhon can fit these groups into his scheme, but we should expect that their actual fit would in practice be less comfortable than theory allows.

It is assumed that people living in close proximity usually have enough common interests to constitute a natural group. Where all do not share similar interests the locale can be divided into any number of homogeneous communities, just as sizable towns already are usually divided into quarters, districts, *faubourgs*, and even small neighborhoods. The last of these, and sometimes also larger locales,

8. *Oeuv.*, VIII, vol. i, 419. For a summary of his plans for federation, see *Oeuv.*, XIV, 545-51.

often have residents conscious of a distinctive community identity and sense of unity. As for geographically extended natural groups, like artisans in a particular trade, they can enter the political and social processes in significant ways without being normal political units. Since a trade organization can engage a "state" in a contractual transaction on precisely the same synallagmatic, commutative basis as that arranged between two states, the trade group suffers no disadvantage.

Each local polity, while retaining complete sovereignty, can join with others to accomplish their common purposes, reconcile differences, and exchange goods and services. Basically these unions are directed to the achievement of specific ends and are contingent upon satisfaction of respective needs, as befits the contractual nature of all such arrangements. Thus each polity can be involved in a complex of varied and changing obligations to others, rather than always remaining in a fixed, uniform system of relations with its neighbors and the rest of the country.

However, there would be many interests and grounds for relationship which would remain relatively constant. For these there would be a "hierarchy" of indefinitely enduring confederations at district, regional, and national levels; Proudhon would like to see the system extended to include continental and universal federative unions as well. ". . . the political center is everywhere, the circumference nowhere." [9]

For these confederations there would be institutional arrangements, based on elections by universal suffrage. The electors would have functions of supervising, revising, and sanctioning the acts of their deputies, as well as selecting them. There would be a legislative body, in one assembly if the constituent "states" were equal in size and importance, or otherwise in two chambers with one apportioned on the basis of importance and the other with equal representation for each state. The people's representatives would choose an executive commission from their own number; the commission would name one of its members as president. Appointment of commissioners, including the president, would be revocable at any time. Similar institutions would exist for confederations at every level.[10]

9. *De la Capacité politique, Oeuv.*, III, 198.
10. This institutional scheme is given in ibid., 216ff.

This arrangement of offices sounds at first very like an unremarkable scheme for a democratic republic of the kind Proudhon had often condemned. Of course he emphatically denies that the appearance of similarity has a real basis, and in fact it does not. This system of institutions for confederations happens to be one of the last things he wrote, possibly an afterthought to add to the apparent practicability of federalism. The core of federative system is not the constitution of a confederation, but the contractual relationship, with complete negation of authority.

The concept of federative government without any authority can best be explained by an example of its functioning. A universally standard currency is important, even necessary, for all communities. The national—or world—legislature would decide the standards, and the executive commission would disseminate them. Actual manufacture of currency would be performed by local communities, or by groups of them pooling their productive resources. If anybody issued money departing from the standard, the executive commission could remonstrate them but not require them to conform.

This example demonstrates both the possibilities and the weaknesses of the concept. The metric system of measurement is an actual example of a set of standards widely but not universally adopted, with adoption by each state voluntary—although use within a state is often mandatory for many applications. Here, at least, Proudhon's approach has proven practicable—but standard weights and measures are a different matter from money. One would expect some states to issue currency debased to less intrinsic value than the standard, with chaos resulting—according to Gresham's law, "Bad money drives out good."

But Proudhon's whole political system is based on the presumption that the spirit of justice is universal. Issuing debased money would be unjust and irrational, and this would not be done. He does not expect that his system could be workable without universal rationality and moral regeneration.

A more serious objection is the recognition that the example of establishing standards just selects a function of conventional government which is exceptionally well suited to the federative scheme. Even if people were habitually just, it is not difficult to imagine situations which Proudhon's system would be unable to handle adequately. For instance, there can easily be divisions between groups where the issues involved are so difficult and complicated that the most just of men cannot agree to a suitably rational solution, or where some of the parties are honestly, stubbornly, and obviously mistaken. One is reminded of some of the marvelously complex trade-union contract negotiations as an example of something like this today. A government with imperative power can arbitrate disputes, a course which is particularly attractive if one or more parties is guilty of obvious error. Proudhon would have to leave such disputes either to voluntary acceptance of mediation or binding arbitration or to no resolution at all. A voluntary approach may be preferable in some matters, like today's labor-management relations, but a chaos of indecision appears all too possible in many other situations.

The difficulty with Proudhon's vision lies in his inability to appreciate the sheer magnitude and complexity of many problems with which society must cope. Modern industrial society does so today only with political authority's absolutely vital contributions. The ties that bind people together are so extensive in industrial economies that very large populations must be involved together; the intricacy of their relationships and diversity of their interests defies the simple rationality of federative contract.

If nothing else, in his system there would be problems of virtually insuperable difficulty arising from the acquisition and allocation of the huge amounts of funds needed to capitalize efficient joint enterprises for industrial production, public works, and public services like education. It would seem that successful introduction of a federative political system in all its particulars—if it were possible at all—would require either universal possession of rational powers far beyond the best yet achieved, or discarding most of the advantages of industrialization in favor of a simple life of small communities and limited economic production and public services. Whether or not the latter course is feasible today, in Proudhon's time putting such limits on productive capacity almost certainly would have kept material deprivation at too high a level for a universal spirit of justice to be realizable. However, if his political system seems inadequate for handling the problems of modern industrial countries, at least it can be said that the performance of existing governments does not inspire great confidence in *their* adequacy, either.

Federative "government" is of course different from the usual proposals of others to replace the tyranny of a centralized national regime by a system leaving much autonomy to local or provincial authorities. These calls for decentralization still leave imperative power to the smaller governments, although they may demand limits on this power, in the name of liberalism and free enterprise.

For Proudhon the only real sovereignty should be that of individuals, with the political hierarchy reversed in order. The confederations of "states" would have fewer functions and "powers" as they increase in size and scope. At each level joint action would include the combination of no more communities than the minimum required to carry out a project.

He asserts that this is the only way that "popular sovereignty" can be more than the illusory abstraction he believes it to have been in Rousseau's conception and in the 1793 republican constitution. The People can achieve real sovereignty only by acting themselves directly in a wide variety of associations to accomplish important purposes. The collective force of people acting in voluntary association is the true power of the sovereign polity.

In response to criticisms of confederation claiming that historically such unions have proven unstable and subject to rapid disintegration, Proudhon insists that centralized states have achieved stability only by means of coercive, despotic force. We have seen that he believes that all states based upon force and institutionalizing injustice are bound to be torn apart and destroyed by the irreconcilable antagonisms always generated within them. He thinks that his confederations would survive simply because they are just.

The usual sources of political instability would not exist in a federative system because in it the differences between men form the basis and even the object of the forms of political organization. Instead of being divisive and disruptive, differences are set in conditions of dynamic balance. With diversity welcomed, intolerance is eliminated. If there should be war-like strife within the polity, federative government would be unable to contain it. If the function of government is to control warring parties inside the nation and to maintain and advance the country's power abroad, then confederation is not the answer—but Proudhon has concluded that such is not the business of government. For his purposes federalism is the only way to achieve genuine unity in the nation, with all people closely tied by the links of their interdependence and those felt by all those who know themselves equal in status and dignity.

The most divisive antagonisms in historical experience arise from economic injustice; the most important human associations are economic in character. Thus, although we speak of the collective force of a sovereign people when describing a political system, nearly all associations and contractual obligations occurring in the context of political organization are primarily economic in purpose and impact.

While the customary terms of discourse in political philosophy make it convenient for Proudhon to discuss his federalism as a purely political theory in these customary terms, he makes it quite clear that the distinction is artificial. Political organization, relationship, and contract are not actually different from economic ones, and all are "social" as well. This is why the trade organization can negotiate with a federative "state" on precisely the same basis as another state does.

All human transactions of any kind should take place according to the form of synallagmatic, commutative contract, although in friendly relationships where there is no conflict the need may not exist for an actual, express agreement. The "golden rule" becomes "reciprocal benefit through mutual guarantees." Thus Proudhon calls his philosophy "mutualism," or sometimes "guarantism." Federalism is just a special case of mutualism, usually as applied to questions traditionally said to be political in nature.[11] It is the organization of a mutualist society; if the merits of the federative political system are to be appraised, they must be judged in terms of the values and hopes of the whole theory of mutualism. No political innovations can succeed if the economy and the social organism are not reestablished on the basis of mutuality.

> As irreproachable as the federal constitution may be in its logic and in practical guarantees it offers, it will sustain itself only as far as it does not encounter incessant causes of dissolution in the public

11. Proudhon also speaks sometimes of "fédération agricole-industrielle" as the system of economic organization corresponding to "fédération politique."

economy. In other words, the buttress of economic *droit* is necessary for political *droit*. If the production and distribution of wealth is given up to chance; if the federative order serves only to protect capitalist and mercantile anarchy; if through the effect of this false anarchy Society finds itself divided into two classes, one of proprietors-capitalists-entrepreneurs, the other of proletarian wage earners; one of the rich, the other of the poor—then the political edifice will always be unstable. The working class, the most numerous and most poor, will end by perceiving there only a deception; workers will join together against the bourgeoisie, who on their side will join together against the workers; and we shall see the confederation degenerate, if the people are the stronger, into unitary democracy, if the bourgeoisie triumphs, into constitutional monarchy.[12]

It would be difficult to specify in detail the ways in which an ideal mutualist society would operate, and Proudhon does not really attempt to do so. Practice would have to be improvised for each new occasion, for that after all is the essence of the whole approach. Systematic planning in detail is antithetical to the requirements for liberty and spontaneity.

Much of the practice of mutuality can be established by determining the opposites of practices he rejects altogether. Thus all income should be derived from productive labor, with none from property rentals, interest and dividends on invested capital, financial speculation, or profits in commerce beyond those serving to compensate the businessman for his work. Prices would depend solely on real value, which is determined only by the amount of labor involved in the product or service offered. There would be no master-servant relations. No one would possess more property than he can and does use productively, and possession would not entail absolute rights to the property; the ruling principle would be the right of every man to possession of an equitable proportion of existing productive property, if he needs it in order to sustain himself by the kind of labor he has himself chosen.

Joint economic enterprises like factories would be no larger and no more closely tied to others than needed for efficiency through division of labor; monopolies would be precluded. By division of

12. *Oeuv.*, XIV, 354.

labor and specialization of functions each man would work in the job best suited to his capacities and preference, while mutualist co-ordination would permit coherent operations without special advantage to anyone. All those associated in joint enterprise would assume responsibility individually and collectively to their fellow workers and to the public at large, freely undertaking obligations to deal with one another fairly on the basis of equivalent value of goods and services.[13]

Proudhon believes that there is a "right of labor" [14] by virtue of which the product of human industry belongs to the producer. The "product" to which each worker has a personal right is that form which he himself gives to material; with the division of labor, many can share rights to the actual articles produced. There is supposed to be an equivalent right for useful services which do not actually create a material product. The idea of the right of labor includes his theory that in a just economy the only criterion of value is the quantity of labor expended. It is on this basis alone that the required equivalence in exchange is determined. The right of labor also serves to define the relationship between workers in collective endeavor and as the basis for rejecting any system whereby workers are simply wage-earners with no interest in the disposal of the product. All men working together ought to be equal associates who share in the rewards, both material and immaterial, which result from creation of a product and its sale.

The material rewards should be distributed among associated workers without regard to any differentiating criterion except the quantity of labor expended by each man. Other distinctions ordinarily made between the work of different men, such as varying levels of difficulty and of talent required, are immaterial and an offense to personal dignity. An architect may have more excep-

13. A number of writers have drawn from Proudhon specific suggestions for the reorganization of industrial practice. For a notable example, see Daniel Guérin, "Proudhon et l'autogestion ouvrière," in *L'Actualité de Proudhon,* ed. Centre National d'Etude des Problèmes de Sociologie et d'Economie Européennes (Brussels, 1967), 67–87; also in Guérin's *Pour un Marxisme libertaire* (Paris, 1969), 99–128.

14. He distinguishes the "right *of* labor" from the "right *to* labor." The latter, which is a major point in his criticism of property, is expressed as a right of every man to the means and opportunity to work for the sustenance of himself and his family. Others cannot rightfully deny him such means of sustenance as farm land, when they do so only for the sake of increasing or maintaining their economic advantages over him.

tional talents than a hod-carrier, but both are needed to erect a building. A day of labor is equivalent to a day of labor, whatever the nature of the work. If the architect needs an extra reward, then he should draw ample satisfaction from his possession of special talents constructively used and from the respect of others for his abilities. In a just society the greatest rewards of work and the main sources of a man's satisfaction should be immaterial, while material rewards would be required only to satisfy the physical needs common to all. Proudhon's plan to distribute the material fruits of labor according to relative amounts of work results from his theory of value and equivalence, not from a bourgeois notion that the harderworking man is more "deserving."

The organization of the new society around a network of economic relations is said by him to have the advantage of providing a central theme and purpose, both for the orientation of men toward progress and increased solidarity and for the creation of those guiding rational principles which would serve in the traditional role of laws. In this way "law" can be constructive and creative instead of negative and punitive. Instead of repression, it offers a basis for organization; instead of sanctions, it provides guarantees. Such positive law is supposed to require no authority to enforce it, simply because rational men should be glad to adhere to it.

That he discusses mutualist society with so much emphasis on problems of labor, production, property, and exchange in commerce should not be surprising, since Proudhon has always maintained that these questions are the core of all social affairs. Twenty years earlier he had said that to constitute society is to organize labor and that society should not be constructed on the model of the family but on that of the workshop. In another place he said that the organization of economic forces should replace political functions and workshops replace government. In his final statements his conception is more sophisticated and complex than in these simple assertions, but his mature theory amounts to the same propositions with further elaborations.

One could with reason object that his emphasis on economic relationships, vital as they are, fails to take adequate account of important human needs. Even though most collective projects require joint labor and a pooling of material resources, many such group efforts are desirable for reasons largely irrelevant to economic functioning. Parks and other community recreation facilities are examples. Surely human needs, individual as well as social, are far from satisfied just by realization of economic and political justice.

Here Proudhon's economic emphasis is faulty; he is a poor psychologist. His understanding of the forces operative in human relationships and of what men need in order to be happy is penetrating within the scope of what he reconsiders; yet, like most philosophers, he hardly thinks of many of the things vital to the human spirit and condition.

Still, although his failings in this area are patently apparent, these criticisms speak more to the improbability of realizing the spirit of justice as he conceives it than they do to the feasibility of mutualism when that spirit is universal. His theory is that those things he does consider are the ones which divide men and harm them most profoundly. Consequent lack of equilibrium, strife, animosity and other passions—above all those primarily economic in origin—prevent the regular satisfaction of all human needs, including those Proudhon does not mention or even know of.

Mutualist contract—social, economic, and political—is the basis for achieving the equilibrium which is the prerequisite for everything else. Through the dynamic balance of mutualism the diverse elements of society can achieve a unity which ties everything together with bonds at once strong and subtle, complex in structure but simple in the quality of each link. With liberty, equality, and genuine social solidarity the moral and spiritual regeneration of mankind becomes possible. Not only would political tyranny and material deprivation be eliminated, but also men will be able to seek happiness and self-fulfillment in every aspect of life and do so for the first time without bars to success at every turn. Mankind may not ever be able to satisfy all of its needs or be idyllically happy, but that should be the result of a man's own inability to do or be more and of natural forces external to man. It should never happen that other men prevent an individual from achieving what his capacities otherwise permit. Rather, the potential of each one should be increased and his attainments be both greater and more satisfying through the effects of collective force and amicable social relations.

This touches on a matter skirted a number of times in this and preceding chapters without ever being fully engaged: the central role of *work* in Proudhon's conception of human nature, and thus in his entire philosophy. Throughout his writings he emphasizes how labor is a vital part of life as necessary for spiritual fulfillment and moral development as for providing material needs. He repeatedly stresses the nobility and dignity of labor, especially manual labor, though he does not think other work less important if it makes a positive contribution to society or to the spiritual self-fulfillment of the man performing it. He sees labor in terms of its creative function and as the way a man realizes his potential. Proudhon thinks of talents as capacity to create and thus sees fulfillment of potential as a matter of creative production also.

He usually thinks of "products" fairly concretely, although intellectual and aesthetic work, parenthood, and contributions to growth of a more just society can also be creative in his view. His concrete idea of productivity is linked to his emphasis on manual labor, making it difficult for him to appreciate adequately the vital positive role played in the economy by workers who provide services not directly related to the shaping of concrete products. As a result he thinks of workers in an ideal society mainly as craftsmen and farmers, a bias that detracts from the relevance of his mutualist theory to industrialized economies.

When Proudhon attacks the capitalist system, it is not only because its economic exploitation results in material poverty, social instability, and political tyranny. Capitalism degrades the worker and prevents him from fulfilling himself through his labor. Work is onerous only when the worker is in a servile position, the conditions of labor imposed upon him by a master who may be either his employer or someone with coercive economic power over him, like the owner of his land or the merchant who can force him to sell his produce at a less than equitable price.

Man and his labor are free by their nature, and they have to cast off the bonds of external necessity. With mutualism the bonds imposed by men themselves are eliminated; the limits on freedom originating in nature constitute challenges that man can confront boldly and joyfully, gradually overcoming them or finding better ways to come to terms with them. Then labor becomes a liberating process, as a man conquers natural limits and expands the scope and power of his activity. Though his work may be hard, it is spontaneous, done because he wants to achieve and create, in tasks he has chosen himself; it is no longer a burden undertaken because the alternative is to perish.

With the preceding as background, it is easy to see how Proudhon arrives by his own route at a critique of what Marx, using quite a different philosophical method to reach similar conclusions, calls the "alienation" of labor. The Frenchman's conception is an explanation of how capitalist industry makes labor exceptionally repugnant, without even the limited degree of fulfillment attainable by a tenant farmer or an impoverished artisan forced to sell his products and buy his materials at disadvantageous prices.

In the first place, the wage worker is separated from his product, deprived of his interest in its disposal. He is reduced to performing an operation instead of being recognized as a vital participant in collective production; his wage rate is determined by his needs for subsistence and the degree of competition among employers for labor services—not by the value he has contributed to the product. His compensation is not equivalent to his worth, and he has little or no reason to be proud of what he is doing or to be conscious of his creative function.

Moreover, as the work of production is further divided and its mechanization advanced, each worker is "worth" less in relation to the value of the products as determined by capitalist accounting, since machines and other workers have assumed much of his function. Proudhon believes that this development of mechanized industry necessarily results in real wages being forced downward, although, unlike Marx, he does not have a thorough explanation of how and why this should happen.

The excessive division of labor means that each worker's task in the productive process is so narrowly restricted that he is no longer able to conceive of it as creative; this restriction is greatly advanced by mechanization, with men often doing no more than tending machines which do the work of actually forming the product. In cottage industry a spinner can turn raw fiber into thread and see the weaver next to him make the thread into cloth; in the big mod-

ern textile factory a man's (or, more likely, a child's) role in spin-
ning is limited to changing bobbins and tying threads, and he can
feel no relation to the final product.

When labor's role is so restricted, the training of the worker is
also restricted and excessively specialized. This deepens his subjugation, both because with few skills he is less able to find alternatives
to an onerous job and because an education thus limited prevents
him from fully realizing his potential. So too does the loss of creative consciousness resulting from routine, overspecialized work and
the separation of workers from their products. The possibilities for
workers in large, mechanized factories seem very meager indeed.
Wage laborers in smaller enterprises may also find it difficult to
fulfill human potential because products are taken from those who
make them, but at least trouble there is less grave and more easily
reduced. After stating that liberation of labor in agriculture and
small factories presents no great problems, Proudhon writes:

> Then there remain the mills, works, factories, workshops and
> shipyards, all that today is called *grande industrie*. . . . There,
> manual skill being replaced by the perfection of the apparatus, the
> roles of man and material are inverted: the spirit is not in the
> worker, it has passed into the machine; what ought to be the worth
> of the worker has become for him a brutalization.[15]

Labor's creative character stems from the relation of worker to
his task and product: work must translate his conceptions to actuality. If his actions in labor follow freely from his ideas and
from his entire consciousness, then the effort is creative, a function
of the human spirit. Proudhon's view contrasts with a more common one—that labor ordinarily does not create, but merely changes
the form or location of material. On the other hand, he regards
even simple tasks as potentially creative, and not just because ideas
are thereby given material substance. In labor the worker can ac-
tualize his conception of what he is to be for himself and for the
others in his community.

15. *Oeuv.*, VIII, vol. iii, 91. Some of the following comparison of Proudhon
with Marx originates with Pierre Naville; I have altered his analysis substantially,
however, as well as adding to it. I think Naville misinterprets Proudhon in some
important ways. Pierre Naville, *De l'Aliénation à la jouissance* (Paris, 1957), 300–
304, 348–55.

Thus the bondage of the working man is much more than his subjugation and the theft of his products by capitalists and landlords. The denial of opportunity to realize the human spirit constitutes the true slavery, and this is the consequence of the whole system of relationships in the productive process, not just of the unequal, tyrannical power of bosses and proprietors.

Here Proudhon's vision approaches that of Marx, though they remain distinct in particulars as well as in overall orientation. When the anarchist speaks primarily in terms of economic *injustice*, he is far from the other's view, for he is appealing to principle as determinant criterion. Marx insists that moral law cannot be ascertained apart from actual social process, or employed to judge the latter. But here Proudhon's effort to describe the situation in terms of a structure of social relationships is more than moral judgment, and it comes much closer to the other man's thought.

Proudhon's ideas about the denial of the human spirit and those about the appropriation of the products of labor by capitalists resemble Marx's conception of alienation, though the latter theorist articulates his own ideas much more fully and precisely. It is necessary here to recognize, however, the variations in their respective views of labor itself.

The anarchist sees labor as naturally free—not the sorry burden mankind must suffer, as in most traditional belief. For him free labor is the vehicle for fulfillment of human potential. The evil of labor is imposed upon it and can be eliminated, through social revolution. But for Marx labor *is* an imposed burden—"free labor" is a contradictory juxtaposition of terms. The conditions of labor vary with the prevailing mode of production, and the very historical developments which have constituted the exceptionally onerous contemporary conditions have also created the means of their transformation.

Marx believes that labor is "alienated" in modern capitalist industry because the worker is separated from the productive process; his work is no longer an expression of self, no longer a primary mode of relating to nature and other men. But in modern industry labor has also become a general, social activity, and is no longer narrowly individualistic—it has become collective rather than personal endeavor. As such it is also slavery, but the way out of subjugation cannot be return to a narrow individualism. Instead, the *social* character of production will continue to develop while the conditions of the activity are transformed, through social revolution. Then "labor" can become "free activity," spontaneous and self-fulfilling.

Both Marx and Proudhon focus on the central importance of man's productive activity; both look forward to spontaneity, self-realization, and liberty through social revolution, and both see individual needs in terms of social structure and change. But the anarchist focuses on the individual and regards society as a collection of single beings necessarily bound to one another. His conception of historical process is an elementary one; though important for him as a general vision, it contributes little to his conception of what society is. Marx, however, sees society as a much more distinctive entity—not the collective "person" Proudhon rejected in his attacks on democracy, but a structure whose complex of particular relationships constitutes the determinants of what it is to be an individual. Marx sees the dynamics of society very differently also: as in his idea of labor's historical transformation from personal to social activity, he thinks that the essential character of society and of human existence is subject to fundamental change. Proudhon sees only a process where particular relations are rearranged, without so basic a transformation; his insistence that governments from absolute monarchy to democracy are but variants on the theme of tyranny is the familiar example.

Thus, while their conceptions about labor and man's liberation are remarkably close in spirit, the two men's theories remain quite distinct in their development. In recent years Marx's humanism, including the concept of alienated labor, has attracted an unprecedented interest and stimulated much new thought, revitalizing the Marxist tradition. Perhaps the spirit of this humanism has proved still more attractive than its rationale and, if this be so, then his French antagonist may offer more than that tradition has yet admitted. The German's version is the more potently reasoned, but Proudhon's moralistic humanism has its own species of power, one that we may be more receptive to now than before, especially since it admits concerns which provoke us today but found little place in Marx's system.

The need to isolate particular aspects of Proudhon's thought in order to facilitate explaining and clarifying them can make it difficult to see how they fit together. Creativity and realization of human potential form a unifying theme for all of his philosophy. The place of this theme is indicated by the following passage from *De la Justice.*

> Human life attains its fulfillment, the soul is *ready for heaven,* as Masillon says, when it has satisfied the following conditions:
>   1. Love, paternity, family: extension and perpetuation of the being by carnal generation, or reproduction of the subject in body and in soul, person, and will.
>   2. Labor, or industrial generation: extension and perpetuation of the being by his action on nature. For as I have said above, man also has a love for nature; he unites himself to it, and from this fecund union comes forth a generation of a new order;
>   3. Social communion, or Justice: participation in collective life and in the progress of humanity. . . .
>   Labor and Justice do not replace each other at all, do not take each other's place.
>   If these conditions are violated, existence is uneasy; man being able *neither to live nor to die,* belongs to misery.
>   If on the contrary these conditions are realized, existence is full; it is a festival, a song of love, a perpetual enthusiasm, an endless hymn to happiness.[16]

With so grand a vision of what the future can offer, it is easy for Proudhon to express enthusiasm for the prospects of actually putting his mutualist theory into universal practice: the system is so attractive, how can men long resist it? He says that, while limited in initial application, mutualist association is not exclusive; it will grow as it receives increasing numbers of people drawn by its incomparable advantages. Mutualism can develop with an irresistible force, assimilating all into its system. One industry reorganized on a mutualist basis will tend to bring into its pattern of guarantees

16. *Oeuv.,* VIII, vol. ii, 436.

those industries with which it has immediate relations, and the system thus extends itself indefinitely. Mutualist society grows by a like pattern. In this process humanity as a whole is transformed, and the generations to come will be increasingly imbued with a new spirit. Egoism and all the passions and prejudices that now tear society asunder will gradually disappear and the spirit of justice will be ever more firmly and widely established. Once well-rooted, mutualism will never be given up and there will be no more retrograde movement for mankind, only forward progress to new achievements and better harmony.

This is a pleasant picture for the enthusiast, but not a realistic one. Proudhon knows that the transformation cannot be so easy or certain. The point of this optimistic description of the transition to Justice is not that events will actually progress so smoothly and readily but that, as far as positive movement is accomplished, its realization will have the overall form given above.

The reciprocal guarantees envisaged are best suited to just a few men in association, and are most readily adopted by them. What they begin, others can join or emulate. Although there are many barriers to the sudden, total transformation of society, elements of it can take on new forms without having to break down these obstacles. In a political and economic system which is unjust overall, seeds of something new can take root and flourish until they have such strength that under their influence the most resistant parts of the system begin to change. This, in outline, is the only way Proudhon thinks true revolution can come about.

All of this is still remote from the immediate problems of the revolutionary cause and of the workers upon whom the hopes of the movement rests. However, mutualist philosophy is more than a plan for the future: it is the theory from which revolutionary practice must be derived. Proudhon's ideas for a working-class revolutionary movement can be applied without much knowledge of the rest of this theory. His conception of the movement did prove close enough to the predispositions of many workers for Proudhonism to be important for some time without his whole philosophy being well or widely known. Nevertheless, neither the strength nor the faults of his conception can be well understood unless it is considered as part of his whole theory of mutualism and justice. In each of the preceding three chapters important aspects of his ideas on the revolutionary workers' movement were discussed at some length. Next I shall try to bring all the various strands together without excessive repetition of previous discussions.

twelve: The Revolutionary Movement

"Power to the People!"
—Revolutionary slogan recently current in the United States

I do not want the plebeian Hercules any more than the Hercules of government.[1]

THE FIRST MAJOR assumption of Proudhon's view of the movement is that there exists a struggle between classes divided by economic differences and that the whole dynamics of revolutionary action derives its force and center of focus from this conflict. The other major assumption is that the working classes are the agency whose transformation will make the revolution. If these ideas seem commonplace, it should be remembered that at this time they were still fresh; Proudhon, Marx, and Engels in their respective ways broke new ground in advocating them.

It will be recalled that Proudhon thinks economic differences the main cause of all social instability, with disruptive conflict the inevitable consequence of economic inequality. The supposed unity of a nation under strong government, even when there exist wide prosperity and a semblance of peace, is a sham; antagonistic social divisions show the only reality. The situation is not reformable, and the prevailing system will be wracked by strife until it falls

1. *La Guerre et la paix, Oeuv.,* VI, 22.

309

and is replaced by another. The inequality of the economy produces class distinctions, and from them arise the principal conflicts; privileged classes require strong government, one completely dominated by them, to maintain their advantage. In so doing they not only increase oppression but also introduce additional factors for instability, such as party factionalism. Always trying to preserve the *status quo*, the privileged classes resist the irrepressibly dynamic forces which press for change, thus causing hostility and open strife to increase. Since the Revolution of 1789 the bourgeoisie has been dominant, and under their yoke there is no hope of real progress for the masses, the naïve materialist optimism of liberal economists and reformers notwithstanding.

These points should be familiar to us from previous discussions, and they have been repeated often in varying forms in the rhetoric of countless speakers in the revolutionary workers' movement, which began to grow significantly from about the time of Proudhon's death. However, as just stated the points are not sharply enough defined for a militant movement. They seem to present little more than a picture of a fragmented, strife-torn society, with some of the fragments sharing certain interests and advantages or afflictions and weakness. Can there be accommodations struck between the disjoint pieces to create overall social unity and harmony? If the oppressed are in an intolerable situation which does not improve, how can they effect change when they are so weak and lack the institutional framework whereby dominant groups unite their separate strengths?

The position which Proudhon, like so many later revolutionaries, arrives at is the conclusion that the division between the privileged and the oppressed is too absolute for accommodations to be realized, and that the oppressed must unite to form a concerted movement. Despite the nature of his criticisms of the bourgeoisie and *their* revolutions, it was not until the late 1850's that he came to unequivocal expression of this position. Only a few years earlier he had been looking expectantly to Caesarism, education with a lifting up of the masses, and electoral activity as offering hopeful though limited possibilities within the capitalist system. However, from 1857 (when he first advocated abstention from elections) onward, he adhered to this more militant position, writing in *De la Capacité politique des classes ouvrières:* ". . . there is complete divergence, profound schism between Power, the Opposition, the upper classes on the one hand, and the laboring and ignorant masses on the other: that is the truth, which is not acknowledged, of our epoch." [2]

In his writing of this final period he repeatedly insists upon the reality and importance of class difference and on the extent of the separation. The distinct classes which he identifies and the relations between them require some clarification. In the first instance his is a two-fold division of society, but he also recognizes finer distinctions. On the one side are entrepreneurs, speculators, profiteers, and people living on unearned income from property and invested capital; all have incomes much above average. On the other side are those who earn their incomes, which they receive entirely in wages or salary.

But this description, while separating the exploiting from the exploited, puts together in the latter group both impoverished plebeians and people whose salaries are relatively comfortable. Effectively omitted are small businessmen whose modest profits could be called no more than a fair return for their labor. Thus Proudhon also divides society into three more meaningful groups: the bourgeoisie—a privileged class with *unearned* income; the middle class—privileged, with *earned* income; [3] and the working class, or proletariat. If this scheme is to be completely sensible in his terms of discourse, presumably anyone with a very large "earned" income or salary has not really earned all of it and belongs in the upper group, while someone with a modest unearned income to supplement his earnings would be in the middle class, although probably with many of the prejudices of the most privileged class.

The identity of the third class, the proletariat, offers some prob-

2. *Oeuv.*, III, 73.

3. Frequently in French usage, including that of Proudhon, rather than indicating the whole of the class called the "bourgeoisie" or "middle class" in English, the word *bourgeoisie* refers to just its upper, more affluent, and powerful portion. *La haute bourgeoisie* approximates this restricted meaning, but bears an additional connotation of exceptional power, wealth, and status. *La classe moyene* includes the lower portion of the bourgeoisie, and others who might not be considered definitely bourgeois but who are above plebeians in wealth and status. The *petite bourgeoisie* is roughly equivalent, but the term also bears the connotation of livelihood gained in small business or of attitudes specific to small businessmen. The different usage of English can cause confusion, but the class distinctions are imprecise in either language.

lems. As has been noted before, Proudhon often finds it convenient to refer broadly to all of those who are poor and exploited, taken together and called plebeians. In some instances he means the third class to include all plebeians, while in others he is thinking primarily of urban workers, or industrial workers in particular, or of wage workers in both city and country. The ambiguity is a natural one, for Proudhon was a good Latinist, and in classical Rome the words *plebs* and *proletarius* both referred to the lowest class of citizens without distinction as to type of labor. It is primarily because of Marxian thought that we have come to identify the proletariat of industrial workers as a distinctive class and regularly use "proletariat" in this more restrictive sense.

Despite the ambiguity arising from his indefinite use of classificatory words, Proudhon certainly recognizes that there are differences among plebeians which are important to his analysis—and the needed distinctions seem clear to him, even if they are not always easy for the reader to perceive. He knows that rural plebeians and even those of provincial towns have different interests and prejudices from those of workers in the larger cities; after the elections of 1848, and especially the strong rural support for Louis-Napoleon, he could hardly expect revolutionary ardor in most parts of the countryside. In particular, he recognizes how peasants' interests in the land give them reason to share with capitalists and *rentiers* a fear of any real or imagined threat to property. He also appears to have some sense of the innate popular conservatism and distrust of the big city common in the provinces.

With urban plebeians his distinctions are less certain; it would not occur to him to suppose that a portion of the urban poor lies largely outside the revolutionary "constituency," since all the poor suffer and have something to gain from mutualist association. He does not set to one side an inert "rabble" or *Lumpenproletariat*, or various nonindustrial workers like domestic servants. Neither does he have a clear concept of the possibly different circumstances of self-employed artisans who also are businessmen and employers.

However, he does lay greatest stress on the revolutionary role of industrial workers, especially those in large enterprises. They suffer the greatest degradation through denial of their human creativity, and they can most readily form viable, constructive mutualist associations. Moreover, unlike peasant freeholders, they have few reasons of self-interest or tradition to remain conservative or egoistical when confronted by the challenge of revolutionary mutualism. Should workers outside the industrial establishment desire to follow the mutualist path, the new society is open to them. Eventually they will come in and add their strength to that of the industrial proletariat.

Thus the main efforts of the revolutionary movement must be concentrated upon industrial workers, but it can also embrace others who have reason to make a common cause with factory labor. Indeed, the ultimate success of the movement depends on its inclusion of all those disparate elements who suffer from present injustice. Their numbers include most of the population, and it is only through mass support that the movement can effectively challenge the entrenched strength of the dominant bourgeoisie.

In particular, Proudhon looks to the peasantry, saying that the *démocratie industrielle* of Paris and the other large cities must seek the points of union existing between it and the *démocratie des campagnes*.[4] He sees a sounder basis for alliance than just the fact that plebeians in both town and country have a hard lot. Peasant farmers must protect themselves from the exploitive activities of bourgeois capitalists, entrepreneurs, official functionaries, merchants, and big landowners. As property owners, small farmers also fear the "communist" tendencies of the urban workers' movement, but this would not divide them from the city if the communist ideal is replaced by one of mutualism. The peasant's conception of and need for property differs sharply from that of the bourgeois landowner. The latter seeks rental income and the pride of possession of an estate; the former wants land of his own to work on, independent of burdens of rents, mortgage interest, and the dues once imposed by feudal obligations. Even when owning his land and clear of debt, the peasant farmer suffers at a disadvantage in his commercial exchanges with the bourgeoisie. Thus, although both peasant and bourgeois own property, their interests are antagonistic, and the peasant cause is the same as that of industrial labor: opposition to the bourgeois economic order and replacement of it by mu-

4. This paragraph and the next two summarize and discuss a section on the peasants' role, *Oeuv.*, III, 66–71.

tualist association and guarantees. "The *Marianne* of the fields is the counterpart of the *Social State* of the cities." [5]

Because of the wide distribution of lands made during the first French Revolution and confirmed by Emperor Napoleon I, farmers support the present Empire, associating the securing of their allodial [6] rights with the imperial regime and the name of Bonaparte. This support is reinforced by their hostility to the bourgeois opposition parties and by the new prosperity which many farmers enjoy despite their being exploited. The prosperity results from better markets for agricultural produce—and the better market is due to industrialization, with the consequent increase of urban population and improvement, through railroad and inland waterway construction, of transportation facilities for distribution of farm products. Farmers associate rising prosperity with the imperial regime, although it deserves very little credit for it. While for the rural masses Napoleon is still the enemy of the old regime who protects them from bourgeois "feudalism," Proudhon says the Napoleonic idea is quite worn out and the old regime far away.

Vast new problems confront society, and the Empire is powerless to solve them. The interests of town and country plebeians in the problems are similar, as are the courses they should take to serve their interests. Instead of supporting the emperor because he opposes the excesses of the bourgeoisie, or supporting the opposition because it fights Bonaparte, peasants and workers should act for themselves, together. The first thing a revolutionary movement must do is withhold electoral support from parties whose primary interests are not those of the masses, and direct any popular electoral action to the service exclusively of the people's interests. The chasm between the bourgeoisie and plebeians is too great for any alliance of expediency to bridge the gulf; an attempt at one will benefit only the stronger party—the bourgeoisie. The same can be said of an alliance of plebeians with Napoleon, since he has neither the desire nor the ability to serve the true interests of the people.

Although Proudhon excludes the possibility of accommodation with the bourgeoisie, he thinks the situation different with the mid-

5. Ibid., 69.
6. "Allodial" is a term used to denote freehold property owned without any obligation to pay rent, services or other dues; opposed to "feudal."

dle class of those with modest earned incomes. He believes that many in this class are subject to increasing impoverishment and reduction to proletarian status. They too are abused and exploited in the present economic order, and their position will grow worse with increased industrialization. Those of the middle class whose position is thus threatened should recognize that if they are to save themselves they need to join their cause to that of the proletariat and press with them for change toward mutualism. On their part, the workers should recognize that they need to seek alliance with the middle class, or the latter may support the haute bourgeoisie, adding to the latter's ability to resist successfully the strength of the working class.

In concentrating on the industrial proletariat while recognizing the revolutionary potential of the petite bourgeoisie, Proudhon's sociology of revolution corresponds to that of the Marxian tradition. The middle class can be an ally of the proletariat, but it also has interests and prejudices antagonistic to those of the workers. Insofar as members of the middle class become *déclassés* or fear that this will happen, they can be partners. There may sometimes be other reasons for temporary partnership. However, they can be relied on only to a limited extent, except when they lose their former attitudes altogether and identify themselves with the proletariat completely. In these points Proudhon's thinking does not differ appreciably from Marxian ideology. However, he does not have as well-defined a theory of the ruin and "proletarisation" of the petite bourgeoisie by monopoly capitalism, nor does he have reason to propose, as Marxists have, a proletarian-bourgeois alliance in order to replace a "feudal" or imperialistic regime by a liberal or nationalist democracy, in preparation for a socialist revolution.

While Proudhon's definition of class identities is not precise enough for rigorous analysis of the class struggle, the imprecision results from the fact that the class differences and identities themselves have never been very distinct. This has always made analyses based on ideas about social class quite difficult and even of questionable validity or utility. Nevertheless, however vague class distinctions may be, making them still permits insights too valuable for many students of society to discard social-class morphology.

In comparison with Marxists Proudhon enjoys a certain advantage in class analysis applied to philosophy of revolution. Because of his greater flexibility in general, and because he is less definite about the identity and revolutionary role of any class, his concept of the revolutionary effects of class struggle is more adaptable to changing or altogether different social, economic, and political conditions. For Marxists both the largely unexpected course of development of Western industrial capitalism and the circumstances of pre-industrial and agrarian countries have presented grave problems for the theory and practice of revolution. As a direct result, Marxist movements have been perpetually perplexed and convulsed for eighty years or more. While for a number of reasons Proudhonism's appeal to potentially revolutionary populations has been limited, in it there are no comparable barriers to its being adapted indefinitely, thus enabling it to encompass these new problems.

I have observed on a number of occasions that Proudhon did not understand the problems of modern industrialized society well enough, and that his viewpoint is basically that of the pre-industrial artisan or peasant. Now I can qualify these conclusions substantially, although they still should stand as stated if the qualifications are understood. It can be said that his perception and treatment of industrial society's problems improved greatly in his last years. Not only is there his development of an ideology of revolution based upon the industrial proletariat, but also his ideas about the future prospects and plight of peasants and middle class, under the impact of industrialization, reflect a degree of insight that we might well not have expected from him. Nevertheless, his final understanding of problems peculiar to industrialized society does not go nearly far enough—and it could not do so, given his fundamental preconceptions and intellectual limitations.

There is a peculiar aspect of Proudhon's discussion of the workers' movement that should be noted and explained. Although he has unequivocally repudiated central government and the electoral process, many of his suggestions for proletarian action refer specifically to matters of electoral politics, or at least are couched in terms most appropriate to these matters although there is a wider reference as well. In part, this is a consequence of the fact that Proudhon is writing in response to the question of workers' participation in the contemporary elections of the imperial government in France.

However, there is more to his approach than this topical concern. The organization of workers in mutualist associations is only one side of the movement he envisions. The other side is political action within the existing system. This action is not to be taken in order to improve the system or better the lot of the masses while in it; a wholly new structure must replace the old one before the people can make real progress. They act in the present political context in order to make it possible to erect that new structure.

In discussing the political capacity of the working classes, Proudhon points out that there is a difference between legal and real capacities. The first is conferred by law and assumes the existence of the second. The assumption is wrong; the real political capacity of the people is very small at present—and legal capacities like universal suffrage have very little value when men remain profoundly unequal despite them, misusing even the rights they have.

The people have not voted responsibly, or in their own interests. They adhere to almost all the false ideas of the time, admiring orators rather than reason. They are vulnerable to flattery, charlatanism, and banal, affected, sentimental appeals. Thanks to their ignorance, impatience, and violent, primitive emotions and instincts, they are inclined to embrace authoritarian government, knowing only to acclaim those who master them. They place their trust in a man, not in the principles which alone can save them.

> Left to itself or led by its tribunes, the multitude never established anything. It has its face turned to the rear: it forms no tradition, no spirit in consequence, no idea which acquires the force of law. Of politics it understands only intrigue, of government only profligacy and force, of justice only revenge, of liberty only the faculty of setting up idols for itself which it demolishes the next day.[7]

Plainly Proudhon does not share the belief of more romantic revolutionaries that nothing more is required than a call to the people to unite and fight for their common cause. He does not think

7. *Oeuv.*, XIV, 302ff.

that the people are prepared to do this, or that they are noble and good; he does think that they *can* change, and that they *will* change because unlike the bourgeoisie they have nothing to lose in doing so.

Therefore the greatest task of the revolutionary movement is to create a real popular political capacity. In accomplishing this, more will be produced than ability to act positively in the political arena. The way to political capacity is also the route to a new social orientation and the realization of a universal spirit of justice.

Proudhon's definition of justice as respect for the dignity of every man takes on added significance here, for it is essentially proletarians' consciousness of their own dignity that he hopes to develop as the foundation of the workers' movement. He observes that in their collective weakness and dependence on the possessing classes plebeians have always been regarded as inferior in quality. By habit and custom they have shared much of this contempt for their own class, remaining in a state of perpetual abnegation. Despite the firm establishment of their inferior status, Proudhon thinks that changing conditions since 1789 have made it possible for them to rise above it in spirit even before their economic and political situation improves. Indeed, they *must* rise above it in spirit first. In the first place, this means casting off common habits of dependency, indolence, irresponsibility, and other traits which contribute to contempt for workers. But these are just the effects of more basic attitudes, or the lack of them, and it is these fundamental qualities on which the movement must concentrate.

> In order that there be political capacity in a subject, individual, corporation, or collectivity, three fundamental conditions are required:
> 1. That the subject have *consciousness* of himself, of his dignity, of his value, of the place that he occupies in society, of the role he fills, of the functions to which he has right to claim, of the interests he represents or personifies;
> 2. As a result of this consciousness of himself in all his powers, that this subject affirms his idea, that is, that he knows how to represent to himself through understanding, to translate through speech, to explain through reason, in its principle and consequences, the law of his being;
> 3. That from this idea, finally, posited as profession of faith, he

can, according to the need and the diversity of circumstances, always deduce *practical* conclusions.[8]

He adds that there would be differences of degree on these points among various men, but these differences do not mean that only some are politically capable. Capacity is not defined by particular aptitude in the handling of public affairs or by exceptional civic zeal. Whoever combines the three specified conditions is politically capable, despite differences in degree.

What Proudhon states as the conditions for political capacity amounts to a generalization of what he regards as the necessary conditions for a working-class movement. To be conscious of oneself as a member of a collectivity: translated into requirements of the movement, this condition says that the proletariat must become conscious of itself as a distinct class with its own, different interests —and each worker must become conscious of his class identity and shared interests. A confident recognition of one's own dignity and admission of the dignity of one's fellows is the central quality of this proletarian consciousness, in combination with an understanding of the differences of the workers' interests from those of the bourgeoisie.

This understanding is part of the second condition, which translated into the terms of this context requires that workers have an idea of who they are, as individuals and as a class, an idea of where they are in relation to the rest of the social, economic, and political system, and an idea of where they are going. This means that they must have a thorough, rational philosophy, no longer acting and reacting by habit, prejudice, and emotion. Of course that philosophy is Proudhon's. Finally, the last condition is that they be able to draw from this rational understanding the practical conclusions of how they should act, for themselves and not for the bourgeoisie, in order to create a new order.

Proudhon believes that elements of what he asks for have existed in every group of men, including the proletariat. The working class has acquired self-consciousness—he says this dates from 1848 —and it has its own distinctive ideas. Nevertheless, the conscious-

8. *De la Capacité, Oeuv.,* III, 89ff. Much of the material discussed in this section on the consciousness and capacity of the workers can be found in *Oeuv.,* III, 85–92.

ness, the ideas, and the consequences drawn from them have not developed far enough. Workers have not yet been able to act intelligently in politics or to make effective through unity their sense of collective identity. The purpose of the movement is to achieve the required development.

In his emphasis on proletarian class-consciousness and solidarity Proudhon was one of the first to enunciate what was to become the major theme in the organization and action of socialist and trade-union movements. Viewed in retrospect, this aspect of his thought may well be the part least subject to challenge and the most important historically. His simultaneous emphasis on proletarian use of ideas is more problematical.

His conception is one of ideas made universal *throughout* the class—*not* just of ideas to serve the *leadership*, with extension of some in much simplified form to the masses. Recalling Georges Sorel's remark that Marxism gives the proletariat a philosophy of *arms*, Maxime Leroy has observed that Proudhon tried to give it a philosophy of *heads*.[9] Experience, however, has made most of us more skeptical than Proudhon about the possibilities of people ever becoming as rational as he hopes, even if they are led to reason by such a movement as he envisions.

At least he does not have the problems common among other revolutionary ideologues about what roles are to be played by intellectuals, by leaders generally, or by some sort of "vanguard of the proletariat" or select party organization. These questions simply have no relevance to his conception. For him, there would be no "leaders" in any strict sense, even though workers might select someone from their midst with special oratorical talent to speak for them, or another of their number who has special administrative talent to handle routine management functions in a mutualist association. Such men would not be true leaders but only persons specializing in what they are best able to do, just as a tailor makes and mends clothing. True leaders are followed because others trust their judgment, or simply because they *are* leaders. If workers act as someone says they should, they must do so only because each of

9. Introduction, ibid., III, 29.

them has thought the matter over rationally and decided that it is wise to take the course of action offered.

The same remarks apply to the intellectual in the movement. His class identity matters only if it results in ideas inappropriate to the proletariat. He too is a "craftsman" exercising a special talent: he may be able to originate ideas that would not occur to men of other abilities. All should be able to understand his intellectual creations, however, and can adopt them as their own or reject them as they will. Although the discovery of ideas may be a specialized function in society, action ought to be inseparable from ideas: when all are "men of ideas," the role of the intellectual presents no problems.

Even though there is reason for skepticism about Proudhon's expectations concerning the universal development of rational thought in the working class, his hopes should be understood for what they are. That there would be a growing use of ideas is not just an initial assumption on the basis of which the rest of the program for a workers' movement is based. This growth should be both the consequence of what has gone before and the prerequisite for what is to come. Many in the Enlightenment tradition have reasoned that man is inherently rational, that true ideas will be embraced by the rational man, and that therefore, when we have discovered the true ideas, all we need do is undertake an energetic educational program to drive out false ideas and teach the truth.

Proudhon is not so naïve as to follow such simple reasoning, although he *does* assume that all men are inherently rational. Conventional schooling, the popular press, street-corner orators and the like can be important, but only as accessories. Moral education within the family is vital, but this nurture cannot originate change, nor can it be the prime locus for intellectual development. The education of the people must be centered in their work and, above all, in the experience of the movement itself.

Proudhon rejects the usual distinctions between high and popular cultures, science and lore, theory and practice. Literary and theoretical instruction should have their places, but only as parts of a polytechnic education in which schooling, work, and other experiences are fully integrated. Learning a trade becomes simultaneously reasoned study and practical apprenticeship, the cultivation of both intelligence and skill.[10] Then ideas and practice can be unified and the human spirit realized.

Since in Proudhon's view work is the primary vehicle of man's self-expression and growth, this polytechnic education is essential if men are to accomplish what he hopes for them, but it must be complemented by education through the experience of the revolutionary movement. It is this experience itself which should produce the maturing of social consciousness and the moral regeneration necessary for real revolution to occur.

Experience with mutualist organization will both convince people of its advantages and teach them how to improve its forms. The more workers assert themselves as a class, the more they will become conscious and confident of their dignity and merits as individuals and as members of the proletariat. Every collective political action will strengthen this process.[11] As they redevelop social relationships within the working-class community on a basis of mutual reciprocity and proletarian brotherhood, their solidarity will increase and their sense of justice mature. With solidarity and intensification of just sentiments, social responsibility also will be more actively felt. All of this teaches and reinforces the ideas of justice and leads to the transformation of these ideas into an inner spirit of justice animating every worker. Every factor interacts with the others in an accelerating process of development.

The urban working class has to take the initiative; its example will draw allies from the rest of the lower classes and even from the middle class. As their numbers and collective strength grow, the balance of weight in the political and economic orders will shift in their direction. Eventually the shift will have gone too far for effective resistance, first in one area, then in another. Gradually resistance should crumble and end. The transition will not be

10. For an analysis of this polytechnic education, see Aimé Berthod, "La Philosophie du travail et l'école," *Proudhon et notre temps,* ed. Amis de Proudhon (Paris, 1920), 53-98.

11. Proudhon says relatively little about the kinds of collective economic action (like strikes and boycotts) that organized labor has taken. He would probably approve, but with the qualifications expressed by his condemnation of violence and by his conviction that the only purpose of collective action by workers within the capitalist system should be to increase working-class self-consciousness and solidarity while preparing the way to a wholly new system.

pinpointed in time, for the transformation of society must be an unending process and thus the revolution is never complete.

Proudhon thinks the revolution is inevitable, but it may be too long delayed—and if the people do not take his proposed course or if it does not develop as he would wish, they will probably rush headlong into violent insurrection with its disastrous consequences. When both were in prison Proudhon had become well acquainted with Auguste Blanqui, that indefatigable and uncompromising revolutionary conspirator who was directly involved in most of the popular insurrections in France over the span of half a century. Proudhon had great respect for his intelligence and courage, despite the great differences in their respective approaches. Blanqui sought simply to destroy the existing system in one cataclysmic conflagration, confident that some happy form of socialism would arise spontaneously from the ashes. In 1851 Proudhon wrote that the other's ideas, however violent and inadequate, had enormous force because they expressed popular urges so well. "Blanqui is the incarnation of popular vengeance." [12] If Blanqui prevails, Proudhon is sure, there can be little hope of progress.

Proudhon's negative attitude toward violent insurrection divided him from a rival socialist for whom he seems to have had more personal respect than any other, Blanqui. It also divided his thought from the Marxist tradition. After his death many anarchists and most workers failed to share this attitude. Anarchists could not make violence really effective because they refused on principle to organize their efforts with martial discipline and obedience to the direction of leaders. Workers for the most part gravitated to a Marxist-oriented leadership which would promise rapid victory, and perhaps vengeance as well. When and where the hopes of rapid victory were frustrated, many followed a more moderate, reformist leadership of socialists, mostly Marxists, whose limited though real successes have not yet brought the millennium either.

While Marx, Proudhon, and their disciples were irreconcilably divided by philosophical attitudes and personal antagonisms, they had a broad common ground in their concentration upon proletarian action built upon the development of class consciousness and

12. Letter to Langlois, August 14, 1851, *Corresp.*, IV, 83. Quoted at greater length above, p. 195.

solidarity. Differences such as theirs can fade into relative unimportance in the course of historical development, and this common emphasis could have been the basis of a fruitful blending of Proudhon's thought and Marx's, but their different view of the class struggle itself made this union difficult or impossible.

Marx himself is not definite about the pace or violence of the revolutionary process, but the implications of his conception of class struggle have naturally led to theories of revolutionary cataclysm those men not restrained by countervailing inclinations or ideas. Although the notion has been modified in its reformist variants, Marxism has regularly contended that bourgeois resistance to socialism and proletarian demands for genuine equality will not decline: the class struggle will end only with the *victory* of the proletariat over the bourgeoisie. This last notion is alien to Proudhon's thought, despite his insistence on the breadth of the division between the two classes. He wants the progressive weakening of the bourgeoisie's power and the assimilation of the class into the mutualist order. "Victory" of one class over another suggests a reversal of positions, with proletarians dominant at least until with the passage of time class distinctions and class-determined attitudes have disappeared. Proudhon does not want the struggle to be a war with this result and the likely concomitant violence. "I do not want the plebeian Hercules any more than the Hercules of government. . . ."

In short, although he sees it as likely to occur, he thinks the transformation of class struggle into class war would be disastrous. Likewise, the struggle must end not with class "victory" but with reconciliation and merging of classes under egalitarian conditions of dynamic equilibrium.

In the experience of the past century, the romance of revolutionary violence has proven to be far more attractive to militant revolutionaries than any pacific path to millennium. Successful execution of their programs has required that these militants organize in such ways that many essential anarchist principles must be rejected. Thus Lenin and Mao have been far more influential than Proudhon, although each approaches him at certain points. The only really significant blending of his theory with that of Marx occurred in syndicalism. In the thought of the most influential syndicalist theorist, Georges Sorel, this blend has been achieved at the cost of discarding Proudhon's requirements for pacific and gradual transformation. When these requirements are rejected, much of his integral logical consistency, as well as his spirit, is lost.

Moderate socialists in the Marxian tradition might reasonably be expected to have gone furthest to join the insights of Marx and Proudhon, but until quite recently little has been done along these lines.[13] There are pacifists who owe something to Marxian thought, but any influence upon them of Proudhon as well must have been very indirect. One might guess that there is a line of influence by way of Leo Tolstoy. There are some contemporary anarchists—Paul Goodman for one—who seem to have absorbed the thought of both Proudhon and Marx without doing serious violence to either, but it would be hard to say that any have made serious attempts to join the two, as Sorel did. Proudhon and Marx are at once so far apart that the divergence of the traditions stemming from each is natural, and so close that it should be possible for contemporary socialists to base new theory upon the philosophies of both men. Each has a power which the passage of years has tarnished but not destroyed.

Neither man foresaw how adaptable capitalism and liberal bourgeois democracy could be in the face of the challenges confronting them. Neither recognized how this flexibility could enable at least the first industrialized nations to improve the material conditions and increase the apparent political power of the proletariat enough to minimize the likelihood of revolution in these countries. Nevertheless, both examined and found insights into problems that still plague the Western world, and the thought of both has substantial relevance to the non-Western world which neither understood.

If serving as the basis of the ideology of movements which gain and retain political power is proof of practicability, then Marx's

13. One might call Georges Gurvitch an exception. His extensive writing on this subject was discussed and cited above, p. 101. Some other exceptions are cited by Georges Guy-Grand in a brief review of works on Proudhon, in his *Pour connaître la pensée de Proudhon* (Paris, 1947), 210–17. Recent writing, most notably Gurvitch's later work and Pierre Ansart's *Sociologie de Proudhon, Marx et l'anarchisme*, and *Naissance de l'anarchisme* (Paris, 1967, 1969, 1970) have tried to do much more of this. I do not know if any of the authors involved could properly be called Marxist. Gurvitch sometimes seems to be playing sophisticated games against Marx, with Proudhon as his foil.

philosophy is the more readily applicable to actual conditions. Still, only the most dogmatic of Marxists would claim that the ideology's application to practice in any of its variant forms has yet proved able to fulfill revolutionary expectations.

Proudhon's federalist politics look as if they would be impossible to put into practice. His entire mutualist approach may be inspired in certain ways, but it has an inescapably utopian appearance. At least he does not share the usual rosy optimism of other utopians of his time. He once wrote, "The twentieth century will open the era of federations, or humanity will begin again a thousand years of purgatory." [14] With more than two-thirds of the twentieth century gone by, it cannot yet be said that he was altogether wrong.

14. *Oeuv.*, XIV, 355ff.

thirteen: Epilogue

> How many roads must a man walk down
> Before you call him a man?
> —From a song popular in the 1960's

The people do not read me, and without reading me, they hear me.[1]

WHEN PIERRE-JOSEPH PROUDHON died in January, 1865, there was not much of a socialist or workers' movement in France, or anywhere else for that matter, except in Great Britain. Even in Britain, then by far the most industrialized country, socialism was temporarily moribund, both trade unionism and the cooperative movement having turned away from their initial orientation in that direction.

Nevertheless, from the historian's viewpoint the decade of the 1860's marks the beginning of substantial growth, in France particularly and in other countries as well, of what in time were to become important labor and socialist movements. The formation in late 1864 of the International Working Men's Association, later often called the First Socialist International, contributed significantly to this, although the I.W.M.A.'s direct role in organizational

1. Bob Dylan, "Blowin' in the Wind," copyright 1962; letter to Dr. Cretin, May 21, 1858, *Corresp.*, VIII, 47.

growth probably was much less important than the part played by its activists in shaping the forms the movements were later to take. Also playing a role were spurts in the industrialization process at this time in several countries, as well as other developments related only remotely if at all to industrialization, such as the appearance of a new kind of radical intelligentsia in Russia.

At this time repressive legal curbs on the organization of trade unions as well as on other groups of supposedly revolutionary character helped limit growth of any movement in France and most of the rest of the Continent. Under the prevailing circumstances most delegates to conferences of the I.W.M.A. actually represented only themselves or at most rather small, often secret groups. For this reason socialist and labor history at this stage consists largely of the thought and actions of a relatively few individuals, some of whom became quite influential in the formation either of mass organizations or of more limited groups which had significant impact on historical events.

Many of these individuals were Proudhonists, or at least were significantly influenced by Proudhon's thought. Thus it is possible to say much about Proudhonism in the early growth of socialist movements, in terms of the convictions of various individuals involved. Much more could be said about Proudhon's influence in later stages as well. However, any attempt to do so either must be arbitrarily truncated or expand into a lengthy history of anarchism as a whole, and of most of the socialist and labor movement in France and major phases of the movement in other countries. Not only is this not the place for either sort of history, but also it would be virtually impossible at most points to say how much significance should be attributed to Proudhon's influence. Ideas which he advocated most often were not adopted in the form he had given to them. Others either started with his thought and altered it, with other concepts and experiences contributing to produce something rather different, or they arrived independently at convictions resembling Proudhon's. Many were wholly unacquainted with his philosophy, although they might have been strongly affected by ideas derived in part from his.

It happens that his theory was so wide-ranging and germane to the problems of socialism and labor that almost any position taken would coincide with his at certain points. Rather than trying to specify Proudhon's actual influence, we shall concentrate here primarily on indicating the ways in which various elements of his thought could in later years have appeal for people, mainly in France, whether or not that appeal was felt directly.

If "the movement" in France can be said to have had a beginning, the June Days of 1848 might be named, because they were so important in separating the proletarian cause from that of the largely bourgeois republican revolutionary tradition. The major role of Proudhon and his popular journalism in effecting this shift in revolutionary outlook was discussed at length in Chapters 5 and 6, and need not be repeated here. However, while this repudiation of a tradition and common cause with bourgeois republicans had to precede growth of a proletarian movement, positive steps to initiate that growth were slow and uncertain at first.

A significant positive step, and perhaps a better point to mark "the beginning," occurred when a delegation of French workers traveled to London to visit the International Exhibition of 1862. Some of them, including one of the more outstanding of their number, Henri Tolain, were mutualists consciously and closely following the ideas of Proudhon. While there they initiated conversations with British trade-unionists and German expatriates associated with Karl Marx. Later several of them returned to London and resumed the talks, discussing possibilities of international organization. In September, 1864, a small group of French workers including Tolain, Charles Limousin, E. E. Fribourg, and Eugène Varlin went to yet another London meeting, where they proposed and the conference adopted a resolution founding the International Working Men's Association.[2] Tolain, Limousin, and Fribourg became the first French correspondents of the International, and the bureau they established in Paris was the first center of the movement in France.

These three were "orthodox" Proudhonists. Tolain was briefly

2. Different sources give conflicting information on the number and identities of the French delegates to the founding conference. In the view of one French scholar, Proudhonists were predominant in the I.W.M.A. for its first two or three years. While their "predominance" is debatable, they were particularly important then. J.-L. Puech, *Le Proudhonisme dans L'Association Internationale des Travailleurs* (Paris, 1907).

the major figure in the nascent movement; he was a model of Proudhon's ideal worker: industrious, sober, studious, a skilled artisan of solid proletarian, Parisian family background. In the 1863 elections he had unsuccessfully led a move for worker candidacies, and he was probably the chief author of the 1864 Manifesto of the Sixty, which declared the cause of an independent, self-conscious proletariat.[3]

Tolain and his group were, if possible, more Proudhonist than Proudhon. They wanted elimination of the State and an egalitarian economy, with individual property possession on the basis he had advocated and with each man enjoying the full fruits of his labors. They sought cooperative associations for production on a voluntary, mutualist basis rather than under state auspices. There were actually some small workers' associations begun, but mainly for talk, self-improvement, and mutual assistance, not for production or concerted political action; Napoleon's regime permitted "friendly societies" of workers to exist, as long as they seemed quite innocuous. (Limited toleration of such proletarian activities as are here described appears to have developed because Bonaparte hoped the workers might serve as a partial counterpoise to the bourgeois Opposition.) The mutualists expected that capital for the new economy would be provided by gratuitous credit arranged by a People's Bank. The Bank, patterned on Proudhon's unsuccessful experiment of 1848–49, would be an autonomous institution established as part of the elimination of the State. Also following their master in his attitude toward the family, this workers' group opposed female labor and women's rights.

Such conceptions were well suited to intelligent working men like Tolain and his friends. Earning their livings as craftsmen, they were better informed, better read, and more actively curious and concerned about their world than the average of their fellows. That world was in a stage of rapid transition to large-scale industry, with the bitter hardship for all workers that always accompanied this process. The position of artisans was an anomalous one. They were likely to be better off than less-skilled workers, if their jobs had not been taken over by machines, as those of the hand-loom weavers had. However, their advantage was usually small and often men-

3. See pp. 222ff.

aced by mechanization and the competitive threat that big factories represented to small workshops. Artisans were at ease with the latter and feared industrialization's menace. Attempts to break machines were common during the time of transition, as if destroying the new contraptions might exterminate their breed permanently, or at least relieve the grief that change brought. The more intelligent and curious craftsmen, however, went beyond fear to contemplation and debate about what could be done to bend the course of industry's development to make it less harmful to their people. They were prepared both to speculate about constructive alternatives and to plan and work for them.

Such men—of whom Proudhon was one by outlook as well as background—were too much the neophytes in a strange world to understand it well. They still had their roots in the craft shop or the small factory where labor was less dehumanized and relations between employees more personal, even intimate; many had peasant roots as well. Although they regarded the problems offered by industrialization with the interest of men trying to anticipate the future and confront it boldly, the situation was still too full of novelties for them to grasp all its implications. In time familiarity with industrial capitalism would make most of those in the movement more set in their attitudes and pragmatic in their thinking; whatever seemed impractical would be discarded by most, and the purpose determining action would be the resolute prosecution of the class struggle by the most effective means at hand.

Before this familiarity and its peculiar militancy developed, proletarian concepts could still revolve around ideals of what *ought to be* if the world is to be just. Afterward the focus would be what *must be done* if present misery is to be ended. In the France of the Second Empire, however, the ideas of intelligent workers like Tolain could be and usually were a blend of realism and utopia. Proudhon's philosophy is just this, and it spoke directly to the workers' condition as none before him had.

For these reasons anarchism, whether directly inspired by Proudhon or by other leaders, has most often been a significant force among skilled workers in an economy in transition to large-scale industry. As such anarchism has itself proved to be a transitional phase in the development of genuinely powerful proletarian political movements. It also retained somewhat more lasting influence among a few groups of craftsmen whose skills were still needed in an industrialized society but who opposed it and felt among themselves a sense of collective identity. The most notable such groups were among the watchmakers of Proudhon's home territory—the Jura region of France and Switzerland. Influenced especially by Mikhail Bakunin and later by Peter Kropotkin, anarchists of the Jura played important roles in the First Socialist International and a lesser but still significant part in the second one.

In the French labor movement the ascendancy, if it can be called that, of Tolain and the "orthodox" Proudhonists was short lived. Eugène Varlin, also in that delegation to the founding conference of the First International, and others like him soon displaced them. Varlin followed enough of Proudhon's concepts to have been called a Proudhonist by some, but unlike the "orthodox" ones he soon became much interested in mass proletarian organization, as well as in small mutualist associations. He went on to become the outstanding organizer of the French trade-union movement in these first years, extending the movement's appeal to unskilled and semi-skilled workers more definitely and energetically than his predecessors had done.

Varlin did, however, retain Proudhon's federalist conception and the associated hostility to centralization of both government and labor organization. With this went a rejection of coercive authority in any form and repudiation of concepts of revolutionary dictatorship associated with Blanquists and Jacobins. Likewise, he rejected Blanquist ideas of a revolutionary elite, saying with Proudhon that no one could represent the people. Varlin's approach foreshadowed that of syndicalism.

From 1867 or 1868, Varlin was the real leader of the French section of the International, and the "orthodox" mutualists were pushed aside. They did remain important in some of the craftsmen's associations, though, and reasserted themselves both nationally and internationally in later years. Since we are taking Varlin and Tolain as exemplars of two strains of Proudhonism, there is a certain symbolic significance in their different fates in that great dividing point of the revolutionary movement, the Paris Commune of 1871. Tolain played a secondary though significant role in the early stages, before civil war began: he was assistant mayor of the Eleventh Arrondissement of Paris, a major working-class district, and was one of four candidates from the workers' list to be elected to the National Assembly in February, 1871. Remaining with the Thiers government at Versailles when the fighting began between Government forces and the Commune of Paris, he tried futilely to reconcile the opposed sides and later to mitigate the severity of the bloodbath to which the victorious Versaillese treated the Communards. He was expelled from the International for his "treason," and lived until 1897. Varlin, on the other hand, was one of the most important Communard leaders and a hero of its later legend; he acted with intelligence, resolution, courage, and restraint. Captured by the Versaillese, he was brutally tortured and mutilated, then shot.

After the Commune "orthodox" Proudhonists, including Tolain, remained active but comparatively ineffectual. They continued to propose gratuitous credit, to little avail; workers' associations grew in importance, but it was others with rather different ideas who gave these groups their significance. The theories of Proudhon were not discarded; there were many who adopted them in part, while conscious of a debt to him, but like Varlin they modified the theory, adapting some concepts to their new perceptions of conditions, ignoring some of Proudhon's ideas, and retaining others intact. Some of these latter-day "disciples" were anarchists, some were not, and for others the "anarchist" identification is debatable, depending on one's criteria and the variations with time of the men's beliefs. There were still others who knew no debt to Proudhon, although their ideas were much the same as some of those who did.

The experiences of "orthodox" Proudhonists is relevant to an assessment of the significance of their master's philosophy, with respect to the problems actually faced by the movement in the formative half-century between his death and World War I. I have repeatedly emphasized the importance of taking Proudhon's theory as a whole, saying that removal of an idea from its context distorts it. Tolain and others like him seem to have taken the elements in the integral context intended, and it did not get them very far. Does this mean that Proudhon's philosophy is as utopian as, say, Fourier's—interesting as speculation and statement of ideals, perhaps significant in stimulating others to further thought, but in the form given not particularly germane to the real world?

Perhaps—but even if this be so, the experience of "orthodox" Proudhonists may not demonstrate it. One can only speculate about what Proudhon would have said and done had he lived two decades longer, but it does not seem likely that he would have adapted his views as little as did these closest disciples. His was the restless, creative, speculative mind; intellectually they were followers, not innovators. When he said mutual credit would be a panacea, they believed in it and tried unflaggingly to put it into practice. His concrete proposals and his attacks on the established order were more readily understood and seized upon than his abstract conceptions of justice and the foundations of *droit*. They were craftsmen who learned how to use new tools, but they lacked the capacity to modify them or fashion others when the occasion demanded. Like many craftsmen they preferred to use the tools they knew, and thought further innovations represented a debasement of their pure art.

Whatever else he was, Proudhon was flexible. He never discarded his mutual credit scheme, but after disappointing experience he no longer thought it a major instrument for initiating revolutionary change; he simply regarded it as one important institution in any future mutualist society. Likewise, as conditions or his perception of them changed, he several times altered his opinion about the attitude toward elections that workers should take.

His convictions on matters of principle could neither be wholly altered nor pushed into the background for the sake of expediency. They could and did develop as he learned and reflected more. On matters of practice he was less committed; concrete proposals were offered as applications of principle, according to rational analysis of existing conditions. If conditions changed or new proposals seemed to apply principles better, he was ready to alter his thoughts on practice.

"Orthodox" Proudhonists do not seem to have realized it, but his proposals for mutualist arrangements are first of all *models* and are programs for practice only insofar as men change and grow in the spirit of justice. As models he thinks them vital guides for planning and effecting action, but actual practice has to be devised anew as each fresh situation is encountered. It seems reasonable to guess that a still-living Proudhon would have adopted positions more like Varlin's than Tolain's. Thinking that for some time to come the possibilities for development of small mutualist associations would be too restricted, he probably would have preferred to emphasize growth of proletarian consciousness and collective strength through mass organization of labor, both in trade unionism and in politics. Federalist organizational structure, associations for mutual assistance and self-improvement, and long-term goals would help to maintain an adherence to the principles of mutualism.

If such was the perspective of Proudhon's philosophy for proletarian practice, then his thought was certainly "in the main stream" of the movement in France, and many of those in the movement were Proudhonists in effect, whether or not they knew or acknowledged it. Nevertheless, there were matters of principle —especially those relevant to revolutionary violence—which he himself would have been unwilling to compromise and from which the movement diverged, some segments doing so more than others.

Other uncompromising anarchists saw their influence wane, especially in the course of struggle with Marxists. This was not wholly a matter of anarchism having too little value to the movement. Much of the bitterness and the strength of Marxists' urge to overcome the anarchists resulted from personal animosities and the way the more dogmatic Marxists sought to eliminate *any* different views. They fought more effectively, and their victories were not altogether due to the virtue of their cause. Nevertheless, even had there been no internecine battles of this sort, it is difficult to see how Proudhon's influence could have remained ascendant, even if he or loyal and intellectually creative disciples had lived well into the twentieth century. Ideals such as his could not remain both intact and popular, given the mood and conditions with which the movement waxed strong.

To clarify further the bearing Proudhon's ideas had on the labor movement in France, it is helpful to look at the response of Proudhonists to the experience of the Commune. Many of the Communards were Proudhonists actively engaged in the struggle, rather than following Tolain's example of withdrawal. Of those who survived the massacres, imprisonment, and exile, many returned to help rebuild the movement in the difficult years after, although some discarded much or all of their earlier anarchist beliefs.

So traumatic an event as the experience of the Paris Commune often does much to shape the convictions of those involved and to confirm their previous faiths. According to differences in the latter, interpretations of the experience vary widely; anarchists saw the commune very differently than did Marxists or Blanquists.[4] They regarded it as a revolt against the State and centralized authority. The people of Paris had acted upon their right to govern themselves, free both of bourgeois domination and of national government. They particularly emphasized the localism of the Commune: Paris as a whole was independent, and organization within the city was based on the smaller communities, including spontaneous natural groups as well as the mayors and councils of the pre-existing *arrondissements*. Despite the demands of crisis, no dictatorship or other imperative authority for the city was established; popular, localized democracy remained the rule until the end.

Thus federalism, as Proudhon had conceived it, was the common ideal of many of the survivors. On the future of the movement they were divided. Those we have called orthodox Proudhonists concentrated on concrete remedies like mutualist production cooperatives and gratuitous credit, without a very clear notion of how the bourgeois order and State could be eliminated or so much weakened that mutualist institutions could be established widely. They tended to shy away from trade unionism, except for local mutual-aid societies and clubs. Possibly the best way of distinguishing them from their master is to suggest that they could not grasp his grand vision of a movement gathering strength and effecting the moral regeneration of its members until transformation of society becomes a reality.

Others, probably more numerous and certainly more influential, shared the federalist, anti-authoritarian ideal, but did not adhere to Proudhon so closely. Many had begun as anarchists and retained federalist, anti-authoritarian attitudes while diverging from their original views in other respects until no longer recognizable as anarchists.

4. Some of the following comments are suggested by the remarks of G. D. H. Cole, *A History of Socialist Thought* (London, 1953–60), II, 166–69.

In part the divergence was a matter of sometimes incompatible attitudes about individualism and collectivism. As we have seen in Proudhon's philosophy, individualism and collective spirit and action are quite compatible in theory, and perhaps in practice as well. But when it comes to committing oneself to action directed toward revolution, the natural tendency appears to be to emphasize one, at the expense of the other if the need seems to arise. The difference between anarchists and socialists of a more collective bent can be explained wholly in terms of their ideas, but it also appears to involve something akin to visceral responses. The anarchist reacts against the prospect of collective organization where the individual might be submerged or coerced. Another man may prefer federalist safeguards against organizational tyranny, but perhaps he feels the cause of the collective in time of struggle to be so vital that demands for individual liberty are often "viscerally" rejected as selfish, foolish, or traitorous. He may start as an anarchist, but as his experience in the cause grows he is unlikely to remain one. When the revolution is complete, there should be a stateless society; but now collective strength must be increased, not subordinated to individualism.

Some of the Proudhonists who survived the Commune focused their attention on the organization of the workers' movement, in effect learning more from *De la Capacité politique des classes ouvrières* than had the "orthodox" mutualists. They concentrated on the formation and strengthening of workers' organizations, including trade unions. Although some of these Proudhonists were in opposition to the "collectivists" following in the path of Eugène Varlin, there is no clear line of demarcation between such Proudhonists and Varlin's collectivist followers, who were the forerunners of syndicalism.[5] Many individuals went from anarchism to this "proto-syndicalism" as events developed.

The latter sought collective "ownership" of the land and the means of production, but not state ownership. The collectives should be local communes or federative agencies that the communes

5. Trade unionists of this type may reasonably be called syndicalists, and often have been. However, although closely related to later revolutionary syndicalism, before 1892 syndicalists had not yet developed their views as far as those identified with syndicalism at the end of the century and after. Those speaking of syndicalism usually are thinking of this later, militantly revolutionary form.

establish and control themselves. Production operations should be carried out by cooperative associations arising from the trade unions. The communes themselves would be based upon trade unions working together under federative arrangements at both local and national levels.

This is not significantly different from what Proudhon envisaged; it just puts heavier stress than he did on the role of the *syndicats* (unions). Collective "ownership" would be at variance with his conception only if farms were operated communally, without individual land possession. Even that difference is easily reconciled. Proudhon takes collective operation to be the only conceivable possibility where much division of labor is needed, as in factories.

These predecessors of syndicalism have been distinguished from Proudhonism by historians because they joined Marx in opposing Proudhonists who did not share an inclination to collectivism. They were also in accord with him in regarding the Paris Commune as historically important because there the proletariat had asserted itself as never before. Although it failed to secure its revolutionary goals, it was in this view the most significant act of revolution before 1917.

However, they opposed Marx's views about "centralism" and the revolutionary state, remaining federalist and anti-authoritarian. Although subject to further evolution, their ideas and attitudes prevailed in French trade unionism until the Communist party was formed and grew strong in the 1920's. Syndicalist attitudes, especially hostility to authority and bureaucratic organization both in the nation and in the movement, have remained potent in France, even in Communist unions. Although available evidence is sketchy, such attitudes seem to have been common, even characteristic, at the level of the rank and file, whether or not repudiated by the leadership. These attitudes have contributed much to the chronic turbulence of the French labor movement. Their role in politics, as far as that is distinguished from labor-union activity, has been less profound but nonetheless significant.

The role actually played here by Proudhon's ideas would be difficult to determine, except where pivotal figures have been intellectuals who thoughtfully articulated their own concepts and what they thought of him. Certainly there is a connection between Proudhon and early union organizers like Varlin, but both the nature of the link and its later consequences are obscure.

Nevertheless, it is clear that Proudhon's opposition to authority and his ideas about proletarian class pride, solidarity, and sense of distinctive identity and interests have had a continuing wide appeal for French workers. They may not have known that he expressed these concepts, but they believed in them, spontaneously or because someone else had advocated them. Of his ideas these lived on after his death, for when someone did give them fresh expression, it struck a responsive chord in the proletariat. Thus a sort of Proudhonism could go on, and find renewed life, even where full-blown anarchism was a lost cause.

Renewed life was found in the 1890's when Fernand Pelloutier and others gave to syndicalism the strength of ideas and spirit that made it much more than nascent trade unionism. Before then the *syndicats* had been less than a major force themselves. The organization of labor suffered a severe setback from the repressions that followed the fall of the Commune, and until 1884 laws sharply curbed the growth of trade unions. Even then labor was slow to gain the drive or the degree of coherence it exhibited later. Although in the unions themselves the attitudes of most were probably not far from Proudhon's, the political expression of the workers' movement in socialist party development was going away from him. There was always a sort of division between socialist parties and the *syndicats*, with undercurrents of antagonism, despite their close ties.

Something of the political fortunes of Proudhonism can be seen from a sketch of the socialist factional divisions. A nationwide unified socialist party was first established in 1880, with Jules Guesde as the moving force in its formation. While in exile after the Commune, Guesde had lived with anarchists and apparently had anarchist leanings himself. After returning to Paris in 1878 he discarded anarchism, rapidly becoming an orthodox Marxist. He was the principal French Marxist leader for many years and might be called an example of the extreme of apostasy from anarchism.

Guesde's united party began to split up rapidly. Soon there were many separate parties or discernible groupings: Guesdists (the Parti Ouvrier Français—Marxist, with centralized organization), Possibilists (the Parti Ouvrier Socialiste),[6] Allemanists (the Parti Ouvrier Socialiste Révolutionnaire—split off from the Possibilists in 1890), anarchists, mutualist trade-unionists, Blanquists (the Parti Socialiste Révolutionnaire),[7] and a variety of groups and individuals who took positions intermediate between the other factions.

The chief issue causing the initial divisions was the objection of a majority of those involved to the efforts of Guesde to build a tightly knit, centralized party organization on the model of German Marxism. This repelled both moderates and those with federalist inclinations. Anarchists and mutualists did not form their own parties, of course, but many played roles of some significance in the *syndicats* and the other parties. Anarchism, however, became weaker politically as other socialist groups grew stronger both in organization and in appeal to new recruits.

The major faction opposing Guesde was the Possibilists, led by Paul Brousse, who forced the Marxists out of the once united party in 1882. Brousse was another apostate from anarchism, but he retained elements of his former beliefs while adopting a very gradualist position. He stressed local initiative and autonomy, a sort of federalism. Rather than waiting for proletarian seizure of power, he wanted socialist control to be assumed step by step—as each becomes "possible"—first, the existing public institutions, then privately owned industries. Compromise and cooperation with bourgeois parties were readily acceptable.

Possibilists regarded trade unions as important instruments in this process and were willing to help the *syndicats* to develop in the ways the latter wanted. Guesdists, on the other hand, thought unions could not help the proletariat until capitalism had been overthrown. Labor unions were useful only to school the workers in understanding of the class struggle, and as a recruiting ground and supporting base for the party. Guesdists tried to force policies on the unions, a practice which contributed much to the Guesdists' eventual loss of influence over the *syndicats* and their federations.

Brousse's party included a sizable, relatively radical element which did not accept his increasingly moderate politics, supporting him only because of his opposition to Guesdist centralism. Many

6. Initially the Parti Ouvrier Socialiste Révolutionnaire.
7. Initially the Comité Central Révolutionnaire.

of these were close to a syndicalist position, believing that the unions could be the main agencies of proletarian revolution. Jean Allemane, the leader of the party left-wing and a former Communard, advocated direct action by the unions and total independence of the proletariat from the bourgeoisie. He attacked reliance on parliamentary action and strongly supported the concept of a revolutionary general strike, an idea which gained currency in France during the mid-1880's, to the consternation of Marxists. In 1890 the Allemanists left Brousse's party to form their own, taking with them the Possibilists' bases of influence in the *syndicats*.

The ideas of Allemane mentioned here show an obvious affinity to those of Proudhon, although the two men might have had some differences over union policies and the revolutionary general strike. Naturally enough, many Allemanists easily made a transition to syndicalism when that movement developed a few years after they separated from the Possibilists.

This revolutionary syndicalism, or anarcho-syndicalism as it is often called, probably more appropriately, certainly has close connections to anarchism. Indeed, where the region involved has had a substantial trade-union movement, anarchists and syndicalists have often been virtually indistinguishable.[8] The entire preceding discussion in this chapter may be summed up by saying that French history in the three decades after Proudhon's death shows that ideas such as he advocated remained continuously current and important in both socialist politics and trade unionism during that period. These ideas were to become bound up in syndicalism, and remain significant to the extent that the latter has been so. I have already pointed out that many of the concepts are similar to Marxist doctrines. The present review of the movement's history indicates that all of these ideas were able to remain current independently, without their being urged by Marxists active in the movement.

The first great leader of revolutionary syndicalism, and the one who defined and established its ideas and goals, was Fernand Pel-

---

8. Some anarchists, especially those giving exceptional emphasis to individualism, remained hostile to syndicalism. On the other hand, some syndicalists have been primarily trade-union militants with few anarchist concepts. There is some reason to make a distinction between "anarcho-syndicalism" and "syndicalism" without the prefix, thus recognizing some of these differences. However, such a distinction is not required here, and would complicate the discussion needlessly.

loutier. He was personally a most remarkable and impressive young man, and he had an enormous impact on workers and intellectuals alike during nine short years before his death in 1901, at the age of thirty-four. Initially a Guesdist, Pelloutier broke with that party in 1892, simultaneously enunciating syndicalist principles and acting upon them. He made the *bourses de travail*, originally simply labor exchanges, the chief centers of militant proletarian action. The Fédération des Bourses de Travail, formed by him in 1892, became the main vehicle for the proliferation and practice of his views. After some years of rivalry and several false starts, the F.B.T. was merged with the national confederation of trade union organizations in 1902. The amalgamated body, the Confédération Générale de Travail, was strongly, but not uniformly, syndicalist in coloring.

While a brief summary of Pelloutier's ideas cannot do them justice, they are so strongly reminiscent of Proudhon's that much of the sketch might be extracted from *De la Capacité politique des classes ouvrières*. The former Guesdist adopted his new course after becoming disillusioned with political parties and parliamentary action, both because of distaste for politics itself and a recognition that party factionalism divided the proletariat—the last a particularly characteristic view of Proudhon's. He sought to make direct *industrial* action by the workers themselves the means for accomplishing revolutionary transformation of society. While accepting the by then common notion of the general strike as the great revolutionary act that would effect the change, unlike many others he did not conceive of it as a spontaneous act, to occur when the time was ripe and itself making possible establishment of socialism. Rather, he believed that workers first had to grow in self-consciousness, solidarity, and *élan* so that they would have the strength to bring about the transformation. Likewise, they had to grow in moral and practical capacities to handle their own affairs, in order to make the new society functionally successful and just.

The needed development of the proletariat would be accomplished through the educational experience of a movement based upon the *bourses de travail*, which Pelloutier regarded as more natural and spontaneous collectivities than trade unions. In the *bourses* working men with common interests could be drawn together, not merely for organized union and political activity, but even more for social life, mutual aid, and moral education. There they could grow in class consciousness and pride, in self-reliance, in collective *élan*, and in self-discipline. Through educational activities they should produce men from their midst capable of assuming the managerial and technical functions until then performed by the bourgeoisie.

> But as he himself warned . . . their principal aim should be to teach the proletariat not to lose sight of its moral purpose in its struggle for emancipation. By setting itself the task of preserving and cultivating a strictly proletarian self-sufficiency, the bourses would not only rescue the worker from his bondage to industrial capitalism, but would also serve to rebuild his character and elevate him from his function as a machine to "an intelligence manning and mastering the machine and rising above it." [9]

Many syndicalists, including Victor Griffuelhes, their leader after Pelloutier's death, professed a belief that speculation on the forms of post-revolutionary society would be useless utopianism. They were concerned only with the struggle. For Pelloutier, a vision of the future society was a necessary, integral part of his revolutionary philosophy. What he saw was mutualism like Proudhon's, with federative organization based upon local *syndicats* of producers.

The only significant elements of possible difference between Pelloutier and Proudhon are the former's greater emphasis on the role in the future society of *syndicats* and his notion of the general strike. The first of these matters represents just a slight, natural evolution of Proudhon's conception of mutualism and is wholly compatible with it. The idea of the general strike is more problematical. Proudhon did not object to massive collective action, and his discussions of the people's right of resistance include a foretaste of the idea of the general strike, including as they do a sug-

9. Alain Silvera, *Daniel Halévy and His Times* (Ithaca, 1966), 152. Silvera refers here to Pelloutier's *Histoire des bourses de travail* (Paris, 1902). Silvera's book includes extensive discussion of intellectual life and thought during this period; many of my subsequent observations on intellectuals in this period are based on Silvera's interpretation.

gestion of the possibility of a spontaneous, universal outbreak of popular resistance.[10] However, his objections to revolutionary violence and cataclysmic overturn of the pre-existing order put him at odds with most syndicalist militants.

With Pelloutier's version of the general strike concept Proudhon should have had little or no reason to quarrel, since here the strike is just the decisive step in a continuous process of transformation. Daniel Halévy, who greatly admired both men, saw in them the heart of French socialism.

> The greatest result of Pelloutier's work, [Halévy] maintained in 1947, was to have demonstrated the enduring significance of Proudhon's socialist ideas. "By typifying beyond doubt the most thoroughly Proudhonian figure, in the militant sense of the word, of our times," he had also inspired a whole generation of syndicalists with the most vital legacy in the French socialist tradition.[11]

However, as influential in the movement as was the thought of Pelloutier, the ideas and attitudes of syndicalists varied widely. Hostility to politics, parties, and centralism, and an emphasis on direct industrial action by the workers have been the common theme of syndicalism. Beyond that, other ideas such as those which Proudhon and Pelloutier had advocated were widely current, but hardly universally so.

Many activists in the movement were like Griffuelhes, having no theoretical bent and little appreciation for the niceties of Pelloutier's philosophy. Some, most notably Emile Pouget, were apocalyptic anarchists who thought that the act of revolutionary victory would somehow by itself create a new morality and justice. Although sharing many ideas with Pelloutier and Proudhon, they lacked the pair's vision of revolution as an extended process of moral regeneration. Griffuelhes, Pouget, and others of their types concentrated their attention on militant action, often with a fondness for the violent stroke against the bourgeois enemy, like industrial sabotage. On the other hand, there were many syndicalist intellectuals, of whom Hubert Lagardelle was perhaps the most distinctive, who followed Pelloutier much more closely while introducing some modifications of his thought.

10. For instance, *Oeuv.*, VII, 292–303.
11. Silvera, *Daniel Halévy and His Times*, 150.

The best known and probably the most original of syndicalist theorists, Georges Sorel, admired both Pelloutier and Proudhon, and he retained many, even most, elements of their philosophies. However, he was also deeply influenced by Marx and by philosophers who did not usually have much affect on other syndicalists— Henri Bergson and Friedrich Nietzsche were two of those most important to Sorel. As a consequence of both his originality and the different ideas to which he responded, he gave new shapes to the ideas of Pelloutier and Proudhon. These new shapes have the general form and content of the old ones, but they are nevertheless markedly different at many points.

To attempt even the most succinct possible summary of Sorel's complex and frequently altered philosophy would lead the present discussion too far from its purpose. I shall just indicate the elements of Proudhon's philosophy, in addition to those already mentioned with respect to Pelloutier, which particularly appealed to Sorel. He liked Proudhon's views on the need for heroic qualities— vigor, courage, *élan*, a readiness to rush boldly into the fray. Likewise he found congenial the other's views on contradiction and opposition of interests as the very essence of the life experience. (His views on contradiction are closer to Proudhon's than to Marx's.)

Sorel goes from there to draw upon Proudhon's concepts of constructive antagonism, tension, and resulting dynamism, developing his own theory of violence. Incorporated here is a notion of a moving spirit and moral regeneration of the proletariat probably more like the other's grand philosophical vision than is Pelloutier's more action-oriented view. Sorel found Proudhon's moral attitudes extremely attractive: to the former, the Comtois ex-printer represented in his life and thought all that was admirable and virtuous in the French people.

However, where in his version of all this Proudhon repudiates physical violence, Sorel regards it as essential to the whole conception and to the practice of revolutionary syndicalism. When he speaks of "violence," he means heroic action and dynamism in physical combat, as well as in the restricted sense of "struggle" intended by Proudhon. Thus Sorel's concept of proletarian action is antipathetic here to the other's pacific approach. He regards the general strike as the culminating act of revolution, the sort of cataclysmic finale Proudhon thought likely to be disastrous. And, in his concept of the role of the "myth of the general strike" in effecting the desired changes in the popular spirit, Sorel also goes far from Proudhon.

In addition, Sorel was attracted to Proudhon's criticisms of democracy and of doctrinaire rationalism. His own views are quite different here, however, although he adopts some points of the other's critique. In many respects he owes much to Proudhon, and he acknowledges a debt possibly larger than he owes. But he is too original and different to be called, as he often has been, a Proudhonist.

Sorel and his closest intellectual disciple, Edouard Berth, believed their ideas to be an effective combination of the best elements of the philosophies of Proudhon and Marx; they also believed there to be a closer relation between the two great ideologues than I have been willing to admit. How well they have performed the combination I will not argue here. However, this "Marxification" of Proudhon's thought became the vehicle by which the latter has been able to have some impact on certain Marxist intellectuals. Sorel probably did not have a very great influence on the French syndicalist movement in its peak period before World War I. Nevertheless, he is the only theorist of syndicalism who has been widely read since then; most scholars know the movement's ideas only through Sorel. To many Marxists he may seem just about the only remotely acceptable writer in the syndicalist and anarchist traditions.[12] Thus we find that Antonio Gramsci, the major leader and theoretician of the Italian Communist party in the 1920's, thought Sorel impressive (the feeling was mutual) and through him acquired some respect for Proudhon. Early in his career Gramsci had occasion to collaborate with anarchists and anarcho-syndicalists, but by 1920 he had definitely denied that anarchism could be an appropriate ideology for the proletariat. This does not seem to have diminished his respect for Sorel and Proudhon, though.[13]

12. Some Russian anarchists and "semi-anarchists" have gained limited acceptance in Soviet historiography and philosophy because they helped to build the Russian revolutionary movement.

13. Antonio Gramsci, "Sorel, Proudhon, DeMan," *Oeuvres choisis* (Geneva, 1959), 110–20; John M. Cammett, *Antonio Gramsci and the Origins of Italian Communism* (Stanford, 1967), 123–28.

Sorel was involved in the particularly lively intellectual life of Paris around the turn of the century. There were a number of intimate circles, often closely interrelated with one another and frequently centered upon common gathering places, like bistros and book shops, and upon intellectual reviews such as Charles Péguy's *Cahiers de la quinzaine*, with which Sorel was associated. Many of those involved in the various circles then or later gained great distinction in literary criticism, the writing of fiction, or other intellectual endeavors. The links between groups and individuals are both fascinating and bewildering; men with quite disparate viewpoints could have close affinities on certain matters. Thus one finds both ties and profound differences between men like Péguy, Sorel, Berth, Maurice Barrès, Daniel Halévy, André Spire, Julien Benda, Charles Maurras, Anatole France, and Romain Rolland.

The Dreyfus Affair and its aftermath effected deep changes in the outlooks and relationships of most of these intellectuals, dividing them and polarizing differences. Many were Jewish, some feeling their Jewish identities important only as a result of the Affair, and some were outspokenly anti-Semitic. Yet for most of them anti-Semitism was a less important issue than the bearing the Affair had on their conceptions of politics. Some acquired deep political concerns only under the impact of the Affair; many passed on from disinterest or moderate political views to relatively radical positions, both conservative and socialist. A number were drawn to the syndicalist movement. Nevertheless, the entangled network of close intellectual and personal ties continued to extend across the gap between the opposite sides in the Dreyfus Affair and the polarization of political viewpoints which followed it.

Few if any of these intellectuals had views which match those considered characteristic of any of the factions in contemporary politics or the syndicalist movement. Most of them defy any attempt at description by standard political labels; although most had definite political views, they were intricate ones, including elements from seemingly disparate sources that twisted theoretical patterns out of their "usual" shape.

Many were deeply affected by the ideas of Proudhon. The intricacy both of the source and of their own concepts is suggested by the fact that from their milieu came both the Cercle Proudhon and the Amis de Proudhon. The latter were by and large syndicalist and socialist in their sympathies; they were essentially the same men who edited the Rivière edition of Proudhon's works.[14] The Cercle Proudhon (see description above, p. 274.) was an arm of the reactionary and royalist Action Française, which was then in a "radical" phase, seeking to establish a working-class following and to attract syndicalist intellectuals. Georges Sorel, Edouard Berth, and Georges Valois had already moved from revolutionary syndicalism or anarchism to association with the Action Française, and in their minds the movement was wholly consistent with their original principles. Berth contributed to the *Cahiers du Cercle Proudhon*, using the pseudonym Jean Darville. Valois was a major figure in both the Cercle and the Action Française; in the 1920's he broke with the latter, formed a short-lived fascist party, then moved back toward the left. One of the principal Amis de Proudhon, Daniel Halévy, was an early and vigorous Dreyfusard—the Action Française had originated from an anti-Dreyfusard impulse—and he would best be labeled socialist and republican. Despite this, and despite his belonging to a prominent Jewish family, he was also a friend and admirer of Charles Maurras, the chief of the Action Française and reaction's best ideologue, a vigorous anti-Semite, and the man who had equipped the anti-Dreyfusard side with plausible intellectual weapons. Halévy even lost his place in the Académie Française through defending Maurras at the latter's treason trial after World War II.[15]

These examples could readily be multiplied. Those cited should suffice to indicate the complexity of convictions involved here. Men like Maurras and Halévy could share many important beliefs but use them to adopt seemingly opposed positions, and a Sorel or a Valois could make major shifts in his primary political associations without changing his most basic principles and ideas. These

14. Under the impact of syndicalism and the repelling spectacle of current politics, there was literally a flood of scholarly writing on Proudhon and on his contemporary importance, the greatest part concentrated in the period roughly 1909 to 1912. Formed at about this time, the Amis de Proudhon did much of their writing on Proudhon after World War I. Their number included radical republicans as well as socialists. See C. Bouglé's preface to their joint work, *Proudhon et notre temps* (Paris, 1920). Some of the group met at weekly intervals for many years (Boris Souvarine, Paris, letter to the author, October 4, 1965).

15. Silvera, *Daniel Halévy and His Times*, 206.

intellectuals' distinctive perceptions of contemporary society and culture were the primary determinants of their political ideas and attachments, but the latter did little in turn to define the shape of these perceptions. Consequently the bases of their various political positions cannot be well understood in terms of the familiar categories of partisan politics—and we have to go beyond such categories to comprehend the cultural process of which they were a part. Examining their responses to Proudhon could help to reveal the process; this is not the place to attempt this, but we can briefly indicate the principal areas of appeal they found in Proudhon's thought.

Many liked his attacks on Jacobinism and, more broadly, on parliamentary democracy. Some were opposed to democracy of any type, but more common was a distaste for its forms in the Third Republic, often combined with a desire for popular democracy in some socialist form. This distaste differed substantially in quality before the Dreyfus Affair and after, especially in reaction against Combist politics. A number were drawn to Proudhon's ideas on the organization of the proletariat; this fit with a common preference for a temperate approach, as did his distrust of apocalyptic revolution.

His ideas on social integration were important to them, though their own conclusions often were actually different. Like him, they believed that modern society had been atomized by economic and political practices, and that the creation of natural community was essential. And they admired his emphasis on heroic qualities as essential to society; for the "conservatives," however, the heroic ethic and natural community were to be jointly the basis—and consequence—of a restored, integral nation under authoritarian rule.

Proudhon's emphasis on the need for popular moral regeneration made a wide impression, and not just among syndicalist sympathizers. Others also gave much attention to the common man, some to peasants in particular, with urban proletarians regarded merely as uprooted peasants. They sought the vital core of the French spirit and tradition; this could easily be a conservative pursuit, but it also was a passion of the politically "neutral" and of men on the left, often with a humanitarian strain drawn in part from Tolstoy. Lovers of popular culture frequently thought its different regional forms endangered by centralized government, and this could also increase their sympathies for Proudhon. "Socialists" among them believed his libertarianism to be a principal strand in the tradition of French socialism. (See, for instance, the remarks of Halévy cited above.)

This all seems to have been part of a more general contemporary pattern, a questioning of accustomed uses of reason which I mentioned at the end of Chapter 4. The pattern is evident in distaste for the political and industrial developments of the several decades then just past, an antipathy shared by both "conservative" and "radical" admirers of Proudhon. They tended to regard the supposed promise of these developments as illusory, and in this connection rationality became suspect in various ways. Their attraction to popular culture, their seeing the common man as unspoiled or at least readily rehabilitated, and their emphasis on popular moral regeneration are signs of this suspicion: they were celebrating what modern rationalized culture scorned or ignored. Yet like Proudhon they were too much a part of that culture to repudiate it altogether. Unlike avant-garde poets and artists of the time, these intellectuals continued to express themselves in conventionally rational forms of discourse, and for the most part they did not direct their attacks against reason as such. They were ambivalent, and the significance of their attitudes remains enigmatic. I think, however, that this Proudhon revival will have to be examined in the context of a presumed process of profound intellectual disturbance.

Relatively little has been said here of Proudhon's influence in specifically anarchist circles. The importance and appeal of his ideas there can be assumed, although most often there are other figures, like Bakunin and Kropotkin, whose somewhat different concepts have more direct and substantial force. Some aspects of Proudhon's philosophy have also been influential among nonanarchists in other countries besides France, but examination of these very complex and diverse lines of filiation cannot be accomplished with sufficient brevity.

However, something should be said in passing about populism in Russia, a movement which began in the 1860's and, although evolving fitfully, was *the* Russian revolutionary movement until Marxism was imported after 1890. Populism continued until its latter-day proponents were suppressed, exiled, or converted after 1917; even then its effects as a major formative force on Russian Marxist thought left a marked imprint on Communist ideology, especially in its effects on Lenin's thought.

Although basically anarchist in its ideas, populism differed markedly from Western anarchism, having many peculiarly Russian qualities. Oddly, Bakunin and Kropotkin were less influential on Russian populism than they were on anarchism in the West, where they lived in exile and were active in anarchist circles. Proudhon was the theorist having the greatest effect on populists, especially in the movement's early years. Nicholas Mikhailovsky and Alexander Herzen, the most influential populist intellectual leaders, both found in Proudhon their most important source of ideas. "By the mid sixties Proudhon had already become probably the most important single ideological influence on the radical intelligentsia. His influence was decisive on Mikhailovsky and his closest friends." [16] In his *Roots of Revolution*, Franco Venturi attributes to Proudhon a great influence on many later figures also. The reasons for his attractiveness are too numerous to go into here,[17] but it should be noted that they were rather different from in the West and that in some respects the populists remained closer to Proudhon's own spirit than did most Frenchmen influenced by him.

We close this epilogue's review of Proudhonism in various movements and milieus by returning to France and quoting a comment which gives added perspective to our discussion of the ways in which ideas advocated by Proudhon affected the French labor and socialist movements. In his *Marxism in Modern France*, George Lichtheim observes that academic historians, particularly those outside France, have seldom understood adequately the late nineteenth- and early twentieth-century development of the movements, or the filiation of ideas in them. He concludes:

16. James H. Billington, *Mikhailovsky and Russian Populism* (Oxford, 1958), 22; see also 129–32, 170–72, et passim; Martin Malia, *Alexander Herzen and the Birth of Russian Socialism, 1812–1855* (Cambridge, 1961), 322–25 et passim. After 1900 a specifically anarchist movement developed in Russia, with Bakunin, Kropotkin, and contemporary Western anarchists most influential.

17. Billington gives them in some detail, esp. 22–23. See Franco Venturi, *Roots of Revolution*, trans. Francis Haskell (London, 1960).

In consequence, the formative period between 1880 and 1905, when the French labor movement—by way of innumerable splits, dissensions, and doctrinal quarrels—worked out its characteristic attitude to major issues of state and society, tends to be treated as a mere propadeutic to the political upheavals that followed. Yet for anyone concerned with the manner in which basic attitudes (as distinct from mere ideological notions) determine the character of political movements, these years are crucial, for it was then that French Socialism received the stamp it has never lost.[18]

This is not to say that Proudhon was chiefly responsible for the stamp given to French socialism, even indirectly. I do insist, though, that ideas first given thorough theoretical elaboration by Proudhon play, by a variety of means, a vital role in this formative period, along with other concepts advocated both by him and Marx, as well as notions he had little to do with. Furthermore, a historical interpretation of the movement in France which fails to recognize the significance of the ideas first propounded by Proudhon, and of the related attitudes, will also fail to comprehend the history very well.

In a carefully done and thoughtful study (1910) of the relationships between syndicalism and Proudhon's thought,[19] Gaëtan Pirou stresses the view that the actual historical filiation between the two is not only inherently uncertain but also a less important issue. He suggests that there are profound "analogies," probably largely unconscious, between the thought and attitudes of syndicalists and those of Proudhon—analogies which he examines and documents at length—and that these are vital. During and after World War I, the revolutionary syndicalist movement and "state of mind" declined and gave way to Communist and reformist approaches, although some postwar C.G.T. leaders (Léon Jouhaux for one) ac-

18. George Lichtheim, *Marxism in Modern France* (New York, 1966), 15. Lichtheim's criticism of other historians seems overstated, but his emphasis on the period's importance is valid. He himself might think my emphasis on Proudhon is overstated.

19. *Proudhonisme et syndicalisme révolutionnaire* (Paris, 1910). Also, see Edouard Droz, *P.-J. Proudhon, 1809-1865* (Paris, 1909), 15-92. Droz's discussion helped lead to a number of others about Proudhon's contemporary relevance. The best of these, written when conditions had changed (1920), is *Proudhon et notre temps,* the joint product of the Amis de Proudhon.

knowledged a great intellectual debt to Proudhon.[20] Just how far a Proudhonist or syndicalist "state of mind" remained important at the level of the rank and file would be difficult to determine, and not much attempt has been made to do so.[21] As a guess, such a state of mind probably has been more significant than party and union leaders would like to admit. In any event, these ideas and attitudes could hardly have failed to shape French labor and social movements profoundly.

Despite their importance, ideas closely akin to Proudhon's have obviously been much less significant for the development of socialism, both evolutionary and revolutionary, than has been Marxism in its many variant forms. The actual reasons are not hard to see, if one is willing to go beyond the snap judgment or uninformed prejudice that Proudhon was a fool or an advocate of bourgeois egoism. Marxist ideologies were usually more attractive to the potential rebel because they seemed better adapted to the immediate problems of the movement. Instead of fretting like Proudhon about moral regeneration and the inner logic of ideals, most preferred to concentrate upon questions of power and its conquest. In a world where only power seems really to count, matters of equity appear inconsequential to those desperate in their lack of power. Moreover, when social conflict generates deep-seated, commonly felt animosities, the rhetoric of irreconcilable combat, destruction of the enemy, and apocalyptic renewal is both more satisfying and more suitable for generating loyalty and enthusiasm than Proudhon's conception of mutual reciprocity, his pacific moralism, and his skepticism.

Marx's remarkable analytic system with its appearance of scientific certainty is much more likely to persuade the rational mind and produce conviction, even dedication, than Proudhon's relatively

20. As examples of testimony to this effect, see Robert Pinot, "La Confédération Générale de Travail et les idées proudhoniennes," *Revue hebdomadaire*, XXIX, 18 (May 1, 1920), 3–34; Bernard Georges and Dénise Tintant, *Léon Jouhaux, cinquante ans de syndicalisme* (Paris, 1962), 1, 3–4.

21. Annie Kriegel touches on this in her "Le Syndicalisme révolutionnaire et Proudhon," in *L'Actualité de Proudhon*, ed. Centre National d'Etude des Problèmes de Sociologie et d'Economie Européennes (Brussels, 1967), 47–66. This article is the best of recent writing on the topic; the volume which includes it is a record of a centennial symposium on Proudhon, held in Brussels in November, 1965; it includes much excellent material.

diffuse, unsystematic, confusing, and idealistic philosophy. This is all the more true because the German's knowledge and understanding of the industrial economy were far more profound than Proudhon's. For many decades the latter's concepts about economic relationships seemed too little relevant to the reality of industrializing societies to merit much serious attention. However, economic development and the problems of the so-called Third World have in recent years exposed the severe limitations of Marx's conception also; a century after its initial publication *Das Kapital* has become an anachronism, although it is still illuminating.

By now it should be possible for us to recognize that the strength of Proudhon's ideas does not depend upon the quality of his economic "science." (To a lesser degree this observation is applicable to Marx's philosophy as well.) Certainly capitalism has proved more able to ameliorate the material conditions of the masses than either man expected. But both were concerned with more than empty stomachs and tuberculous, wizened children. Both, and Proudhon in particular, wanted above all for men to be able to live in genuinely just conditions, with spiritual as well as material satisfaction and unhindered opportunity to fulfill their human potentials. With material deprivation and the struggle for power the most immediate problems, for a long time most of those on the left have tended to ignore this humanist concern, or to leave it very far in the background. Recently some have rediscovered it; if they find the young Marx's humanism attractive, then Proudhon deserves their close attention also.

When the conquest of power was the all-consuming passion, it was only natural that movements should evolve in the direction of ever more powerful organizations, and hence well-disciplined and centrally controlled ones. The insistent refusal of anarchists, anarcho-syndicalists, and other libertarian groups to do likewise inevitably resulted in their virtual or total eclipse under the impact of the power of more authoritarian and disciplined competitors. The way Communists prevailed over anarcho-syndicalists in the Spanish Republic of the 1930's is the classic example.

Yet the power-oriented movement has given us tyranny on the one side and the heavy hand of dull, frustrating, and maddening socialist party and union bureaucracies on the other.

Communist, socialist, and trade-union power groups now may bask too complacently in self-satisfaction with past successes, while grubbing doggedly and unimaginatively to maintain their positions and continue a smoothly progressive evolution, somehow failing to confront basic dilemmas. Alternatively they grope desperately, often frenetically, for fresh solutions to two types of problems: those of industrial society in a relatively affluent stage, and those of societies which have rebelled against old masters while yet only beginning to industrialize. For all, whatever their outlook, mere conquest of power proves to be far from satisfactory, and the classic image of struggle to the death between bourgeoisie and proletariat is increasingly less relevant to the actual conflicts of the contemporary world.

Thus the stage is set for more substantial innovations in both theory and practice on the left than at any time since the initiation of Communism in the early 1920's, and probably since the development of Marxism a century ago. Innovations are already in process, although it is too early to tell how significant they will prove to be or how responsive to the actual demands of this decade and those to come. Since much of the current theoretical ferment arises in reaction against the rigidly doctrinaire discipline of the past, Proudhon's rejection of "absolutism" should be especially attractive.

In another direction, nonsocialist thought and practice have proved more capable of progressive development than most on the left had thought possible. The former have also shown themselves to be more adaptable than had been expected concerning changing conditions and more responsive to demands of rebellious and critical elements—or at least better able to divert or dull the brunt of their attacks. On the other hand, "progressive," liberal, but nonsocialist forces have discovered that neither the increase and extension of affluence nor that of democratic polities and constitutional guarantees have produced a mode of life as satisfactory as they had hoped for. Moreover, many of them are coming to believe that the problems confronting them cannot be solved with the ease that, with their simple Enlightenment-born faith in progress, technology, and liberal economics, they once expected.

As they reexamine old faiths, these "progressive" liberals are often doing no more than haltingly enunciating a growing awareness of the shortcomings of democracy and "free enterprise" that Proudhon expressed incisively and thoroughly long ago. Much of what comes forth in the United States as the criticism of "thoughtful liberals," the "new politics," and the "new left" is only a confused, half-blind reprise of what he said, and said much better, with a firmer, more integrated understanding—although few recognize the affinity. Even the Catholic Church which Proudhon fought so hard has begun to come around, with the Papal encyclical *Populorum Progressio* (1967) taking a position surprisingly close to his, including some similar criticism of property.[22]

The kaleidoscope of patterns of rebellion in "advanced" industrialized countries shifts too rapidly for a brief appraisal of Proudhon's relevance. Nevertheless, we can see that many of his attitudes are repeated among rebels today. Resentment against the often heavy hand of authority finds more forms of expression every year, and the urge for individual spontaneity and autonomy is reflected even more in popular culture than in politics. Where rebellion was once directed chiefly against State, Church, and the "class enemy," there is now much more sympathy for what Proudhon recognized: that repression of the human spirit can be imposed by other authoritative institutions and doctrines—such as universities, the press, or "science"—acting according to their own inner logic, as well as in roles of handmaidens to the State.[23] And, lest enthusiasts suppose that the times are ripe for realization of Proudhon's revolutionary hopes—or those of Marx—the reactions of a confused and frightened public to recent displays of rebellion confirm his gloomy view of the people's counterrevolutionary qualities.

The times have changed too much for Proudhon to be the sole oracle of the modern age. Neither should the most ardent Proudhonist claim for his philosophy the extent of strength and total

22. Since World War II a number of Catholic writers, most notably Henri du Lubac and Pierre Haubtmann (both of whom are clerics), have found in Proudhon an expression of ideas they believe to be highly compatible with Church doctrine.

23. For a recent view of anarchism's role among rebellious youths, see Paul Goodman, "The Black Flag of Anarchism," *New York Times Magazine*, July 14, 1968, pp. 10, 11, 13, 15, 16, 18, 20, 22; also in *Anarchism*, ed. Robert Hoffman (New York, 1970).

clarity of understanding that followers of Marx have often claimed for their master. Indeed, Proudhon would have been the first to insist that his theories would require much modification to be applicable a century and more after his death.

Nevertheless, it is clear, both from the directions in which modern politics is groping—or tumbling—and from the methods and ideas against which many now react, that Proudhon's philosophy is more germane to current concerns than ever before. This is true because his ideas are relevant to problems which have continually beset modern man, and at the same time they have not been as specific to immediate conditions which later changed as the concepts of his contemporaries usually were. Most of his critics in the nineteenth century—and many of them since—rejected his views out of hand either because of Marx's attacks or, more often, because they looked no further than the dictum that "property is theft," the notions about free credit, or other superficialities, and thought them foolish, dangerous, or at least impracticable. As I have tried to show, those who go only that far miss most of what the man has to say. Even if free credit, the exchange system stemming from his labor theory of value, or many of his other more obvious suggestions are technically unsound, his fundamental concepts are hardly altered by this. He may have had too little understanding of many of the problems of human psychology and society, but despite his limitations his understanding was sufficiently profound and universal to demand our closest attention. Strike away all the anachronisms and the other unquestionably faulty features, and the remainder retains its integral force and cogency.

Men have tried to make a better world through manipulation of the instruments of power, changes in laws and political organization, reconstruction directed by governmental and corporate institutions, technological innovation and economic growth, popular enlightenment and education, and deliberate elimination of disruptive conflict. All have helped, but none has fulfilled its promise. Proudhon thought illusory the supposed promise of all of them except, with qualifications, enlightenment.

It would be too much to say that men have fully recognized the limits of these approaches, or that they are near discarding their more futile or obnoxious variations. However, they are beginning to take more critical stances and explore alternative routes. Proudhon can serve as an invaluable guide.

In the end, most complaints about the condition of man amount to objections about the way human dignity is denied and unrealized in the existing order—and that is what Proudhon's philosophy is all about. Instead of slogans like "Power to the people," "Black Power," "Imperialist go home!" "participatory democracy," or any of the other familiar shibboleths of countless factions, we could better begin with Proudhon's "Justice is spontaneous respect for human dignity."

Bibliography

PART I: THE WORKS OF PROUDHON

A. The "Rivière edition"

Oeuvres complètes de P.-J. Proudhon, nouvelle édition, ed. C. Bouglé
and H. Moysset (Paris: Marcel Rivière, 1923–1959), 15 vols. in 19,
in 8º.

This is the best edition of Proudhon's works, despite some textual
faults; it has a thorough critical apparatus and excellent, lengthy
introductions by a number of fine scholars. Publication was ter-
minated before completion of the edition, but most of his important work is included. The following list gives the major contents of each volume; many of the volumes also contain briefer
pieces, including letters, newspaper articles, and other relevant
documents. The publisher did not number the volumes: in library
cataloging and binding they are ordinarily numbered in order of
their publication. Hereafter this edition is indicated by the abbreviation "Riv."

1. *Système des contradictions économiques, ou philosophie de la
   misère,* 2 vols., 1923. Introduction and notes by Roger Picard.
2. *Idée générale de la révolution au XIXᵉ siècle,* 1924. Introduction
   and notes by Aimé Berthod.
3. *De la Capacité politique des classes ouvrières,* 1924. Introduction
   and notes by Maxime Leroy.
4. *Candidature à la pension Suard. De la célébration du Dimanche.*

Qu'est-ce que la propriété?, 1926. Introduction and notes by Michel Augé-Laribé.

5. *De la création de l'ordre dans l'humanité, ou principes d'organisation politique*, 1927. Introduction and notes by C. Bouglé and Armand Cuvillier.

6. *La Guerre et la paix, recherches sur le principe et la constitution du droit des gens*, 1927. Introduction and notes by Henri Moysset.

7. *Les Confessions d'un révolutionnaire pour servir à l'histoire de la révolution de février*, 1929. Introduction and notes by Daniel Halévy.

8. *De la Justice dans la révolution et dans l'Eglise*, 4 vols., 1930. Introduction by Georges Guy-Grand, *étude* by Gabriel Séailles, notes by C. Bouglé and J.-L. Puech.

9. *La Révolution sociale démontrée par le coup d'état du deux décembre. Projet d'exposition perpétuelle*, 1936. Introduction and notes by Edouard Dolléans and Georges Duveau.

10. *Deuxième Mémoire sur la propriété. Avertissement aux propriétaires. Programme révolutionnaire. Impôt sur le revenu. Le Droit au travail et le droit de propriété*, 1938. Introduction and notes by Michel Augé-Laribé.

11. *Du Principe de l'art et sa destination sociale. Galilée. Judith. La Pornocratie ou les femmes dans les temps modernes*, 1939. Introduction and notes by Jules-L. Puech.

12. *Philosophie du progrès*, introduction and notes by Théodore Ruyssen. *La Justice poursuivie par l'Eglise*, introduction by Jules-L. Puech; 1946.

13. *Contradictions politiques. Les Démocrates assermentés et les réfractaires. Lettre aux ouvriers en vue des élections de 1864. Si les traités de 1815 ont cessé d'exister?*, 1952. Introduction and notes by Georges Duveau, Jules-L. Puech, and Théodore Ruyssen.

14. *Du Principe fédératif. La Fédération et l'unité en Italie. Nouvelles Observations sur l'unité italienne. France et Rhin* (fragments), 1959. Introductions: "Fédéralisme et Proudhonisme," by Georges Scelle; "Le Fédéralisme dans l'oeuvre de Proudhon," by J.-L. Puech and Théodore Ruyssen; other introductory material and notes by Puech and Ruyssen.

15. *Ecrits sur la religion* (includes many short pieces and fragments), 1959. Introduction and notes by Théodore Ruyssen.

Carnets de Proudhon, cited in the next section, were planned as part of this edition, and were published by the same firm, but do not seem actually to belong to the *Oeuvres complètes*. Except for these *Carnets*, whose publication is in progress, there are no plans to complete the Rivière edition.

B. Other collections

Oeuvres complètes de P.-J. Proudhon (Paris: A. Lacroix, Verboeckhoven, et Cie., 1867–70), 26 vols. in 18°. Vol. VI also issued by C. Marpon & E. Flammarion (n.d.), in 18°.

A more complete edition than that of Rivière, there are some omissions, including all of the works published posthumously. It has no critical apparatus or introductory material. Hereafter this edition is indicated by the abbreviation "Lac."

Oeuvres posthumes de P.-J. Proudhon (Paris & Brussels: A. Lacroix; Paris: Garnier, 1866–75), 8 vols. in 18°.

Unfinished manuscripts edited and published by Proudhon's friends. A large number of other posthumous publications, not included here, are cited below. Hereafter this edition is indicated by the abbreviation "O. P."

Correspondance de P.-J. Proudhon (Paris: A. Lacroix, 1875), 14 vols. in 8°.

Additional letters are cited in Part I-D below.

"Carnets," 11 MS. vols., Bibliothèque Nationale (Paris), Collection des Manuscrits, Nouvelles Acquisitions Françaises, nos. 14265–75.

Notebooks written between 1843 and 1862, containing a wide variety of valuable material. The following table gives the years covered by each *carnet* with the manuscript collection number in parentheses.

I	(14265) 1843–45	VII	(14271) 1848–50
II	(14266) 1845–46	VIII	(14272) 1850–51
III	(14267) 1846	IX	(14273) 1851–52
IV	(14268) 1846–47	X	(14274) 1852–54
V	(14269) 1847	XI	(14275) 1854–62
VI	(14270) 1847–48		

Carnets de Proudhon, edited, with full critical apparatus, by Pierre Haubtmann (Paris: Marcel Rivière, 1960–), 3 vols.

Includes the first seven and part of the eighth of the *carnets*. Vol. I (1960), 1843–46; Vol. II (1961), 1846 to February 24, 1848; Vol. III (1968), 1848 to August 13, 1850. More than 1,800 pages remain unpublished; the preparation of this portion is in process.

"Archives Henneguy-Fauré-Frémiet." The name given by Pierre

Haubtmann to MSS. in the possession of Proudhon's descendants (see my Preface). Included are MSS. of most of his published works (with annotations and corrections), rough drafts of unfinished, unpublished work, notes, and letters by and to Proudhon. All are described, with lengthy extracts, by Haubtmann in two 1961 theses cited below in Part II. The most interesting items, cited more fully in Part I-E below, are the "Cahiers de lecture," the "Cours d'économie," and "La Pologne." As far as I know, this collection has been made accessible only to Haubtmann, although "La Pologne" was available to some others many years ago.

Proudhon library. His personal library, with his notes in book margins, is in the Bibliothèque Municipale de Besançon, *dons* 34.904–35.913.

Mélanges: Articles de journaux, vols. XVII–XIX of the Lacroix edition of the *Oeuvres complètes.*

> Reproduces most of the newspaper articles written by Proudhon between 1848 and 1850, with some omissions and deletions, the latter made because of government censorship. Other articles appear in vol. VI of this edition; the major deletions are reproduced in vol. VII of the Rivière edition.

C. Works first published by Proudhon or his literary executors

Les Actes des apôtres (Brussels, 1868), O.P.; in Riv., XV.

"Actes de la révolution: Résistance: Louis Blanc et Pierre Leroux," published with "Qu'est-ce que le gouvernement? Qu'est-ce que le dieu?" (Paris: *La Voix du peuple,* 1849), 62 pp. in 18°, in Riv., II. Articles from Proudhon's newspaper.

Amour et mariage (Paris: Lacroix, 1876), 251 pp. in 18°; in Riv., VIII; Lac., XXIV. Consists of two additional studies first published in the 1860 edition of *De la justice.*

"Au Président de la république. Le Socialisme reconnaissant" (Paris, 1850), 8 pp. in 4°. From *La Voix du peuple.*

Avertissement aux propriétaires, ou lettre à M. Considérant, 3ᵉ mémoire (Besançon & Paris: Prévot, 1842), 115 pp.; also (Paris: Garnier, 1848), 100 pp.; and (Paris: Marpon-Flammarion, 1849); in Riv., X; Lac., II.

"Banque du peuple" (Paris: Boulé, 1849), 16 pp. in 4°; printed with "Rapport de la commission des délégués du Luxembourg," and other materials (Paris: Garnier, 1849), 52 pp. in 18°.

La Bible annotée (Paris: Lacroix, 1866; 2nd ed., 1866), O. P., xii, 419 pp. in 18°; 3rd ed. also including *Les Actes des apôtres* and other fragments (Brussels: Lacroix, 1867); Riv., XV.

"Candidature. Citoyen Proudhon aux électeurs catholiques!" (Paris: Beaulé & Maignand, 1849), single sheet folded, in fol.

Césarisme et Christianisme, ed. J.-A. Langlois (Paris: Marpon & Flammarion, 1883), 2 vols. in 18°. Publication of notes written (1852–54) for a universal history which got no further, except in other works.

Les Confessions d'un révolutionnaire pour servir à l'histoire de la révolution de février, 1st ed. (Paris: *La Voix du peuple*, 1849), 106 pp. and table, in 4°; 2nd ed. issued simultaneously (Paris: Garnier, 1850 [1849]), 381 pp. in 18°; 3rd ed. (Paris: Garnier, 1851), 327 pp. in 18°; in Riv., VII; Lac., IX.

Contradictions politiques: Théorie du mouvement constitutionnel au XIXe siècle (Paris, 1870), O. P.; in Riv., XIII.

De la Capacité politique des classes ouvrières (Paris: E. Dentu, 1865), O. P.; two more editions in 1865, one in 1868, one in 1873; in Riv., III.

"De la Concurrence entre les chemins de fer ct les voies navigables" (Paris, 1845), 48 pp.; from the *Journal des économistes*, X (May, 1845), 157–202; 2nd ed. (Paris: Garnier, 1848), 77 pp., in Lac., II.

De la Création de l'ordre dans l'humanité, ou principes d'organisation politique (Besançon & Paris: Prévot, 1843), 582 pp. in 12°; 2nd ed. (Paris: Garnier, 1849), 454 pp. in 18°; in Riv., V; Lac., III.

De la Justice dans la révolution et dans l'Eglise (Paris: Garnier, 1858), 3 vols. in 18°; new edition, revised and augmented with two more *études* (Brussels, 1860); another edition with yet another *étude* (Paris: Michel Lévy, 1861); in Riv., VIII; Lac., XXI–XXVI.

De la Solution du problème social (Paris: Garnier, 1848); contains three pamphlets: "Solution du problème social," "La Démocratie," and "L'Organisation du crédit"; the last was published separately, and is cited below; in Lac., VI.

De l'Utilité de la célébration du Dimanche considérée sous les rapports de l'hygiène publique, de la morale, des relations de famille et de cité (Besançon: Bintot, 1839), 104 pp. in 12°; 2nd ed., rev. (Besançon: Prévot, 1841), 128 pp. in 16°; 3rd ed. (Besançon: Prévot, 1845), 92 pp. in 8°; 4th ed. (Paris: Garnier, 1850), 84 pp. in 18°; in Riv., IV; Lac., II.

Les Démocrates assermentés et les réfractaires (Paris: E. Dentu, 1863, 1864), 96 pp. in 18°; in Riv., XIII; Lac., XVI.

"Démonstration du socialisme théorique et pratique pour servir d'instruction aux souscripteurs et adhérents à la Banque du Peuple" (Paris: Boulé, 1849); 8 pp. in 4° oblong.

"Discours du citoyen Proudhon prononcé à l'Assemblée Nationale dans sa séance du 31 juillet, en réponse au rapport du citoyen Thiers sur la proposition relative à l'impôt sur le revenu" (Paris: Pilhes, 1848), 8 pp. in fol., and 15 pp.; in *Le Moniteur universel* (1848), pp. 1772 and 1826–30; also published with other material as "Proposition relative à l'impôt . . ." and as "Rapport du . . . ," q.v.; in Riv., X; Lac., VII.

"Le Droit au travail et le droit de propriété" (Paris: L. Vasbenter, n. d. [1848]), 12 pp. in fol.; article from *Le Peuple;* reissued (Paris: Garnier, 1848, 1850), 60 pp. in 18°; in Riv., X; Lac., VII.

Du principe de l'art et sa destination sociale (Paris: Garnier, 1865; Lacroix, 1875), O. P., viii, 380 pp. in 18°; in Riv., XI.

Du Principe fédératif (Paris: E. Dentu, 1863) 324 pp. in 18°, and (Paris: Bossard, 1921), 223 pp. in 16°; in Riv., XIV; Lac., VIII.

Encyclopédie catholique (Paris: Société de l'Encyclopédie Catholique, 1839). Proudhon wrote 29 or 30 articles in vol. II; 17 are reproduced in Riv., XV.

Essai de grammaire générale, first printed as an epilogue to a reissue of N. Bergier's *Eléments primitifs des langues* (Besançon: Lambert, 1837); published separately (Besançon: Bientôt, 1850); extracts in Riv., XV.

"Etudes sur l'école hollandaise," *Revue trimestrielle* (Brussels), XXI (January, 1859), 276–89. Review of a book by W. Burger (Théophile Thoré), *Les Musées de la Hollande, Amsterdam, et la Haye.*

"Les Evangiles." Title used in reference to notes published as part of *La Bible annotée*, q.v.

"Explications présentées au Ministère Public sur le droit de propriété" (Besançon, n.d. [1842]), 24 pp. in 8°; in Riv., X; Lac., II.

La Fédération et l'unité en Italie (Paris: E. Dentu, 1862), 143 pp. in 18°; new ed. (Paris, 1862); in Riv., XIV; Lac., XVI. Two articles first published in *L'Office de publicité* (Brussels), July 13 and September 7, 1862, with additional material.

France et Rhin, ed. Gustave Chaudey (Paris, 1867), O. P.; 2nd ed. (Paris: Librairie Internationale, 1867), vi, 260 pp. in 12°; in Riv., XIV.

"Garibaldi et l'unité italienne," *L'Office de publicité* (Brussels), September 7, 1862; in his *La Fédération et l'unité en Italie*, q.v.

Gratuité du crédit. Discussion entre M. F. Bastiat et M. Proudhon (Paris: Guillaumin, 1850), 192 pp. in 16°. An exchange of letters first published in *La Voix du peuple; Intérêt et principal,* cited below, is almost the same, but lacks a final letter from Bastiat.

La Guerre et la paix. Recherches sur le principe et la constitution du droit des gens (Paris: E. Dentu, 1861) 2 vols.; in Riv., VI; Lac., XIII, XIV.

Idée générale de la révolution au XIXe siècle (Paris: Garnier, 1851), viii, 352 pp., 2nd ed., 1851, the same; in Riv., II; Lac., X.

Idées révolutionnaires, preface by Alfred Darimon (Paris: Garnier, 1849), xxviii, 268 pp. in 18°. A selection of outstanding articles by Proudhon from *Le Peuple.*

Intérêt et principal (Paris: Garnier, 1850), 198 pp. in 18°; in Lac., XIX. See *Gratuité du crédit,* above.

La Justice poursuivie par l'Eglise (Brussels: Office de Publicité, 1858), viii, 184 pp. in 18°; in Riv., XII; Lac., XX.

Lettre à M. Blanqui. 2e Mémoire sur la propriété (Besançon: Prévot, 1841), 188 pp. in 18°; published with *Qu'est-ce que la propriété?* (Paris: Garnier, 1848); in Riv., X; Lac., I.

"Liberté, égalité, fraternité, mutualité" (Paris: Dondey-Dupré, n.d.), single-sheet poster seeking subscriptions for Proudhon's Banque du Peuple.

Les Majorats littéraires (Brussels: Office de publicité, 1862), 166 pp. in 18°; 2nd ed. (Paris: E. Dentu, 1863), 262 pp. in 18°; in Lacroix, XVI.

"Les Malthusiens" (Paris: Boulé, 1849), 8 pp. in 8°; also (Paris, n.d.), 7 pp.; in Riv., VII; article reprinted from *Le Représentant du peuple,* August 11, 1848.

Manuel du spéculateur à la bourse, 1st ed. written in collaboration with Georges Duchêne and Charles Beslay (Paris: Garnier, 1854), viii, 353 pp. in 18°; 2nd ed., revised, augmented, corrected (Paris: Garnier, 1855), viii, 416 pp. in 18°; 3rd ed., the first that bore Proudhon's name, further revised (Paris: Garnier, 1857), xii, 499 pp. in 18°; 5th ed. (Paris: Garnier, 1857), xii, 511 pp. in 18°; in Lac., XI.

"Mazzini et l'unité italienne," *L'Office de publicité* (Brussels), July 13, 1862; in his *La Fédération et l'unité en Italie,* q.v.

"Le *Miserere,* ou la pénitence d'un roi. Lettre au R. P. Lacordaire sur son carême de 1845," *Revue indépendante,* XIX (March, 1845), 203–29; published separately (Paris: Boulé, 1849), 8 pp. in fol.; in Riv., XV; Lac., II.

"MM. Considérant et Proudhon jugés par eux-mêmes" (Paris: G. Dairnvaell, 1849), 16 pp. in 18°. Articles from Considérant's *Démocratie pacifique* and Proudhon's *Le Peuple*.

Nouvelles observations sur l'unité italienne (Paris: E. Dentu, 1865), 69 pp. in 18°; articles first published in *Le Messager de Paris*, November, 1864, in 5 issues; in Riv., XIV; Lac., XVI.

"L'Organisation du crédit et de la circulation," first published as part of *De la solution du problème social* (see above); 2nd ed., separate (Paris: Garnier, 1848), 43 pp. in 8°; 3rd ed. (Paris: Garnier, 1849), 43 pp. in 8°; in Lac., VI.

"Pétition au Sénat [May 11, 1858]" (Paris: Bry, 1858), 7 pp. in 8°; in Riv., XII; Lac., XX.

Philosophie du progrès (Brussels: A. Lebègue, 1853), 156 pp. in 8°; in Riv., XII; Lac., XX.

La Pornocratie, ou les femmes dans les temps modernes (Paris: Lacroix, 1865, 1875), O. P., vii, 269 pp. in 18°; in Riv., XI.

"Procès des citoyens Proudhon et Duchêne (avec discours de Proudhon à la cour d'assises de la Seine, 28 mars 1849)" (Paris: Boulé, 1849), 8 pp. in fol.

Projet d'exposition perpétuelle, written in 1855, first published with *Théorie de la propriété*, cited below; in Riv., IX.

"Proposition à l'Assemblée Nationale pour l'organisation d'un service de transport entre Avignon et Chalon-sur-Saône" (Paris: Boulé, 1850), 7 pp. in 8°.

"Proposition relative à l'impôt sur le revenu, présentée le 11 juillet, 1848, avec discours du 31 juillet" (Paris: Garnier, 1848), 66 pp. in 18°; in Riv., X.

"La propriété littéraire," *L'Office de publicité* (Brussels), September 26 and October 24, 1858.

    This topic is covered in his *Majorats littéraires*, q.v. Unable to determine whether these articles are included in the book.

Qu'est-ce que la propriété? ou recherches sur le principe du droit et du gouvernement. 1e Mémoire (Paris: J.-F. Brocard, 1840), xii, 244 pp. (Besançon: Prévot, 1841); with *2e Mémoire* (Paris: Garnier, 1848), 155 pp. in 18°; also (Paris: Garnier-Flammarion, 1966); in Riv., IV; Lac., I.

"Rapport du citoyen Thiers et discours du 31 juillet 1848" (Paris: Garnier, 1848), 87 pp. in 18°; in Riv., X; also in "Proposition relative à l'impôt . . ." and "Discours du citoyen Proudhon . . . ," q.v.

Les Réformes à opérer dans l'exploitation des chemins de fer (Paris: Garnier, 1855), 392 pp. in 18°; in Lac., XII.

"Réponse de M. Proudhon à M. Considérant et son réplique" (Paris: 1849), 2 folded folio sheets; this is the same as "MM. Considérant et Proudhon," cited above.

Résumé de la question sociale, ou banque d'échange et banque du peuple (Paris: Garnier, 1848), xx, 116 pp. in 18°; in Lac., VI.

La Révolution sociale démontrée par le coup d'état du deux décembre (Paris: Garnier, 1852), 6 editions in the same year, with the 5th and 6th adding a letter from Proudhon to the Prince Président de la République; all 283 pp. in 18°, except the last two, xii, 283 pp.; in Riv., IX; Lac., VII.

Si les traités de 1815 ont cessé d'exister? (Paris: E. Dentu, 1863), 108 pp. in 18°; 2nd ed., ibid.; 3rd ed., ibid., 1864; in Riv., XIII; Lac., VIII.

Système des contradictions économiques, ou philosophie de la misère (Paris: Guillaumin, 1846), 2 vols.; 2nd ed. (Paris, 1850); in Riv., I; Lac., IV, V.

Théorie de la propriété (Paris: Lacroix, 1866, 1871), O. P., iv, 310 pp. in 18°.

Théorie de l'impôt (Paris: E. Dentu, 1861), 400 pp. in 18°; in Lac., XV.

D. Letters in other places besides the collected correspondence

"Cinq lettres inédites à son ami Jouvenot," *Revue d'Alsace,* nouvelle série, XI (1882), 433–44.

(*Compte-rendu* of a typographers' banquet, September 16, 1849, with a letter of Proudhon), apparently published (Paris, 1849); see below, "Letters to Mme Guichon de Grandpont . . ."

"Correspondance de Proudhon avec son cousin Melchior Proudhon," ed. M. Lambert, *Bulletin de l'Académie des Sciences, Belles-lettres, et Arts de Besançon* (1910), 340–676.

"Deux Lettres inédites de P.-J. Proudhon à Victor Considérant," ed. Aimé Berthod, *La Révolution de 1848,* Bulletin de la Société d'Histoire de la Révolution de 1848, XX (March–April, 1923), 19–38.

"Deux Lettres inédites de Proudhon," ed. Arthur Lehning, *International Institute of Social History, Bulletin* (1950), no. 1, 31–42; also published separately (Amsterdam, 1950).

(Five letters to Charles Beslay), in Beslay's *Mes Souvenirs* (Paris, 1873), 213–14, 479–82.

(Four letters to Auguste Nefftzer, 1852–60), in René Martin, *La Vie d'un grand journaliste, Auguste Nefftzer* (Besançon, 1948 & 1953), 2 vols., I, 157–58, 191; II, 27, 29–30.

"From the Letters of P.-J. Proudhon," in Alexander Herzen, *My Past and Thoughts*, trans. Constance Garnett, rev. Humphrey Higgens (London: Chatto & Windus, 1968), II, 813–15; IV, 1791–96.

Two letters, and most of two more, first printed in Herzen's paper, *Poliarnaia zvezda*, in 1859, and also available in Russian editions of his works.

"La Jeunesse de Proudhon. Une Correspondance inédite," ed. Adolphe Court, *Revue moderne*, XLVIII (1868), 385–423, 648–76; XLIX (1868), 53–77.

Letters which were later included in the collected correspondence.

(Letter to Alfred Darimon, September 21, 1862), in Darimon's *Histoire d'un parti: L'Opposition libérale sous l'empire (1861–1863)* (Paris, 1886), 278.

(Letter to Charles Edmond [pseudonym of Karol Edmond Chojecki]), in Edmond's *La Florentine* (Paris, 1856).

(Letter to Gagne, undated), *Le Figaro*, XII, 1040 (February 2, 1865), 6.

(Letter to Georges Duchêne, December 30, 1860), in Alfred Darimon, *Histoire d'un parti: Les Cinq sous l'empire (1857–1860)* (Paris, 1885), 428.

(Letter to Monsieur J., October 3, 1861), in "Proudhon en Belgique" (article signed "E. R.," the pseudonym of P.-E.-A. Poulet-Malassis), *La Petite Revue*, III, 6 (February 25, 1865), 14–15.

(Letters to Guillemin and others), MSS., Bibliothèque Municipale de Besançon, No. P 644. Thirty-three letters, of which the last is by his daughter Catherine; may be included in the publication cited below, "Quelques lettres inédites."

(Letters to Joseph Droz, November 26, 1838, and to Prince Napoleon, August 10, 1851), MSS., Internationaal Instituut voor Sociale Geschiedenis, Amsterdam.

(Letters to Mme Guichon de Grandpont, October 14, 1836; to Hoddé, March 17, 1853; to Lebègue, December 14, 1862, and to the typographers of Paris, September 16, 1849), MSS., Institut Français d'Histoire Sociale, Paris.

(Letters to the editor of *Le Moniteur universel*), September 20, 1848, p. 2528; October 17, 1848, p. 2884; November 2, 1848, p. 3064; November 4, 1848, p. 3092; April 3, 1849, p. 1224.

(Letters to the Gauthier brothers), MSS., Collection Delestre. Copies of unpublished originals, 235 to the Gauthiers, mostly to Victor Gauthier, 1843 to October 20, 1848, and one to Monsieur X, June 8, 1841. Haubtmann says these are the most important letters yet unpublished. (See Haubtmann's "P.-J. Proudhon, sa vie et sa pensée," vol. VII.)

"Lettre à Madame J. d'Héricourt," *Revue philosophique et religieuse* [Jan.?], 1857.

"Lettre à M. Rouy, rédacteur-en-chef de *La Presse*, 29 mai 1863," in Riv., XIII, 93–104.

"Lettre au procureur impérial . . . , 10 nov. 1858," *L'Etoile belge*, February 1, 1859; in his *Correspondance*, VIII, 234, and Riv., XII, 165n–168n.

"Lettre aux ouvriers en vue des élections de 1864," in Riv., XIII, 313–26.

"Lettre inédite de Proudhon," *Revue littéraire de la Franche-Comté*, II (1864). Stated date improbable, unverifiable.

"Lettre du citoyen Proudhon à un de ses amis de Besançon . . . 10 avril 1848" (Paris: Bintot, 1848), 4 pp. in 4°. Said to be an extract from a letter published in the *Franc-Comtois*, and explaining his candidacy for the National Assembly; in *Correspondance de P.-J. Proudhon*, II, 299–304.

Lettre inédite de Proudhon," *Les Nouvelles Littéraires*, August 4, 1934.

"Lettre inédite de Proudhon à Ad. Crémieux," ed. E. Charavay, *Revue politique et littéraire*, V (1896), 171–73.

"Lettre inédite sur Napoléon Ier (17 sept. 1858)," in Alberto Lumbroso, *Miscellanea napoleonica*, Sér. II (Rome, 1896).

Lettres à Gustave Chaudey et à divers comtois, 1839–64, ed. Edouard Droz (Besançon: Dodivers, 1911), 107 pp. in 8°; also in *Mémoires de la société d'émulation du Doubs*, Sér. 8, V (1910), 157–258.
    Includes several unpublished fragments and a letter of Gustave Courbet on Proudhon's death.

Lettres à sa femme (Paris: B. Grasset, 1950).

"Lettres inédites de P.-J. Proudhon," to M. Sauvage (1849) and Léon Laurent-Pichat (1856), ed. Yves Lévy, *Le Contrat social*, IX, 2 (March–April, 1965), 108–9.

Lettres au citoyen Rolland, 1858–62, ed. Jacques Bompard (Paris: B. Grasset, 1946).

"Lettres au Prince Napoléon—lettres, notes et fragments," in C.-A. Sainte-Beuve, *P.-J. Proudhon, sa vie et sa correspondance, 1838–1848* (Paris, 1872), 307–50.

"Proudhon à Auguste Blanqui," *Amateur d'autographes*, March, 1913, 81–84. This letter, dated July 17, 1841, is not to Auguste Blanqui, but to his brother Adolphe, a prominent economist.

"Proudhon et les Lyonnais. Lettres inédites," ed. A. Bertrand, *Séances et travaux de l'Académie des Sciences Morales et Politiques*, CLXI (1904), 211–42; also published separately (Paris, 1904); same title listed as being in *La Renaissance latine*, August 15, 1904—unable to verify contents.

"Proudhon expliqué par lui-même—lettres inédites de Proudhon à M. N. Villiaume (24 et 29 jan. 1856) sur l'ensemble de ses principes et notamment sur sa proposition: La Propriété, c'est le vol" (Paris: Alcan-Lévy, 1866), 16 pp. in 8°.

"Quatre Lettres inédites de Proudhon," ed. Daniel Halévy, *Mouvement socialiste*, XXXIII B, 5–12.

"Quelques Lettres inédites," *Revue politique et parlementaire*, XXXI (March, 1902), 575–93; XXXII (April–May, 1902), 98–110, 323–44. To Guillemin, 1845–63.

"Quelques Lettres inédites de P.-J. Proudhon," ed. Henri Martineau, *Le Divan*, XXXIX (1947), April–June, 85–92; July–September, 142–48; October–December, 208–22. Fifteen letters.

(Seven letters to Auguste Javel), in Javel's "Proudhon dans ses relations intimes," *Revue socialiste*, XLI (1905), 257–75, 414–32, 568–88.

(Thirty-two letters to Pierre-Jules Hetzel), in A. Parménie and C. Bonnier de la Chapelle, *Histoire d'un éditeur et ses auteurs: P.-J. Hetzel* (Paris, 1953), passim.

"Treize Nouvelles Lettres inédites de P.-J. Proudhon," *L'Actualité de l'histoire* (1954), no. 9, pp. 15–25. Excerpts of letters written 1844–56, probably to Maître Renaud of Besançon. Other Proudhon letters in the same journal and year, no. 7, pp. 29–34, and in one other issue around the same time.

"Trois Lettres inédites de Proudhon" to Auguste Javil [February 8, 1842; October 12, 1848; January 14, 1850] (Lons-le-Saunier, 1871), 14 pp. in 8°.

(Twenty letters to diverse correspondents), MSS., private collection of A. Valat.

(Two letters to G. Ferrari), in "Lettere di Giuseppe Ferrari a Pierre-Joseph Proudhon, 1854–61," ed. Franco Della Peruta, *Annali di Istituto Giangiacomo Feltrinelli: 1961* (Milan, 1962), 267.

(Two letters to Jenny d'Héricourt, October 8 and December 2, 1856), in her *La Femme affranchie* (cited in part II, below), I, 128–42; in Riv., XI, 326n–330n.

E. Other items written by Proudhon

(Agreement for the foundation of *La Voix du peuple;* written by Proudhon and Alexander Herzen, who furnished necessary funds, dated August 14, 1849), in A. I. Gertsen, *Polnoe Sobranie Sochinenii i Pisem*, ed. M. K. Lemke (Petrograd, 1915–25), V, 292–96.

Almanach des associations ouvrières pour 1850, ed. Proudhon and others (Paris, 1849); includes "Maximes"—an extract from his *Célébration du Dimanche*—and another piece, pp. 71–75, 97–99.

"Les Annotations Feuerbach," in Pierre Haubtmann, *P.-J. Proudhon: Genèse d'an antithéiste* (Paris and Tours: Mame, 1969), 247–58.

"Appel au conseil d'état sur les actions de jouissance des canaux," written in August, 1843; not known whether this was published or whether there is an extant manuscript.

"Biblia Proudhonia," ed. Daniel Halévy, *L'Indépendance*, July 1, 1911, 343–63.

"Cahiers de lecture," MSS., 41 vols., 1826–42, 1844, Archives Henneguy-Fauré-Frémiet. Described, with extracts, in Pierre Haubtmann's unpublished thesis, "P.-J. Proudhon, sa vie et sa pensée," q.v.

"Carnets de Proudhon," *La Grande Revue*, L (August 10 & 25, 1908), 417–43, 625–48; LI (September 25, 1908), 209–36. Extracts—see part I-B for details on the whole.

"Ce que serait la révolution sociale, par Proudhon" (Paris: Librairie de la Société Bibliographique, 1877), 4 pp. in 24°; extracted from Lac., XVII, 65, and V, 310.

Commentaires sur les mémoires de Fouché, with "Parallèle entre Napoléon et Wellington," and notes on the treaties of 1814–15, ed. Clément Rochel (Paris: P. Ollendorf, 1900), 290 pp. in 8°.

"Cours d'économie," MS., 1850–55, 3 vols., Archives Henneguy-Fauré-Frémiet. Described, with extracts, in Haubtmann's "Philosophie sociale de Proudhon," q.v.

"Le Dossier d'un polémiste. Pages inédites," *La Revue*, LXX (1907), 433–48; LXXI (1907), 37–48, 215–28, 361–73. Fragments.

Le Droit au travail à l'Assemblée Nationale—recueil complet des discours, ed. Joseph Garnier (Paris, 1848), includes speech by Proudhon, 388–405; a letter by him to *L'Union*, July 13, 1848, 431–45; and one to *Le Moniteur universel*, 445.

"Le 'Feuillet Boutteville,'" 1862 MS., in Pierre Haubtmann, *P.-J. Proudhon: Genèse d'un antithéiste* (Paris and Tours: Mame, 1969), 232–45.

"Galilée: Scénario d'un drame," ed. Edmond Lepelletier, *La Nouvelle Revue*, XCI (February 15, 1895), 498–522, and 719–38; in Riv., XI, 283–301.

Jésus et les origines du Christianisme, ed. Clément Rochel (Paris:

G. Havard, 1896), iv, 323 pp. in 8°; in Riv., somewhat abridged, XV, 475–600.

"Judith" (scenario of a drama found in the *carnets*), in Riv., XI, 296–301.

"Un Mariage en commerce" (rough sketch for a comic drama), in Riv., XI, 295.

"Napoléon et Wellington," ed. Clément Rochel, *Cosmopolis*, IV, 10 (October, 1896), 115–36; 11 (November, 1896), 447–94; 12 (December, 1896), 775–91. See *Commentaires*, cited above.

Napoléon Ier, ed. Clément Rochel (Paris: Montgredien, 1898), lxxxvi, 271 pp. in 18°; first published in *La Nouvelle Revue*, XCVII (November 1 & 15, December 1, 1895), 5–26, 225–46, 449–77.

Napoléon III, ed. Clément Rochel (Paris: P. Ollendorf, 1900), 447 pp. in 8°.

"Une Page inédite (29 mai 1860)," ed. Georges Gazier, *Mémoires de la société d'émulation du Doubs*, Sér. 7, VIII (1903–4), and in Gazier's "Les Maisons natales de Fourier et Proudhon" (Besançon, 1905).

"Pages inédites de P.-J. Proudhon," ed. Georges Gazier, *Bulletin de l'Académie des Sciences, Belles-Lettres, et Arts de Besançon*, 1926, 183–96; in Riv., X.

> Variations between the original manuscript of *De l'Utilité de la célébration du Dimanche* and the 1841 (second) edition, which is the earliest published version extant.

"Pages inédites sur la Pologne," *Grande Revue*, CIII (July, 1920), 16–22; with article by Léon Abensour, "P.-J. Proudhon et la Pologne," 3–15. Excerpts from the next item.

"La Pologne, considérations sur la vie et la mort des nationalités," MS., written in 1862, 950 pp. plus 350 sheets of notes, Archives Henneguy-Fauré-Frémiet. Described in Pierre Haubtmann's unpublished thesis, "P.-J. Proudhon, sa vie et sa pensée," q.v. Also described briefly in C. Bouglé, "La Sociologie de Proudhon," *Bulletin de la Société Française de Philosophie*, XII (April, 1912), 182ff.

"Polémique contre Louis Blanc et Pierre Leroux, novembre 1849–janvier 1850," title given by the editors of the Rivière edition to a series of articles originally published in *La Voix du peuple*; in Riv., II, 353–459.

(Un Procès-verbal de la discussion du comité des finances, 15 & 17 juillet 1848), MS., Archives Nationales, C. 278, versement de la Chambre des Deputés. Discussion between Proudhon and Adolphe Thiers; resumé given in Riv., VII, 27–31.

"Proudhon et Marx," in Riv., I, vol. ii, 415–23. Proudhon's marginal notes in his copy of Marx's *La Misère de la philosophie;* the same notes are incorporated in the text of Marx's book, the editions published by A. Costes (Paris, 1950) and by Pléiade (Karl Marx, *Oeuvres* [Paris, 1965], I, 1–136).

"Recherches sur les catégories grammaticales et sur quelques origines de la langue française" (1839); treatise written for the Prix Volney— about half published in the *Journal de langue française.* While the editors of the Rivière edition believed this work to have been lost (Riv., XV, 85), it is in the Archives Henneguy-Fauré-Frémiet, and the next item is the same piece, despite the slight difference in title.

"Recherches philologiques sur les catégories grammaticales," autograph MS., with notation "mémoire qui a obtenu une mention honorable au concours Volney, le 3 mai 1839," Bibliothèque Municipale de Besançon, no. 1375, 52 sheets, written on both sides.

"La Royauté du peuple souverain," extract from *Qu'est-ce que la propriété?* (Paris: *Temps nouveaux,* no. 53, 1912), 8 pp. in 16⁰.

(Speech in the National Assembly, in the debate on authorization of his prosecution for attacks on Louis-Napoleon), *Le Moniteur universel,* February 14, 1849, 495–96.

(Speech in the National Assembly offering amendment to the proposed constitution), *Le Moniteur universel,* September 25 & 28, 1848, pp. 2593, 2631.

F. French selections from Proudhon's works

Abrégé des oeuvres de Proudhon, ed. Hector Merlin (1st vol. anonymous) (Paris: E. Flammarion, 1896–1906), 3 vols.

"Le Christianisme et l'église, ou le boulevard de l'autorité," ed. Manuel Devaldès (Herblay: Impr. de l'Idée Libre, 1930), 46 pp. in 8⁰.

"Dieu, c'est le mal!," ed. Manuel Devaldès (Conflans-Ste.-Honorine: Editions de l'Idée Libre, 1927), 36 pp. in 8⁰.

Les Femmelins: Les Grandes Figures romantiques (Rousseau, Béranger, Lamartine, Mme Roland, Mme de Staël, Mme Necker, G. Sand), Collection du Cercle Proudhon, no. I (Paris: Nouvelle Librairie Nationale, 1912), 107 pp. in 16⁰.

Justice et liberté, ed. Jacques Muglioni (Paris, 1962).

Lettres de P.-J. Proudhon, ed. Daniel Halévy and Louis Guilloux (Paris: Grasset, 1929), 364 pp. in 16⁰.

Oeuvres choisies, ed. Jean Bancal (Paris: Gallimard, 1967).

La Pensée vivante de Proudhon, ed. Lucien Maury (Paris, 1945), 2 vols.

P.-J. Proudhon, étude et choix de textes, ed. Joseph Lajugie (Paris: Dalloz, 1953).

Portrait de Jésus, ed. Robert Aron (Paris: Pierre Horay, 1951). Extracts from Proudhon's works, mainly unfinished ones, arranged to reconstitute the life of Jesus which he planned but did not complete.

Proudhon, ed. C. Bouglé (Paris: F. Alcan, 1930), 156 pp. in 16°.

Proudhon, ed. A. Cuvillier (Paris, 1937).

Proudhon. Textes choisis, ed. Alexandre Marc (Paris, 1945).

"Proudhon et l'enseignement du peuple," ed. Aimé Berthod and Georges Guy-Grand, Collection des "Amis de Proudhon" (Paris: E. Chiron, 1920), iv, 29 pp. in 8°.

[Proudhon moraliste, ed. Gabriel Séailles, Collection des "Amis de Proudhon" (Paris, 1920).] Publication announced, but probably did not actually appear.

Textes choisis, ed. Bernard Voyenne (Paris, 1952).

G. English translations

"An Anarchist's View of Democracy," in Anarchism, ed. and trans. Robert L. Hoffman (New York: Atherton Press, 1970), excerpts from "Solution du problème social."

General Idea of the Revolution in the Nineteenth Century, trans. John Beverley Robinson (London: Freedom Press, 1923; New York: Haskell, 1970, and Howard Fertig, 1970). Somewhat abridged.

"The Malthusians" (London, 1886); reprinted from The Anarchist.

Proudhon's Solution of the Social Problem, ed. Henry Cohen (New York, 1927); selections on mutual banking, with commentary by Charles A. Dana and William B. Greene.

Selected Writings of Pierre-Joseph Proudhon, ed. Stewart Edwards, trans. Elizabeth Fraser (Garden City, N.Y.: Doubleday, 1969).

System of Economical Contradictions, or the Philosophy of Misery, trans. and published by Benjamin R. Tucker (Boston, 1888), vol. 1 only, no more published.

What Is Property?, trans. and published by Benjamin R. Tucker (Princeton, Mass., 1876; London, 1902?; New York, 189–; reprint editions, New York: Howard Fertig, 1966, and Dover, 1970).

PART II: WORKS ABOUT PROUDHON

Of the authors cited below, a remarkably large number have been celebrated men of letters, politics, and journalism. However, very little of what was written about Proudhon during the nineteenth century can help today's scholars to understand him, although insights into the times can be gained from these older pieces. Most of them are distorted by political bias, and many are frank polemics. As a result of several stimuli, including the syndicalist movement and some complex interactions in Parisian intellectual circles, during the decade immediately before World War I there was a great upsurge of scholarly interest in Proudhon. A large number of books and articles resulted, many of them excellent. A number of the men who first wrote about him then continued to do so later, and much of the quality and quantity of work on him is due to them. There has been a steady but small stream of writing by later scholars, most of it of less distinction.

Many of the best of the authors from this decade, the ones most prolific in writing about him, formed a group calling itself the Amis de Proudhon. Most of them were widely respected, even distinguished, scholars. In addition to publishing a number of fine studies of Proudhon individually, they produced one admirable collection of articles, *Proudhon et notre temps*, and, most important, served as editors of the Rivière edition of his *Oeuvres complètes*. Their introductions and notes for the volumes in this edition constitute some of the most valuable work on Proudhon. Their names are given in Part I-A of this bibliography. Of recent authors who were not a part of this group, among the most outstanding have been Pierre Haubtmann, Georges Gurvitch, and Pierre Ansart.

Two of the most distinguished of the Amis de Proudhon, Daniel Halévy and Edouard Dolléans, have written the best published biographies of him, both making excellent use of his correspondence and *carnets*. The latter were not available to many of those who have written about Proudhon, having been placed in a public depository only after the death of his daughter Catherine in 1947. Dolléans's *Proudhon* is primarily a consideration of his intellectual life. Halévy wrote a number of biographical studies of Proudhon, two of them especially illuminating: *La Jeunesse de Proudhon* and *Le Mariage de Proudhon*. (The second covers more than the title suggests.) Halévy's work reflects a deep understanding of its subject, but covers only limited portions of his life. The great critic C.-A. Sainte-Beuve wrote a fine study of one decade in Proudhon's career: *P.-J. Proudhon, sa vie et sa correspondance, 1838–1848*.

Relatively little has been written about Proudhon in English, and most of that says hardly anything that is not treated far better by the French authors just cited. There are a few articles which provoke in me the reaction, "I wish I had said that!" An article by Nicola Chiaromonte and three by Aaron Noland come immediately to mind in this regard. George Woodcock's biography, *P.-J. Proudhon,* is competent but better suited for general reading than for scholarly study. Apart from Henri du Lubac's *The Un-Marxian Socialist,* which is a translation from the French, the only serious scholarly book of merit in English is Alan Ritter's recent *The Political Thought of Pierre-Joseph Proudhon.* Ritter's scholarship is thorough, and some readers have liked the book, though I did not. Examining his subject in terms of issues currently important in American political science, he abstracts Proudhon from the historical context, a method which I believe seriously distorts the anarchist's ideas.

No very thorough bibliography of works by Proudhon or about him has been published. The following listing attempts to be comprehensive, regardless of the value of the items cited or their relevance to the present monograph. Included are books and articles specifically about Proudhon and others which devote substantial attention to him. Many of the latter no doubt have been overlooked, as have a number of newspaper articles and ephemeral anarchist publications. Where possible the relevance, significance, and accuracy of citations first noted in other sources have been carefully verified, and missing information has been added. Where entries here do not include all the usual information, it is usually because someone else's citation of the item could not be verified. When an unverified item appears dubious for any reason, the questioned portion is enclosed in brackets.

Abensour, Léon. "P.-J. Proudhon et la Pologne," *Grande Revue,* CIII (July, 1920), 3–15.

Adam, Juliette. *See* Lambert, Juliette.

Adler, Georg. *Die Grundlagen der Karl Marx'schen Kritik der bestehenden Volkswirtschaft* (Tübingen, 1887), 169–201.

Alas, Leopoldo. *Proudhon* (Madrid, 1912).

Albert-Petit, A. "Proudhon et les socialistes," *Journal des débats,* August 15, 1910, pp. 1–2.

Allen, Mary B. "P.-J. Proudhon in the Revolution of 1848," *Journal of Modern History,* XXIV (1952), 1–14.

Alph, D. "P.-J. Proudhon," *Le Figaro,* XII, 1037 (January 22, 1865), 2.

Amis de Proudhon. *Proudhon et notre temps.* (Paris, 1920).

Analisis del socialismo y exposicion clara . . . (Paris, 1852). Includes section on Proudhon.

Ansart, Pierre. *Naissance de l'anarchisme: Esquisse d'une explication sociologique de Proudhon* (Paris: Presses Universitaires de France, 1970).

―――. *Sociologie de Proudhon* (Paris: Presses Universitaires de France, 1967).

―――. *Marx et l'anarchisme, essai sur les sociologies de Saint-Simon, Proudhon, et Marx* (Paris: Presses Universitaires de France, 1969), 1–17, 141–325, 359–539.

Armand, F. *P.-J. Proudhon et le Fouriérisme* (Paris, 1929); from *Revue d'histoire économique et sociale*, XVII (1929), 437–97.

Antonelli, Etienne. "Autour d'une Renaissance Proudhonienne," *Wissen und Leben*, Jg. III, vol. 6 (1910), 562–68.

Arnauld, M. "Deux livres de P.-J. Proudhon," *Nouvelle revue française*, X, 527–45.

Aron, Robert. "Karl Marx et les socialistes français," in *De Marx au Marxisme* (*1848–1948*), ed. Robert Aron (Paris, 1948), 55–84.

[(Article on Proudhon and Communist China), *The Observer*, November 9 or September 11, 1958.]

(Article on Proudhon's *Révolution sociale*), *L'Assemblée nationale*, August 9, 1852.

Arvon, Henri. "Proudhon et le radicalisme allemand," *Annales des économies, sociétés, civilisations*, VI, 2 (1951), 194–201; also in *Revue de la pensée juive* (1951), no. 7, 112–23.

Assezat, J. "Ste.-Beuve et Proudhon," *Revue bleue*, 1873, 399–404.

Aucuy, Marc. *Les systèmes socialistes d'échanges*, thesis (Paris, 1908), Ch. 2, pp. 114ff.

Audebrand, Philibert. *Lauriers et cyprès. Pages d'histoire contemporaine* (Paris, 1903), 269–95.

―――. *P.-J. Proudhon et l'écuyère de l'Hippodrome, scènes de la vie littéraire* (Paris, 1868).

Augé-Laribé, Michel. Introductions for Riv., IV, 3–8, 19–30, 99–118; X, 3–20, 157–66, 251–54, 289–300, 337–42, 408–14.

―――. "La Marianne des champs," in *Proudhon et notre temps*, ed. Amis de Proudhon (Paris, 1920), 99–131.

Auger, Lazare. *A quelles conditions la république (ou une monarchie) est possible . . . Réponse aux confessions d'un révolutionnaire* (Paris, 1849).

Amoudrez, Madeleine. *Proudhon et l'Europe. Les idées de Proudhon en politique étrangère* (Paris, 1945).

Aulnis de Bourouill, J. d'. "Proudhon en zijn stelsel van economische contradictiën," *Onze Eeuw. Maandschrift voor Staatkunde, Letteren, Weltensschap en Kunst*, II (1905), 378–404.

Ayomonier, Camille. "Un Ami bordelais de P.-J. Proudhon," *Revue philomathique* (Bordeaux), XLI (1938), 145–63.

Bachelin, Henri. *P.-J. Proudhon, socialiste national (1809–1865)*, 4th ed. (Paris, 1941).

Baile, F. "Proudhon d'après sa correspondance," *Bibliothèque universelle* (Geneva), LVIII (1875), 414–43.

Bancal, Jean. "La Démocratie industrielle de Proudhon," *Revue de l'action populaire*, no. 190 (July, 1965), 823–40.

————. "Proudhon et la propriété," *L'Europe en formation* (Paris), May, 1965.

————. "Proudhon: La Propriété, la démocratie économique et le fédéralisme mutuelliste," *L'Actualité de Proudhon*, ed. Centre National d'Etude des Problèmes de Sociologie et d'Economie Européennes (Brussels, 1967), 17–46.

————. "La Socio-économie de Proudhon," *Cahiers de l'Institut de Science Economique Appliquée*, Sér. M, Cahier 23 (April, 1966), 3–138.

Barbey d'Aurevilly, Jules Amédee. *Sensations d'art*, in his *Les oeuvres et les hommes*, vol. VII (Paris, 1886), 1–14.

[————. *Les Philosophes et les écrivains religieux*, in his *Les Oeuvres et les hommes*, vol. I? (Paris, 1887).]

Barral, Jean. "Von Proudhon zu Silvio Gesell" ([Erfurt]: Freiland-Freigeld, n.d.).

Barrès, Maurice. "De Hegel aux cantines du Nord," *Le Journal*, November 30, December 7 and 14, 1894; 3rd ed. (Paris, 1904), 29–37.

Bart, B. F. "Michelet and Proudhon," *French Studies*, IV (1950), 128–41.

Bartier, John. "Proudhon et la Belgique," *L'Actualité de Proudhon*, ed. Centre National d'Etude des Problèmes de Sociologie et d'Economie Européennes (Brussels, 1967), 169–227.

————. "Proudhon et ses amis belges," *Bulletin de la Société d'Histoire Moderne* (Séance du 5 Déc. 1954), LIII, 11/12 (1954), 13–15.

Basso, L. "Ritorno a Proudhon e Bernstein," *Rinascita*, VII, 2 (February, 1960), 121–26.

Bastiat, Frédric. *See* Part I-C above, under *Gratuité du crédit* and *Intérêt et principal*.

[Baudoucourt, J.-M. *Proudhon;* not in the catalog of the Bibliothèque Nationale or other listings examined.]

Baudrillart, Henri J. L. "M. P.-J. Proudhon en 1848," in his *Publicistes modernes* (Paris, 1863), 353–403.

————. "P.-J. Proudhon: Sa Correspondance et son historien [Sainte-

Beuve]," *Revue des deux mondes,* CIII (February 1, 1873), 584–616.
———. *La Propriété* (Paris, 1867). A defense against Proudhon and others.
———. "Du principe de la propriété," in his *Etudes de philosophie morale et d'économie politique* (Paris, 1858), II, 39–70.
Bauer, Edgar. "Proudhon," *Allgemeine Literatur-Zeitung* (Charlottenberg), V (April, 1844), 37–52.
Beauchery, Auguste. *Economie sociale de P.-J. Proudhon* (Lille, 1867).
Beauquier, Charles. "P.-J. Proudhon," *Revue littéraire de Franche-Comté,* V (1867), 65–82.
Bergmann, Heinrich. "Uber Proudhon und die Proudhon-Forschung: Zum 150. Geburtstag P.-J. Proudhons," *Geist und Tat,* XIV, 3 (1959), 78–81.
———. "Pierre-Joseph Proudhon. Zu einem neuen Auswahlband aus Proudhons Werk," *Geist und Tat,* XIX (1965), 50–51.
Bernard, Michel. "Visées eschatologiques dans les doctrines de Cournot, Proudhon, et Marx," thesis in law, Grenoble, 1954.
Bernès, Marcel. "La morale de Proudhon," in his *Etudes sur la philosophie morale au XIXᵉ siècle* (Paris, 1904).
Bernstein, Edouard. "Proudhon als Politiker und Publizist," *Neue Zeit,* Jahrgang XIV, Bd. II, Nr. 46 (1896), 609–21. This may be just translations from Proudhon, as later published by Bernstein in *Dokumente des Socialismus* (Berlin, 1902–3), I, 26–33; II, 267–76, 328–33, 377–81, 423–26.
Bertauld, A. "Théorie de la propriété par Proudhon" (a *compte-rendu*), *Revue critique de législation et de jurisprudence,* XXVII (1865), 549–61.
Berth, Edouard. "Le Centenaire de Proudhon," *Mouvement socialiste,* 3ᵉ série, IV (January 15, 1909), 49–55.
———. *Les Derniers Aspects du socialisme* (Paris, 1923), 78–110; revised and augmented edition of his *Nouveaux Aspects.* . . .
———. *Guerre des états ou guerre des classes* (Paris, 1924), passim, and esp. "Proudhon, Marx, Georges Sorel," 154–96.
———. *Les Nouveaux Aspects du socialisme* (Paris, 1908), 32–64.
———. "Le Procès de la démocratie," *Revue critique des idées et livres,* XIII, 72 (April 10, 1911), 9–46.
——— (writing under the pseudonym "Jean Darville"). "Proudhon," *Cahiers du Cercle Proudhon,* 1 (1912), 8–28.
———. "Proudhon en Sorbonne, *Indépendance,* III (April 1, 1912), 123–40. Opposing Bouglé's identification of Proudhon as a sociologist; Bouglé was a Sorbonne professor.

————. "Proudhon et Marx," *Du "Capital" aux "Réflexions sur la violence"* (Paris, 1932), 69–168—much of the rest of the book also deals with Proudhon; "Proudhon et Marx" also in Berth's *Révolution prolétarienne* (Paris, 1926).

———— (writing under the pseudonym "Jean Darville"). "Satellites de la ploutocratie," *Cahiers du Cercle Proudhon,* no. 5/6 (1912), 177–213.

Berthod, Aimé. "L'Attitude sociale de Proudhon," *La Révolution de 1848,* V (January–February, 1909), 783–815; also published separately (Lyon, 1909).

————. "L'Idée proudhonienne de la révolution," *Grande Revue,* CXII (1923), 481–93.

————. Introduction for Riv., II, 5–92.

————. "La Philosophie du travail et l'école," *Proudhon et notre temps,* ed. Amis de Proudhon (Paris, 1920), 53–98.

————. "Proudhon et les associations ouvrières," *Revue des études coopératives,* II (1922), 13–31.

————. *P.-J. Proudhon et la propriété. Un Socialisme pour les paysans* (Paris, 1910).

————. "Saint-Simon, Fourier, Proudhon," in his *Tradition philosophique et la pensée française* (Paris, 1922), 162–79.

————. "Les Tendances maîtresses de P.-J. Proudhon," *Revue socialiste,* XLIX (February & March, 1909), 120–37, 218–38.

————. "La Théorie de l'état et du gouvernement dans l'oeuvre de Proudhon," *Revue d'histoire économique et sociale,* XI (1923), 270–304.

[Bertrand, A. "Proudhon et les Lyonnais," *La Renaissance latine,* III (August 15, 1904), 226ff.; see this title in Part I-D, above.]

Beslay, Charles. *Mes Souvenirs* (Paris, 1873), 200–214, 479–82, et passim.

Besse, Dom. "Un Socialiste anti-démocrate," *L'Univers,* 1913, 22/8.

Besson, Edouard. *La Correspondance de P.-J. Proudhon dans ses rapports avec la Franche-Comté* (Besançon, 1878).

Bjoerklund, C. *P.-J. Proudhon, han liv och idéer* (Stockholm, 1915).

Blanc, Louis. "L'Etat-anarchie du citoyen Proudhon," *Le Nouveau Monde,* January 15, 1850.

————. "Hommes du peuple, l'état c'est vous! Réponse au citoyen Proudhon," *Le Nouveau Monde,* November 15, 1849.

[————. Article in *Revue du progrès social et littéraire,* August 18, 1840.]

Blanqui, Adolphe. (Report on Proudhon's first *mémoire* on property to the Académie des Sciences Morales et Politiques, August 29, 1840), *Le Moniteur universel*, September 27, 1840, pp. 2020–21.

Boas, George, ed. *Courbet and the Naturalistic Movement* (Baltimore, 1938), passim, esp. George Boas, "Courbet and His Critics," 45–57. Courbet was a close friend of Proudhon's; this discusses the latter's ideas on art as social criticism.

Boborykin, P. D. (writing as "D—eva"). "Posledniia desiat' let zhizni P.-Zh. Prudona," *Vestnik Evropy*, 1878, no. 6, pp. 522–77; no. 9, pp. 28–82.

———. "Pier-Zhozef Prudon," *Vestnik Evropy*, 1875, no. 3, pp. 154–85; no. 5, pp. 78–114; no. 7, pp. 32–77; no. 12, pp. 573–601.

Bochard. "Le Problème de la valeur et les théories de Proudhon et de Karl Marx," *Bulletin des sciences économiques et sociales*, Comité de Travail Historique, Congrès de 1897, 251–63.

Boixe, Prosper. *Théorie de l'impôt de M. Proudhon* (Paris, 1862).

Bonafous, H. "Lettre à Barbès . . . à tous les électeurs de France. M. Proudhon" (n.p., n.d. [1849]).

Boniface, Joseph (pseudonym of Louis-Joseph Defré). "La Belgique Calomniée. Réponse à P.-J. Proudhon" (Brussels, 1862).

———. "Joseph Boniface à P.-J. Proudhon. 2ᵉ réponse" (Brussels, 1862).

Bonjean, L. B. *Socialisme et sens commun* (Paris, 1850).

Bonnin, A. (Articles concerning Proudhon's writings on Italian unity), *La France*, September 25 & October 21, 1862.

Bose, Atindranath. *A History of Anarchism* (Calcutta: World Press Private, 1967), 115–48.

Bouglé, Celestin Charles A. "L'Alliance franco-allemande (1844)," in his *Chez les prophètes socialistes* (Paris, 1918).

———. "Bilan de Proudhonisme," *Revue de l'histoire économique et sociale*, XIX, 375–94; also in his *Socialismes français* (Paris, 1912), 139–65.

———. "La Méthode de Proudhon dans les premières mémoires sur la propriété (1840–1842)," *Revue d'économie politique*, XXIV (1910), 712–31.

———. "Pacifisme de Proudhon," *Grande Revue*, LXVII (June, 1911), 521–38.

———. "Pierre-Joseph Proudhon," *Encyclopaedia of the Social Sciences* (New York, 1930–35), XII, 575–76.

———. "La Première Philosophie de Proudhon," *Revue du mois*, X (October, 1910), 424–34.

———. "Le Progrès intellectuel de Proudhon avant 1848," *Revue du mois*, XII (September 10, 1911), 273–87.

———. "Proudhon écrivain," *Le Figaro*, January 7, 1911.

———. "Proudhon fédéraliste," *Revue du mois*, XX (1919), 502–13; also in *Proudhon et notre temps*, ed. Amis de Proudhon (Paris, 1920), 239–55.

———. "Proudhon sociologue," *Revue de métaphysique et de morale*, XVIII (September, 1910), 614–48.

———. "La Résurrection de Proudhon," *Revue de Paris*, 17ᵉ Année, tome V (September 15, 1910), 357–80.

——— et al. "La Sociologie de Proudhon," report of a meeting held February 10, 1912, *Bulletin de la Société Française de Philosophie*, XII (April, 1912), 169–214.

———. *La Sociologie de Proudhon* (Paris, 1911).

———. "Die soziologen Anschauungen Proudhons in den 'Contradictions économiques,'" *Archiv für die Geschichte des Sozialismus und der Arbeit*, I (1911), 98–119.

Boulen, Alfred-Georges. *Les Idées solidaristes de Proudhon* (Paris, 1922). Written to provide an exposition of the ideas of Léon Bourgeois.

Bourdeau, J. *Socialistes et sociologues* (Paris, 1905), 65–73.

Bourgeat, Jacques. *Proudhon. Père du socialisme français* (Paris, 1949).

Bourgeau, Pierre. *P.-J. Proudhon et la critique de la démocratie*, thesis, University of Paris (Strasbourg, 1933).

Bourgeois, Nicolas. *Proudhon, le fédéralisme et la paix*, thesis, Faculté de Droit, University of Paris (Paris, 1926); also in his *Les Théories du droit international chez Proudhon* (Paris, 1927).

Bourgin, Georges. "Notes d'archives pour les commentaires de Proudhon" (Paris, n.d.).

———, and Bourgin, Hubert, *Le Socialisme français de 1789 à 1848* (Paris, 1912), 76–82.

Bourgin, Hubert. *Fourier: Contribution à l'étude du socialisme français* (Paris, 1905), 545–50, 556–605 passim.

———. "P.-J. Proudhon," *Grande Encyclopédie*, XXVII, 833–39.

———. *Proudhon* (Paris, 1901).

Bourguin, Maurice. "Des Rapports entre Proudhon et Karl Marx," Université de France, Séance de rentrée des Facultés de Lille, 3 novembre 1892 (Lille, 1892); also in *Revue d'économie politique*, March, 1893; and in *Le Contrat social*, IX, 2 (March–April, 1965), 96–107.

Bouzareingues, Cl. Girou de. "Proudhon imprimeur," *Bibliographie de*

France, 154ᵉ année, 5ᵉ série, no. 29 (July 20, 1965), 221–27; no. 30 (July 27, 1965), 231–36.

Bowle, John. "Proudhon's Attack on the State," in his *Politics and Opinion in the Nineteenth Century* (New York, 1954), 152–67.

Boyenval, A. "Proudhon et la sophistique, à propos d'un livre récent [that of Desjardins, cited below]," *Réforme sociale,* October 16, 1896, 525–38.

Brandwajn, Rachmiel. "La Langue et l'esthétique de Proudhon," Göttingen, Philosophy faculty dissertation, August 22, 1947; *Wroclawskie Towarzystwo Naukowe,* Seria A (Humanistyczna), no. 30 (1952), 1–116.

Bravo, Pedro, ed. *Socialismo premarxista: Babeuf, Saint-Simon, Sismondi, Fourier, Owen, Leroux, Blanc, Blanqui, Proudhon, Weitling* (Caracas, 1961); an anthology.

Bremer, Karl Heinz. "Napoleon III und Proudhon," in his "Der Sozialistische Kaiser," *Die Tat,* XXX (June, 1938), 164–66.

Bresson, Jacques. *Liberté du taux de l'intérêt . . . avec . . . un examen du système de banque d'échange de M. Proudhon* (Paris, 1848).

Breynat, Jules. *Les Socialistes depuis février* (Paris, 1850), 93–128. 3rd ed. of his *Les Socialistes modernes.*

Brogan, Denis W. *Proudhon* (London, 1934).

Brunello, Bruno. "Ferrari e Proudhon," *Rivista internazionale di filosofia del diritto,* XXVIII (1951), 58–75.

Buber, Martin. *Paths in Utopia,* trans. R. F. C. Hull (London, 1949; Boston, 1958), 24–37 et passim.

Butchart, Montgomery. "Marx and Proudhon," *The Criterion,* XVII (April, 1938), 445–56.

"Calomnie, Mme." "Lettre de Mme Calomnie au citoyen Proudhon pour le recommander aux électeurs" (Paris, 1848).

Carr, E. H. "Proudhon: Robinson Crusoe of Socialism," in his *Studies in Revolution* (New York, 1964), 38–55.

Casals, Victor María. "Consideraciones a raiz de un centenario: Pierre-Joseph Proudhon," *Revista de instituta de ciencias sociales* (Barcelona), 1965, no. 5, 231–42.

Castille, Hippolyte. *P.-J. Proudhon* (Paris, 1858), one of his series, *Portraits historiques au 19me siècle.*

Castagnary, Jules A. "Comment Proudhon a quitté Bruxelles," in his *Les Libres propos* (Paris, 1864), 281–90.

Cauvain, Henri. (Untitled *compte-rendu* on Proudhon's *Révolution sociale*), *Le Constitutionnel,* August 5, 1852, p. 3.

Centre National d'Etude des Problèmes de Sociologie et d'Economie Européennes. *L'Actualité de Proudhon: Colloque des 24 et 25 novembre 1965* (Brussels: Editions de l'Institut de Sociologie de l'Université de Bruxelles, 1967).

Ce que peuvent nous apprendre les disciplines françaises: Saint-Simonisme, Fouriérisme, Proudhonisme (Paris, 1919).

Cercle Proudhon. *Cahiers du Cercle Proudhon*, 6 numbers in 4 issues (in 8°), 1912; 1 issue (in 12°), 1914. The Cercle Proudhon was closely associated with the Action Française; see the text for more details.

Chabrier, Jacques. *L'Idée de la révolution d'après Proudhon*, thesis, University of Paris, Faculté de Droit (Paris, 1925).

Cham (pseudonym of Amédée de Noé). *La Banque Proudhon et autres banques socialistes* (Paris [1849]), 60 caricatures, including 49 of Proudhon.

———. *P.-J. Proudhon en voyage* (Paris [1849?]), 60 caricatures, including 53 of Proudhon.

———. *Proudhoniana, ou les socialistes modernes commentés et illustrés. Album dédié aux propriétaires* (Paris [1848]); includes 35 caricatures of Proudhon. Cham also did other Proudhon caricatures not included in these three pamphlets.

Chanson, Paul. "Proudhon et la propriété chrétienne," *L'Atelier*, July 17, 1943.

———. "Le Suffrage rationnel," *L'Atelier*, August 28, 1943.

Charles-Brun, J. "La Doctrine de Proudhon," in Jean Hennessy and J. Charles-Brun, *Le Principe fédératif* (Paris, 1940).

Charnay, M. "Mutuellisme," *Grande Encyclopédie*, XXIV, 650–51.

Châteaugiron, Denis de. *L'Anti-Proudhon* (Rennes, 1860).

Chaudey, Gustave. (Article on Proudhon's *La Guerre*), *Le Courrier du dimanche*, July 21, 1861.

Chauvelot, Barnabé. "Les Faux savants: P.-J. Proudhon," *La Revue du monde catholique*, V (1863), 148–55, 211–17; VI, 257–73.

———. *Proudhon et son livre, La Révolution sociale* (Paris, 1852).

Ch'ên, Kuei-hsi. *La Dialectique dans l'oeuvre de Proudhon*, thesis, University of Paris (Paris, 1936).

Cherbuliez, A. E. "Lettres à M. Proudhon, sur le droit de propriété" (Paris, 1849); from the *Journal des économistes*, XXII (December, 1848).

Chevallier, J.-J. "Le Dernier Mot de P.-J. Proudhon," *Revue des deux mondes*, March 1, 1965, 30–45.

————. "Le Fédéralisme de Proudhon et de ses disciples," in Gaston Berger et al., *Le Fédéralisme* (Paris, 1956), 87–127.

Chiaromonte, Nicola. "P.-J. Proudhon: An Uncomfortable Thinker," *Politics*, III (January, 1946), 27–29.

Clément, Henry. "Proudhon et ses doctrines sur la propriété," *La Réforme sociale*, Sér. 6, X (November 16, 1910), 565–83.

Cogniot, Georges. "Le Centenaire de 'Philosophie de la misère,'" *La Pensée*, no. 9 (October–December, 1946), 27–35; no. 10 (January–February, 1947), 43–54.

————. "Proudhon et la démagogie bonapartiste: Un Socialiste en coquetterie avec le pouvoir personnel" (Paris, 1958).

Cole, G. D. H. *A History of Socialist Thought* (London, 1953), I, 201–18, et passim.

Colins, César de. *De la Justice dans la science hors l'Eglise et hors la révolution* (Paris, 1860), 3 vols.

————. *A M. P.-J. Proudhon sur son ouvrage intitulé, De la Justice dans la révolution et dans l'Eglise* (Paris, 1858).

————. *Qu'est-ce que la science sociale?* (Paris, 1853), I, 234–336.

Communism and Free Trade, or Theory and Practice Exemplified, Being a Glance at the Proudhonian and Manchester schools ("by an Attentive Observer") (London, 1849).

(*Compte-rendu* of C. Bouglé, *La Sociologie de Proudhon*), *Journal des économistes*, April 15, 1912, pp. 160–61.

(*Compte-rendu* of the first *mémoire* on property), *Revue politique, industrielle, scientifique et littéraire*, October 11, 1840.

Comte, Auguste. Two letters to Proudhon, reproduced in Pierre Haubtmann, "La Philosophie sociale de Proudhon," q.v.

Constandse, Anton L. *Anarchisme van de Daad* (The Hague: Kruseman, 1969), 37–40.

Coquelin, Charles. "Du Dernier Ouvrage de M. P.-J. Proudhon. Idée générale de la révolution au XIXᵉ siècle," *Journal des économistes*, XXX (December, 1851), 359–67.

Costes, A. "Les Vicissitudes de l'édition Lacroix des oeuvres complètes de P.-J. Proudhon," *Revue d'histoire économique et sociale*, XXXVI (1958), 444–63.

Courbet, Gustave. "Proudhon auf den Totenbett. Lithographie," *Kunst und Künstler*, XXVIII, heft 2 (1929), 83. Reproduction of a Courbet lithograph; the same picture also appears as the frontispiece in Jean Maitron, ed., *Dictionnaire biographique du mouvement ouvrier français* (Paris, 1964–), III. Courbet executed several portraits of Proudhon, of which the best known and most interesting is "Proudhon et sa famille," in the Petit Palais, Paris.

Croome, Honor. "La Propriété, c'est le vol," *The Spectator*, CLXXXVII, no. 6430 (September 21, 1951), 354–55.

Cuvillier, Armand (pseudonym of G. d'Ardillon Pervieax). Introduction to Riv., V, 5–31.

———. "Marx et Proudhon," in A. Cornut, A. Cuvillier, Paul Labérenne, and L. Prenant, *A la lumière du Marxisme* (Paris, 1937), II, 151–238; also in Cuvillier's *Hommes et idéologies de 1840* (Paris, 1956), 145–226; Proudhon is also discussed in the latter book, 138–44.

———. *Proudhon* (Paris, 1937). Biographical and analytic introduction, with a selection of texts.

Cuvillier-Fleury, Alfred A. (Article on Proudhon and his *Confessions*), *Le Journal des débats*, November 11, 1849; and in his *Portraits politiques et révolutionnaires*, 3rd ed. (Paris, 1889), II, 46–63.

———. (Article on Proudhon's *Révolution sociale*), *Le Journal des débats*, September 12, 1852.

Dagnino, M. *Ensayos criticos sobre algunas teorias filosóficas de la Divinidad (Spinosa . . . Proudhon)* (Genova, 1874).

Dallari, Gino. "L'Idea della guerra nel pensiero di un socialista: P.-J. Proudhon," in his *Guerra e Giustizia* (Milan, 1918), 187–261.

Dallmayr, Winifried R. "Proudhon et la coexistance, une interprétation de 'La Guerre et la paix,'" *Revue internationale d'histoire politique et constitutionnelle*, XXIII (1956), 205–17.

Dameth, C.-M.-H. (attributed to Dameth, published anonymously). *Défense du fouriérisme. Réponse à MM. Proudhon, Lamennais, Reybaud, Louis Blanc, [etc.]* (Paris?, 1841). Actually a response only to Proudhon. His third *mémoire* on property was itself written in response to this tract; a detailed résumé is given in Riv., X, 159–64.

Dana, Charles A. "Proudhon and His 'Bank of the People'" (New York, 1896); first published in Dana's *New York Tribune*, then in William Henry Channing's weekly, *The Spirit of the Age*, 1849.

Daniels, Alfred. "Welt jenseits von Kapitalismus und Kommunismus. Eine Einführung in die Lehre Proudhons," *Gemeinschaft und Politik*, XII (1964), 272–86.

Daudet, Léon. "Proudhon et la révolution sociale," in his *Flammes* (Paris, 1930), 53–89.

Delimal, N. Odilon. "L'Empereur, le pape, et la démocratie. Lettre à M. Proudhon" (Brussels, 1862).

Delord, Taxile. (Article on Proudhon's arguments in *Les démocrates assermentés*), *Le Siècle*, May 9, 1863.

Demoinet, Ferdinand. *L'Idée de l'état chez les théoriciens anarchistes*, thesis, University of Paris, Faculté de Droit (Paris, 1941), 25–83.

Denis, Hector. "Proudhon et les principes de la banque d'échange," *Annales de l'Institut des Sciences Sociales de Bruxelles*, Année I; in German, "Proudhon: Die Principien der Tauschbank," trans. J. Borchardt, *Zeitschrift für Volkwirtschaft, Soz.-Pol., und Verwaltung*, V (1896), 283–95.

Depitre, E. (*Compte-rendu* of Droz, *P.-J. Proudhon*), *Revue d'histoire des doctrines économiques*, 1909, no. 2, 212ff.

"Le Dernier Livre de Proudhon" [on *La Pornocratie*], *Revue des deux mondes*, 3ᵉ période, XI (1875), 467–74.

Derome, Léopold. "Proudhon et son oeuvre," *Revue de France*, Année V, vol. 13, no. 38 (1875), 370–90.

Deschanel, Emile. "Les idées de Proudhon sur la femme," report by R. Van der Berg of a lecture by Deschanel, *Revue des cours littéraires*, VII (1870), 282–84.

Desjardins, Arthur. "Conférence St. Thomas d'Acquin. Proudhon conférence faite par M. Arthur Desjardins . . . à Besançon, le dimanche 12 décembre 1897" (Besançon, 1898).

———. *P.-J. Proudhon* (Paris, 1896), 2 vols.

———. "Proudhon après le coup d'état," *Séances et travaux de l'Académie des Sciences Morales et Politiques*, CXLV (1896), 425–43.

———. "Proudhon et le christianisme," *Correspondant*, CLXXXII (1896), 3–31.

———. "Proudhon, sa vie, ses oeuvres, sa doctrine," *Correspondant*, CLXXI (1895), 820–27.

———. "Le Socialiste Proudhon et le nihiliste Herzen," *Séances et travaux de l'Académie des Sciences Morales et Politiques*, CXLIII (1895), 820–27.

Dessaint, J. "Proudhon ou Karl Marx," *Nouvelle Revue*, Ser. 4, XLIII (1919), 97–106.

Dessirier, J. B. *Le Système Social de P.-J. Proudhon* (Paris, 1849).

Diehl, Karl. *P.-J. Proudhon. Seine Lehre und sein Leben* (Jena, 1888–96), 3 vols.

———. *P.-J. Proudhon. Seine Lehre und sein Leben*, inaugural dissertation, Philosophy Faculty, University of Halle (Halle, 1888); a preliminary version of vol. 1 of the preceding item.

———. *Proudhons praktische Vorschläge zur Lösung der sozialen Frage*, dissertation, Philosophy Faculty, University of Halle (Halle, 1890); Ch. 2, vol. 2 of Diehl's three-volume work on Proudhon, cited above.

Dietz, Jean. "L'Actualité de Proudhon," *L'Alsace française* (Strasbourg), Année X, no. 40 (October 5 & 12, 1930), 297–303.

Dillard, Dudley. "Keynes and Proudhon," *Journal of Economic History*, II (1942), 63–76.

———. "Proudhon, Gesell, and Keynes: An Investigation of Some 'Anti-Marxian Socialist' Antecedents of Keynes' *General Theory of Employment, Interest, and Banking*," Ph.D. dissertation, University of California, Berkeley, 1940.

Dimier, Louis. *Les Maîtres de la contre-révolution au XIXe siècle* (Paris, 1907); lectures on Proudhon delivered at the Institut de l'Action Française, February–June, 1906.

Dolléans, Edouard. "A propos d'un nouveau livre sur Proudhon [Droz, P.-J. Proudhon]," *Revue d'économie politique*, May, 1909, 321ff.; also printed separately (Paris, 1909).

———. *Histoire du mouvement ouvrier* (Paris, 1936–53), 3 vols., passim.

——— and Georges Duveau. Introduction for Riv., IX, 7–106.

———. *Proudhon* (Paris, 1948).

——— and J.-L. Puech. *Proudhon et la révolution de 1848* (Paris, 1948).

———. "La Rencontre de Proudhon et de Marx (1843–1847)," *Revue d'histoire moderne*, XI (January–February, 1936), 5–30.

Dommanget, Maurice. *Les Grands Educateurs socialistes: Proudhon* (Paris, 1950).

Donoso Cortès, J. F. M. *Ensayo sobre el catolicismo, el liberalismo y el socialismo* (Madrid, 1851; Buenos Aires, 1943); conceived in part as a response to Proudhon.

Douglas, Dorothy W. "P.-J. Proudhon: A Prophet of 1848," *American Journal of Sociology*, XXXIV (1929), 781–803; XXXV (1930), 35–59.

———. (Review of Henry Cohen, ed., *Proudhon's Solution of the Social Problem*), *American Economic Review*, XVIII (1928), 721–22.

Domergue, Gabriel. "Proudhon et le féminisme," *La Quinzaine*, Année VIII, vol. XLIX, 174 (January 16, 1902), 222–35.

Draper, Hal. "A Note on the Father of Anarchism," *New Politics*, VIII, 1 (Winter, 1969), 79–93.

Dréolle, Ernest. (Article on Proudhon's *Si les traités*), *La Patrie*, December 2, 1863.

Droz, Edouard (lyrics), and Ratez, E. (music). "Hommage des petits bousbots à Proudhon et à Fourier," choral music sung by school children at the soirée given at the Kursaal de Besançon, June

25, 1904, by the Université Populaire in honor of Fourier and Proudhon. MS., Bibliothèque Municipal de Besançon.

Droz, Edouard. *P.-J. Proudhon* (Paris, 1909).

Drumont, Edouard. "Proudhon et Karl Marx," in his *Les Tréteaux du succés: Figures de bronze ou statues de neige* (Paris, 1901), 315–32.

Dufresne, A., and Pelloutier, F. "Proudhon philosophe," *Revue socialiste*, XXX, 178 (October, 1899), 463–85.

Dumay, Gabriel. *Etude sur la vie et les travaux de Proudhon* (Autun, 1878); originally published in the *Mémoires* of the Congrès Scientifique de France, 42nd session.

Duprat, Jeanne. "La Conception proudhonienne des facteurs économiques de la guerre et de la paix," *Revue internationale de sociologie*, XXXVII (March, 1929).

———. "L'Evolution de la conception du travail," *Revue internationale de sociologie*, XXXIX (1931), 217–46.

———. "Le Paupérisme, facteur de bellicisme d'après Proudhon," *Annales de l'Institut International de Sociologie*, XVI (1932), 241–54, and in her *Sociologie de la guerre et de la paix* (Paris, 1932).

———. ["Proudhon, penseur original," *Revue mensuelle*, January-February, 1931.]

———. *Proudhon; sociologue et moraliste* (Paris, 1929).

Duprat, M.-J. "P.-J. Proudhon, et le mutuellisme," *Bulletin de la section sciences économiques et sociales, Comité des Travaux Historiques et Scientifiques*, 1932, 101–29.

Dupré, Louis. *The Philosophical Foundations of Marxism* (New York, 1966), 181–88 et passim.

Duveau, Georges. (*Compte-rendu* of books on Proudhon by Guy-Grand, Dolléans, and Haubtmann), *Cahiers internationaux de sociologie*, V (1948), 181–83.

———. Introductions for Riv., IX (with Edouard Dolléans), 7–106; XIII, 1–30, 327–50.

———. *La Pensée ouvrière sur l'education pendant la seconde république et le second empire* (Paris, 1948), 134–38, 146–55, 199–201, 318–22, et passim.

———. "P.-J. Proudhon pendant la 2ᵐᵉ République," *La Révolution de 1848 et les révolutions du XIXᵉ siècle*, XXXIII, 29–39.

———. "Proudhon, Bakounine et les réactions ouvrières des années 60," *Esprit*, April, 1937, 5–14.

Eltzbacher, Paul. *Der Anarchismus* (Berlin, 1900), Ch. 4.

Ely, Richard T. *French and German Socialism in Modern Times* (New York, 1883), 124–42.

"Encore un mot sur la publication des oeuvres posthumes de Proudhon," *La Petite Revue*, 108 (1865), 29–31.

Engels, Friedrich. (Notes on Proudhon's *La Guerre et la paix*), in Russian translation, *Arkhiv Marksa i Engel'sa* (Moscow), 2nd series, X (1948), 35–39.

———. "Vorwart zur ersten deutschen Ausgabe *Das Elend der Philosophie*" (Stuttgart, 1885), with additional brief preface for the 2nd German ed. (1892), in Marx and Engels, *Historische-kritische Gesamtausgabe* (Moscow, 1927–35), I, vol. VI, 119–228.

———. "Wie Proudhon die Wohnungsfrage löst," in his *Zur Wohnungsfrage*, first published in *Der Volksstaat* (Leipzig), 1872; in Marx and Engels, *Werke* (Berlin: Dietz, 1958–67), XVIII, 213–32.

Engländer. "Der Sozialismus in Frankreich seit der Februar-Revolution: Proudhon," *Deutsche Monatschrift*, 1850 & 1851.

Epple, Paul. "Von Proudhon zu Silvio Gesell," *Fz. Freiwirtschaftliche Zeitung* (Erfurt), 1933, no. 31, 1–48; no. 32, 1–47.

Estignard, Alexandre. *Portraits franc-comtois* (Paris, 1887), 3 vols.; includes Proudhon.

Faguet, Emile. *Politiques et moralistes du dix-neuvième siècle* (Paris, 1900), III, 115–84; this sketch of Proudhon first appeared in the *Revue de Paris*, III (1896), 308–80.

———. "Jésus selon Proudhon," *Revue politique et littéraire*, V (1896), 810–14.

Faucher, Léon. "Du Communisme et du socialisme," in his *Mélanges d'économie politique* (Paris, 1856), II, 426–45; also in Henri Baudrillart, *Lectures choisies d'économie politique* (Paris, 1884), 74–83.

Febvre, Lucien. "Une Question d'influence. Proudhon et le syndicalisme contemporain," *Revue de synthèse historique*, XIX (1909); 179–93; published separately (Versailles, 1909).

Fernand-Demeure. "P.-J. Proudhon d'après ses lettres," *Le Nouveau Monde*, XI, 462–68.

Ferrari, Aldo. "Il pensiero socialisto europeo antico e moderno," *Nuova Rivista Storica*, XIII (1929), 420–52 (Proudhon, 433–36).

Ferrari, Giuseppe. "P.-J. Proudhon," *Nuova Antologia*, X, pt. 1 (1875), 809–47; also in *Pensiero e voluntà*, III (1926), 214–16, 235–40, 264–67, 287–88, 334–36, 380–84; in his *La disfatta della Francia* (Modena, 1943); and in C.-A. Sainte-Beuve, *P.-J. Proudhon* (Milan, 1947).

Ferraz, Marin. "Proudhon ou le socialisme semi-rationaliste," in his *Etude sur la philosophie en France au XIXe siècle* (Paris, 1877, 1882), 427–71.

Fichte, Immanuel Hermann. *System der Ethik* (Leipzig, 1850–53), I, 800–820.

Filippov, M. "Prudon kak ideolog melkoi burzhuazii," *Nauchnoe Obozrenie*, 1898, no. 2.

Florence, Jean. "Pierre-Joseph Proudhon," *La Phalange*, IV, 32 (1909), 690–95.

Földes, Bela. "Proudhon," *Közgazdasági Szemle*, X (1910), 663–93.

Forcade, E. "La Guerre du socialisme. I. La Philosophie révolutionnaire et sociale. MM. de Lamennais et Proudhon. II. L'Economie politique révolutionnaire et sociale," *Revue des deux mondes*, December 1 & 15, 1848.

Foucher de Careil, L. A. "L'Economie politique et la dialectique de Proudhon," *Journal des économistes*, 2ᵉ série, XLVIII (December, 1865), 388–401.

Fournière, Eugène. "Le Centenaire de Proudhon," *Revue socialiste*, XLIX (January, 1909), 1–4.

———. "Fourier et Proudhon," *Revue socialiste*, XL (1904), 129–45.

———. "Les Systèmes socialistes (de St.-Simon à Proudhon)," *Revue socialiste*, XXXVII (1903), 129–52, 257–87, 385–414, 663–90; XXXVIII (1903), 150–79, 257–86, 395–423, 513–46.

———. *Les Théories socialistes au XIXᵉ siècle, de Babeuf à Proudhon* (Paris, 1904); essentially the same as the preceding item.

Frablan. "Schopenhauer et Proudhon, moralistes," *Revue socialiste*, XVIII (1893), 331–34.

France. Chamber of Deputies. MS. documents concerning prosecution of Proudhon in 1849. Archives Nationales, C908.

Franck, Adolphe. "Droit de la nature et des gens: La Paix et la guerre," lecture reported by Oscar Muller, *Revue des cours littéraires*, I (1863–64), 1–4, 22–24, 32–34.

Franco, Augusto. "Ritorno a Proudhon," *Divenire sociale*, I, 14 & 15 (July 16 & August 1, 1906).

Franz, J. "Der Doctrinaire philosophische Idealismus in der Socialen Frage. Eine Antwort auf Mülbergers 'Die Theorie der Anarchie,'" *Neue Gesellschaft* (Zürich), 1878.

"A French Anarchist," *Fraser's Magazine*, LXXXV (1872), 277–88.

"The French Revolution of 1848," *North American Review*, LXXX (1855), 273–306; article on Proudhon's *Confessions* and books by others.

Friedmann, Georges. "Proudhonien? Optimiste?" *Sociologie de travail*, IV (October–December, 1962), 395–98.

Fubini, Ranzo. "Rileggendo Ferrari: Ferrari e Proudhon," *Giornale degli economisti e rivista di statistica*, LII, 1 (1937), 1–17.

Gall, Jean. *Essai sur la pensée de P.-J. Proudhon—ses idées morales, religieuses et sociales*, thesis, Faculty of Protestant Theology, University of Toulouse at Montauban (Montauban, 1897).

Galland, Pierre. "Proudhon et l'ordre," *Cahiers du Cercle Proudhon*, no. 1 (January–February, 1912), 28–33.

Gamache, Pierre. "La Vie, les idées, l'oeuvre de P.-J. Proudhon d'après sa correspondance. Essai de classement méthodique de la correspondance de P.-J. Proudhon," MS., 1424 pp., Institut français d'histoire sociale, F°45. Elaborate classification of topics and names in 1,871 letters, with many extracts. Described by Gamache in *L'Actualité de l'histoire*, 10 (January, 1955), 42–43.

———. "Treize Lettres inédites de P.-J. Proudhon à un notaire," *L'Actualité de l'histoire*, 9 (1954), 26–30; comments on letters published in the same issue (see "Treize Nouvelles Lettres," above, section I-D).

Gandon ("Ouvrier Cordonnier"). "Que serait une société sans dieu, sans gouvernement, et sans propriété? Ou Vue finale du Proudhonisme, etc." (Paris, 1851).

Garnier, Joseph. (Sketch of Proudhon), in *Le Droit au travail à l'Assemblée Nationale*, ed. Jos. Garnier (Paris, 1848), 388ff.; accompanying material by Proudhon, cited above in section I-E as *Le Droit au travail*, etc.

———. "Ouvrages de M. P.-J. Proudhon," *Journal des économistes*, VI (October, 1843), 290–96.

Gastineau, Benjamin. *Les Génies de la liberté* (Paris, 1865), 137–56.

———. *Les Socialistes. P.-J. Proudhon, sa vie, ses oeuvres. Avec les discours prononcés sur la tombe de Proudhon* (Paris, 1865).

Gaultier, P. "Proudhon," *Revue bleue*, May 25, 1912, pp. 666–69; *compte-rendu* of Bouglé, *La Sociologie de Proudhon*, q.v.

———. "Proudhon et la science sociale," *Bulletin du Comité des Travaux Historiques et Scientifiques*, Ministère de l'Instruction Publique et des Beaux-Arts, 1912, 125–30.

Gaussen, Yvan. *Du fédéralisme de Proudhon au félibrige de Mistral* (Nîmes, 1928).

Gazier, Georges. "Les Maisons natales de Fourier et de Proudhon," *Mémoires de la Société d'Emulation du Doubs*, 7e série, VIII (1903–4); and published separately (Besançon, 1905).

George, William Henry. "French Political Theory since 1848, with Special Reference to Syndicalism," dissertation, Harvard University, 1921, Harvard College Library, pp. 194–215.

Gide, Charles, and Rist, Charles. *Histoire des doctrines économiques,* 7ᵉ édition, rev. & aug. (Paris, 1947), I, 322–57 et passim.

Gillouin, René. "Le Mysticisme social. Fourier. Proudhon," *Grande Revue,* CV (March, 1921), 57–70.

Ginzburg, Leone. "Garibaldi e Herzen," *La Cultura,* XI, 4 (1932), 726–49.

Girardin, Emile de. "Question du jour," *La Presse,* November 11, 1864; and in Riv., XIV, 205–6.

––––––. "L'Unité italienne et l'union italienne," *La Presse,* November 25, 1865; and in Riv., XIV, 250–52.

Giraud d'Hubert, J. "La Propriété est un vol. Lettre au citoyen Proudhon" (n.p., 1848).

Goriely, Georges. "Proudhon et les nationalités," *L'Actualité de Proudhon,* ed. Centre National d'Etude des Problèmes de Sociologie et d'Economie Européennes (Brussels, 1967), 151–61.

Gramsci, Antonio. "Sorel, Proudhon, de Man," in his *Oeuvres choisies* (Geneva, 1959), 110–20.

Grand-Carteret, John. "Proudhon et la caricature," *Franche-Comté et Monts-Jura,* December, 1922.

"La Grande Synthèse de P.-J. Proudhon," *La Critique philosophique,* II (1872), 375–83.

Gray, Alexander. *The Socialist Tradition* (London, 1946), 230–56.

Grégoire, Ernest. *Proudhon au tribunal de la pénitence* (Paris, 1850).

Grégoire, H., and Poinsot, M. C., eds. "Le Centenaire de Proudhon," *Grande Revue,* LIII (January 10, 1909), 132–43; a six-page *mémoire* by Grégoire and Poinsot, followed by short notes by a number of others.

Grewe, Wilhelm G. "Krieg und Frieden: Proudhons Theorie des Völkerrechts," *Zeitschrift für Politik,* XXX (1940), 233–45.

Grilli, C. "Due sistemi di economica politica (P.-J. Proudhon e A. Loria)," *Rivista internazionale di scienze soziale,* November, 1909, 340–90.

Grimala Lubanski, Henry. *La Vérité sur les lettres de M. J. Proudhon* (Turin, 1862); diatribe of a Polish emigré against Proudhon.

Grondahl, Britta. *Pierre-Joseph Proudhon, socialist, anarkist, federalist* (Stockholm, 1959).

Grossmann, Stefan. "Proudhon," *Die Zeit,* nr. 224, January 14, 1899.

Grün, Karl. *Die Sociale Bewegung in Frankreich und Belgien* (Darmstadt, 1845), 401–71.

Guérard, Albert L. *French Prophets of Yesterday* (London, 1913), 172–79.

Guérin, Daniel. *Anarchisme* (Paris, 1965).

———. "Proudhon et l'amour unisexuel," *Arcadie*, December, 1964, January, 1965.

———. "Proudhon et l'autogestion ouvrière," *L'Actualité de Proudhon*, ed. Centre National d'Etude des Problèmes de Sociologie et d'Economie Européennes (Brussels, 1967), 67–87; in his *Pour un Marxisme libertaire* (Paris, 1969), 99–128.

Guéroult, Adolphe. "La Fédération et l'unité en Italie par P.-J. Proudhon," *L'Opinion nationale*, October 28 & 30, 1862.

[Guesde, Jules. "Anarchie et socialisme," *Le Socialiste*, February 27, 1886.]

Guia, M. "Proudhon et la proprietà," *Pagine libere*, nr. 15, 78–87.

Guillaume, James. (Anarchism according to Proudhon), written in French, translated into Russian by Zaytsev, published by Bakunin (Zurich, 1873?); apparently no publication in French.

———. "Proudhon communiste," *La Vie ouvrière*, August–September, 1911, 306–12.

Guiral, Pierre. "Mesure de Proudhon," *Revue d'histoire moderne et contemporaine*, VIII (1961), 161–68.

Gurvitch, Georges. "La Dialectique chez Proudhon," in his *Dialectique et sociologie* (Paris, 1962), 96–117.

———. "Les Fondateurs français de la sociologie contemporaine: II. P.-J. Proudhon," mimeographed Cours de Sorbonne, 1952–53 (Paris: Centre de Documentation Universitaire, 1955).

———. *L'Idée du droit social* (Paris, 1929), 327–406.

———. "Pour le centenaire de la mort de Pierre-Joseph Proudhon. Proudhon et Marx: Une confrontation," mimeographed Cours de Sorbonne, 1963–64 (Paris: Centre de Documentation Universitaire, 1964).

———. *Proudhon* (Paris, 1965).

———. "Proudhon et Marx," *Cahiers internationaux de sociologie*, XL (1966), 7–16; and in *L'Actualité de Proudhon*, ed. Centre National d'Etude des Problèmes de Sociologie et d'Economie Européennes (Brussels, 1967), 89–97.

———. "Proudhon und die Gegenwart," *Archiv für Rechts- und Wirtschaftsphilosophie*, 1928, 537–62.

Guy-Grand, Georges. "Aspects de la justice selon Proudhon," *Revue philosophique de la France et de l'étranger*, CIX (1930), 286–315.

———. "L'Ere Proudhon," *Proudhon et notre temps*, ed. Amis de Proudhon (Paris, 1920), 1–32.

———. Introduction for Riv., VIII, 5–167.

————. "Nietzsche et Proudhon," *Grande Revue*, LIX (January 25, 1910), 146–62; and in his *La Philosophie syndicaliste* (Paris, 1911), 195–237.

————. "La Philosophie populaire selon Proudhon," *Revue de l'histoire économique et sociale*, XVIII (1930), 93–114.

————. *Pour connaître la pensée de Proudhon* (Paris, 1947).

————. "Proudhon critique littéraire et philosophe," *Grande Revue*, LXXVII (February 25, 1913), 793–813.

————. "Proudhon: L'Eglise et la religion," *Europe*, XXI, 617–30.

————. "Proudhon est-il philosophe?" *Revue bleue*, LXVIII (1930), 268–73.

————. "Sur la pensée politique de Proudhon," *Revue philosophique de la France et de l'étranger*, CXLIII (1953), 99–106.

[Hack, F. "P. J. Proudhon," *Tübinger Zeitschrift*, 1865.]

————. "Proudhon. Einer Beitrag zur Geschichte des Socialismus," *Zeitschrift für gesammte Staatswissenschaft*, XXVII (1871), 363–92.

Haedelt, Werner. *Die Asthetik Proudhons*, dissertation, Munich University (Krefeld, 1958).

Halévy, Daniel. *Essais sur le mouvement ouvrier en France* (Paris, 1901), 279–88.

————. Introduction for Riv., VII, 5–55

————. *La Jeunesse de Proudhon* (Paris, 1913).

————. *Le Mariage de Proudhon* (Paris, 1955).

————. *Proudhon d'après ses carnets inédits (1843–1847)*, "Hier et Demain," no. 9 (Paris, 1944).

————. "Proudhon-Péguy," *Terre des Hommes*, February 2, 1946.

————. "Proudhon, Sorel, Péguy," *Fédération*, November, 1947.

————. "Sur l'interprétation de Proudhon," *Journal des débats*, January 2 & 3, 1913, p. 3.

————. *La Vie de Proudhon, 1809–1847* (Paris, 1948); includes his *La Jeunesse de Proudhon*, Sainte-Beuve's *P.-J. Proudhon*, and appendices and comments by Halévy.

Hamerton, P. G. "Proudhon as a Writer on Art," *Fortnightly Review*, IV (1866), 142–83; and in his *Thoughts* (1871).

Hammacher, Emil. *Das Philosophische-ökonomische System des Marxismus* (Leipzig, 1909), 79–86 et passim.

Hamon, H. D. *Études sur le socialisme* (Paris, 1849).

Harbold, William H. "Progressive Humanity: In the Philosophy of P.-J. Proudhon," *Review of Politics*, XXI, 1 (January, 1969), 28–47.

Harley, J. H. "Proudhon and the Labor Movement," *Socialist Review*, III (1909), 273–83.

Harmel, Maurice (pseudonym of Louis-Antoine Thomas). "De Proudhon à Marx," *La Clairière*, I (August 15, 1918).

———. "P.-J. Proudhon," *Portraits d'hier*, I, 10 (August 1, 1909); published separately (Paris, 1909).

———. "Proudhon et le 'Contrat social,' " *La Clairière*, December 15, 1918, pp. 1641–54.

———. "Proudhon et le mouvement ouvrier," *Proudhon et notre temps*, ed. Amis de Proudhon (Paris, 1920), 33–52.

———. ["Le Testament de Proudhon," *La Clairière*, March 1, 1919.]

Haubtmann, Pierre. " 'Forces productives' et 'forces collectives': De l'Affinité des concepts sociologiques chez Marx et Proudhon," *Cahiers internationaux de sociologie*, IV (1948).

———. *Marx et Proudhon: Leurs Rapports personnels 1844–1847. Plusieurs Textes inédits* (Paris, 1947).

———. "La Philosophie sociale de P.-J. Proudhon," MS., *thèse complémentaire*, University of Paris, Faculté des Lettres et des Sciences Humaines, 1961; Bibliothèque de l'Université de Paris, W–1961(5).

———. "P.-J. Proudhon et la pensée allemande," thesis, Institut Social de Paris, 1958.

———. "P.-J. Proudhon, sa vie et sa pensée," thesis, University of Paris, Faculté des Lettres et des Sciences Humaines, 1961; Bibliothèque de l'Université de Paris—Sorbonne, W-1961; 8 vols.

———. *P.-J. Proudhon. Genèse d'un anti-théiste* (Tours and Paris: Mame, 1969); thesis in theology, Gregorian University, Rome, 1966.

Heintz, Peter. *Die Autoritätsproblematik bei Proudhon*, Beiträge zur Soziologie und Sozialphilosophie, bd. VII (Cologne, [1956]).

[Héligon. "La Critique du droit de propriété d'après Proudhon," *Revue psychologique soc.*, 1907].

Henriot, Yvonne. (Thesis on Proudhon's anti-feminism), Faculté des Lettres de Besançon.

Hepner, Benoît-P. *Bakounine* (Paris, 1950), 201–14.

Héricourt, Jenny d'. *La Femme affranchie. Réponse à MM. Michelet, Proudhon, E. de Girardin, A. Comte, et aux autres* (Brussels & Paris, 1860), 2 vols.

———. "M. Proudhon et la question des femmes," *Revue philosophique et religieuse*, December, 1856.

———. "M. Proudhon et les femmes," *Revue philosophique et religieuse*, March, 1857.

———. "Réponse de Mme Jenny d'Héricourt à M. P.-J. Proudhon," *Revue philosophique et religieuse*, February, 1857.

Hervé, Edouard. (Article on Proudhon's *La Révolution sociale*), *La Presse*, August 23, 1852; in Riv., IX, 358–64.

[———. "Le Nouveau Crucifiement de N. S. par Proudhon, etc." (1856).]

Herzen, Alexander. *Ego otnosheniya k Mazzini, Garibaldi, Prudonu* (Geneva, 1901).

———. *Byloe i Dumy*, in his *Polnoe Sobranie Sochinenii i Pisem*, ed. M. K. Lemke (Moscow, 1915–25), XIII, 446–64, et passim; *My Past and Thoughts*, trans. Constance Garnett, revised Humphrey Higgens (London, 1968), II, 805–22 et passim.

———. "Pis'ma k P. Zh. Prudonu," *Sochinenia*, ed. M. K. Lemke, VI, 181–82, 533–36; VII, 127–40; VIII, 195–201; X, 265–67.

———. "Proudhon et 'La Voix du peuple,'" *Revue blanche*, VIII, 46 (May 1, 1895), 391–95; trans. Miceslas Goldberg, first appeared in Herzen's paper, *Poliarnaia zvezda*, 1859.

Herzkowiza, R. "P.-J. Proudhon et le 'Monde primitif,'" *Revue de l'histoire économique et sociale*, XXI (1933), 301–18; also printed separately (Paris, 1934).

Hoffman, Robert. "Marx and Proudhon: A Reappraisal of Their Relationship," *The Historian*, XXIX, 3 (May, 1967), 409–30.

Huard, A. *De l'Injustice dans la révolution et de l'ordre dans l'Eglise . . . réfutation de P.-J. Proudhon . . .* (Paris, 1858).

Hugentobler, A. *Dialogues des morts entre Proudhon et Colins* (Neuchâtel, 1867), and in his *Extinction du paupérisme* (Paris, 1871), 231–382.

Isambert, Gaston. *L'Idée socialiste en France de 1815 à 1848* (Paris, 1905), 316–70.

Isambert [Gaston?]. (Article on Proudhon's *Si les traités*), *Le Courrier français*, December, 1863.

Jackson, John Hampden. *Marx, Proudhon, and European Socialism* (London, 1957).

———. "Proudhon: A Prophet for Our Time," *Contemporary Review*, CLXV (March, 1944), 156–59; and in *Why?*, III, 4 (September–October, 1944), 6–8.

———. "The Relevance of Proudhon," *Politics*, II (October, 1945), 297–99.

Jacowski, Morris. "MM. Proudhon et Montalembert, la Pologne et le constitutionnel" (Paris, 1861).

Janin, Jules. *Histoire de la littérature dramatique*, 2nd ed. (Paris, 1855), II, 165–71.

Javel, Auguste. "Proudhon dans ses relations intimes," *Revue socialiste*, XLI (1905), 257–75, 414–32, 568–88; includes seven unpublished letters from Proudhon.

Jean-Desthieux, François. *La Leçon de Pyrrhus. La Paix n'est pas faite. De Proudhon à Wilson* (Paris, 1920).

[Jolivet, R. "Trois Critiques de l'humanité cartésienne: Proudhon, Cournot, Nietzsche," said to be in *Revue thomiste*, XIX, 164–93, but is not there.]

Joll, James. *The Anarchists* (London, 1964), 61–83, et passim.

Jostock, Paul. "Proudhon," *Staatslexicon* (Freiburg, 1961), VI, 558–60.

Junius (pseudonym of Gaëtan Delmas). "Curiosités révolutionnaires. Le Citoyen Proudhon devant l'Assemblée Nationale. . . . Exposé de la doctrine du citoyen Proudhon, son projet de décret . . ." (Paris, 1848).

La Justice en Pologne et réponse à M. Proudhon (Paris, 1863); on Proudhon's *Si les traités de 1815.* . . .

Justification et réhabilitation de M. Proudhon (Paris, 1850), by "un nouveau prétendant."

King, Preston T. *Fear of Power* (London, 1967), 43–67.

Kriegel, Annie. "Le Syndicalisme révolutionnaire et Proudhon," *L'Actualité de Proudhon*, ed. Centre National d'Etude des Problèmes de Sociologie et d'Economie Européennes (Brussels, 1967), 47–66.

Kropotkin, Peter. *Ethics: Origin and Development*, trans. Louis S. Friedland and Joseph R. Piroshnikoff (New York, 1924), 268–79.

Kuntz, Henri. *Un Procès de presse à Besançon en 1842* (Besançon, 1897).

———. *P.-J. Proudhon* (Besançon, 1897).

La Barre, A. de. "Un Anarchiste bourgeois: Proudhon," *Mouvement socialiste*, XXXII, no. 6, 504–12.

Labrusse, Laurent. *Conception proudhonienne du crédit gratuit (le mutuellisme)*, thesis, University of Paris, Faculté de Droit (Paris, 1919).

Labry, Raoul. *Herzen et Proudhon* (Paris, 1928).

Lacroix, Jean. "Proudhon ou la souveraineté du droit," in his *Itinéraire spirituel* (Paris, 1937).

Lagarde, Edmond. *La Revanche de Proudhon, ou l'avenir du socialisme mutuelliste*, thesis, University of Paris (Paris, 1905).

Lagardelle, Hubert. "Proudhon et néo-monarchistes," *Mouvement socialiste*, Année XIV, vol. 31 (January, 1912), 65–69.

Lagrange, Henri. "Proudhon et l'ordre européen," *Cahiers du Cercle Proudhon*, no. II (March–April, 1912), report on a conference of the Cercle Proudhon; also reported in *L'Action française;* May 3, 1912; and in *Démocratie sociale,* May 5, 1912.

Lair, Maurice. "Proudhon, père de l'anarchie," *Annales des sciences politiques,* XXIV (September 15, 1909), 588–618.

Lajugie, Joseph. "P.-J. Proudhon," *Revue d'histoire économique et sociale,* XXXVII (1959), 477–80.

La Logique, Madame de (pseudonym of Carl August Candidus). *Mes Griefs contre ces messieurs.* Dossier no. 1 (Leipzig, 1863).

Lambert, Juliette (pseudonym of Juliette La Messine—Mrs. Edmond Adam—who also wrote as J. Adam). *Idées anti-Proudhoniennes, sur l'amour, la femme et le mariage* (Paris, 1858); rev. ed., with a critique of Proudhon's *La Guerre et la paix* added (Paris, 1861).

Lambert, Maurice. "La Correspondance de Proudhon" [in publication cited as "Mém. de Besançon," probably the series given in the next item], 1910, 340–66.

———. "Proudhon et l'Académie de Besançon," *Procès-verbaux et mémoires,* Académie des Sciences, Belles-Lettres, et Arts de Besançon, CIX (1910), 132–81.

La Messine, Juliette (pseudonym J. Lambert, q.v.).

Landauer, Carl. *European Socialism* (Berkeley and Los Angeles, 1959), I, 59–68.

Landry, Adolphe. *L'Utilité sociale de la propriété individuelle* (Paris, 1901).

Lanfrey, Pierre. "P.-J. Proudhon," in his *Etudes et portraits politiques* (Paris, 1863); reprint of two articles in *Revue nationale,* November 10, 1862, and an unknown 1863 date.

Langelütke, Hans. *Tauschbank und Schwundgeld als Wege zur zinlosen Wirtschaft* (Jena, 1925); extract from the next item.

———. "Zins- und geldtheoretische Grundlagen der Tauschbank und des Schwundgeldes. Vergleichende Darstellung und Kritik des Zirkulationsreform P. J. Proudhons und Silvio Gesells," dissertation, Freiburg University, 1923.

Langlois, Amédée-Jérôme. *L'Homme et la révolution, huit études dédiées à P.-J. Proudhon* (Paris, 1867), 2 vols.

———. "P.-J. Proudhon, sa vie et son oeuvre" (Paris, 1875); separate issue of his preface to Proudhon's collected correspondence.

Largeron, l'Abbé. "Proudhon et sa morale," *Le Correspondant,* LXX (1867), 512–33.

Larivière, C. de. "P.-J. Proudhon," *Revue politique et parlementaire,* IX (1896), 164–73.

Latouche, Peter. *Anarchy!* (London, 1908), 11–19.

Lavergne, Léonce de. "Le Libéralisme socialiste, les écrits de M. Proudhon," *Revue des deux mondes*, XXII (June 15, 1848), 842–61.

Lecouturier, H. "La Science du socialisme universel suivie de: Le Dieu de Proudhon" (Paris, 1850); a critique of Proudhon's "Dieu, c'est le mal!" *Le Peuple*, May 7, 1849.

Lédermann, László. *Fédération internationale. Idées d'hier, possibilités de demain* (Neuchâtel, 1945).

Lepelletier, Edmond. "Proudhon auteur dramatique," *La Nouvelle Revue*, XCII (1895), 498–522, 719–38; includes Proudhon's previously unpublished scenario *Galilée*, cited above, part I-E.

Leroux, Pierre. "Politique et socialisme," *La République*, November 11, November 18, November 25, and December 2, 1849; a polemic against Proudhon; Proudhon's side in Riv., II.

Leroy, Maxime; Bourgin, Hubert; Bouglé, C.; et al. "Ce que peuvent nous apprendre le fouriérisme et le proudhonisme," report of conference, *Libres entretiens*, 11e série, no. 2 (January 19, 1919), 24–50.

Leroy, Maxime. *Histoire des idées sociales en France* (Paris, 1946–54), I, 469–518; II, 282–97 et passim.

———. Introduction for Riv., III, 5–43.

———. "Le Retour à Proudhon, *Grande Revue*, XVI, 7 (April 10, 1912), 609–15.

———. "Stirner contre Proudhon," *La Renaissance latine*, February 15, 1905; and in *Le Contrat social*, I, 5 (November, 1957), 282–86.

[Leroy-Beaulieu, Paul. "Proudhon d'après un livre récent," *Journal des économistes*, said to be in the issue of March 7, 1896, but not there.]

[Lévy, Michel. *Proudhon, sa vie, sa correspondance* (1872).]

Lévy, Yves. "Proudhon contre les arts et la littérature," *Le Contrat social*, IX, 2 (1965), 110–12.

Lewis, Wyndham. "Proudhon and Rousseau," in his *The Art of Being Ruled* (New York & London, 1926), 343–88.

Lichtheim, George. *The Origins of Socialism* (New York, 1969), 83–98 et passim.

———. *A Short History of Socialism* (New York: Praeger, 1920), 56–63 et passim.

———. "Socialism and the Jews," *Dissent*, July–August, 1968, 321–23, 337–38.

Loin, Arsène. *Le Philosophe Proudhon, esquisse de sa philosophie* (Brussels, 1862).

Loria, Achille. "Pier Giuseppe Proudhon nel centenario della sua nascita," *Nuova Antologia*, CXL (March 16, 1909), 177–85.

Loris, E. (Author of a tract signed "Un Patriote belge," attacking Proudhon for his articles on Italian unity, 1862.)

Lossier, Jean-G. *Le Rôle social de l'art selon Proudhon* (Paris, 1937).

Losson, E. *Philosophie de la mort, à la mémoire de Proudhon* (Brussels, 1865).

Loudon, E. "Proudhon," *Le Correspondant*, XXVI (1850), 329–46.

Louis, Gustave. "Coup-d'oeil sur les doctrines de M. Proudhon" (Paris, 1848).

Louis, Paul. *150 Ans de pensée socialiste* (Paris, 1938–39), I, 201–22.

———. *Histoire du socialisme en France*, 5th ed. (Paris, 1950), 110–17.

Lourdoueix, J. H. Lelarge de. *Le Dernier Mot de la révolution. M. Proudhon réfuté* . . . (Paris, 1852).

———. (Probable author of an article on Proudhon's *La Révolution sociale* . . .), *La Gazette de France*, August 14, 1852.

Loüys, Edouard. "Pierre-Joseph Proudhon et Jean-Jacques Rousseau," Sorbonne thesis, Bibliothèque de l'Université de Paris, 1955.

———. "Proudhon et l'idée de progrès social, ou l'unité de la pensée proudhonienne," Sorbonne thesis, Bibliothèque de l'Université de Paris, 1955. Loüys gives summaries of his theses in "Proudhon," *Information historique*, XVII, 5 (1955), 195–96.

Löwith, Karl. *Meaning in History* (Chicago, 1949), 60–66.

Lu, Shi Yung. *The Political Theories of P.-J. Proudhon*, dissertation, Columbia University (New York, 1922).

Lubac, Henri du. "Proudhon anticlérical," *Cité nouvelle*, February 25, 1943.

———. "Proudhon contre le 'mythe de la Providence,' " in his *Traditions socialistes françaises* (Neuchâtel, 1944).

———. *Proudhon et le Christianisme* (Paris, 1945); trans. by R. E. Scantlebury as *The Un-Marxian Socialist* (London, 1948).

Magnin, Antoine. "P.-J. Proudhon et la Franc-maçonnerie, documents publiés à l'occasion de l'inauguration de sa statue, 14 août 1910" (Besançon, 1910).

Maitron, Jean. *Histoire du mouvement anarchiste en France (1880–1914)* (Paris, 1951), 27–36 et passim.

Malassis, P.-E.-A. Poulet (writing under pseudonym "E. R."). "Proudhon en Belgique," *La Petite Revue*, VI (1865), 9–21, 45–50, 73–78.

Malnoury, Louis. *Les Procès de l'histoire comtoise* (Besançon, 1930). Includes Proudhon's 1842 trial.

Malon, Benoît. *Histoire du socialisme* (Paris, 1882–85), II, 324–99.

———. "Karl Marx et Proudhon," *Revue socialiste*, V (January, 1887),

15–22; a translation, with notes and preface, of Marx's letter to J.-B. von Schweitzer, "Uber Proudhon," q.v.

———. *Le Socialisme intégral* (Paris, 1890), I, 167–92.

"Manifeste néo-communiste, publié sous le signe du machinisme intégral, par un de la masse" (Talence, 1938).

Marbot, l'Abbé. "Le Socialiste Proudhon, conférence du 12 mars 1884" (Marseille, 1884).

Marchal, Charles. *P.-J. Proudhon et Pierre Leroux, révélations édifiantes* (Brussels & Paris, 1850).

Marchegay, Henri. *La Liberté des proudhoniens, les libéraux, c'est l'esclavage* (Mayenne, 1868).

———. *Silhouette de Proudhon* (Paris, 1868).

Marsico, Rodolfo Guido de. "La Dottrina etico-giuristica di P. J. Proudhon," *La Sintesi*, II (1921), 141–68.

Martin, J. Luis. "Proudhon y Donoso Cortés ante la propriedad privada," *Revista de filosofia* (Madrid), XXIV, nos. 94–95 (1965), 317–44.

Marx, Karl. *Die heilige Familie oder Kritik der kritischen Kritik* (Frankfurt-am-Main, 1845); in Marx and Engels, *Werke* (Berlin: Dietz, 1958–67), II, 23–36, 39–56, 165, 166.

———. (Letter to Pavel Annenkov on Proudhon, written in French, Brussels, December 28, 1846); first published in *M. M. Stassiulevich i ego sovremenniki v ich perepiske* (St. Petersburg, 1912), III, 445ff.; also in *Mouvement socialiste*, XXXIII (March–April, 1913), 141–54; in German trans., *Neue Zeit*, XXXI, pt. I, 23 (March 7, 1913), 821–30; in Marx and Engels, *Werke*, IV, 547–57.

———. (Letter to Proudhon, May 5, 1846), in Riv., VII, 432–34.

———, and Friedrich Engels. "Lettres inédites de Marx et Engels sur P.-J. Proudhon," *Mouvement socialiste*, XXXV (January–February, 1914), 5–23; letters and extracts of letters from an edition of their correspondence then just published by Dietz. There are a number of other mentions and discussions of Proudhon in their correspondence.

———. *Misère de la philosophie* (Paris & Brussels, 1847); the first complete German edition, *Das Elend der Philosophie*, trans. Eduard Bernstein and Karl Kautsky, preface and notes by Friedrich Engels (Stuttgart: J. H. W. Dietz, 1885), includes some changes indicated by Marx; 2nd German ed. (1892) has an additional brief preface by Engels; the edition published by A. Costes (Paris, 1950) includes the correspondence between Marx and Proudhon, the latter's marginal notes in the book, Engels's prefaces, and the letter to von Schweitzer cited below.

————. (Note on the *Misère de la philosophie*), *L'Egalité*, April 7, 1880; reprinted in *Annali di Istituto Gianciacomo Feltrinelli*, I (Milan, 1958), 204–5.

————. "Proudhons Rede gegen Thiers," *Neue Rheinische Zeitung* (Cologne), August 5, 1848; in Marx and Engels, *Historische-kritische Gesamtausgabe* (Moscow, 1927–35), part I, vol. VII, 273–76.

————. "Uber Proudhon" (letter to J. B. von Schweitzer, January 24, 1865), *Der Sozial-Democrat*, February 1, 3, & 5, 1865; also in Marx and Engels, *Werke*, XVI, 25–32. Written in response to a request for a sort of memorial notice on the occasion of Proudhon's death.

Mason, Edward S. *The Paris Commune* (New York, 1930), 30–44 et passim.

Mattabon, J. A. "La Propriété est-elle le vol? Lettre à M. J. Proudhon sur son mémoire *Qu'est-ce que la propriété?*" (Paris, 1848).

Mattfeldt, R. *P. J. Proudhons Theorie des Kapitals und sein soziales Kreditsystem*, dissertation (Berlin, 1920).

Maurras, Charles. "A Besançon," *Cahiers du Cercle Proudhon*, 1 (January–February, 1912), 3–8.

————. "Proudhon," in his *L'Action Française et la religion catholique* (Paris, 1913), 154–69; extract in *Action Française*, December 20, 1913, p. 1.

Maury, L. "Sur Proudhon," *Revue bleue*, LXVI (1928), 278–80.

Meissner, Alfred. "Proudhons revolutionäres Programm," and "Sociale Schulen: 3) Proudhon," in his *Revolutionäre Studien aus Paris* (Frankfurt-am-Main, 1849), II.

Menezes, Djacir. *Proudhon, Hegel e a dialética* (Rio de Janeiro: Zahar, 1966).

Menger, Anton. *Das Recht auf den vollen Arbeitertrag in geschichtlicher Darstellung* (Stuttgart, 1886), 21–23, 70–78, 81–83, et passim.

Menzel, Adolf. "P.-J. Proudhon als Soziologe," *Festschrift für Carl Grünberg zum 70. Geburtstrage* (Leipzig, 1932), 312–42.

————. "P.-J. Proudhon in neuer Beleuchtung," *Archiv für Sozialwissenschaft und Sozialpolitik* (Tübingen), LXVIII (1933), 730–40.

Méric, L'Abbé Elie. *Les Erreurs sociales du temps présent* (Paris, 1884).

————. "Proudhon et le divorce," *Revue du monde catholique*, LXXII (1882), 477–91, 651–65.

Michel, H. *L'Idée de l'état* (Paris, 1896), 395–416.

Michel, J. "Quelques notes sur l'ouvrage de M. Proudhon, *De la Justice . . .*" (Paris, 1859).

Mikhailovsky, Nikolai K. (Proudhon and our publicists), *Knizhnyi Vestnik*, X, 8 (1866), 506.

Milsand, J. "L'antichristianisme de Proudhon," *Revue des deux mondes*, XVI (December, 1852), 1148–73.

Mirecourt, Eugène de (pseudonym of C. J. B. Jacquot). "Lettres à M. P.-J. Proudhon, en réponse à son livre *De la Justice* . . ." (Paris, 1858).

———. "Proudhon," one of his series, *Les Contemporains* (Paris & Brussels, 1855, 1856, 1858, 1870); a clerical polemic—Proudhon's *De la Justice* was written partly in response to this tract.

Mitchell, Robert. (Articles on Proudhon's *Si les traités* . . .), *Le Pays*, December 5, 6, & 21, 1863.

Molinari, G. de. "M. Proudhon et M. Thiers," *Journal des économistes*, XXI, 86 (August 15, 1848), 57–73.

———. "Système des contradictions économiques," review article in the *Journal des économistes*, XVIII, 47 (November, 1847), 383–98.

Morin, Frédéric. (Article on Proudhon), *Avenir national*, June 13, 1865.

Morino, L. "Marx e Proudhon," in Istituto di studi filosofici, *Atti del congresso internazionale di filosofia* (Milan, 1947), I, 435–37.

Moysset, Henri. Introduction for Riv., VI, i–xciv.

"M. Prudhon [*sic*]: Contradictions économiques," *Blackwood's Magazine*, LXV (1849), 304–13.

Muckle, Friedrich. *Die Geschichte der sozialistischen Ideen im 19 Jahrhundert* (Leipzig, 1917), II.

———. *Die grossen Sozialisten* (Leipzig, 1920), I, 111–31.

Muglioni, Jacques. "La religion de Proudhon," *Revue socialiste*, CXXXII (1959), 398–408.

Mülberger, Arthur. "Eine deutsche Schrift über Proudhon," *Frankfurter Zeitung*, November 13, 1887.

———. *Der Irrtum von Karl Marx, Aus Ernst Buschs Nachlass herausgegeben* (Basel, 1894; Stuttgart, 1908).

———. *Kapital und Zins. Die Polemik zwischen Bastiat und Proudhon* (Jena, 1896).

———. "Aus meinen Proudhons-Kollektaneen," *Deutsche Worte* (Vienna), 1896.

———. *P.-J. Proudhon, Leben und Werke* (Stuttgart, 1899).

———. *Studien über Proudhon. Ein Beitrag zum Verständnis der sozialen Reform* (Stuttgart, 1891; Leipzig, n.d.).

———. "Die Theorie der Anarchie," *Die Neue Gesellschaft* (Zurich), March, 1878, 291–311.

———. "Von und über Proudhon," *Die Wage* (Berlin), 1878–79.

———. "Ein Wahlmanifest Proudhons. Ein Beitrag zur Vorgeschichte der Commune," *Die Neue Gesellschaft* (Zurich), Jg. 1, V (February, 1878), 251–62.

———. *Zur Kenntnis des Marxismus* (Leipzig, 1894), 19–34.

Munier, H. "L'Opposé du misérable principe de Proudhon (n.p., n.d. [1848?]).

Naville, Pierre. *De l'Aliénation à la jouissance* (Paris, 1957), 291–355.

Nefftzer, Auguste. (Article on Proudhon's *Fédération et l'unité en Italie*), *La Presse*, October 26 & 28, November 1 & 6, 1862. See also the correspondence between Proudhon and Nefftzer, cited in part I-D under "Four letters to Auguste Nefftzer."

Nettlau, Max. *Der Anarchismus von Proudhon zu Kropokin* (Berlin, 1927), 5–20, 51–64, 75–87.

———. *Die Forfrühlung der Anarchie* (Berlin, 1925), 143–83.

Nikodemos. "Proudhon," *Die Zukunft* (Harden), CI (1918), 219–46.

Noland, Aaron. "History and Humanity: The Proudhonian Version," *The Uses of History*, ed. Hayden V. White (Detroit: Wayne State University Press, 1968), 59–105.

———. "Proudhon and Rousseau," *Journal of the History of Ideas*, XXVIII, 1 (January–March, 1967), 33–54.

———. "Proudhon: Socialist as Social Scientist," *American Journal of Economics and Sociology*, XXVI (July, 1967), 313–28.

Noyelle, H. "La Notion de justice dans l'oeuvre économique de Proudhon, la valeur et l'égalité," *Revue d'histoire des doctrines économiques et sociales*, XI, 2 (1923); printed separately (Reims & Paris, 1923).

Nyblaeus, Axel. *Om Statsmaktens grund och vasende. Med anledning . . . Proudhons skrift: "Les Confessions d'un révolutionnaire"* (Lund, 1864, 1882).

Opitz, T. *Proudhons neueste Schrift: Theoretischer und praktischer Beweis des Sozialismus* (Leipzig, 1849).

Oppenheim, Heinrich B. "P. J. Proudhons Philosophie der Gesellschaft," *Die Opposition*, ed. K. Heinzen (Mannheim, 1846), 148–80.

Oppenheimer, Ludwig. "Die Einheit des Proudhonschen Systems," dissertation, Berlin, 1923; extract in *Jahrbuch d. Diss. d. Phil. Fak. Berlin*.

Orano, Paolo. *Il patriarchi del socialismo* (Rome, 1904).

Osgood, Herbert L. "Scientific Anarchism," *Political Science Quarterly*, IV, 1 (March, 1889), 1–36; printed separately (Boston, 1889).

Ott, Auguste. *Traité d'économie sociale* (Paris, 1851), 535–44.

Oualid, W. "Proudhon banquier," *Proudhon et notre temps*, ed. Amis de Proudhon (Paris, 1920), 132–56.

Ozynaki. "Monsieur Proudhon" (Paris, 1864).

Paepe, D. de. "La Mort, sa conception physiologique et morale chez P.-J. Proudhon," *Revue scientifique*, 4ᵉ série, VII (January 23, 1897), 106–8.

Pareto, Vilfredo. *Systèmes socialistes* (Paris, 1902–3), I, 353–56, 380–85.

Passage, H. du. "Avec Marx ou Proudhon: Nationalisation des transports et la confiscation des terres," *Revue études*, July 5, 1920; published separately with the title, "Marx ou Proudhon? Les Ascendants intellectuels de la C. G. T." (Paris, 1920).

Pavićević, Radovan L. *Država kao konfederacija komuna. Kritika Prudonovich shavatanja* (Beograd, 1969).

Pellétan, Eugène. "Les Confessions d'un révolutionnaire par P.-J. Proudhon," *La Presse*, IV, no. 1887 (November 18, 1849), 1–2.

———. "Proudhon et ses oeuvres complètes," *Revue des deux mondes*, LXI (January 15, 1866), 328–52.

Pelloutier, Fernand. See Dufresne, A., and Pelloutier, F.

Pelvey, L. (Article on *De la Justice*), *L'Observateur*, April 28, 1858.

Perelman, Chaim. *Justice et raison* (Brussels, 1963), 66–72.

Périé, Raphaël. "Devant ta mort: Le Pape Léon et le Tonnelier," *Pages libres*, III, 136 (August 8, 1903), 109–16.

Pertchik, L. "Iz istokov mezhdunarodnoi kommunisticheskoi partii. O pismakh Marksa i Engel'sa k Prudonu i Kotgenu, 1846," *Bol'shevik*, III (1933), 62–68; *Kommunisticheskii Internatsional*, VI (1933), 40–44. Presumably concerns the letter of Marx (May 5, 1846) cited above.

Peruta, Franco della. "Un capitolo di storia del socialismo risorgimentale: Proudhon e Ferrari," *Studi Storici*, III (1962), 307–41.

"Petites Lettres de la province. Lettre I. Sur M. Proudhon" (Paris [ca. 1849]).

Petrus (pseudonym), ed. *Proudhon e a cultura portugesa*, textos de Amorim Viana [et al.] 1825–1965 ([Lisbon?]: Editorial Cultural Portugal, 1967–), 5 vols.

Pey, Alexandre. " 'De la Capacité politique des classes ouvrières,' par P.-J. Proudhon," *Revue contemporaine*, Année XIV, Sér. 2, vol. XLVIII, no. 83 (1865), 172–75.

Pfau, Ludwig. "Proudhon und die Franzosen," in his *Freie Studien* (Stuttgart, 1866, 1874), and his *Gesammelten Werken* (Stuttgart & Leipzig, 1888), VI.

Picard, Roger. Introduction for Riv., I, vol. i, 5–32.

———. "Proudhon et l'impôt," *Action nationale*, Série nouvelle, X

(1920), 205–20; and in *Proudhon et notre temps*, ed. Amis de Proudhon (Paris, 1920), 157–74.

Pickles, W. "Marx and Proudhon," *Politica* (London), III (1938), 236–60.

———. "Les Tendances proudhoniennes dans la France d'après la guerre," *Revue de l'histoire économique et sociale*, XXIII (1937), 289–309.

"Pierre-Joseph Proudhon," *Dictionnaire biographique du mouvement ouvrier français*, ed. Jean Maitron (Paris: 1964–), III, 256–61.

Pillon, François (probable author). "Abstention" and "Anarchie," *Grand Dictionnaire universel du XIXe siècle*, ed. Pierre Larousse; mainly descriptions of Proudhon's ideas.

———. "L'Antithéisme de Proudhon," *La Critique philosophique*, 1874: II, 289–301; 1875: I, 4–17.

———. "P.-J. Proudhon. Sa Vie et sa correspondance, 1838–1848, par Sainte-Beuve," *La Critique philosophique*, 1872: II, 345–52.

Pinot, Robert. "La Confédération générale du travail et les idées proudhoniennes," *Revue hebdomadaire*, Année 29, V, 18 (May 1, 1920), 3–34.

———. Review of Proudhon's "La Pornocratie," *La Critique philosophique*, 1875: II, no. 39, 202–8.

Pirou, Gaëtan. "Les Interprétations récentes de la pensée de Proudhon, *Revue d'histoire des doctrines sociales et économiques*, 1912, 133–65.

———. "Proudhonisme et Marxisme," *Revue du mois*, XX (1920), 237–56; and in *Proudhon et notre temps*, ed. Amis de Proudhon (Paris, 1920), 175–202.

———. *Proudhonisme et syndicalisme révolutionnaire*, thesis, University of Paris (Paris, 1920).

"P.-J. Proudhon, et notre temps," *Le Pont* (édition française, Berlin), III, 18 (1943), 3.

Plamenatz, John. *The Revolutionary Movement in France* (London, 1952).

Plée, Léon. (Article on Proudhon's *La Révolution sociale*), *Le Siècle*, August 19, 1852; and in Riv., IX, 364–70.

Plekhanov, G. V. "Proudhon," in his *Anarchism and Socialism*, trans. Eleanor Marx Aveling (Chicago, 1918), 53–77.

Pleshcheev, A. N. (Article on Proudhon), *Otechestvennye Zapiski*, 1873, no. 11.

[Poitevin, E. "La Crise économique: Solution proudhonienne," *Le Fédéraliste*, 1933.]

Poitou, Eugène. *Les Philosophes français contemporains et leurs systèmes religieux* (Paris, 1864), 53–67.

Polonskaia, K. "Zabytyi epizod ideinoi bor'by 60-kh godov. Chernyshevskii i Prudon," *Izvestiia Akademii Nauk SSSR, Otdelenie Literatury i iazyka*, XXVI, 1 (1967), 28–40.

Pomian, F. (pseudonym of V. Puissant). "Lettre sur l'opuscule de P. J. Proudhon: Si les traités de 1815 ont cessé d'exister" (Brussels, 1864).

Poncheville, Thellier. "L'Oeuvre révolutionnaire jugée par Proudhon," in his *L'Ouvrier aux siècles passés* (Arras, 1884).

Pontmartin, Armand Ferrard de. "P.-J. Proudhon," in his *Nouvelles samedis* (Paris, 1878), II, 89–104.

Portael, A. (pseudonym of Albert Laporte). *Napoléon III, M. Proudhon, l'Italie et la Belgique* (Liège, 1862).

Portelette, Constant. *La Pologne en 1815, réponse à M. Proudhon* (Paris, 1864).

[*Portraits de Bakounine et Proudhon* (Paris, 1887?). Anarchist tract advertised in another, published by *La Révolte*, 1892; I can find no other record of this item.]

Potter, Agathon de. *De la Propriété intellectuelle . . . examen des Majorats littéraires de M. P. J. Proudhon* (Brussels, 1863).

———. *Qu'est-ce que la guerre et la paix? Examen de l'ouvrage de M. Proudhon sur la guerre et la paix* (Brussels, 1862).

"Les Précurseurs. Proudhon" (Paris, 1943).

Prélot, Marcel. "Pierre-Joseph Proudhon," *International Encyclopedia of the Social Sciences* (New York: Macmillan and The Free Press, 1968), XII, 604–7.

Pressensé, Edmond de. "La Ruine sociale, réponse à M. Proudhon, ni matérialisme, ni jésuitisme" (Duclon, 1852).

Prevost, J. M. Constantin (presumed author). *De la Déomanie au XIXe siècle* (St.-Simon, Enfantin, Comte, Proudhon) (Toulouse, 1860).

———. "Proudhon, jugé et traité selon des doctrines métaphysiques; réfutation comico-sérieuse de ce grand pamphlétaire par un solitaire rustique et illettré" (Paris [Toulouse?], 1858).

Prévost-Paradol, L.-A. (Untitled article on Proudhon's *La Guerre*), *Le Journal des débats*, July 5, 1861, 3.

Procureurs généraux d'Aix, Limoges et Besançon au Garde des Sceaux, et al. A dossier with nine items relative to the trial and seizure of *De la Justice*, including letters from these officials, Archives Nationales: Bb[18] 1578.

Proudhomme (pseudonym). "Lettre au Citoyen Proudhon" (n.p., n.d. [Paris, 1848]).

"Proudhon," *Grand Dictionnaire universel du XIXe siècle,* ed. Pierre Larousse (Paris, 1875), 315–20.

"Proudhon, der Original-Sozialdemokrat," by "H. B.," *Magazin für Literatur des Auslandes,* XXXIV, 13 (1865).

"Proudhon und das geistige Eigentumsrecht," *Magazin für die Literatur des Auslandes,* XXXI, 53 (December 31, 1862), 623–26.

Puech, Jules-L. "Le Centenaire de Proudhon," *Revue de la paix,* XIV, 1 (January, 1909), 8–21.

———. "Le Fédéralisme dans l'oeuvre de Proudhon," introduction for Riv., XIV, 24–76.

———. Introductions for Riv., XI, 1–36, 303–24; XII, 133–70; XIII, 305–12.

———. "Proudhon et la guerre," *Action nationale,* nouvelle série, IX (1919), 300–330; and in *Proudhon et notre temps,* ed. Amis de Proudhon (Paris, 1920), 203–28.

———. *Le Proudhonisme dans l'Association Internationale des Travailleurs,* with appendix, "Le Sens de l'internationale proudhonienne" (Paris, 1907).

[———. "Quelques récents commentateurs de Proudhon" (Paris, 1950).]

———. "Proudhon et le fédéralisme des peuples," *La Tradition socialiste en France et la Société des Nations* (Paris, 1921), 181–201.

Putlitz, G. H. Gans zu. *Proudhon; sein Leben und seine positiven Ideen* (Berlin, 1881).

Quack, H. P. G. *De Socialisten: Personen en Stelsels* (Amsterdam, 1899–1901), 6 vols.; see esp. IV, 100–236.

Rahn, Kurt Walter. "Die Guesdisten und ihr Kampf gegen den Proudhonismus in der Französischen Arbeiterbewegung von 1876 bis 1882," dissertation, Humboldt University, Berlin, Philosophy Faculty, 1956.

Raphael, Max. "La Sociologie de l'art chez Proudhon," *Proudhon, Marx, Picasso* (Paris, 1933).

Ralea, Michel. *Proudhon: Sa Conception du progrès et son attitude sociale,* thesis, University of Paris (Paris, 1932).

Rambaud, J. *Histoire des doctrines économiques,* 2nd ed. (Paris, 1903), 620–727.

Rappoport, C. "P.-J. Proudhon et le socialisme scientifique (1809–1909)" (Paris, [1909]).

Ratuszny, Anton. *Tolstojs soziale Anschauungen, insbesondere sein Eigentumslehre und ihr Verhältnis zur Lehre Proudhons*, dissertation, Freiburg University, 1907 (Lemburg, 1905).

[Rau, A. "P.-J. Proudhon und Ludwig Feuerbach," trans. E. Wachler, *Deutsche Zeitschrift* (Berlin), said to be in issue of July 2, 1900, but not in this volume.]

Reclus, Elisée. "De la Mutualité, P.-J. Proudhon. Travail et capital. Formule de conciliation," *L'Association*, no. 8, 1865.

Réfutation de la guerre et de la paix de Proudhon (Paris, 1886).

Reichert, William O. "Pierre-Joseph Proudhon: One of the Fathers of Philosophical Anarchism," *Journal of Human Relations*, XIII (1965), 81–92.

Renard, Georges. *La République de 1848 (1848–1852)*, in *Histoire socialiste*, ed. Jean Jaurès (Paris, 1901–8), IX, 247–62, 332–45.

Renaud, Hippolyte (tentatively identified as the author of an article defending Fouriérism against criticisms in Proudhon's first *mémoire* on property), *L'Impartial* (Besançon, October 8, 1840); Proudhon's second *mémoire* is in part a response to this.

Renouvier, Charles. "Introduction. De la philosophie du XIXᵉ siècle en France," *L'Année philosophique*, I (1867), 1–108; Proudhon discussed, 60–74.

———. *Philosophie analytique de l'histoire* (Paris, 1896), IV, 213ff.

"Réponse au Représentant Proudhon par un des disciples" (Paris, n.d. [1848]).

Reyntiens, N. "La Correspondance de Proudhon," *Revue de Belgique*, VIII (December 15, 1874), 322–32.

Rhillon. "Qu'est-ce que la propriété? Selon P.-J. Proudhon" (Paris, 1923).

[Richet, Charles. *La Passé de la guerre et l'avenir de la paix* (Paris, 1907).]

Richter, Walter. "Proudhons Bedeutung für die Gegenwart," *Abhandlungen zur Wissenschaftgeschichte und Wissenschaftsoziologie und eine Studie über Proudhon*, ed. W. Richter, E. Rothäcker, and K.-A. Haeger (Bremen, 1951).

Ridley, F. F. *Revolutionary Syndicalism in France* (Cambridge: Cambridge University Press, 1970), 25–32.

Rieff, Philip. "A Jesuit Looks at Proudhon. Competition in Damnation," *Modern Review*, III, 2 (January, 1950), 166–71; review article on du Lubac's book, q.v.

Rifflet, Raymond. "Conclusions," *L'Actualité de Proudhon*, Centre Na-

tional d'Etude des Problèmes de Sociologie et d'Economie Européennes (Brussels, 1967), 229–51.

Rist, Charles. "La Pensée économique de Proudhon," *Revue d'histoire
économique et sociale*, XXXIII (1955), 129–65.

———, and Charles Gide. *See* Gide, Charles, and Rist, Charles.

Ritter, Alan. *The Political Thought of Pierre-Joseph Proudhon* (Princeton: Princeton University Press, 1969).

———. "Proudhon and the Problem of Community," *Review of Politics*, XXIX (October, 1967), 457–77.

———. "Proudhon: Realist, Radical, Moralist," dissertation, Harvard
University, 1966; Harvard College Library.

Rittinghausen, Moritz. *La Législation directe par le peuple, ou la véritable démocratie* (Paris, 1851); first published as three articles in *La
Démocratie pacifique*.

Robinson, John Beverley. "The Economics of Liberty" (Minneapolis,
1916); a brief summary of Proudhon's thought.

Roland, Pauline. "Réponse d'une morte à P. J. Proudhon," *L'Espérance*,
II (1858).

Rosenthal, Léon. "Les Destinées de l'art social d'après P. J. Proudhon,"
Revue internationale de sociologie, II, pt. 2 (1894), 689–703; printed
separately (Paris, 1894).

Rocher, A. "Qu'est-ce que le travailleur? Rien! Que doit-il être? Tout!
Résumé de Proudhon—Qu'est-ce que c'est la propriété?" (Geneva
[1873?]).

Rostu, Georges du. *Proudhon et les socialistes de son temps*, thesis, University of Paris (Paris, 1913).

Rota Ghibaudi, Silvia. *Proudhon e Rousseau* (Milan: Dott. A. Giuffre,
1965).

Les Rouges Jugés par eux-mêmes . . . (n.d., n.p.); includes Proudhon.

Rousseau, Jean. "P.-J. Proudhon," *Le Figaro*, XII, 1038 (January 26,
1865), 2–4.

Rousseaux, André. "Proudhon et nous," *Le Figaro littéraire*, August 22,
1942.

———. "Actualité de Proudhon," *Le Monde classique* (Paris, 1946), II,
185–99.

Roussel, Auguste. "L'Avenir; au citoyen P.-J. Proudhon (Paris, 1850).

Rozenberg, David Iachevich. *Istoriia politicheskoi ekonomii* (Moscow,
1936), III; on nineteenth-century French writers, including Proudhon.

Rüdenberg, Ernst. *Entstehung und Beziehung der Sozialtheorien von*

P.-J. Proudhon und Karl Marx bis zur Feb. Rev. 1848, dissertation (Frankfurt, 1927).

[Runge, H. "Pierre Joseph Proudhon," *Staatslexicon,* ed. Rolleck and Welcher (1865)].

Ruyssen, Théodore. "La Guerre et la paix," *Le Contrat social,* V, 2 (March–April, 1961), 96–100.

——. Introductions for Riv., XII, 5–43; XIII, 105–40; and XV, 7–76.

Sá, Victor de. *Amorim Viana e Proudhon* (Lisbon, 1960).

Sabatier, Camille. *Socialisme libéral ou morcellisme* (Paris, 1905).

——. "Syndicalisme proudhonien," *Dépêche de Toulouse,* November 16, 1910.

Saint-Michel, L'Archange. "Réponse à Satan au sujet de M. Proudhon" (Paris, 1848).

Sainte-Beuve, C.-A. *P.-J. Proudhon, sa vie et sa correspondance, 1838–1848* (Paris, 1872).

——. "Proudhon étudié dans ses correspondances intimes (1ᵉ partie, 1838–1848), *Revue contemporaine,* XLVII (October 31, 1865); a preliminary publication of part of the preceding item.

Sand, George. "Sur Proudhon et Jules Janin," *Souvenirs et idées,* (Paris, 1904), 39–49.

Santonastaso, Giuseppe. [L'antifemminismo della litteratura rivoluzionaria," *La Fiera Letteraria,* December 26, 1946.]

——. *P.-J. Proudhon* (Bari, 1935); rev. ed. (Milan, 1954).

——. "Proudhon e la proprieta," *Rivista internazionale di filosofia del diritto,* XIII, 575–82.

——. *Il socialismo francese da Saint-Simon a Proudhon* (Florence, 1954).

Sarraz-Bournet, (M.?). *Une Evolution nouvelle du socialisme doctrinal: Le Socialisme juridique,* thesis, Grenoble, Faculté de Droit (Chambéry, 1911), 48–60 et passim.

Satan (pseudonym of Georges Marie Mathieu Dairnvaell). *Histoire de M. Proudhon et de ses principes* (Paris, 1848); said by Proudhon to be a government publication (comment in his *Carnet,* VII, 29 [October 2, 1848]).

Scelle, Georges. "Fédéralisme et proudhonisme," introduction for Riv., XIV, 9–23.

Schapiro, J. Salwyn. "Pierre-Joseph Proudhon, Harbinger of Fascism," *American Historical Review,* L (1945), 714–37.

——. *Liberalism and the Challenge of Fascism* (New York, 1949), 332–69.

————. (Review of du Lubac's book, q.v.), *American Historical Review*, LIV, 3 (1949), 586–87.

Schatz, Albert. *L'Individualisme économique et social* (Paris, 1907), 491–505.

Scherer, Edmond. "M. Proudhon ou la banqueroute du socialisme," *Bibliothèque universelle* (Geneva), II (1858), 481–514; and in his *Mélanges de critique religieuse* (Paris, 1860).

Schlesinger, Paul. "Proudhon et Sade," *Mercure de France*, June 1, 1951, 373–74.

Schnerb, Robert. "Finances proudhoniennes. Ni impôts, ni emprunts. Organisation du crédit!," *Revue socialiste*, February, 1947, 169–79.

————. "Marx et Proudhon, devant le coup d'état du 2 décembre," *Revue socialiste*, 1947, 526–36.

Schulze, Williband. "War Proudhon Anarchist?" *Deutschlands Erneuerung*, XXIII (January, 1939), 14–21.

Schumacher, Heinz. *Proudhons Mutualisierung des Kredits*, dissertation, Frankfurt (Gelnhausen, 1935).

Séailles, Gabriel. "La Philosophie de la justice," published as part of the introductory material for Riv., VIII, vol. i, 168–83.

Seillière, Ernest. *La Philosophie de l'impérialisme* (Paris, 1903–8), III, 205–323.

Sergent, Alain, and Harmel, Claude. *Histoire de l'anarchie* (Paris, 1949), 117–48.

Seymour, Henry. "P.-J. Proudhon, a Biographical Sketch" (London, 18—); reprinted from *The Anarchist*.

Simon, Jules. "Proudhon, de Desjardins," *Journal des savants* (April, 1896), 185–95; *Revue des revues*, XVII (May 15, 1896), 311–19.

Silberner, Edmund. "Proudhon's Judeophobia," *Historica Judaica*, X, 1 (April, 1948), 61–80.

Silvera, Alain. *Daniel Halévy and His Times* (Ithaca: Cornell University Press, 1966); details about the wide and deep interest of *fin de siècle* intellectuals in Proudhon.

Simon, Yves. "Notes sur le fédéralisme proudhonien," *Esprit*, April, 1937.

Sluchevsky, Konstantin Ivanovich. "Prudon ob iskusstve, ego perevodchiki i kritiki," *Iavlenniia russkoy zhizni pod kritikoii estetiki* (St. Petersburg, 1866–67).

Snell, R. "P. J. Proudhon," *Revue socialiste*, XIV (December, 1891), 671–82.

Socalist Revolutionary Party, Russia. *Anarkhiia po Prudonu* (Kiev, 1907), *Izdaniie Sotsial'no-Revolutsionnoi Partii*, III.

[Sokolov, N. V. (and V. Zaytsev). *Otshchepentsy*, suppressed by the censor, to have been published in St. Petersburg, 1866, but it is not clear whether it appeared; published as *Die Abtrünnigen* ([Zurich], 1872).]

Soltau, Roger. *French Political Thought in the Nineteenth Century* (London, 1931; New York, 1959), 268–91.

Sorel, Georges. "Essai sur la philosophie de Proudhon," *Revue philosophique*, XXXIII (1892), 622–38; XXXIV (1892), 41–68.

———. "Exegèses proudhoniennes," *Matériaux d'une théorie du prolétariat*, 2nd ed. (Paris, 1921), 415–49.

———. (Review of the collection of Proudhon's *Lettres à divers comtois*), *Indépendance*, February 15, 1912.

———. *Introduction à l'économie moderne*, 3rd ed., rev. and augmented (Paris, 1922).

———. "Proudhon," *La Ronda* (Rome), I (September, 1919), 5–17.

———. "Proudhon e la rinascita del socialisma," *La Ronda*, III (1921), 727–46.

———. *Les Illusions du progrès* (Paris, 1911), 254–64 et passim.

———. "Quelques mots sur Proudhon," *Cahiers de la Quinzaine*, 2e série, XIII (1901), 21–30.

———. *Réflexions sur la violence* (Paris, 1908).

Souvarine, Boris. "P.-J. Proudhon: Cent Ans après," *Le Contrat social*, IX, 2 (March–April, 1965), 86–94.

Spoll, E. August. *P. J. Proudhon. Etude biographique* (Paris, 1867).

Stakitch, Vladislav D. *La Doctrine française du crédit mutuel. Proudhon, Saint-Simonisme. Crédit populaire*, thesis, Faculté de Droit, University of Paris (Paris, 1924).

Stavenhagen, Gerhard. "Pierre Joseph Proudhon," *Handwörterbuch der Sozialwissenschaften* (Stuttgart, Tübingen, & Göttingen, 1964), VIII, 638–41.

Stein, Lorenz von. *Der Sozialismus und Communismus des heutigen Frankreich* (Leipzig, 1842); 2nd ed., enlarged (Leipzig, 1848), II, 397–421 et passim.

———. *Der Geschichte der sozialen Bewegung in Frankreich von 1789 bis auf unsere Tage* (Leipzig, 1850), III, 1–36, 103–8, 123–24, 147–68, 343–81; this is the 3rd ed., rev. and enlarged, of the preceding title.

Steklov, Iurii M. *Prudon, otets anarkhii (1809–1865)* (Petrograd: Izdanie Petrogradskogo Soveta rabochikh i soldatskikh deputatov, 1918).

Stockhausen, Viktor von. *Die Wertlehre Proudhons in neuer Darstellung* (Bern, 1898).

Sudan, Elisa. *L'Activité d'un socialiste de 1848*, thesis, Bern (Fribourg, 1921).

Sudre, T. R. L. A. *Histoire du communisme* (St.-Denis, 1849), 403–65.

Taillandier, Saint-René. "L'Athéisme allemand et le socialisme français: M. Charles Grün et M. Proudhon," *Revue des deux mondes*, XXIV (October 15, 1848), 280–332.

Tarbouriech, Ernest. *Essai sur la propriété* (Paris, 1904).

Tavernier, E. "Proudhon. L'Homme et l'oeuvre," *Le Correspondant*, Année 82, CCXL (nouv. sér.: CCV) (August, 1910), 446–65.

Tcherksoff, W. (Cherkezov, V. N.). *Précurseurs de l'Internationale*, Bibliothèque des *Temps nouveaux*, XVI (Brussels, 1899), 114–32.

Thabault, Roger. "L'Amour et le mariage, selon P.-J. Proudhon," *Grande Revue*, CXXI (July, 1926), 103–39.

Theinert, Benno. *P.-J. Proudhon. Versuch einer Lösung des sozialen Problems (Tauschbank)* (Zürich, 1920).

Thibaudet, A. "Proudhon, Saint-Simon, et nous," *La Nouvelle Revue française*, XXXIII (January 15, 1932), 90–103.

Thibert, Marguerite. *Le Féminisme dans le socialisme français de 1830 à 1850*, thesis (Paris, 1926), 167–92.

Thier, Erich. "Marx und Proudhon," *Marxismusstudien*, ed. Iring Fetscher (Tübingen, 1957), II, 120–50.

Thiers, Adolphe. "Rapport fait au nom du Comité des Finances sur la proposition du citoyen Proudhon relative à la réorganisation de l'impôt et du crédit," *Le Moniteur universel*, July 27, 1848, p. 1772; reprinted with Proudhon speeches, cited under "Rapport du citoyen Thiers . . . ," in part I-C, above.

Thomas, Albert. "La Sociologie de Proudhon" (critique of Bouglé's book of this title), *L'Humanité*, January 25, 1912.

Thonissen, Jean-Joseph. *Le Socialisme depuis l'antiquité jusqu'à la constitution française du 14 janvier 1852* (Louvain, 1852), II, 152–84.

———. *Socialisme et ses promesses* (Brussels, 1850), II, 29ff.

Thuriet, C. "Le Dernier Voyage de Proudhon à Besançon," *Annales francs-comtoises*, September–October, 1896; printed separately (Besançon, 1896).

Thureau-Dangin, Paul. *Histoire de la monarchie de Juillet* (Paris, 1884–1892), VI, 125–41.

Tissot, J. "Examen de la théorie de M. Proudhon sur la propriété," *Revue de droit français et étranger*, VI (1849); separately printed (Paris, 1849).

————. "Proudhon," *Revue littéraire de la Franche-Comté*, II, 257–73.

Traub, Karl. *Das Problem Eigentum und Gemeinschaft*, thesis (Tübingen, 1936).

Troubat, Jules. "Mme P.-J. Proudhon, née Louise-Euphrasie Piégard, 26 oct. 1822—8 juillet 1900" (Chartres, 1900); funeral oration for Proudhon's wife.

Tugan-Baranovsky, Mikhail Ivanovich. *P. Zh. Prudon, ego zhizn' i obshchestvennai a deiatel'nost'* (St. Petersburg, 1891).

Turgeon, Charles. "Essai sur la conception de l'histoire et du progrès d'après Proudhon," *Revue d'économie politique*, XXIX (1915), 232–58, 337–64.

Valbert. "Le Dernier Livre de Proudhon," *Revue des deux mondes*, September 15, 1875, p. 467.

[Vallein, V. Series of articles on Proudhon, *L'Indépendant* (Saintes), October and November, 1862.]

[Valois, Georges. "La Direction de l'oeuvre Proudhonienne et le cas Halévy," said to be in the *Cahiers du Cercle Proudhon*, September–December, 1913, but it is in none of the *Cahiers*, and there were no issues of this journal in 1913.]

————. "Pourquoi nous rattachons nos travaux à l'esprit proudhonien," *Cahiers du Cercle Proudhon*, no. 1 (January–February, 1912), 34–47.

————. "De Quelques Tentatives d'agression contre le cercle Proudhon, *Cahiers du Cercle Proudhon*, 2ᵉ série, no. 1 (January–February, 1914), 72–94.

Vaugeois, Henri. "Les 'Femmelins' par P.-J. Proudhon," *Action française*, January 6, 1913, p. 1, and in his *Notre Pays* (Paris, 1916), 102–6.

Verleger, Hilde. *Staat und Steuer bei Proudhon*, dissertation, Frankfurt (Neurode, 1933).

Vermorel, Auguste. *Le parti socialiste* (Paris, 1870), Bk. IV, Ch. 3.

Veuillot, Louis. "Proudhon," *Revue de monde catholique*, XI (1865), 421–28.

————. "M. Thiers et M. Proudhon," *Mélanges religieux, historiques, politiques et littéraires* (Paris, 1859–61), III, 418–31.

————. "Du Nouveau Livre de M. Proudhon," *L'Univers*, August 23, 25, 27, & 29, 1852; in Riv., IX, 371–84.

Vialatoux, J. "La Justice selon Proudhon," *Economie et humanisme*, XVI, 106 (1957), 400–404.

Viaud, Francis. "Un Précurseur. Proudhon" (Paris, n.d. [1952]).

"La Vie de Proudhon" (by "G. D."), *Année politique et économique*, XXIII, 95 (1950), 443–44; about Halévy's book on Proudhon.

"La Vie et l'oeuvre de P.-J. Proudhon," *Encyclopédie socialiste syndicale et coopérative de l'internationale ouvrière,* ed. A. C. A. Compère-Morel et al. (Paris, 1912), I, 194–251.

Viette, F.-J. *Etude sur la correspondance de Proudhon* (Besançon, 1875).

Villat, Louis. "Proudhon et ses amis: Précisions nouvelles et documents inédits," *Mémoires de la Société d'Emulation du Doubs,* Ser. 9, V (1926), 55–78.

Vincent, Albert. "Le Bilan de la démocratie," *Cahiers du Cercle Proudhon,* no. 2 (March–April, 1912), 98–104.

———. "La Famille chez Proudhon et dans la démocratie," *Cahiers du Cercle Proudhon,* nos. 3 & 4 (May–August, 1912), 134–49.

———. *Les Instituteurs et la démocratie,* Collection du Cercle Proudhon, no. 2 (Paris: Nouvelle Librairie Nationale, 1912; augmented edition, 1918).

Viviani, René. "Discours prononcé à l'inauguration du monument Proudhon," *Le Journal des débats,* August 15, 1910, pp. 2–3.

Voyenne, Bernard. "Le Fédéralisme de Proudhon," *L'Actualité de Proudhon,* ed. Centre National d'Etude des Problèmes de Sociologie et d'Economie Européennes (Brussels, 1967), 141–50.

———. "L'Organisation européenne selon St.-Simon et P.-J. Proudhon," *La Table ronde,* no. 113 (1957), 116–23.

———. "Proudhon, le fédéralisme et l'Europe," *Communauté européene,* no. 12 (1965).

Vrau, Jules. "P.-J. Proudhon und seine Schriften," *Unsere Zeit,* III (1859), 562–84.

———. *Proudhon et son système économique* (Paris, 1853).

Vuillaume, A., and MM. Grosjean, Viviani, Couyba. "Inauguration du monument élevé à la mémoire de P.-J. Proudhon, Besançon, 10 août 1910" (Paris, [1910]).

Walras, Léon. *L'Economie politique et la justice. Examen critique et réfutation des doctrines économiques de M. P.-J. Proudhon* (Paris, 1860).

Walter, H. E. "Pierre-Joseph Proudhon," *Der Druckspeigel,* XXII, 2 (1967), 764–66.

Watkins, Frederick M. "Proudhon and the Theory of Modern Liberalism," *Canadian Journal of Economics and Political Science,* XIII, 3 (August, 1947), 429–35.

Wauterniaux. *Le Socialiste. Livre 1: Proudhon* (Liège, 1893).

Weill, Georges. *Histoire du mouvement social en France, 1852–1924,* 3rd ed., enlarged (Paris, 1924), 35–40 et passim.

Weiss, Charles. MS. journal, Bibliothèque Municipale de Besançon. Contains much about Proudhon.

Weiss, J.-J. (Article on Proudhon's *La Guerre*), *Le Courrier du Dimanche*, 16 July 1861.

Werckmeister, Karl, ed., *Das neunzehnte Jahrhundert in Bildnessen* (Berlin, 1898–1901), III, plate 271. Lithographic portrait of Proudhon, by Catier, from a drawing by A. Colette.

Woodcock, George. *Anarchism* (London, 1963), 98-134 et passim.

———. "Pierre-Joseph Proudhon," *The University Libertarian*, no. 5 (Winter, 1958), 10–11.

———. "Pierre-Joseph Proudhon," *Encyclopedia of Philosophy* (New York & London, 1967), VI, 507–8.

———. *P.-J. Proudhon* (London & New York, 1956).

———. "Proudhon, an Appreciation," *Dissent*, II, 4 (Autumn, 1955), 394–405.

———. "Proudhon and His Mutualist Theories," *The Writer and Politics* (London, 1948).

———. "The Solitary Revolution: Proudhon's Notebooks," *Encounter*, XXXII, 3 (September, 1969), 46–55.

Zastenker, N. E. "Ideinoe bankrotsvo sovremennogo neoprudonizma," *Voprosy Istorii*, XLIII, 9 (1968), 76–94.

Zenker, E. V. *Anarchism: A Critique and History of Anarchist Theory*, trans. from the German (London, 1888), 26–81.

Zhukovsky, Yuri. "Prudon i ego ekonomicheskaia sistema protivoretchii," *Sovremennik*, CVI, CVII, CIX (February, March, & July, 1865), 185–222, 1–36, 163–206.

———. *Prudon i Lui Blan* (St. Petersburg, 1866).

Zoccoli, E. *L'Anarchia* (Turin, 1907), 69–96.

Zola, Emile. "Proudhon et Courbet," *Mes Haines* (Paris, 1913), 31–39; article first published in 1866.

Index